EARNING WHAT YOU'RE WORTH?

The Psychology of
Sales Call Reluctance®

EARNING WHAT YOU'RE WORTH?

*The Psychology of
Sales Call Reluctance®*

George W. Dudley
Shannon L. Goodson

Behavioral Sciences
Research Press, inc.

INTERNATIONAL

Dallas
1995

Published by Behavioral Sciences Research Press, Inc.
12803 Demetra Drive, Suite 100
Dallas, Texas 75234

Inside Design by Gary E. Minnich
Editorial Supervision by Theresa M. Donia

Some names, anecdotes, and case studies included in this book are fictional inventions. When necessary, the names of real people, companies or events have been altered to conceal their identities.

Cataloging-in-Publication Data

Dudley, George W., 1943-
    Earning what you're worth?: the psychology of sales call reluctance / George W. Dudley & Shannon L. Goodson -- 2nd ed.-- Dallas, Tex. :
Behavioral Sciences Research Press, 1995.
    p. cm.
    2nd rev. ed. of: The psychology of call reluctance.
1986.
    Includes bibliographical references and index.
    Preassigned LCCN: 95-77660.
    ISBN 0-935907-05-X (hc)
    ISBN 0-935907-06-8 (pbk)

    1. Selling--Psychological aspects. 2. Telephone selling--Psychological aspects.
I. Goodson, Shannon L. 1952- II. Dudley, George W., 1943-
Psychology of call reluctance. IV. Title.

HF5438.8.P75D83 1995   658.85
                        QBI95-20274

10 9 8 7 6 5

Printed in the United States of America

Dedicated to the memory of

Jayne Wheeler

1932-1994

Contents

1
The Faces of Call Reluctance   1

Chapter 1   2

The Invisible Man

2
The Prescriptions

3
Appendix
The Research   339

FOREWORD

Singapore—My company, Service Quality Centre, exists to help other companies achieve service excellence through Service Quality Management and customer-service training. So why write the foreword to a book on sales? From my perspective, this book is not merely about sales. In a sense, it too is about service quality management. One of the most compelling reasons for sustaining a customer care and Service Quality Management program is to maximise sales potential.

Winning new business in today's hotly competitive marketplace starts or stops with making quality contacts with current and prospective buyers. As we move toward the 21st century, cultivating our current customer base has become as important as finding and selling new clients. Both depend upon initiating contact on a consistent daily basis with current and future customers. Not everyone can comfortably make those contacts. This book can help identify who can, who can't, why and what to do about it.

Although contact initiation is critically important, it has evaded most formal customer service programmes. *Earning What You're Worth?* can remedy that. It provides individuals and sales-driven organizations alike with key insights and measurement concepts necessary to benchmark and continuously improve sales productivity by assuring frequent customer contact.

Like many other professional sales managers before me, *Earning What You're Worth?* has changed how I think about managing, and about what I do. But before I could learn new ways of thinking, I had to undergo some basic re-training. For example, sales call reluctance is not just about making cold calls, nor merely overcoming phobic phone etiquette. Sales call reluctance is far more pervasive, and costly, than that. It can impair everyone from senior corporate officials to order fulfillment personnel, the customer service staff and, of course, salespeople. The financial consequences defy precise calculation.

If you are serious about maximising your formal customer service programme, boosting your market share or increasing sales, the formula is here, in the following pages. I urge you to read this book, mark it up and consult it regularly. You won't be disappointed. I know I wasn't.

Debbie Teo, Divisional Manager, Business Development
Service Quality Centre

PREFACE

The pulsating beat of modern industry does not easily yield the time that is necessary to monitor advances in the behavioral sciences. Instead, business people must often wait for months and even years before benefiting from the fascinating theories and functional technologies spawned by this rich and broad scientific discipline. Typically, information from the behavioral sciences trickles into the business community only through speeches, books and cassettes produced by men and women who serve as self-appointed interpreters. Calling themselves motivation or performance experts, these interpreters seem to pop up in some industries like mushrooms pop up from the ground. Relying on information based on hearsay and informal sources like newspaper and magazine accounts, these interpreters are essentially entertainers. Few have the skill, background or interest to search out and read primary scientific source material themselves. The result is incomplete or misunderstood information passed on to uncritical business consumers as factual and representative. Due to faulty transmission, information capable of making dramatic differences in the way important considerations are managed is watered down or garbled in transit. Nowhere is this more evident than in the management of the fear of self-promotion, or call reluctance (fear of self-promotion that interferes with the prospecting activity of salespeople). Some entire industries have failed to benefit from the modern technology available to manage call reluctance because they simply don't know it exists. And they don't know it exists because the sources they use to keep them up-to-date and informed on such matters—their interpreters—also don't know it exists.

Recently we had the opportunity to observe this futile and wasteful process at an industry convention. A consultant was speaking from the main platform about maximizing sales performance. Over the last 15 years of studying the fear of self-promotion, we have heard many such speeches. The patter and technique of this particular consultant were typical and predictable.

In our experience, there always seems to come a humorous point during call reluctance presentations when the speaker (we'll call him Tom) seems to have enough control over both subject and audience to bring time itself to a standstill. We can still recall how Tom did it...

The audience was filled with eager anticipation as the presentation neared its end. Everyone grew noticeably tense, like small children with full bladders. Then Tom, radiating sincerity, unexpectedly stopped for emphasis. He grinned knowingly to himself, gazed off into the unfocused distance, closed his eyes, and contemplatively stroked his meticulously trimmed beard. He began to gesture as if something really momentous was about to be said, which from all appearances was in the process of being providentially revealed to him. With pupils dilated with excitement, the audience waited for what seemed like an eternity. Tom then began to dispense mentalistic words of wisdom like amphetamines for confused and bewildered call reluctant spirits. "Remember, we've all experienced call reluctance," he said, lowering his voice to whispering solemnity. "Everybody has it. But," he continued, his words sharpening and his voice growing louder, "call reluctance is nothing more than the fear of rejection; and you can beat it if you'll just do three things for me: Learn to relax while you work, learn to laugh at yourself, and learn to distinguish between being turned down personally and just having your ideas turned down."

The audience applauded politely. Many looked disappointed. Some looked transfixed. The master of ceremonies rose to reclaim the microphone. "That's really heavy," he chanted reverently. "We've really struck some deep chords here today. I hope you all heard Tom's message because he really knows our heads. If we go back and share this with our sales force, we'll have the best year ever!"

Most of the audience left quickly. But a faithful few lingered worshipfully around Tom. Most were asking him about his $250 per day Personal Performance Workshop. Tom was in rare form. Not a tall man, he stood as erect as he could to broadcast his "power gaze" and optimize his "command presence." He dropped names and slung out answers to questions with the speed and agility of a verbal food processor. One manager, a pop psych groupie, finally managed to get Tom's attention. Enraptured, he testified that his career had been scarred by the fear of rejection. But now he was completely restored. He could feel it. He knew it and "just had to share it with the group" (a phrasing we suspected he might have picked up during group psychotherapy). But this was obviously not this manager's first outing into pop psych matters. He had been there before. Many times. Maybe one too many times. Sporting an out-of-focus, thousand-mile-stare and beaming a beatified smile, he looked to us like he had just swallowed a near fatal dose of Valium and couldn't remember how to change the expression on his face.

This feature plays daily. Millions of salespeople and their managers eat McWisdom served up by Tom and other proprietors of the mental fast food industry. Tom's a heavy. But is he your brother?

If you have call reluctance or manage people who have it, he's not. The residue of faulty and incomplete information which he unintentionally leaves behind is one of the reasons that call reluctance remains the problem it is in some industries. Clamoring tightly together in a room to hear people like Tom brings to mind the medieval practice of crowding into churches to pray for delivery from the plague, thereby assuring its rapid and unhindered spread.

We, along with other behavioral scientists using sophisticated new research methods, have discovered the reasons for call reluctance. We have developed powerful new training procedures to neutralize it. Years of research, development and field testing are all included on the following pages. This is the first attempt to bring the bulk of our work on call reluctance directly to you. We hope you find it worthwhile and enjoyable.

George W. Dudley   Shannon L. Goodson

ACKNOWLEDGEMENTS

Some people think scientific scholarship cannot occur outside the theory-soaked departments of academic institutions. That is not true. There is a long, impressive tradition of independent scholarship which pre-dates the modern university and is not dependent on nor constrained by it. We are part of that ancient tradition.

However, a project such as this book, supported by original research spanning three decades and stretching to several countries, could not be completed alone. It wasn't. Independent scholarship does not necessarily mean solitary scholarship. We have many people to thank.

Our approach to formal personality assessment has been influenced by the formative work of Henry A. Murray, and two modern pioneers, Douglas N. Jackson and R.B. Cattell. Neuroscientist Carol A. Dudley at the University of Texas Southwestern Medical Center helped upgrade our understanding of important brain functions.

The entire staff of Behavioral Sciences Research Press were enormously helpful. A project like this could not be completed without their persistent encouragement and ready help.

We are particularly indebted to Anna K.H. Dowe. Anna is a graduate student in psychology at Southern Methodist University, and our research assistant. She has done an extraordinary job collecting, organizing, analyzing and interpreting research data. She is a credit to her university and makes us look smarter than we are. Thank you, Anna.

If the quality of our writing seems to be improving, it is because it has been edited by Theresa M. Donia, a gifted writer in her own right. Terry has worked hard (not always with our cooperation) to make our words more accessible to more people. We think she succeeded and look forward to working with her as a co-author of future projects.

We are also grateful to our small but growing network of international associates for helping us obtain some of the research samples used for our studies. But we are most indebted to the tens of thousands of sales and non-sales professionals in more than ten countries who allowed us to poke, probe, measure and observe—because they wanted to earn what they were worth. Ultimately, this book is a tribute to them.

1

THE FACES
OF
SALES
CALL RELUCTANCE

The thick-skinned fearlessness expected in salespeople is more fiction than fact. It turns out that many salespeople are struggling with a bone-shaking fear of prospecting. This fear tends to persist regardless of what they sell, how well they have been trained to sell it, or how much they personally believe in the product's worth.

Chapter One

THE INVISIBLE MAN

THE WAY WE WERE

It's a typical Monday evening at the United Metro Insurance Agency. Nancy, an agent for three weeks, sits at her desk. Now and then she glances at a nearby wall clock. She knows that prospecting for new business is critical if she is to succeed in her new sales career. But that awareness is not enough to immunize her against an involuntary, heart-pounding fear she can't understand or control.

The selection psychologist who evaluates prospective agents for the United Metro Agency strongly recommended Nancy for a career in life insurance sales. The standard paper-and-pencil psychological test administered during the selection process awarded her its highest score. She has the personality, intelligence and motivation to succeed in sales. She has been armed with newly sharpened interpersonal skills, an array of aggressively competitive new products, access to expensive state-of-the-art portable computers, and expert support from the home office. But Nancy is like the caterpillar who said to the butterfly as it winged effortlessly overhead, "You'll never get me to go up in one of those." Though equipped by nature and nurtured for success, prospecting scares her to death and keeps her career from ever getting off the ground.

But today she is determined to get an appointment. So she draws a few deep, self-assuring breaths and reaches for the first card in her prospect card file.

"I know what to say and how to say it," she reminds herself. Then she dials the number. As the phone rings on the other end, her resolve strengthens but her composure weakens. Her breath rate increases. Each breath becomes shallower than the one before. Her memory, usually saber-sharp, becomes murky and clouded over. Struggling desperately to conceal her discomfort, she begins her presentation in a voice which is now barely audible.

"Hello, my name is Nancy . . ."

Bob is another story. He's been an automobile salesman for four years. In the beginning, everyone expected him to be a heavy hitter, and although his initial production rose steadily, it soon leveled off to a disappointingly low plateau. His sales manager sent him to a number of highly touted seminars and workshops to remedy the problem. His attitude, never really a problem, improved, but his production did not; it currently remains frozen at a level considerably below his talent, market and ability.

Bob's dealership even sponsored an extensive market analysis to help its salespeople target additional prospects, thereby making them less dependent on floor traffic. But Bob refuses to make sales calls on some of his targets. Instead, he indignantly points out that some of these "so-called targets" are actually members of his own family.

"Real salespeople," according to Bob, "never make calls on members of their own family."

Larry is a sales veteran. He has fought in the trenches since 1980 selling computer hardware/software products. He is undeniably dedicated and extremely capable in every respect except one—prospecting. While he has changed over the years as a sales professional, his production has not significantly grown. It remains at 1981 levels. Nonetheless, Larry likes to boast that he can "sell anybody, anytime, anyplace," and he probably can unless they happen to be physicians, lawyers, accountants or other up-market professionals and decision makers. Unfortunately for Larry, these groups represent the prime market for his company's new product line.

Larry has been asked, begged and ordered to direct his sales calls to the company's primary market. He either can't or won't. He has been sent to psychiatrists, stress managers, and the best sales training seminars in his industry. He has listened to exhortations from motivational speakers, read inspirational books, and learned how to establish eye contact. But he is still downsighted. He can only set his prospecting sights in one direction, downward. His overworked rebuttal is, "I don't make calls on them SOBs."

Willie Doesn't Live Here Any More

A few years ago, salespeople were presumed to be male, outgoing, fearless and audacious. That was the stereotype. Sales executives, trainers, consultants, motivational speakers, psychologists, the buying public, and salespeople themselves uncritically accepted the prevailing stereotypical view of the sales profession and the people in it.

Times changed. Women joined the men's club. They discovered that sales positions offered the opportunity to go further, faster, than non-sales careers. Sales training programs, which previously showcased crude, miracle-mongering novelties like "body language," developed a less manipulative, more collaborative approach to selling. Products became more sophisticated, specialized, competitive and complex. But what about the back-slapping stereotype? It stayed the same.

In *Death of a Salesman*, Arthur Miller crafted the image of an anchorless drifter who was shiftless, self-centered and superficial. With Willie Loman's "smile and a shoeshine" character, Miller's fictional salesman was projected onto the awareness of an entire culture. His story blended into our popular mythology so completely that fiction and reality became indistinguishable. Today, people actually believe that all salespeople are like Willie Loman.

A few decades ago, psychologists and psychiatrists, never at a loss for words themselves, began to speculate about the inner workings of this curious subspecies—the salesperson. Adjectives were shuffled about in wildly descriptive abandon as they celebrated their insights in a ritual dance of linguistic narcissism. Chanting complex and spooky incantations such as "ambivalence," "sublimated drives" and "meta-motivation," they employed verbal sleight-of-hand to repackage the old stereotype into the new mentalistic language of the times. More light would have been shed on the subject had they accidently bumped their heads together and produced a small spark.

Here's an actual "thumbnail sketch of the life insurance salesperson" as described in one university level psychology textbook:

Didn't choose occupation; stumbled into it.
Ambitious, desires success, money, luxuries.
Likes selling and business.
Dislikes aesthetic and scientific activities.
Aggressively hostile, sociable on a large scale.
Dependent on others for advice and companionship.
Conservative and authoritarian.
Sensitive to criticism.
Doer, rather than thinker.
May exploit others financially.

In their promotional material a few years ago, two psychologists selling sales selection tests to industry characterized the desirable candidate for a sales career with these words:

. . . friendly and outgoing, but when you know him he is arrogant, conceited and not very interested in people . . . but when he begins to talk he can be a most persuasive, charming, convincing individual . . . he gains your confidence and makes you feel like the most important person in the world . . . but don't be fooled, he doesn't really like people . . . to him people are just objects to be twisted, shaped and manipulated.

The picture which emerges is not one of innocent, winged figures, robed in dazzling white. It's more like mild retardates with probable criminal intent.

Are salespeople really the oversocialized, fearless mercenaries they're made out to be? Superficial studies which presume the stereotype described above suggest they are. Furthermore, many current sales selection programs are still biased in favor of the old stereotype. For example, in a recent study of sales selection systems, we found the most common trait measured was high "dominance" (social forcefulness), followed by high "sociability." But modern, in-depth personality studies, which probe deeper than the typical sales selection test, tell another story.

They reveal that salespeople vary considerably from their stereotypes. Armed with a sophisticated array of high-tech assessment techniques, we have found that, as a group, salespeople are barely distinguishable from the general population of adults in terms of forcefulness and sociability. The thick-skinned fearlessness expected of salespeople is fiction, not fact. It turns out that many salespeople are secretly struggling with a bone-shaking fear of prospecting.

Their fear persists regardless of what they sell, how well they've been trained to sell it, how they manage their time and set their goals, or how much they personally believe in their product's worth. The result is a lot of Nancys, Bobs, and Larrys. You may know one. You may manage one. You may be one. Each has an affliction peculiar to direct sales. Technically, this problem is tagged *the fear of self-promotion* because it can interfere with advancing one's interests in many areas of life, not just sales. But when it infiltrates the sales force, it cuts off the vital supply of new business by interfering with the act of prospecting. When that happens, the fear of self-promotion becomes *Sales Call Reluctance.*®

THE INVISIBLE MAN

In direct sales, results are critically linked to the number of contacts initiated with prospective buyers. Figures vary somewhat depending upon industry, product, and skill level, but most sales training professionals agree that the relationship between new contacts and sales success is extremely important. Generally, it takes about 25 contacts to get 12 responses, which result in five sales presentations and three closed sales. Most salespeople already know this. But legions of otherwise capable salespeople fail each year because they are unable or unwilling to translate what they know about prospecting into prospecting behavior.

Our studies show that as many as 80% of all salespeople who fail within their first year do so because of insufficient prospecting activity.

What about veteran salespeople? Our research shows that during their careers, approximately 40% will experience one or more episodes of call reluctance serious enough to threaten their continuation in sales—despite their years of experience, product knowledge, or current income level. In the words of one senior salesperson, "Twenty-eight years a member of MDRT [an international organization of top producing insurance agents], I sell 40-50 lives annually, [produce] approximately 7-9 million dollars annually. I still experience call reluctance." Apparently, experience does not immunize.

Call reluctance is a career-threatening condition which limits what salespeople achieve by emotionally limiting the number of sales calls they make. Some have trouble using the phone as a prospecting tool. Others have trouble initiating face-to-face contact with prospective buyers. Many have trouble doing both.

Earning What You're Worth?

The fear of self-promotion is the general condition which makes call reluctance possible in salespeople. It's found everywhere in motivated, goal-striving people who have trouble promoting themselves. Not limited to salespeople, it keeps competent and deserving people in many walks of life from being recognized for their contributions and, therefore, from earning what they're worth.

- Too modest to "toot his own horn," a loyal and deserving administrator is not promoted to the next higher position because someone less competent, but more visible, gets the job.
- Sacrificially modest about her contributions, a hard-working partner in an accounting firm does not get the end-of-year performance bonus she deserves because another partner, less capable than she, sensed her vulnerability and took credit for some of her accomplishments.
- Uncomfortable using his own social network, a customer service consultant to industry discovers that a friend's company has just purchased a large in-house training contract from a far less technically competent competitor. The fear of self-promotion can make you invisible.

Do Phone Machines
Circumvent Call Reluctance?

Got call reluctance? Maybe crusaders for the ever-present microchip can help. Their pitch: "Leads, leads, leads—without ever having to prospect!" So say the marketeers of these hard-wired, auto-dialing computer prospectors. But aside from growing social disapproval over their use, can these machines really be effective prospecting surrogates?

One sales manager thought so. Perplexed and disappointed by the call reluctance plaguing the human element of his sales force, he waited impatiently for the arrival of his first non-human solution. Costing in dollars much more than it weighed in pounds, it arrived wrapped in the promise that it would not—could not—ever become call reluctant. That's what the manager wanted to hear. That's why he bought it.

But in the realm of human activities, dreams of push-button sales management can be highly perishable. And they were. Three things happened. First, the few leads the machine actually produced were inconsistent with the manager's marketing strategy. Second, the quality of the business he realized from the leads was not what he envisioned—it was poor both in terms of the dollar amount per sale and the length of time the sales remained on the books.

But the third point was to become the most perplexing. Although the overall number of leads did increase, the number of follow-up calls made by his human sales force remained about the same. It seems that our manager overlooked a very basic point. Arguably, machines may be able to generate leads, but in direct sales, people still have to sell. His people couldn't make prospecting calls before the machine arrived, and they couldn't make *follow-up* calls after. The machine was sold after one month of use.

Many people who fear applying self-promotion to advance their career interests are dreamers. Tucked away with the fables and fairy tales of childhood are the innocent expectations they bring with them to their careers. These are not realistic representations of the way things are, but romantic idealizations of what could be if men and women were angels. But they're not. These myths fall into two basic groups: fallacies of recognition and fallacies of reward. Here are some examples.

Idealistic Myth: If you are loyal to your superiors, you can trust them to look out for your welfare.

Practical Reality: You are responsible for yourself. It's not your boss's job to take care of you or your career. Loyalty is nice, but not necessarily symmetric. Just because you choose to be loyal does not mean that others will be loyal to you. So don't be disappointed when you discover they're not. It's more reasonable to expect your company, its owners, and management to *look after their own interests first.*

Idealistic Myth: The hardest working, best producing and most deserving always (eventually) rise to the top.

Practical Reality: Where have you been? Open your eyes. Look around. Are the people who head your organization necessarily the most competent? People who are *perceived* to be the most competent are the ones who typically make it to the top. But they cannot be perceived as competent if their competence is invisible. Getting to the top of any enterprise or organization (you don't already own) requires a two-part approach: competent performance supported by assertive self-promotion. Competent performance without assertive self-promotion creates a recognition vacuum. If you don't take credit for who you are and the contributions you have made, someone else in the organization—probably less deserving—will.

Idealistic Myth: Good work speaks for itself.

Practical Reality: Work gets rewarded from two basic sources. One is the personal satisfaction and feeling of accomplishment you confer on yourself when you know you've done your job well. That's important, but it is also private. The other is public recognition and financial reward.

The Fear of Self-Promotion Down Under

Recent observations suggest that the fear of self-promotion is not limited to a particular department, company, industry or even country. During one of our frequent trips to Australia, we were shown the August 1990 issue of a popular Australian magazine which contained the results of a reader survey.

Seventy percent of the respondents indicated they were not "paid what they were worth." Ironically, of that number, 74% admitted they had never asked for a raise. Of those who did, 81% got some, all or more than what they asked for. The fear of self-promotion can extract its emotional and financial tariffs from the paychecks of hard working and deserving people everywhere.

These are based on the behavior of others and, to a great extent, lie outside your control. These payoffs can be substantial and meaningful, but they are determined by people who are trying to maximize their own rewards by promoting *themselves* as good expense managers or shrewd corporate navigators. Payoffs for *your* good work are likely to be as insignificant and infrequent as you allow.

Like it or not, these and other shopworn platitudes represent the history of effective career management, not modern reality. They have failed the test of time. Today, if you keep your head down and your nose to the grindstone, all that is likely to happen, according to some personnel specialists, is the removal of your nose. While hard workers are often appreciated, they are less often promoted.

NATURAL SELF-PROMOTERS

What do Tom Peters, George Foreman, and Madonna have in common? They're natural self-promoters. They seem to instinctively understand the need to "let their light shine" and are magnetically drawn to opportunities for self-promotion. Unlike most of us, however, they appear to genuinely enjoy the process. You may or may not approve of their style, content, or ambitions, but they are flawless prototypes of effective self-promotion. Observe them in action. There is much you can learn.

First, natural self-promoters are rarely considered the most knowledgeable or technically competent members of their profession. Second, they enjoy income levels as high or higher than if they were! How do they do it?

By sifting through years of accumulated notes, findings, comments, opinions, and other scholarly junk, we were able to factor out the income-attracting secrets of natural self-promoters. These are the elementary tricks of the self-promotion trade, the things natural self-promoters actually do while the rest of us either fall asleep on the sidelines or painstakingly wait for the right time, place, and opportunity.

Three Key Behaviors of Natural Self-Promoters

Although natural self-promoters are, like most groups of people, more different than they are alike, they are inclined to share three common behaviors.

Positioning

"To get ahead in life," the old platitude says, "you have to be in the right place at the right time." Positioning is how natural self-promoters get there. They fully utilize their existing contacts, networks and social systems and remain on the lookout for ways to develop new ones. They know that to rub shoulders with the people who can most significantly affect their careers requires them to move within arms length of those individuals. Getting there takes positioning.

Style

Natural self-promoters know they are not the only people positioning for the best contacts and advantages. Sometimes there's a crowd. So their strategy shifts from getting noticed to getting remembered. That's where style comes in. There are many definitions of style. We define it not in terms of its essence, but in terms of one of its primary functions: Style is what you do that sets you apart from the crowd and gets you remembered.

Consistency

To natural self-promoters, staying in the spotlight is not an impulse or a grim necessity. It's a way of life. Most would never consider deferring this prerogative to the momentary whims, moods and opinions of others. Self-promotion is an important aspect of modern career management. Natural self-promoters know it and constantly practice it.

Ethical Self-Promotion

To some people, all self-promotion is unethical. It's just another name for unrestrained pride, arrogance, boasting, exaggeration and deceit. To them, the term "ethical self-promotion" is a self-contradiction and makes as much sense as a "round square."

Regrettably, a few people do use unethical methods to self-promote. That reflects their values. But it doesn't have to be done that way. *Ethical* self-promotion can be a healthy, rewarding, and even enjoyable process.

Ethical self-promotion is based on the realistic understanding that success in any contact-dependent endeavor requires both effective performance and effective self-promotion. But ethical self-promotion requires an additional element to distinguish it from the blustery schemes and predatory ambitions of unethical self-promoters: At the center of ethical self-promotion lies the desire to self-promote, balanced by a genuine respect for the needs of others.

How to Identify Unethical Self-Promoters

They're easy to spot. In person or in print, they communicate with the high-sounding vagueness common to politicians and university commencement speakers. They identify the need for unshakable commit-

Overcoming the Cinder Block Syndrome

We are frequently asked to speak at conventions and, even more frequently, to do guest spots on radio talk shows. During one such appearance on a popular New York City talk show a listener, obviously one of the great minds of the twentieth century, felt compelled to supplement our information. So he called in. Once on the air, he told his story:

Recently he had attended Dudley & Goodson's presentation on call reluctance at his company's annual convention. According to him, it was great. He learned some things that helped him increase his commissions. But "the best part," he volunteered, "was meeting the two authors themselves. They're not even in sales—they're number crunchers!" Then he cut to the heart of the matter and rested his case: "If it can work for those two, it can work for anybody. I went up to shake their hands after they finished their presentations, and I tell you, those two, added up, have the personality of a cinder block! Like I said, if it can work for them, it can work for anybody."

He's right. But we "two cinder blocks" went from being $14,000 per year researchers to earning salaries well into the six figures, all in less than two years. Now we drive pretentious automobiles, own diamonds, and manage a highly visible and profitable business which allows us to share our good fortune with others through our international group of dealer representatives.

The caller was right. If we can do it, so can you. Successful prospectors don't have to have outgoing personalities. If you're shy you can still learn to overcome call reluctance and prospect effectively—without having to change either your personality or your principles.

ments to moral decency and national pride without so much as giving a hint as to how *they* will vote in the next election. Who are they? They're unethical self-promoters.

Self-promotion is important. It's practiced by many people. But not everyone chooses to do it ethically. Spotting unethical self-promoters, especially among gifted, natural self-promoters, can be frustrating. But it's not impossible.

Most unethical self-promoters tend to repeat certain behaviors. That means they follow patterns that make them predictable. When you

Famous Self-Promoters—
Dr. Sagan to Sir Thomas

During our public appearances we like to ask audiences to tell us whom they most associate with the phrase "self-promoter." As you might expect, certain names are mentioned more often than others. "Excellence" marketeer Tom Peters, media sexpert Dr. Ruth, stargazer Dr. Carl Sagan, pop psychologist Dr. Joyce Brothers, entrepreneur Donald Trump, businessman Lee Iacocca, and motivator Zig Ziglar currently top the list.

The British add Richard Branson, Margaret Thatcher, and Michael Heseltine. In New Zealand, motivational speaker Billy Graham and businessman Bob Jones come to mind. Australians think of Kerry Packer.

Self-promotion, however, is not just a contemporary phenomenon. There have been self-promoters throughout history. Some of the most admired, celebrated, and accomplished historical characters knew the magic of self-promotion. General Douglas MacArthur was a self-promoter, as was politician/statesman Sir Winston Churchill. Scientist Albert Einstein apparently found self-promotion relative to his practical interests, as did psychoanalyst Dr. Sigmund Freud. And then there's Sir Thomas More (St. Thomas to Roman Catholics). Subject of the movie *A Man for All Seasons*, Sir Thomas had his perspective permanently altered by Henry VIII, who beheaded him for stubbornly adhering to his convictions. In his earlier life, More was a skilled self-promoter. Richard Marius, in his authoritative biography *Sir Thomas More*, claims that "few people have enjoyed greater success in advertising their humility."

observe enough of these patterns, we recommend placing your hand firmly on your wallet or purse and moving deliberately toward the door.

How can you spot them before they victimize you? There is no foolproof way to spot unethical self-promoters. But the ancients used an interesting method: In much earlier days, building contractors were given a public opportunity to prove their skills and quality of work. When a new building was almost complete, the builder was asked to participate in a ceremony in which he was expected to stand beneath the building's main support as the finishing touches were added and the scaffolds and braces removed. If the building was designed and constructed as well as the builder claimed, the thrill-seeking spectators showed their approval with applause. If not, the entire structure unceremoniously collapsed on the contractor's head.

Searching for unethical self-promoters after the fact—among the debris of collapsed condominiums, financial empires, and wrecked political careers—may prove effective, but the timing could be better. Here's a checklist of behaviors that can help you spot unethical self-promoters before they spot you. The checklist is adapted from information provided to sales managers who attend our Fear-Free Prospecting & Self-Promotion Management Training Workshop.^{SM}

CAUTION: One, two, or even three of the following characteristics do not provide a reliable indication of an unethical self-promoter. Large clumps of these characteristics, however, could be the behavioral calling card of an individual trying to get what he or she wants *at your expense.*

The 19 Characteristics of Unethical Self-Promoters

- *Compulsive name-dropping*

  Most good salespeople have contacts. Some are impressively well-connected. But unethical self-promoters know *everyone*. They continuously rattle off names for effect. It works like this: Not too long ago we heard about a speaker's sermonette on subjects that ranged from motivation to personal integrity. When his subject drifted to his insights on "the fear of rejection," a perceptive member of the audience interrupted to ask if he was familiar with the call reluctance work of Dudley and Goodson. "Oh, yes!" the speaker assured. "They're personal friends of mine." We have never met the man.

- *Melodramatic use of righteous indignation to assert credibility and integrity*

- *Strategic use of actual and implied intimidation*

- *Inappropriate calmness and atypical composure in situations that would normally provoke anxiety, such as being caught in a lie*

  To unethical self-promoters, these occasions are always "just harmless misunderstandings."

- *Few deep or long-lasting business relationships*

  Most salespeople develop a clientele, whereas unethical self-promoters develop enemies.

- *History of concealed "misunderstandings" and legal problems*

  When a series of legal difficulties is uncovered, we are told that they were never mentioned because they were "unimportant, just misunderstandings." *(See above: "Inappropriate calmness and atypical composure")*

- *Unable to show or sustain genuine emotion*
  Some unethical self-promoters appear emotionally insincere.

- *Deals with tough issues by trying to relativize them*
  Slogans touted by some unethical self-promoters—like "everything is relative," "go with the flow," and "win-win"—can easily decompose into *"everything* is negotiable" or *"everything* is relative." To the unethical self-promoter, nothing is absolute, not even right and wrong—promises made are promises broken.

- *Uses bizarre reasoning and self-delusion to justify unethical behaviors*
  When unethical self-promoters experience fleeting moments of conscience, they cope by denying the unethical nature of their actions. "Everybody does it" or "You'd do the same thing if you had the chance!"

- *Talks long-term, thinks and acts short-term*

- *Employs simplistic, manipulative techniques to gain an advantage*
  "Buy! Buy! Buy!" the subliminal tape whispers beneath inoffensive background music. Trying to establish powerful rapport, they pace their breath-rate to the breath-rate of the prospective buyer. Delivering their presentation in a practiced monotone, they think they will hypnotize their prey into submission. Their gurus promise quick, clean kills. That's what unethical self-promoters want; that's what they thrive on.

- *Considers interpersonal influencers, like charm and endearment, more important than skill-based competencies*

- *Frequently uses words like "openness" and "trust" to deflect lack of integrity*
  Most people do not need to advertise their integrity. Unethical self-promoters do. They use reassuring words and phrases to draw attention to their *words* and away from their actions. "Don't you trust me?" he asked as he rested his hand gently on her right knee. Sometimes words and intentions are not in sync.

- *Uses verbal ambiguity as a manipulative technique*
  Skillfully and carefully avoids detailed discussions whenever possible, thus limiting personal and performance accountability. When inevitable problems due to ambiguous expectations occur, the unethical self-promoter righteously insists that he or she has been taken advantage of.

- *Behavior tailored to look psychologically open, strong, caring and resilient*

    This is not an accurate description of an unethical self-promoter, but it's the impression their persona is fabricated to project.

- *Tainted view of other people*

    To the unethical self-promoter, everyone else is unethical or would be if they had the opportunity. Their gospel is "everybody has a price," "everybody is out for himself," and "if I don't get them, they'll get me!"

- *Expert knowledge of other master manipulators' tools and techniques*

    Unethical self-promoters proudly study other manipulators and the tools and techniques of their trade.

- *Unmoved by threats of being found out*

    Most people on the verge of being exposed for some wrongdoing begin to experience regret. Unethical self-promoters become *more* indignant and self-righteously maintain their innocence to the end.

- *Claims expertise in an unrealistic number of different fields*

    Unethical self-promoters speak authoritatively, without hesitation, on many subjects. We call this Pivoting for Position because its purpose is to establish these individuals as being knowledgeable in as many different areas as necessary. You *will* be impressed.

Ethical Prospecting Guidelines

As you prospect for new business, are your tactics ethical? That's not an easy question. Sometimes it's difficult to tell. Unlike some self-certain religious marketeers, salespeople do not always have moral absolutes to lean on. Like the blind searching for their canes, salespeople must occasionally feel their way through moral obstacles and ambiguous situations. In the frenzy for new accounts and larger market shares, shiny moral guidelines can lapse into tones of amoral gray.

So how do you know if your prospecting methods are ethical? Here are some guidelines you can use to gauge your prospecting ethics. All do not apply in every situation, but they apply frequently enough to serve as a reasonable basis for self-examination.

Consider each of the questions below very carefully. Then answer each question with either "yes," "no," or "maybe."

Do other people stand to gain from your prospecting tactics?

Do your prospecting tactics have a positive influence on your own well-being and self-esteem?

Would you approve if another salesperson used the same prospecting tactics on you or a member of your immediate family?

Do your prospecting tactics really help move you closer to your short- and long-term goals?

Are your prospecting tactics legal?

Would people in general approve of how you prospect for new business?

Are your prospecting tactics good business?

Do your prospecting tactics really feel right?

Do you have more "yes" answers than "maybe's" or "no's?" If you do, then your prospecting efforts are probably thoughtful and purposefully ethical. But two other dangerous possibilities must be considered.

These questions are difficult for most sales professionals to answer at all, let alone quickly. If you moved through each of the questions rapidly and effortlessly, you may be disinterested in the subject, self-deluded to the extent that you are out of touch with the ethical implications of your behavior, or so ashamed of *your* prospecting (not to be confused with prospecting itself) that you must distance yourself from anything that reminds you of how you really feel. That's called denial. Take a moment. Think about it.

If you answered "maybe" more often than "yes" or "no," you could be experiencing some difficulty committing to anything. Or your ethical values may be in transition and presently unclear. But if you often find yourself choosing "I don't know" alternatives during self-discovery tasks such as this, it could mean something else: Frequent use of "I don't know" or "I don't care" could indicate an overriding need to freeze out critical discussion and self-examination. Ever wonder why?

If you answered more "no's" than "yes's" or "maybe's," then you are probably either a backslapping, silver-tongued devil of a con-man (or woman), a transactional analyst desperately needing work, or psychologically at home among the guilty, always pointing an accusing finger at yourself.

How to Ethically Prospect and Self-Promote

You work hard and perform your job well. You can, and should, take pride in that. God also knows you have integrity, talent and ability. Not a bad audience, that.

But if you want to be recognized and financially rewarded for your contributions, you must first make those contributions visible. Visibility precedes recognition, and it's much too important to be left to accident or chance.

Only when your contributions are recognized can you be rewarded. Not until. Rewards like money, attention, power, and prestige are the aftermath of recognition.

This arrangement is not necessarily fair. It's not the way we were raised, nor is it the way we would personally prefer. But it's the way big incomes are earned. Competent craftsmanship may or may not result in visibility. But visibility attracts recognition, and recognition draws rewards.

There are many sources which can teach you how to prospect and self-promote more effectively. However, beneath their wit and studied efforts to appear innovative, most are antiquated and suffer from indistinguishable sameness. In sifting through dozens of available guidebooks, we have uncovered a few shining exceptions. Offering straightforward, practical advice on achieving and managing visibility, the following books, in our judgment, represent the cream of the crop for readability, usability and marketing savvy:

Speak For Yourself, published by the BBC (British Broadcasting Company)

Marketing Yourself, by Dorothy Leeds

PPR (Personal Public Relations), by John A. Chestara

Guerrilla P.R., by Michael Levine

High Visibility, by Irving Rein, Philip Kotler, and Martin Stoller

We recommend these titles to consultants, physicians, psychologists, sales managers, lawyers, salespeople, and other professionals whose success depends upon the quality and frequency of contacts with other people. If you don't know how to make contact with large numbers of prospective buyers, these books can teach you. But experience has repeatedly demonstrated that, for most sales professionals, *knowing how* to make contacts is not the problem. The problem is emotionally allowing themselves to *apply* what they *already* know.

FOUNDATIONS OF CALL RELUCTANCE

At its center, call reluctance pulsates with behavioral patterns of escape and avoidance. Each pulse possesses career-stopping force. But before we can effectively attack these forces, we need to understand more about behavior. Today, numerous definitions of behavior are in use, each the product of a pet theory or conceptual model.

Some of these models existed long before the advent of modern behavioral science. Many have been added since. Here are a few examples:

Religious: The Devil makes you do it.

Cosmic: The position of certain celestial bodies at the time of your birth determines your present prospecting behavior.

Environmental: Shaped by rewards and punishments, you learn it.

Chemical: Your behavior is the emotional footprint left by obscure chemical events in your brain.

Pop psych groupies will be disappointed. The behavioral model we use lacks sex appeal. Bearded consultants and ambitious graduate students will find it altogether too unmysterious to describe in low, churchly voices. But we use it because it is, as Dr. J. R. Haynes, former chairman of the Department of Psychology at the University of North Texas, likes to say, "simple, straightforward and self-evident." More than that, our behavioral model works by providing a jumping off point for subsequent corrective assaults on call reluctance.

The model we employ says that whatever else a behavior may be, it can be reduced to at least three elements: thoughts, feelings and actions.

Do All Salespeople Have Call Reluctance?

The notion that *all* salespeople have call reluctance is a popular misconception. It's based upon an imprecise definition of what call reluctance really is. True, every salesperson may have a predisposition to one or more forms of call reluctance, but that does not mean they are call reluctant. Presently there are many microorganisms in our bloodstream which predispose us, under certain conditions, to an attack of the flu. But while the genesis of the illness may be present, the actual debilitating symptoms are not.

To decrease the likelihood of contracting the flu, or at least limiting its severity should it occur, health conscious people take vitamins, live healthy lifestyles, and endure flu shots prior to the flu season. Many episodes of call reluctance can be prevented in the same way. Even if you have no symptoms of call reluctance at present, you can still learn which types you are most predisposed to and then apply the precautionary steps provided later in this book. Think of it as immunization for the call reluctance season of your sales career.

Everything we do (actions) is accompanied by thoughts and feelings. These three dimensions may be related in some complex fashion yet unknown. Then again, they may not. Despite what you read elsewhere, no one knows for sure. The evidence is controversial, incomplete and often incoherent. The jury is still out. But we know that call reluctance in salespeople is a problem which usually involves amplified feelings like fear, and can often involve all three behavioral elements.

Where does call reluctance come from? Its origins are multiple and complex. There is no single source, no single "germ" to isolate and destroy. Some forms appear to result from hereditary predispositions. Others have been traced to traumatic early selling experiences, sometimes quickened by ruthlessly high performance pressures. Ironically, call reluctance is most often *taught* unintentionally by the sales training process itself. It can be present at the onset of the career or it can strike years later without warning or apparent justification.

The genealogy of any behavior, including sales call reluctance, can be traced to one or more origins. Knowing where call reluctance comes from can provide critical information about its development, which is key to finding its hidden weaknesses. With this information, we can then fashion specific countermeasures which target its vulnerabilities and exploit its weaknesses like heat-seeking missiles.

Though complex, colorful and diverse, all behaviors, including call reluctance, originate from one of the following sources.

Instincts—Inclinations and reflexes you were born with. These are actions and automatic tendencies you did not learn and were not taught.

Mimic Learning—Things you discovered on your own that you could do. These are behaviors you observed in other people, discovered you could do yourself, and then decided to mimic. We often forget that some of our mannerisms and behaviors reflect *choices* we made as adolescents and children.

Passive Learning—Habits and behavioral styles you unintentionally absorbed from people you regularly interacted with or placed significant value in. These are repeated, predictable behaviors you picked up from parents, sales trainers, managers, consultants and others without even realizing it.

Education and Training—Mannerisms, actions and behaviors you were purposefully taught. These are the attitudes and behaviors you acquired through systematic behavior-shaping enterprises such as education and training.

Synthesized Learning—Things you think, feel and do that are combinations of the four influences above.

The Germ Within

Certain highly toxic forms of call reluctance, like Role Rejection (described in Chapter 3), have been found to be extremely contagious. Contaminated sales managers and trainers have been identified as the primary carriers. Many of them are unintentionally infecting some of their most promising and productive salespeople.

Most salespeople initially learn how to cope with call reluctance from their managers, sales trainers, or training consultants who may be secretly struggling with the problem themselves. Data from management studies using the Call Reluctance Scale, a specialized test constructed specifically to detect all forms of call reluctance, reveals that salespeople who have been exposed to a call-reluctant sales management team are up to 20 times more likely to have toxic levels of call reluctance. When we find elevated levels of Hyper-Pro Call Reluctance (described in Chapter 3) in sales trainers, for example, we also find it in the salespeople they train.

But does that prove that managers pass call reluctance on to their sales force? Couldn't it just as easily be interpreted the other way? It could. But additional observations produced additional evidence.

A few years ago we conducted a pre- and post-hiring study using the Call Reluctance Scale. Our objective was simply to evaluate the presence, severity and types of call reluctance in a typical group of prospective salespeople before they were hired into a large organization. At that time, the prospective salespeople were no more or less call reluctant than anyone else. A few weeks later, however, after they were selected into the organization, it was a different story. Not only did the new group begin to show signs of two types of call reluctance, but the types that showed up were the same two we had previously found in their sales managers, trainers and consultants. They were also the same two types detected earlier in the regional sales vice presidents and later in the senior vice president of sales and marketing. We finally tracked these particular call reluctance strains all the way up to the company president who insisted his call reluctance was inconsequential because he was "not directly involved in sales." Ground zero for call reluctance in that organization was the executive suite.

The salespeople in that study did not have significant amounts of call reluctance prior to their exposure to management. But a few weeks after being hired, they acquired the same types, to approximately the same degree, as their sales managers, trainers and consultants (see research chapter). Where do you suppose their call reluctance came from?

Many forms of call reluctance are highly contagious. Therefore, if you're in sales, watch who you let near your mind. If you're in sales management, watch who you let near the mind of your salespeople.

SEARCH FOR AN ANSWER

Typically, when salespeople first show signs of call reluctance, many well-intentioned but misguided sales managers rush off to seek the aid of priestly exorcists from the psychological fast-food industry. A rich blend of ceremonial ritual, mysterious jargon and evangelistic zeal quickly reassure the manager that the offending case of call reluctance will soon yield to a 45-minute inspirational cassette or be soothed away by the gentle incantations of a stress manager or the hypnotic ocean sounds of a subliminal tape. However, due to prohibitive costs and less-than-spectacular results when dealing with genuine call reluctance, most managers do not err in this direction more than once or twice. They learn that inspirational cassettes cannot coax it away. Threats cannot scare it away. And if you ignore it, it won't just go away.

If Nancy, Bob and Larry are like most salespeople, their early training conveyed the implicit attitude-shaping message that prospecting is a scourge, a necessary evil, inexorably associated with any career in direct sales. And these attitudes may have been fatalistically fixed by exposure to cynical sales managers or veteran salespeople who never learned how to overcome the problem themselves. Therefore, to Nancy, Bob and Larry, call reluctance comes with the territory.

Veteran salespeople will recall that a few years ago sales training programs were porous, brittle structures welded together by untested speculation and ancient sales training folklore. Genuine research was the exception. When consultants claimed to have "researched" a topic, they really meant they had an interest in the subject or had read about it in a popular article. Until 1970, there was no systematic research conducted on the subject of call reluctance. *Anywhere.*

Fortunately, most of the old, time-worn sales training practices, and the superficial stereotypes on which they were based, are now being edged out by newer, client-based approaches like psychologist E.O. Timmons' Sales Dynamics Program.

Call Reluctance Contaminators
Ranked by Estimated Potency

- Traumatic early selling experience
- Sales trainers
- Sales managers
- Outside consultants, speakers, trainers
- Other call-reluctant salespeople
- Internally created sales training programs and materials
- Externally created sales training programs and materials (including industry sanctioned materials)
- Commercially available sales training materials (including self-help books, tapes, workshops, etc.)
- Company policies, procedures and attitude-influencing messages
- Media stereotypes of salespeople
- Formal education (especially university-acquired biases and stereotypes about various professions)
- Family
- Friends
- Other sources

These new programs represent significant milestones because they mark the end of the folkloric sales training era and herald the advent of modern behavioral science into the sales training profession. Progress continues.

Since 1970, a small but dedicated group of serious researchers has been attacking call reluctance head-on. Reverberations from the collision can still be heard throughout the sales training profession.

America's telecommunications giant MCI, Australia's high profile Macquarie Bank, England's human resources phenomenon Select Appointments, the courier industry's Loomis, in Canada and Australia, and many other progressive sales organizations world-wide have already put programs in place to aggressively counter call reluctance. They're not waiting for other organizations to clear a path. They're leading the way.

Michael Swinsberg, sales manager for Macquarie Bank's New South Wales Investment Services Division, says his organization now "focuses in on specific types [of call reluctance] as opposed to dwelling on global issues [fear of rejection]."

MCI's director of corporate training, Bonnie Rich, says her company's call reluctance program, Selling With Assertive Tactics (SWAT), is directly linked to production.

"MCI has an exciting history of success over the last few years," Rich says. "If we are going to continue this year, we're going to have to look for ways to continue to improve productivity in our sales reps. We feel that our [call reluctance] program will be a vehicle to help us do that. Prospecting in our business has a direct correlation to success in sales . . . and we're already seeing [the] numbers. That's why we promote our call reluctance program."

Determining Your Call Reluctance Profile

An effective intervention program always begins with an accurate diagnosis. Typically, our modern diagnoses originate from a sophisticated, computer-scored call reluctance test. Sales training departments find the added diagnostic precision provided by this test to be an invaluable aid.

The following two self-diagnostic scales are provided to help individual salespeople get started immediately. Though not as precise as the computer-based technology mentioned above, they are sufficient to help establish a call reluctance profile.

THE PROSPECTING EKG

The following questions have two purposes. First, like a medical EKG, your answers provide an indication of how your prospecting heart is functioning at the present time. Second, you will learn which particular type(s) of call reluctance you may be most susceptible to. So take out a piece of paper and answer each of the following questions as honestly as you can.

1. How many contacts did you initiate with prospective clients during your last full workweek?

2. Approximately how much time do you invest in preparation for each new prospecting contact you make?

3. How many group or seminar-selling presentations did you give or try to schedule last month?

4. How many sales presentations or requests for contacts, referrals or connections did you initiate with your personal friends and acquaintances last month?

5. How many sales-related conversations did you initiate while attending civic, social, fraternal, political or religious meetings during the last month?

6. How many prospecting appointments or sales interviews were you persuaded to reschedule during the last month?

7. How many sales contacts or conversations did you try to initiate last week with professional persons or wealthy, influential people in your community?

8. How many sales-related conversations or requests for contacts, referrals or connections did you initiate during the last three months with members of your own family? *(Skip this question if you do not live in an area where you can visit members of your family with reasonable frequency, or if members of your family are not accessible for other reasons.)*

9. Approximately how many times during the last full workweek did you try to think of new, innovative prospecting methods that would not be demeaning to you or your profession and would not be offensive to prospective buyers?

10. Approximately how many times during the last full workweek did you ask people you know (including your present customers) for names of *other* people you could make a sales call on (referrals)? Approximately how many times *could* you have asked for referrals?

11. Approximately how many phone calls did you attempt to make to prospective buyers during the last full workweek? Approximately how many *could* you have attempted?

12. *Optional*: Describe any circumstances you believe had a significant influence on how you did or did not answer the questions above. Also, if you wish, you may include comments about the questions, the relevance of the exercise to your particular situation, or any other observations you wish to make.

Analyzing Your EKG

Are you normal? What's "normal?" That depends. Prospecting varies from industry to industry, company to company within the same industry, and even among local branches of the same company. Therefore, acceptable prospecting activity in one sales setting could be a serious problem in another. We suggest you solicit the help of your sales manager or trainer if you have one. He or she can bring another perspective to your answers and possibly help you better understand whether they are high, low or average for your sales organization. (The various call reluctance types will be explained in detail in Chapter 3.)

Question 1: A significantly lower-than-average number for your organization could indicate the presence of Doomsayer Call Reluctance—the inclination to habitually worry.

Question 2: Unnecessarily large blocks of time spent preparing to prospect instead of actually prospecting for new business could indicate the presence of Over-Preparation Call Reluctance—the tendency to cope with prospecting discomfort by constantly preparing.

Question 3: A much lower-than-average number for your sales organization could indicate the presence of Stage Fright Call Reluctance— defaulting on mass prospecting opportunities due to discomfort speaking in front of groups.

Question 4: A figure well below what is possible for you or typical for your sales organization may indicate Separationist Call Reluctance—hesitation to call on friends or even to ask them for referrals.

Question 5: A number significantly less than the opportunities available to you could indicate Role Rejection Call Reluctance—guilt and shame associated with being in sales which makes it difficult for you to feel genuine pride for your chosen career or to disclose your profession to others.

Question 6: A larger-than-average number could indicate the presence of Yielder Call Reluctance—habitually yielding your interests to the interests of others in order to avoid appearing selfish, pushy or intrusive.

Question 7: A lower-than-average number, or a number lower than the opportunities available to you, could indicate the presence of Social Self-Consciousness Call Reluctance—the inclination to become intimidated by persons of wealth, prestige, education or social power.

Question 8: If you could have made significantly more contacts than you did, you may have Emotionally Unemancipated Call Reluctance—the hesitation to call on members of your own family or even to ask them for referrals.

Question 9: A higher than usual number here could indicate Hyper-Pro Call Reluctance—a preoccupation with professional images and themes, like credibility, dignity and respect, which interfere with prospecting by equating it to unprofessional hustling.

Question 10: A lower-than-average number for your organization, or a number lower than the actual opportunities available, could indicate the presence of Referral Aversion Call Reluctance—the hesitation to ask people you know, especially existing clients and customers, for the names of new people to contact.

Question 11: A lower-than-average number for your sales organization, or a number lower than the opportunities available, could indicate Telephobia Call Reluctance—hesitation or emotional distress in using the telephone for prospecting or self-promotional purposes.

Question 12: If you wrote, or even thought of writing, a number of critical comments (especially in regard to the questions themselves or how they were asked); if you failed to follow instructions because you concluded that the exercise might be for *others* but certainly not for you; if you catalogued excuses for not making as many contacts as you could or should have, then congratulations. You probably have Oppositional Reflex Call Reluctance, a form characterized by denial, excuse making, intellectual one-upmanship, and compulsive critiquing, even of the people and programs most likely to help you. Lighten up. Give us a chance.

CALL RELUCTANCE SELF-RATING SCALE

Before drawing any final conclusions, let's take a second picture from another angle. Take a few minutes to answer each of the following questions as honestly as you can. Each requires a simple "yes" or "no" response. Write your answers on a separate piece of paper.

1. I probably spend more time planning to prospect than I devote to actually prospecting. Yes or no?

2. I'm probably not really trying to prospect for new business as much as I could or should because I'm not sure it's worth the hassle any more. Yes or no?

3. I probably don't try as often as I could to initiate contact with influential people in my community who might be prospects for the products or services I sell, or at least a source for referrals. Yes or no?

4. I get really uncomfortable when I have to phone someone I don't know, who is not expecting my call, to persuade them to buy something they may not want to buy. Yes or no?

5. Personally, I think having to call people I don't know, who are not expecting my call, to promote a product or service is humiliating and demeaning. Yes or no?

6. To me, self-promotion doesn't really bother me. I just don't apply myself to it very purposefully or consistently. Yes or no?

7. I try to avoid giving presentations before groups if I can. Yes or no?

8. Actually, prospecting doesn't really bother me. I could initiate more contacts if I were not involved in so many other activities which compete for my time and energies. Yes or no?

9. I find myself hesitating when it is time to ask for a referral from an existing client. Yes or no?

10. I tend to need time to "psych" myself up before I prospect. Yes or no?

11. I tend to spend a lot of time shuffling, planning, prioritizing and organizing the names on my prospecting list (or cards) before I actually put them to use. Yes or no?

12. Regularly making cold calls (calling on people I don't know who are not expecting my call and who may not want to talk to me) is really difficult for me. Yes or no?

13. I tend to feel uneasy when I prospect because deep down I think that consistently promoting yourself or your products is not very respectable or proper. Yes or no?

14. To me, making sales presentations to my friends or asking them for referrals is unacceptable because it might look like I was trying to exploit their friendship. Yes or no?

15. I often feel like I might be intruding on people when I prospect. Yes or no?

16. To me, making sales presentations to members of my own family, or even asking them for referrals, is inappropriate because it might look like I was trying to selfishly exploit them. Yes or no?

17. It is very important to me to find innovative, alternative ways to prospect which are more professional and dignified than the methods used by other salespeople. Yes or no?

18. I think that prospecting for new business probably takes more out of me emotionally than it does other salespeople. Yes or no?

19. I do okay in one-on-one sales situations, but I would probably get really nervous if I found out that next week I had to give a sales presentation in front of a group. Yes or no?

20. Highly educated, professional people like lawyers and physicians tend to annoy me, so I don't try to initiate contact with them even though I probably could if I wanted to. Yes or no?

21. Self-help material, like this self-rating scale, is superficial and probably won't teach me anything I don't already know. Yes or no?

22. I have reasonably clear goals, but I probably spend more time talking about them than working towards them. Yes or no?

23. I would probably feel more positive about prospecting for new business if I had some additional training to fortify my product knowledge. Yes or no?

24. I probably could prospect more, but I'm really just marking time until I get to do what I *really* want to do. Yes or no?

Scoring Your Call Reluctance Self-Rating Scale

There are two steps to evaluating the Call Reluctance Self-Rating Scale. Both are quick and easy.

Step One:
Compute your overall call reluctance score by adding up your "yes" responses. Then read the following interpretive summary which is based on your total number of "yes" answers.

Total Number "Yes" Answers	Interpretation
1-2	Indicates one of two conditions: Either you are experiencing no emotional difficulty whatsoever associated with prospecting, or you really are experiencing some distress but you're hesitant or emotionally unable to reveal how much, even to yourself.
3-4	Indicates that you are like most other salespeople. The fear of self-promotion is present but only in low, non-toxic amounts. It may be occasionally annoying but it is not likely to be serious if it remains at this level. It should be manageable by simply emphasizing the markets and prospecting techniques you are most comfortable with and avoiding those which are the most

threatening. This book, however, is still recommended, because it can strengthen your tender prospecting areas, and by so doing open up even more prospecting possibilities later.

5-6
You probably have moderate levels of call reluctance at the present time. One or more forms of call reluctance are currently limiting your prospecting activity to a level beneath your ability. Low prospecting probably keeps you from exploiting the potential of your market. If so, the remaining sections of this book should be personally and financially rewarding.

7-8
Your answers indicate a considerable amount of call reluctance at the present time. Your prospecting may be only a shadow of what it could be or needs to be. But don't despair. Instead, fasten your seat belt and get ready for some serious self-confrontation.

9 or more
Do you glow in the dark? According to your score, you could have enough call reluctance to stop a small sales force. Are you comfortable making calls on *any* prospective buyers?

If your answers are truly indicative of your attitudes toward prospecting then you should consider taking immediate corrective steps. Honestly discuss the problem with your manager if he or she does not already know about it. That's important. Then continue reading. Be certain to follow instructions. This book can help you turn your career around, if you will let it.

One other interpretation is possible. You may be too self-critical. When you took Abnormal Psychology class, were you certain you had all the pathologies described? In church, are you the sinner the clergyman accusingly preaches to? When you complete a test or rating scale like this one, do you think most of the self-critical statements apply to you? If you suspect you might have been too hard on yourself, ease up. Go through the scale again.

Does your score indicate that call reluctance could be holding your career hostage? If it does, look at step two. It will help you pinpoint the type(s) of call reluctance that might be choking off your prospecting ability and endangering your sales career.

Step Two:

Call reluctance never "just happens." It's like a virus. It has a developmental history, comes in a variety of strains, and leaves clues along the way in the form of attitudinal footprints. Use the following chart to review each of your "yes" answers on the Call Reluctance Self-Rating Scale. It will help you determine which particular type(s) of call reluctance you might have, or which strains you could be most susceptible to in the future. For the present, don't worry about what each of the call reluctance types, or the call reluctance impostors, mean. The impostors will be covered in Chapter 2. The twelve types of call reluctance will be described in Chapter 3.

Question Number	Type of Call Reluctance or Impostor	Question Number	Type of Call Reluctance or Impostor
1, 11	Over-Preparation	8	Impostor: (Goal Diffusion)
2, 24	Impostor: (Low Goals)	9	Referral Aversion
3, 20	Social Self-Consciousness	10, 13	Role Rejection
12, 18	Doomsayer	14	Separationist
5, 17	Hyper-Pro	15	Yielder
6, 22	Impostor: (Low Motivation)	16	Emotionally Unemancipated
7, 19	Stage Fright	21	Oppositional Reflex
4	Telephobia	23	Impostor: (Insufficient Training)

Final Word

The Prospecting EKG and the Call Reluctance Self-Rating Scale give you an opportunity to review your orientation to prospecting. Together they work like a flawed, but valuable mirror, reflecting your prospecting image. When you hold up your mirror and look squarely into it, what do you see? Are you looking at the face of call reluctance?

Low prospecting activity means you could have call reluctance. But it does not mean you do. Three essential conditions—motivation, goals and goal-obstructing feelings—must be present before you can conclude that you have authentic call reluctance.

Chapter Two

THE CALL RELUCTANCE IMPOSTORS

Most companies don't take call reluctance seriously until profit projections are decimated by marginal sales caused by persistently low prospecting activity. By then their internal training resources have already begun to disintegrate under pressure for more results. Some organizations cope by instinctively adding more training in the areas of product knowledge, goal-setting, time management, and persuasion skills. Most—even highly parochial sales training departments like those found in banking, insurance, securities and real estate—sooner or later reach the point where the added pressure forces an admission that current practices are not producing acceptable results. Those not indisposed by professional vanity call for help, and often get it. For others it's too late. They've already exceeded their annual sales training budget. Groping for improved sales in the compost heap of old thoughts, stale witticisms, and outrageous claims, they spent every last penny to supply each of their offices with a copy of Mindpower's slick new six-part audio cassette series: "Success Unlimited: How to Win at Sales, Lose Weight Effortlessly, Play Championship Golf, and Find God." What do they get for their money? Bad advice. Impotent techniques. No results. Big trouble.

Heavy artillery is needed to attack call reluctance on both the individual and organizational levels. Unfortunately, some companies still use toy pistols. Billy Broker is a good example.

"They're broke. Fix 'em!" ordered Billy, a scowling, but amiable, real estate trainer who always had a cigar poking out from his face and spoke out of the side of his mouth.

"They used to be heavy hitters, you know. Now they won't prospect. Got call reluctance," he told us, emphasizing each syllable and making it sound as important as a complete sentence.

Billy recalled that he had just paid a locally well-known psychologist to conduct a group call reluctance session for his entire sales force. According to Billy, the psychologist had peculiar, carp-like lips, spoke with a lisp, and drooled as he ordered the agents to stretch out on the training room floor and "relax." It didn't work. The entire sales force uncontrollably rolled around the floor, laughing to the point of pain each time the psychologist spoke. When he instructed them to let their minds "just wander out of your body and relax," they laughed even more. Billy was not amused.

As a prerequisite to attending our Fear-Free Prospecting and Self-Promotion Workshop, one of Billy's backsliding agents completed the Call Reluctance Scale. The results indicated a problem, but it was not call reluctance. On the surface it looked like call reluctance, but we knew from experience that this case would never respond to call reluctance countermeasures. So what was it?

Call reluctance usually plays a high-handed role in prospecting problems, but there are other prospecting suppressors which are not related to call reluctance. They're called *impostors*. Only by recognizing the impostors can you be sure that call reluctance is the cause of your prospecting problem. But before you can understand the impostors, you must first know more about call reluctance.

CALL RELUCTANCE PRODUCT DEFINITION: How Call Reluctance Affects Prospecting Activity

Presentations on call reluctance often surge right past the smoldering issue of how to define it. Instead, they muddle through a stiff and awkward hodgepodge of unconnected thoughts and illogical conclusions until, sooner or later, the audience cannot fail to detect the definitive odor of untreated verbal sewage.

The widespread ploy of evading the issue by ceremoniously conferring a name to the problem, like "fear of failure," and then deftly moving on to other matters is one of the main reasons for the continued confusion, trained ignorance, and general lack of understanding in this area. Fear of Success. Fear of Failure. Fear of Rejection. Call reluctance has enough names. It needs an address.

The most concrete evidence for call reluctance comes directly from the effect it produces on prospecting activity. We use the product definition of call reluctance to describe the problem in terms of its result or *product*: the direct impact of call reluctance on prospecting activity.

Prospecting activity is the *total* number of face-to-face plus telephone contacts initiated with prospective clients. *Genuine call reluctance always results in low prospecting activity*. But what is the definition of low activity?

T-Factor Production Slumps?

Some companies react to call reluctance and production slumps as if they were the same thing. They're not. In our judgment, call reluctance is an emotional short circuit which keeps motivated salespeople with clear performance objectives from being able to comfortably prospect. Production slumps are associated with drops in motivational current, not increases in fear. *Techniques for overcoming call reluctance are useless against production slumps; measures for escaping from a production slump are ineffective against call reluctance.* To explain why, we'll borrow and completely make over a metaphor used in neurophysiology.

To succeed, salespeople must focus their intellect and their senses on the sharp edges of social interaction every day. They are expected to know their products, work their markets, and learn the sales process. They must also maintain surveillance over a whole constellation of subtle behaviors that engineers, technicians, bureaucrats, and proceduralists can safely ignore. Salespeople may be more naturally disposed to tasks like these, but it still takes physical and mental effort. Billions of nerve cells have to fire on cue, then recharge to fire again when needed. In this sense, salespeople are like toilets.

To use a toilet, certain rules of conduct and design must be followed. Like the nerve cells of a salesperson, the toilet's tank must first be filled with water before it can perform its function. Once flushed, you must wait until the tank has refilled before you can use it again. That's how toilets were designed to work and most are indifferent to modern life management techniques like coaxing, temper tantrums, nervous impatience, reckless threats, and positive visualization.

Some sales trainers seem to respect their toilets more than their salespeople. When a sales slump occurs in his sales force, Marty the Motivating Sales Manager recommends the equivalent of sitting on the toilet and furiously pumping the handle. Soon, their arms grow weary and the handles eventually wear out. Despairing, his exhausted salespeople don't even have an additional flush to show for their effort.

Production slumps caused by occasional drops in motivation can take on a variety of appearances. Here are some of the most common ones:

continues

T-Factor Production Slumps? *continued*

- Challenges which typically excite you make you weary.
- You get up in the morning still tired even after a good night's sleep.
- You lose enthusiasm for your work.
- All your work projects begin to blur together.
- Common problems inexplicably become unmanageable.
- You uncharacteristically lose your temper.
- You muddle up sales presentations you have done correctly many times before.
- You can't recall important facts about your products.
- You call your clients by the wrong names.
- Everything you attempt fails to work.
- Your mind seems to drift in and out of focus.
- It becomes difficult to concentrate.

If you notice any of these in yourself, you are probably experiencing a slump. But don't panic. Slumps of this type are normal, necessary and predictable. All salespeople experience them although some experience them more often than others and some experience them less often but more deeply. Either way, they can be your body's way of forcing you to pull your life off the main road, slow down, and catch your breath. If possible, consider changing your routine for a while. Take a different route to work. Emphasize low intensity duties like working on plans and preparing lists. Avoid high risk sales calls until you have passed through the valley of your slump.

Don't ignore the message or try to beat the system by driving faster. Furiously pumping the handle won't get you any more flushes.

"Low" is one of those inherently unstable words. Its definition differs among individuals and organizations. From our admittedly limited perspective, low activity is defined as prospecting activity insufficient to sustain personal or corporate performance objectives. That means you are not initiating contacts with prospective buyers frequently enough to support 1) your own career objectives, 2) the potential of your market, or 3) your organization's performance requirements. In other words, low prospecting activity means trouble.

The product definition of call reluctance is the one most people intuitively use. Uncritically accepted without further clarification, it can be very misleading.

CALL RELUCTANCE PROCESS DEFINITION: Conditions Necessary for Call Reluctance to Occur

Suppose you have a fever. Your fever *could* mean you have the flu. It could also mean you have something else. Low prospecting activity means you *could* have call reluctance. But it doesn't necessarily mean you do. Three essential conditions—*motivation, goals,* and *goal-obstructive feelings*—must be present before you can have authentic call reluctance. If prospecting activity is low and one of these conditions is missing or deficient, you're not call reluctant—you're a call reluctance *impostor.* You must be able to tell one from the other. Your course of action depends upon it. The process definition gives you the edge by providing a systematic way to begin to deal with your specific problem.

Imagine your expensive new radio doesn't work. You take it to a repair shop. There, a skilled technician compares the values observed by taking measurements at key points against the values his schematic diagram indicates should be there. If one of these values is missing or incorrect, the electrician knows he has found your problem, and he knows exactly which circuit is responsible. Armed with this information, he can fix your radio.

The process definition of call reluctance also involves taking measurements from three critical points. These measurements reveal the present status of important mental circuits that influence your prospecting activity. To conclude that your low prospecting activity is due to genuine call reluctance, measurements must first be taken of your 1) motivation, 2) goals, and 3) goal-obstructive feelings.

Motivation

Motivation is a galvanizing buzzword. Any self-help guru worth his jargon uses it. Most pop psych marketeers have their own proprietary definition. But what does motivation mean to you? How do you know when you're motivated and when you're not? How do you use your motivation? One thing is clear: Whatever motivation is, you can't have authentic call reluctance without it.

To assess motivation, most modern sales organizations supplement their informal assessment procedures, such as interviewing and personal observation, with dedicated, formally developed instruments like the Call

Who Cares?

Many salespeople, in tandem with their managers, have the conviction that emotional training problems such as anger, depression, and call reluctance are deadly. We agree that they're never fun and should always be taken seriously. But they're not the most deadly problem faced by sales trainers. That distinction is reserved for a situation which is far more difficult, perhaps even impossible, to deal with—low motivation. It can surface in any of three disconcerting, energy-robbing behavioral addictions: *lethargy*, *disinterest*, or *apathy*. Any one is a career killer.

Salespeople who secretly *don't care* about improving their performance are unreachable. In response, many sales managers and trainers attempt to cope with the situation by doing the "wanting" for these individuals. But that never works. Salespeople must be self-energized; they must do their own "wanting." That's one thing they *must* bring with them to their career. To the unmotivated, there are never urgent performance problems. Unexpected opportunities never beckon. These figments exist only in the minds of excitable managers and trainers.

Other performance-limiting problems such as anger, depression, and call reluctance are different. They are the outward emotional signs of intense, but conflicted, internal wanting. You cannot experience them unless you first deeply want something. As performance problems go, they are perplexing, but they also have a positive side. They indicate the presence of a rich layer of motivational energy. This energy can be tapped to help solve performance problems like call reluctance.

Lethargy, disinterest and apathy darken the outlook. They provide insufficient fuel for enlightenment or improvement. Salespeople with these conditions don't want to improve. Outside of prayer, sales trainers have little to work with. Do you really care about your sales career? How much?

Reluctance Scale and the Motivation Analysis Test. Though not absolutely necessary, these devices bring a valuable, objective dimension to the complex task of measuring the following three aspects of motivation:

Amplitude   This is an extremely important measure called Motivational Level on the Call Reluctance Scale. It calibrates how much physical energy is available to the circuit that drives your prospecting activities. Think of it as the amount of juice behind your desire to prospect and succeed in sales. Some people have more of it than others. Amplitude is a measure of motivational energy, like the volts you need in your wall receptacle to make your television work. If the volts are not there, or are present but at an insufficient level, your television will not work properly. But is this the fault of your television? No. The problem is insufficient power to meet the needs of the application. Why is that so important? What does that have to do with call reluctance? Plenty. Numerous companies continue to experience prospecting problems because they try to wire 50 volt salespeople into 110 or 220 volt sales careers. The result? No prospecting picture. Is the problem call reluctance? No. That's a logical impossibility. You cannot be reluctant to do what you don't *want* to do in the first place. Low motivation is an impostor.

Duration

In order for your television to work, it must also have uninterrupted access to a *stable* energy supply. It can't have 110 or 220 volts one minute, then drop to 40 volts the next. That's true for successful salespeople, too. Therefore, we must try to estimate the variability in the observed motivation. Some salespeople want only to perform at minimal levels. Once those levels are reached, they slack off until the need to perform arises again. During their "down" time, prospecting drops below their potential. In such cases, when prospecting falls off it's due to declining desire, not emotional hesitation. It's an impostor.

Velocity

Some salespeople are high octane individuals whose motivation is transformed into behavior at breakneck speed. Others are more laid back and composed. This is a stylistic difference among salespeople and is useful for predicting performance problems such as low frustration tolerance and burnout. Although helpful in these applications, the measurement of motivational velocity is not necessary to deal with call reluctance.

Increasing Motivation?

Can you *really* motivate anyone? We're asked that question frequently. It's usually intoned with a touch of smug self-certainty suggesting the questioner already knows the answer. Lying in studied repose, the inquisitor awaits an opening through which to expand our knowledge of the beatitudes or self-righteously explain Maslow's often repeated hierarchy of needs.

From our perspective, many sales trainers, writers, public speakers, and people who develop sales training materials continue to depend on the "needs hierarchy" theories of the '50s to understand motivation. To the rest of the world, however, the study of motivation did not end with Maslow's exalted sensitivity training, celebrated nude marathons, or famous hierarchy of needs. Much work has been done since then. Scientific understanding of human systems, such as motivation, has progressed. Today, scientists are discovering new ways to effectively manipulate human energy and drive.

New methods have been developed to arouse the body to higher energy levels. Drugs have been found which function as authentic aphrodisiacs, exhibiting a marked effect on libido (sexual motivation). The new scientific emphasis on food has made us more aware of how vitamins, minerals and other nutrients influence our energy level. Shelves of new bags, boxes, and bottles of nutritional elixirs formulated to heighten our energy levels are readily available. Many people regularly receive vitamin B12 shots prior to entering high energy demand situations. But the drug of choice for today's super achiever is adrenalin.

Much has been discovered about the demotivating influences of a number of common health risks: Excessive drinking, excessive smoking, too much or too little exercise, sleep disturbances, workaholism, mental trauma, chronic stress, physical disease, drugs, and call reluctance all take a toll on physical energy.

Can you motivate another person? Of course. If you are willing to teach them how to become better body managers.

Are you motivated? Do you have enough "want" to propel you to the top? To prospect successfully, motivation is necessary but it is not sufficient in and of itself. There are plenty of motivated salespeople who are not call reluctant but are nonetheless bogged down at marginal prospecting performance levels. This brings us to the second important measurement dimension—goals.

Goals

Motivation is physical energy. Like electricity, which is also a form of physical energy, in order for it to work it must be connected to something. For electricity to be transformed into entertaining sights and sounds it must first be connected to your television. Only then can the electrical energy behind the wall plate be discharged through the wires to the set.

To continue the analogy, goal management is the evaluation and maintenance of the integrity of the connections between an energy source (motivation) and an output device (goals). What's your motivation connected to? How reliable is the connection? *Goal assessment* is the process of finding out. Here's what you should look for.

Target

This is what you want. It provides the meaning behind your prospecting efforts. Where do your motivational wires lead? What is your motivation connected to? Ideally, you should have clearly focused career goals to support your prospecting activities. These goals should be accomplishable where you are now, not somewhere else. Motivation without firm, supportive, accessible goals becomes a mindless struggle without meaning; eventually your drive overpowers your direction. Prospecting becomes mechanistic and tedious, boring you to sleep behind the wheel of your career. Prospecting activity inevitably drops off. But is it due to call reluctance? No. It's due to disinterest.

Strategy

Some salespeople take pride in being able to gratuitously recite their goals and ambitions at the drop of a hat. It impresses people and may even have helped them obtain their current sales position. But if you poke beneath the cloud cover, you don't find much else. No thought. No purpose. No planning. No meaning. Just sketchy dreams and empty ambitions recited for effect. Without a plan for reaching their goals, they easily get distracted, sidetracked or just plain lost. One of the first performance areas to suffer the consequences is prospecting. But salespeople who don't plan are not call reluctant. They're confused.

Are You a Driver or a Striver?

During the '70s, it became fashionable in some circles to insist that good salespeople had to be drivers. The term "driver" had also been used to describe salespeople before that time. But by the '70s it had become part of our cultural vocabulary.

Experience, however, has not been kind to drivers. The concept did not age very well. Eventually, it expired. Why? Because drivers did not live up to their billing. They were praised for being in motion, but nobody bothered to check their direction. The result was a group of forceful salespeople who were unable or unwilling to see or plan ahead, one of the basic elements behind any long-term career management strategy. Consequently, to the disappointment of managers, trainers, and colleagues alike, their commitment to the sales organization, its products, and marketing methods was not long-term. Their tenure was dismal.

Since then, studies based on sophisticated and more universally accepted personality tests have found that drivers need a steering wheel to match their engine size. We call these salespeople "strivers." A striver is a driver with a goal.

Pursuit

Some salespeople target their goals and then spend endless hours constructing elaborate lists, plans, and strategies for reaching them. The trouble is they rarely do anything else. They fail to devote sufficient motivational energy to actually carrying out their plans. There's no target pursuit. Are they call reluctant? No. They just prefer to plan rather than prospect.

Goal-Disruptive Feelings

The third dimension completes the call reluctance triangle. To be call reluctant, a motivated (M), goal-directed (G) salesperson must be ensnared by self-imposed mental obstacles whenever prospecting is attempted.

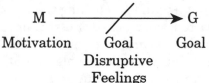

M ————— / ————→ G

Motivation   Goal   Goal

Disruptive

Feelings

Four Conditions for Dynamic Goal Setting

Goals. Some people have them and some don't. Like good shock absorbers, they keep us on track and soften the jolts caused by the ruts and potholes of our careers. Career hazards—distraction, confusion, disappointment, and despair—can jar our careers off course; good shock-absorbing goals provide our careers with purpose and help keep us focused.

There are many excellent sources on how to set and maintain goals. There is much less, however, on their general nature, how they come about, and what makes them effective.

Goals are commitments. S.R. Marks, in an article for the *American Sociological Review*, describes four conditions which encourage commitment.

First is *intrinsic enjoyment* of the activities involved in a particular pursuit; you experience pleasant sensations when you do the things that move you closer to your goal. Actually, you would probably enjoy doing these things anyway, even if they were not associated with a career objective.

The second condition is *loyalty to your colleagues*. Working with a group of people you genuinely like is a strong reason to keep steering the course, even when your career throws you a curve.

Third, *expectations for external rewards* can sharpen your focus and concentrate your energy. Believing there will be a positive payoff for your efforts can pull you through a multitude of dark days.

Finally, *knowing that an undesirable payoff could occur if you fail to focus your energy* can also influence you to move in the right direction.

Goals that stick need a touch of pleasure mixed with a pinch of affiliation, a dab of faith, and a dash of fear.

Let's return to our television analogy. First, to get sound and a picture, we plug the television into an energy source in the wall. If all is well, the energy flows from the wall through the wires to the set where it powers the set to operate. But what if a frayed wire causes a short circuit?

If this happens, the available energy gets diverted at the site of the short and never makes it to the set. The result? No picture. No sound. No way to accurately gauge performance until the short is fixed.

Call reluctance does the same thing. It's an emotional short circuit that causes a malfunction in energized, goal-directed salespeople. Energy destined for prospecting is short-circuited into prospecting *avoidance behavior* which we have identified as call reluctance. Instead of energizing prospecting activity, it's redirected to recalling and reinforcing unproductive, lifelong habits of escape and avoidance. Wishing, waiting, whining, blaming, and pouting are some indicators of a call reluctant short circuit.

THE FOUR GREAT IMPOSTORS

When motivation or goals are missing, you have a prospecting problem, but it is not due to call reluctance. It's an impostor.

Impostors have several important features. First, they always lack one or more of the three essential conditions described above. Second, impostors are always accompanied by low prospecting activity which mimics the product definition of call reluctance given earlier. Third, they will not respond to countermeasures designed to correct call reluctance.

Are you currently prospecting beneath your ability? Are you call reluctant or are you an impostor? It's important to find out. Let's explore each of the impostors in more detail.

Impostor 1: Low Motivation
Low motivation, high goals
All talk, no action

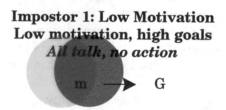

Capsule Summary:

Some salespeople aren't very motivated. Some are motivated but not enough to succeed in direct sales. What about you? If you're not prospecting because you don't want to, then you're not call reluctant; you simply lack motivation. Your low activity might look like call reluctance but the similarity ends there.

Daryl, a headhunter for a large national executive search firm, was not prospecting enough to suit Blair, his manager. Daryl expressed clearly-defined goals, so Blair assumed his low production was due to call reluctance and sent him to one of our Fear-Free Prospecting and Self-Promotion Workshops. Daryl completed the Call Reluctance Scale, the first in a series of assessments administered to workshop participants. The test showed that Daryl was not call reluctant; he was an impostor.

His results (partly reproduced below) indicated that Daryl was *not* hesitant to initiate contact with prospective buyers. His Brake Score (general social inhibition) was lower than his Accelerator Score (social motion) and none of the 12 types of call reluctance were indicated. But his Motivation score was only 10% out of a possible 100%. Salespeople typically score 40%-60% and highly successful ones score above 60%.

Brake Score	15%	Motivation (Level)	10%
Accelerator Score	85%	Goal (Level)	93%
Doomsayer	12%	Goal (Diffusion)	18%
Over-Preparation	27%	Problem Solving	20%
Hyper-Pro	25%		
Stage Fright	7%	Impression Management	33%
Role Rejection	12%	Hedging	12%
Yielder	18%	Response Consistency	88%
Social Self-Consciousness	00%	Oppositional Reflex	00%
Separationist	20%		
Emotionally Unemancipated	5%		
Referral Aversion	23%		
Telephobia	00%		

Daryl *didn't want* to prospect, or close, or learn new products, or take responsibility for his own career, or tolerate the frustrations associated with career growth. He was an impostor. He could not be considered reluctant merely because he would not do what he did *not want* to do.

Probable Origin:

Low motivation can be the by-product of two sources: emotional or physical. Low Motivation Impostors of the emotional persuasion *are motivated* but they divert their energies into not showing it. Angry, disappointed, or both, they publicize their feelings indirectly through displays of apathetic disinterest.

It is not uncommon to find this apathetic disinterest in veteran salespeople who were once effective prospectors and successful producers. This situation is common in companies where managers fail to keep their commitments or where the organization is caught up in helter-skelter reorganization spasms.

The physical source of low motivation is poor energy management. This can include excessive smoking, excessive drinking, too much or too little exercise, physical illness, improper diet, or other physical influences.

Outlook:

The outlook for Low Motivation Impostors depends upon whether the problem's source is physical or emotional. If low motivation is due to apathetic disinterest and the salesperson acknowledges his or her anger, then the outlook for corrective action can be very positive. This depends, however, on management keeping its commitments and the company being sensitive to the effects of corporate change on the sales force. When these conditions are not met, the outlook can disintegrate rapidly.

If the cause of low motivation is physical, then lifestyle changes are necessary to increase the energy supply available for career-related behaviors like prospecting. If those changes are not made, then significant improvement cannot be reasonably expected.

CareerStyle (for both sources of low motivation):

- Satisfied with the way things are; lacks serious ambition
- No sense of urgency
- Rhetorical goal-setting; little behavioral investment in actual follow-through
- Fails to understand why management takes issues, like marginal performance, so seriously
- Satisfied with minimal production quotas; just getting by is sufficient
- Unbothered by poor performance; therefore, acknowledges few performance problems
- Unfinished assignments; poor and erratic appearance
- Frequently late for appointments
- Falls asleep during important meetings
- Attends business conventions to hear jokes and be entertained; gives high approval ratings to inspirational speakers and other stage performers who do not make demands on attention or intellect
- Copes with demands for improved productivity by ignoring the issue as long as possible; when that no longer works, changes companies
- Works hard but in short bursts
- Favors the "cartoon" approach to sales training: short, sensational sales training products on subjects such as "How to Hypnotize Your Clients Without Their Knowing It" or "How to Read Your Client's Mind in 20 Seconds or Less"

Self-Assessment:

Do you tend to become impatient with the rate your career is progressing?

Most reasonably motivated people get frustrated from time to time with their progress. Having placed a high degree of importance upon success, they pursue it with a sense of urgency. Therefore, answers that reflect a total absence of frustration and impatience can indicate a Low Motivation Impostor.

Do you enjoy talking about how successful you will become? Do you spend more time verbalizing your goals than actually working to obtain them?

Low Motivation Impostors enjoy talking about success; they invest considerably less effort in doing the things necessary to become successful.

Are you amazed at the trivial things managers allow to upset them regarding the productivity of their salespeople?

Low Motivation Impostors seem to have trouble understanding why everyone does not just accept the way things are—like they do.

After attending a convention, are you more inclined to remember important information or do you tend to recall only the jokes and funny stories?

Low Motivation Impostors are inclined to remember the jokes.

In your opinion, how much success do most people really need?

Low Motivation Impostors tend to define success in terms that make it less personally desirable and consider those who passionately pursue their career objectives to be workaholics.

How many times have you changed companies or careers during the last five years?

Low Motivation Impostors are inclined to change careers whenever the demand for improved production cannot be ignored or evaded.

What type of sales training subjects and materials do you find most beneficial?

Low Motivation Impostors tend to favor inspirational material that is light on content and accompanied by lots of pictures and unused white space.

Can you give me three *quick* examples of projects you stayed with from beginning to end?

Low Motivation Impostors approach this question in one of two ways: They take more time than most people to come up with an answer, often defaulting to "I can't think of anything right now," or they show little interest in even attempting to answer the question.

When you daydream, do you ever see yourself in relaxed settings such as lying on a beach, fishing at a lake, or just lying in the grass enjoying nature?

Low Motivation Impostors tend to fantasize about escaping the pressures of everyday life and retreating to a more relaxed, serene situation.

Objective Assessment:

A Motivation Level score below 40% on the Call Reluctance Scale indicates a Low Motivation Impostor.

Frequency of Occurrence:

Low Motivation Impostors are not uncommon. Some companies (and industries) have far more than their fair share.

Impostor 2: Goal Diffusion
High motivation, too many goals
Too many irons in the fire

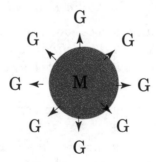

Capsule Summary:

Alan, a bright, exuberant manufacturer's rep, bounced about from subject to subject whenever he spoke. He was, to use his own decorous words, "a Renaissance man." He prided himself on his many interests, relationships, and involvements. When he was evaluated by his company's new sales assessment center, the observers were enchanted by his broad interests and keen intellect. Noting this, and his congenial social skills, the assessors unanimously predicted high sales achievement. Once outside the simulated reality of the assessment center, however, Alan's

"I Don't Give a Damn About Call Reluctance!"

Once, after giving a presentation on call reluctance to a national conference of insurance sales managers, a young manager approached us—not to congratulate us, but to test our mettle.

"I don't give a damn about call reluctance," he said, smiling falsely and looking much like a naughty child about to intentionally belch in church.

"That's interesting," we responded. "First time we've ever met a manager who didn't care."

"Why should *I* care?" he continued. "It's not *my* money; it's the company's money."

Utterly fascinated, we asked, "What company do you work for?" "Big Time Life—best agents, best managers, best products," he said boastfully, his eyes darting about in search of approval from other managers who had began to gather around. Noticing his obvious need to be center stage, Goodson demurred, silently grimaced and turned to speak with someone else. Dudley, a former Marine, who some say suffers from arrested social development, fired back, "Does your company own a stopwatch that counts in microseconds?"

"I guess a company as big as mine has one lying around somewhere," he answered, visibly rattled by the question. "What does that have to do with managing call reluctance?"

"Well, you see," Dudley explained calmly, "that's how we'd measure your tenure if you worked for us. With an attitude like that, you'd be out the door in microseconds."

Judging from the look on his face, we failed the young manager's test. And, he failed ours. We presume all managers *care* about making their company as profitable as possible. Apparently, some don't.

work habits became the subject of immediate concern. He was constantly late for training or did not show up at all. When asked for an explanation, he was unable to acknowledge the problem. If there was a problem, it was not his. He was content. His reflexive reaction to any criticism was smiling disbelief. "Why does everyone have to be so materialistic all the time?" he asked himself.

One day recently, Alan was called at his home by the training manager. Again, he had failed to attend a scheduled sales training class.

MGR: Hi, Alan, I thought we had agreed to begin your training last night at 7 p.m. We were here waiting. Where were you?

ALAN: Gosh, I'm sorry guys. I guess I just plain missed it, didn't I? I went on down to the wine and cheese tasting party at the Fairmont with my girlfriend.

MGR: Wine and cheese tasting party? You missed training for a wine and cheese tasting party?

ALAN: Yeah, I guess so. But it won't happen again. Sorry.

MGR: Okay. Let's see that it doesn't.

Time passed; two evenings later:

MGR: Alan? Where were you last night? I thought you said you would be here on Tuesday evenings for telephone prospecting. What happened this time?

ALAN: Golly, I'm sorry. Guess I'm just not organized enough. I forgot to tell you I take lute lessons every Tuesday evening. Great stuff. You should try it.

MGR: Lute lessons? Well, how about nine in the morning? Can you be here for training in the morning?

ALAN: That would be great....Oh, wait a minute. I don't think I can make it.

MGR: Oh? Why not?

ALAN: Well, a group of us registered for a medieval metaphysical poetry course at the junior college. It meets every Wednesday morning at nine. A friend of mine said it changed her life. Want to sign up with us?

Slam! Dial tone.

Alan *is* motivated. He has energy, but since it's not focused on anything specific, it's not effective. There's no target. No strategy. No systematic pursuit. His prospecting will never get off the ground because it can't compete with "other interesting things to do." Regrettably, Alan will never be accomplished in anything. Instead, he will remain inert—starting much, completing little, interested in everything, mastering nothing. Alan's not call reluctant. He's an impostor.

Some salespeople are adrift in their own possibilities. Seeing life as an adventure, and commitments as a bore, they become addicted to celebrations of their own freedom. Returning to our television analogy, they are like an energy source with 20 televisions simultaneously plugged in. The result? Nothing works like it is supposed to.

Goal diffusion is found in salespeople who convince themselves that boredom can never be tolerated so it must always be avoided. They are emotional and intellectual sensation-seekers who move through religions, social issues, careers, companies, hobbies, and personal relationships with alarming regularity.

Probable Origin:

Corporate cultures are the most frequent triggering mechanisms for Goal Diffusion. Recent Call Reluctance Scale studies conducted within large, high visibility organizations revealed massive Goal Diffusion scores within each company's sales force. Further assessment showed that policies, internal procedures, and endless paper work were cutting into the time, effort, and attention of the sales force. With its efforts diffused, the sales force was unable to focus its energy on selling. When this was pointed out to senior management, no one accepted responsibility and no one could remember how it started. Like primordial ooze, it just evolved.

Every day salespeople for one well-known multinational company are expected to complete forms for the training department, personnel, purchasing, inventory management, sales management, and accounting. If they have time left over to actually prospect and make a sale, they are punished by having to fill out even more forms. In addition, they have meetings to attend, internal phone calls to answer, and endless other demands on their time. The sales force does not know if their primary job is to represent the company's products—and thus attain their sales quotas—or function as administrative assistants, endlessly trying to comply with bureaucratic procedures. The result is confused thinking and scattered actions.

Goal Diffusion can also originate in childhood, though not as often. Children, when mildly conflicted or frustrated, are often placated with a new toy, a trip to the zoo, or a television of their very own. They soon learn that conflict and frustration are justification for seeking out another novelty, another stimulating thing to play with. As adults, conflict and frustration cannot be avoided. Therefore, like most adults these individuals have to cope. How? At the first sign of conflict or frustration they react as they always have: They decide to be bored and cope the way they were taught, by searching for novelty and stimulation. They move from person to person, thing to thing.

One of the most pathetic situations we occasionally encounter are older people who bought into the "do your own thing, go with the flow" mentality characteristic of the '60s. Now, aged and often without direction or resources, they're lost. They did their own thing and went with the flow. They effortlessly (some would say selfishly) floated downstream. Now they can't get back.

Outlook:

When Goal Diffusion is learned during childhood and change is desired, the outlook is extremely positive. When it is due to corporate culture and the organization is willing to do something about it, the outlook is also very positive.

CareerStyle:

- High energy, little focus
- Starts many projects, completes few
- Loses interest quickly
- Continuous need for novelty, stimulation and change
- Very easily bored
- Changes jobs frequently
- Superficially familiar with many subjects
- May have good general overview, but lacks substantive product knowledge
- Multiple interests demand other involvements, some of which conflict with career
- Due to over-commitment, may feel loss of control
- Self-starter with poor follow-through

Self-Assessment:

Do your daydreams tend to center on the theme of simplifying your life?

When Goal Diffusion Impostors become weary of multiple commitments pulling them in many directions, they cope by fantasizing about moving to some simpler place where they can shed the complexity of their lives.

Have you decided what you want to be in life?

Goal diffused people typically have not, regardless of their age. They see commitments, such as prioritized career goals, romantic relationships, or even religious beliefs as being narrow and likely to exclude something interesting that could come their way.

Does the term Renaissance man (or woman), an individual of many interests, apply to you?

In order to cast their overcommitment and underachievement in the best possible light, Goal Diffusion Impostors often like to portray themselves this way.

Do you consider people with clear objectives and priorities to be unsophisticated, narrow, or boring?

Goal Diffusion Impostors can be rigid, elitist, and critical of other people who do not share their values or their lifestyles.

Do you ever unintentionally schedule different activities at the same time, or nearly the same time?

Goal Diffusion Impostors do. With so many activities and interests competing for their attention, they lose perspective and become confused.

Objective Assessment:

Some Goal Diffusion appears to be an unavoidable aspect of the modern sales career. But a Goal Diffusion score of 75% or *higher* on The Call Reluctance Scale suggests a Goal Diffusion Impostor.

Frequency of Occurrence:

Goal Diffusion is common and on the increase. We see more cases today than previously, especially among university-educated salespeople.

Impostor 3: Low Goals
High motivation, low goals
All dressed up, no place to go

$$M \longrightarrow g$$

Capsule Summary:

Some salespeople have plenty of energy but don't know what to do with it. Referring again to our television analogy, these individuals are plugged into an adequate energy source, but one of the connections is either loose, broken, or corroded. The energy can't efficiently move from the source to the television. The TV might work, but if it does it will be erratic and never at full potential until the contacts are fixed or replaced.

In sales, good contacts are needed to connect your energy supply to your objectives and intentions. When that's done, your goals can function properly. Goals supply the focal point for your energy. When they're missing or murky, it's impossible to focus on the things that are important. It becomes increasingly difficult to sustain initiative when you don't know or can't remember why you should be prospecting in the first place. When goals become blurred, prospecting becomes ritualized, mechanical, and soon begins to deteriorate.

Low Goal Impostors have plenty of energy but bad connections. Lacking clear goals to provide meaning to their careers and a reason for working hard, they borrow what appears to be working for *other* salespeople and mindlessly dump their motivation into it. Examples of borrowed goals include recognition, approval of one's parents, and money. These are worthwhile goals, but if they're not *your* goals, the pressures of prospecting and selling will eventually erode them away. When that happens they will no longer provide career direction; performance problems not related to call reluctance, such as burnout and midlife crisis, will rip the rug out from under you. Your prospecting level, though it may remain adequate, could drop well below your ability. On the surface, all of this will look and feel like call reluctance, but it won't be. It's an impostor. Your engine is outperforming your steering mechanism. Suspect this impostor when you can no longer easily answer the question, "What am I prospecting *for?*"

Probable Origin:

Low Goal Impostors can originate from various sources. A small minority of them don't have goals, never have, and never will. This is because they are unable to commit to anything unless it promises a short-term payoff. These salespeople don't have fully functioning commitment faculties, a situation that may ultimately be traced to brain structure, brain chemistry, or a combination of both.

The majority of Low Goal Impostors never learned how to define their goals, select them, and then strive towards them. In a few cases, this is due to the absence of appropriate role models during childhood. More often it's because thoughtful courses in the *life discipline* of goal-setting are not taught in the school system (when it would be most beneficial) or provided later by industry. To compensate for never having learned this discipline, many people simply mimic what seems to be working for others.

Outlook:

The outlook depends upon the origin. If the problem is due to either the absence of an effective goal-setting role model or insufficient exposure to substantive goal-setting procedures, the outlook is very positive. This, of course, presupposes the missing elements will be provided.

CareerStyle:

- Initial production gets off to a quick start, bursts into multiple colors, and then subsides to a fixed plateau

- Plateau Hovering: Performance vacillates erratically around a well-established production plateau

- Goal Misalignment: Failure to consistently apply initiative to presently attainable goals while loitering about waiting for an opportunity to change careers or return to school

- Grass is Greener Syndrome: Perpetually searches the daily newspaper's job listings and recruitment ads

- Prone to job stress, career burnout, and, depending on age, mid-life crisis.

- Overstates loyalty to company, products, and the sales career in order to cover an ambivalent, undecided attitude

- History of attending workshops and seminars on attitude, motivation, and other topics ancillary to sales success (Remember, Low Goal Impostors are *already* motivated. Also, they probably have a positive attitude. What they need are internalized goals to *focus* their high octane energies and positive expectations.)

- Distracted by relatively unimportant side issues like where the sales convention will be held three years from now, how many paid holidays are scheduled for the last half of the year, and whether or not there will be a company picnic this year

- Incentives, reasonably effective for other members of the sales force, fail to significantly increase his/her production

- Initial enthusiasm for new products and marketing aids soon loses steam

- Fails to significantly develop knowledge or skills beyond initial level

- Ambiguous or unclear short- or long-term goals

- Momentarily inspired by motivational presentations

- Talks long-term but acts short-term
- Works to achieve other people's objectives, not really his/her own
- More interested in the company's social activities than daily performance
- May change jobs frequently
- Day-by-day career management philosophy in lieu of long-term goals
- Supervision and frequent reinforcement required
- Does not stay focused on one product
- Undervalues life planning, career planning, or strategic planning of any type (which is exactly what is needed)
- Responds best to short duration, frequently-held sales contests
- May be impulsive, taking imprudent risks without carefully considering the long-term implications
- Often in a hurry but has little to show for it
- Service after the sale may be inadequate or inconsistent

Self-Assessment:

Are you inclined to daydream about finding relationships that will bring order to your life? What about discovering a career which will provide deep-seated loyalties or embarking on a life-long crusade that requires all your energy?

Low Goal Impostors dream about being in circumstances where "meaning" and "purpose" are conferred upon them by the situation they are in, thus delegating to other people or places the responsibility for shaping their lives.

Do you concentrate more on how you *feel* about being in sales than you do the opportunities associated with the career?

In the absence of clear, rational understandings about their careers, Low Goal Impostors overemphasize their feelings.

Are you dependent upon high intensity books and inspirational cassettes to wind you up and get you started?

Low Goal Impostors must purchase their zeal from commercial sources to compensate for their own ambiguous convictions. Incidentally, that's why many Low Goal Impostors tend to have a ready supply of sales clichés and success platitudes.

Objective Assessment:

Goal level scores below 20% on the Call Reluctance Scale suggest a Low Goal Impostor. Scores between 40% and 70% are considered average for people in sales.

Frequency of Occurrence:

Some companies have a disproportionate number of Low Goal Impostors. In general, however, this impostor tends to occur in about 10-15% of all experienced and inexperienced salespeople.

Impostor 4: Information
High motivation, high goals, low training
I'll prospect when I know what to say

$$M \longrightarrow ? \longrightarrow G$$

Capsule Summary:

Some motivated, goal-directed salespeople hesitate to initiate contacts with prospective buyers because they feel they have not been sufficiently trained to ethically represent their products and services.

Probable Origin:

Hesitating to make calls before you have been adequately trained can be an act of conscience and often happens when high quality salespeople are hired into low quality sales organizations. The strip-mining approach to sales training found in these companies often sparks the Information Impostor. (For our purposes, we do not distinguish organizational quality by the type of product or service sold, but rather by the quality of sales management and depth of preparation and training they provide.)

In low quality sales organizations, careers are designed to be short-term infatuations. Therefore, sales training is not provided for the long haul. These organizations don't expect new salespeople to stay, and they don't particularly care when they leave. It is of paramount importance to them, however, that salespeople generate big profits during their short tenure.

Training is rarely formal or systematic in these organizations. Instead, the process unceremoniously begins with "Sign here" and ends with a slap on the back, a shove out the door, and a heartfelt "Sic 'em tiger!"

High quality salespeople expect more. They also *need* more before they allow themselves to feel positive about the products and services they sell. Under these circumstances, their hesitation to initiate contact with prospective buyers could be an act of intellect and integrity—not an act of fear. These salespeople are not call reluctant. They're Information Impostors.

Outlook:

If you're an Information Impostor, your resistance to prospecting can be cleared up quickly and easily by gaining access to the information you need. Just ask your sales manager or trainer for the information you think you need. That should do the trick. But be careful. There could be a call reluctance specter lurking behind the scene (See Over-Preparer, Chapter 3).

CareerStyle:

- Frequent requests for needed information go unheeded or are mechanically delegated to superficial indoctrination techniques

- Complains that training consists of too much indoctrination and not enough substance

- Spends prospecting time trying to acquire needed training and information

- Doubts begin to surface about the integrity of the company, its products, and its sales management

- For ethical reasons, resists calling on family, friends, and community contacts

- Has little respect for management

- Wonders why most of the sales force is new and inexperienced though the company has been in business for a considerable period of time

- Willing to make calls but only after adequate training has been provided

- Was recruited with highly emotional claims and sensational promotions in lieu of factual particulars about the company's training programs and sales materials

Self-Assessment:

Do you spend more and more time pondering the ethics of your career choice, the products you sell, or the company you represent?

Information Impostors do this because they are exposed to practices every day most ethical people would consider questionable.

Do you daydream about being in a respectable setting where there is a clear emphasis on ethical standards?

Information Impostors frequently dream of escaping to just such a place.

Do you pose *hypothetical* questions to friends and acquaintances about sales methods, products, or practices which are cryptically linked to your company's sales methods?

Information Impostors may indirectly raise their concerns in this way to verify their suspicions about the ethics of certain sales practices advocated by their company.

Objective Assessment:

Companies with high-level training programs that suspect isolated episodes of poor training should consider using internally developed tests specifically constructed to assess product knowledge and sales techniques.

Frequency of Occurrence:

Information Impostors are relatively rare. Most sales organizations we have observed attempt to supply their salespeople with enough information to enable them to ethically represent their products and services.

Information Impostor symptoms are found in new salespeople as well as in veterans associated with companies that have been acquired by new owners. Once in a while, we find these symptoms in veterans following a radical alteration of their company's marketing orientation. We have also identified Information Impostors in pyramid sales organizations and other companies that have questionable sales training standards. These organizations seemed unconcerned about who sold their products—or how.

WARNING!

If you suspect you are an Information Impostor, request the information you need. Once you receive the additional information you said you needed, you should be ready to make more calls, *immediately*. If you *still* need more information, ask for that information as well, and continue asking as often as you need to.

If your prospecting activity is low because you are an Information Impostor, you will be "magically cured" by the information you said you needed. For Information Impostors, the problem is the lack of information; once this is corrected, the problem should cease to exist. *Improved prospecting activity should immediately follow.* However, if you still find yourself reflexively asking for more information, then it's obvious that the lack of information was not the problem in the first place. *It's an excuse. You're not an impostor, you're call reluctant.* Your career is being detained by Over-Preparation, one of the twelve forms of call reluctance. Over-Preparation Call Reluctance and the other eleven types are described in Chapter 3.

Goals and Motivation:
How Much Do You *Really* Need?

Are clear goals really important? If so, how important are they? What about motivation? How much do you *really* need? Our research suggests that the relationships between motivation, goals, and success are important, but in a more complex manner than is presupposed by most silver bullet success books that insist upon crystal clear goals and Olympian motivation levels.

Data gathered from several studies may help to clarify the issue. For example, our study (1988) of the insurance industry's Million Dollar Round Table (MDRT) clearly showed that production was positively associated with goal clarity, but within limits. After a certain point, goal-clarifying activities actually interfered with production. Participants, who represented all MDRT production levels, completed the Call Reluctance Scale. Top of the Table producers, the highest MDRT production category, averaged a goal clarity score of 64.11% on a 100% scale. The year this data was acquired, Top of the Table membership required a minimum of $240,000 in commissions. Basic membership required only $40,000 and corresponded with an average goal clarity score of 46%.

A non-MDRT comparison sample consisted of salespeople who represented the same companies and sold the same products at the same time and to the same markets as the MDRT sample. They also had approximately the same insurance sales experience. Their goal clarity score averaged only 38.53%.

There is no question that for these samples, higher production is associated with clearer goals. The differences between these groups are striking, but that's not the end of the story. The Top of the Table group, which included some of the highest producing salespeople in the world, averaged only 64.11%. That certainly shows disciplined daily management of goal-supporting energy, but it fails to support the fiction that high achievers are obsessive, "mission-driven," or have goals which are clearer than those of mortal men and women.

In subsequent interviews we learned that many of the highest producers did not have three- or five-year plans. Many were even uncertain about what they wanted to accomplish in the next five weeks. And, in some cases, high producers were operating exclusively on a daily basis. A few knew what they were trying to accomplish but had no discernible plan of attack. Paradoxically, the producers who were most organized were the over-preparers in the non-MDRT comparison group. They had everything organized and scheduled. These individuals kept neat lists, plans, charts, and schedules to project very lofty goals, but they had very little time left to make calls and few results to justify the time they had invested in preparation.

Perhaps success in sales does not require heroic goals. The discipline to do the things that have to be done on a daily basis may be sufficient. If that is the case, then success becomes accessible to more of us, more often. That is truly unexpected and truly inspiring.

As part of the study some of the Top of the Table producers brought up the role of religious faith in sales success. It became clear to us that these individuals intended to be heard. Religious faith was an important aspect of their career management strategy and they insisted that it be included in any explanation of their higher-than-average, but unspectacular, goal-clarity scores. They reported that they conducted their daily affairs in the reasonable trust that their "future is in better hands than their own."

"I just show up ready and trust the Lord to take care of the details," one said. To us, excessive planning and goal-setting is a sign of call reluctance. To them, it shows a lack of faith. Simplistic? They were some of the highest producers we have ever observed.

What about motivation? Motivation scores were also analyzed in the above study. Like goal clarity, high motivation scores corresponded to high production and clearly distinguished the MDRT sample from the average producers in the comparison group. The Top of the Table producers averaged 74% on motivation while the comparison group averaged only 42%. But like goal clarity, success in sales does not appear to require superhuman levels of motivation. The ability to consistently focus energy

How to Evaluate Call Reluctance "Experts"

The wrong information, or even the right information in the wrong hands, can make prospecting problems worse. So how do you distinguish the help from the hype? You can evaluate the expertise of prospective consultants and speakers by asking a few key questions in advance:

- Can they properly define call reluctance?
- Do they know and use both the "process" and the "product" definitions?
- Do they know how to use the tools necessary to assess the "three essential conditions?"
- Do they know how to recognize all four "impostors?"
- Do they know how to spot all twelve forms of call reluctance?
- Do they know how to match each of the call reluctance types with the countermeasure best suited to correct it?

If the answer to *any* of the above questions is "no," and your prospective consultant or speaker still uses terms like "fear of rejection," fasten your seat belt and hold on to your wallet. You are about to be taken for an expensive and wasteful ride.

on daily, goal-supporting behaviors like prospecting is more important than piston-knocking, super-high motivation scores.

GAMES IMPOSTORS PLAY

Over time, impostors grow comfortable with certain habits of living and coping. Most realize they're not performing at—or even near—their potential. But commitment to effective countermeasures always carries with it some risk and uncertainty. Therefore, impostors cope, like other people, by rigorously avoiding the solutions they need the most. They turn instead to less threatening agencies of change. Often, their patterns of evasion become so complete and predictable that you can infer what they need by observing what they avoid.

Goal-Setting Junkies

Impostors who recite goals, but lack the motivation to reach them, know they have a problem. Ironically, they seek their medicine from among their poison. Dutifully, they sign up for every goal-setting conference, seminar, workshop, or assembly they can find. They stretch their goal-setting vocabulary and refine their goal-setting concepts and procedures. This would be useful if, in fact, goal-setting was their problem. It's not. But at least it's something they're comfortable with. They know a lot about it, and it's not threatening. Have you ever noticed, however, what Low Motivation Impostors dutifully avoid: motivational workshops. They resist the things that could help them the most. Paradoxically, the result is career anemia. They eat a lot, but all the wrong foods.

Inspirational Junkies

Low Goal Impostors need fundamental goal-setting skills. So they attend every motivational workshop they can find. When they're not marching off to a workshop, they're listening to inspirational cassettes. They intoxicate themselves with mindless platitudes, and converse with motivational quips and slogans. But they religiously avoid what they need the most: help setting their goals.

Time Management Junkies

Goal Diffusion Impostors lack the ability to clarify and sort out what is most important in their lives. They know they have an energy allocation problem because they regularly find themselves stretched in too many directions—lost among an assortment of needs, desires, and interests. They never learned how to differentiate between what they would like and what they actually need. Weighted down by fragmentation and chaos, they turn to books on planning and time management for all the answers. None of the solutions stick. So they keep looking. Avoiding their real need for values clarification and priority management, they remain lost in a self-induced maze of planning techniques and time management procedures.

Well represented among marginal producers, the impostors are as lethal to a career in direct sales as authentic call reluctance. They mimic the low production associated with the real thing. But they're missing one or more of the three essential ingredients necessary for genuine call reluctance, and they don't respond to countermeasures designed to correct it.

REMEDIES AND POISONS

Impostor	Remedies				
	Time Mgt.	Values Clarif.	Goal Setng.	Product Trng.	Motivation Training
Low M	NE	NE	P	NE	B
Low G	NE	NE	B	P	NE
Goal Diffusion	NE	B	B	NE	P
Information	P	P	P	B	P

NE   = Not harmful or helpful; probably not effective
B   = Probably beneficial
P   = Poisonous; can make matters worse

The first thing a salesperson, manager, trainer, or consultant should do before treating call reluctance is to rule out the impostors.

But beware. Most pop-psych approaches to evaluating call reluctance fall woefully short. For example, typical selection tests are unable to distinguish authentic call reluctance from other causes of low prospecting activity. Even good tests in the wrong hands can produce misleading results. Therefore, we recommend using only specialized tests and evaluation procedures which may be available through your company's sales training or personnel departments.

Recalculating Losses

Once call reluctance is properly defined, its epidemic impact can be more precisely observed and accurately understood. We know, for example, that up to 40% of the salespeople said to fail each year due to "call reluctance" are actually impostors. In many cases they are the casualties of rigid, but superficial, sales selection programs, which yield grossly inaccurate hiring decisions—with no accountability. In other cases, they are victims of neglect. Their companies, using inexpensive and ineffective rating scales to chart their needs, deploy improper training weapons, and aim them at the wrong training targets. Everybody loses.

Recommendations for Impostors:
A Resource Guide

This book is specifically dedicated to correcting authentic call reluctance. It would not be manageable if we also included corrective measures for impostors. That volume will come later. If you've determined that you're probably an impostor, you should talk to your manager or trainer. If that is not possible, then seek out corrective information and resources on your own. We have provided some initial guidance to help you get started in the right direction. Our list is far from complete and makes no pretense at being exhaustive. It is only meant to be representative of some of the most worthwhile advice currently available.

Low Motivation Impostors

Substance abuse:
  Churches—Some religious organizations sponsor substance abuse programs.
  Industry—Some industries have support groups.
  Social—Some state and local substance abuse resources are available.
Sleep disorders: Consult a qualified physician.
Vitamins: There are several good books on nutrition available in major bookstores and in health food stores.
Stop Smoking: Many reputable groups sponsor programs to help you stop smoking.
Exercise: Excellent exercise books and videos are available.

Stress Management: A Comprehensive Guide to Wellness, by Charlesworth and Nathan
Triggers: A New Approach to Self Motivation, by Stanley Mann
Biofeedback, by Danskin and Crow
  (*Biofeedback training can be obtained through qualified psychologists and other professionals.*)

Goal Diffusion Impostors

Values Clarification, by Simon, Howe, and Kirschenbaum
The Time Trap, by Alec MacKenzie
  (*Workshops on how to set and manage priorities are offered by many universities.*)

Low Goal Impostors

A Christmas Carol, by Charles Dickens; James H. Heineman
What Color Is Your Parachute?, by Richard Bolles
The Three Boxes of Life, by Richard Bolles

Pastoral Counseling: Some churches and denominations provide counseling services which can help in this area.
Some colleges and universities provide career counseling services.

Information Impostors

Product knowledge:
- Consult your sales manager, trainer, consultants.
- Review your company training materials.
- Check with experienced colleagues.
- Search out audio/video and written information about your industry.

Sales Training:
The Best Seller, by D. Forbes Ley
Strategic Selling, by Robert B. Miller, et al
Influence: Science and Practice, by Robert B. Cialdini
Effective Negotiating, by Chester L. Karass
Professional Selling, by Vince Pesce
How To Sell Your Ideas, by Jesse S. Nirenberg
How to Win Customers and Keep Them for Life, by Michael LeBoeuf
Your Public Best, by Lillian Brown
Closing the Sale, by Friedman and Weiss
Money Making Marketing, by Jeffrey Lant

Debunking a Call Reluctance Myth

Back in sales training antiquity (ten years ago), we happened to hear Buford (not his real name), a weather-beaten, crusty old sales manager, speak at his industry's annual sales management convention. A young manager in the audience stood and asked him to comment on call reluctance. Buford immediately affected a weariness he didn't really feel, and theatrically closed his eyes for a long moment like he was privately receiving divine revelation straight from heaven.

"Call reluctance?" he said slowly, stretching each syllable. "You want to know about call reluctance? Well I'll tell you about call

continues

Debunking a Call Reluctance Myth *continued*

reluctance. Show me a call reluctant salesman [they were mostly all men back then] and I'll show you a lazy SOB who doesn't believe in our products or our industry."

Wheezing and fuming, Buford went on, "He ain't got no commitment. That's all you need to know about call reluctance."

With those words, Buford verbally wiped call reluctance from the board like an incorrect answer to an elementary math problem. But he spoke the truth as it was known back then. He held the majority opinion. Fortunately, times have changed. We now know differently.

The process definition of call reluctance firmly establishes that no salesperson can be call reluctant unless he/she is both motivated and committed. *You simply cannot be reluctant to get something you don't want in the first place.* Impostors don't care if they don't meet their prospecting goals. Salespeople with authentic call reluctance care very much. Imagine the pain and energy required to continuously try prospecting day after day regardless of constant distress. What do you think keeps these salespeople going if not motivation and commitment? It's certainly not job satisfaction! Salespeople with authentic call reluctance hang in as long as they can, usually until the system expels them. Impostors leave soon after their first confrontation with sales management.

Sales managers have tried for years to attract motivated and committed salespeople. Ironically, they have always been around. They just happened to be imperfect—they had call reluctance. But thanks in part to great social scientists like Buford, call reluctance was considered a character flaw, an absence of willpower, the wrong attitude, or a lack of commitment to the company or product. The solution was to get the heretic "...right the hell out of the business!"

Companies did. Motivated salespeople who happened to have call reluctance were either branded with a scarlet letter or neglected altogether. It cost both the companies and the salespeople dearly. In many companies and industries, it still does.

The notion that call reluctance is a single condition is a venerable piece of nonsense which has largely been discredited. Twelve different types have been identified so far and there are probably more.

Chapter Three

THE TWELVE FACES OF SALES CALL RELUCTANCE

CONFRONTING THE ENEMY

O ur call reluctance research, the first of its type, was launched in 1970 under the misguided presumption that we were confronting a one-dimensional aggravation, like "shyness" or "timidity." But the view that call reluctance could be condensed to one or two tidy notions, such as "fear of rejection" or "fear of failure," soon broke under the strain of mounting evidence. By 1986, when the first edition of this book was published, nine types of call reluctance had been identified. Since then we have discovered three more. There are probably others.

The custom of downgrading complex behaviors like call reluctance to simple-minded cliches like the "fear of rejection" is a venerable piece of nonsense. For some veteran sales trainers, the practice is still too entrenched to be displaced by objective evidence. Serious practitioners, however, have soundly discredited and permanently discarded these banalities. They know that the dark, mental landscape where call reluctance presides is more complicated than originally thought. It's a province where motivated, goal-directed ambitions are stalked by 12 separate specters, not just one.

Remember Nancy, Bob and Larry, the three real-life cases we used to introduce Chapter 1? Nancy is fighting a form of call reluctance called Doomsayer. It's characterized by a paralyzing preoccupation with mental and physical safety that results in relentless preparation for things that could go wrong.

Doomsayers tend to presume that things are bound to go wrong. They divert too much of their motivational energy to being prepared for the worst. They're perpetually on "red alert." To them, *any* risk taking is distressful. Since initiating contact with prospective buyers requires taking social risks, prospecting becomes difficult, if not impossible, for Doomsayers to do on a regular basis. They must first receive corrective training.

What Is a Sales Professional?

We were prepared. Another live radio interview about our call reluctance research was about to get underway. We were ready.

"What *is* a sales professional?" the pudding-faced, carefully modulated talk show host wondered aloud to her vast audience, affecting an almost perfect sincerity. We were the "guest experts." We were supposed to have a proper answer. We didn't. The question had never crossed our minds. Therefore, sensing the situation, we glanced at each other over our microphones while valiantly trying to stifle the urge to laugh at the absurdity of the situation. Fumbling for words, we managed a feeble answer that was so unmemorable that we immediately wiped it from our minds.

Eventually we composed a better definition based on our work with call-reluctant salespeople.

To us, **a professional salesperson is an individual who has the will and the discipline to make cold calls when necessary, but who has been trained so well that he or she never has to.**

Bob limits himself by refusing to call on friends and relatives, even to ask for referrals. He has two types of call reluctance: Emotionally Unemancipated (excludes family) and Separationist (excludes friends). Typically, salespeople like Bob fashion elaborate, sometimes belligerent, quasi-ethical arguments to excuse their call-reluctant behavior. "Professional salespeople," they moralize, "should *never* involve their family or friends in their business." Some become emotional when pressed to explain the logical justification for their refusal to use the contacts closest to them. And that's the key. In the heat of argument it quickly becomes apparent that their hesitation is not really the by-product of a liberated, intellectual choice. It's the result of a choice-limiting emotional cramp. It's call reluctance.

Larry's sales career isn't suffering from vague psychological aches and pains like the "fear of rejection." He has Social Self-Consciousness Call Reluctance.

Social Self-Consciousness Call Reluctance is an emotional condition that makes salespeople feel inferior to prospective buyers they consider socially or economically better off. Larry habitually permits himself to be intimidated by persons of wealth, education, prestige or power. He copes by avoidance—aiming his prospecting efforts downward. He sustains

---

Variations On a Call Reluctance Theme

The fear of self-promotion is the generic name given to the general inhibitions associated with self-promotion. It can limit the progress of anyone in a contact-dependent career. When it limits the ability of salespeople to prospect, it earns the name "sales call reluctance." When it interferes with the ability of sales managers to contact high quality sources of new recruits, it is called "recruiting reluctance." When it impedes the ability of salespeople to close sales once a presentation has been given, it is called "close reluctance."

Recruiting reluctance and close reluctance are blood relatives of call reluctance. But they also contain important differences. The measurement techniques outlined in this book can also be used to assess both of these career-limiting conditions. The corrective procedures we describe can also be used but may require adjustments.

---

prospecting comfort by sacrificing one of his most lucrative markets. By doing so, he defaults on his performance objectives. It's a bitter trade-off. Social Self-Consciousness is particularly dangerous in salespeople whose companies routinely market to upscale clientele. Without proper training, salespeople with Social Self-Consciousness Call Reluctance can't make the grade.

Terms and Concepts

You must do some heavy spadework, turning up a lot of subsoil, before you can successfully contest call reluctance in yourself or others. Familiarity with a few terms and concepts will give you a better perspective of the call reluctance types that follow.

Popular Name—Nontechnical, widely accepted name for each of the call reluctance types.

Technical Name—Precise, definitive name experts use for each of the call reluctance types.

Abbreviation—Shorthand used by experts when referring to each of the call reluctance types.

Capsule Summary—General overview of each type of call reluctance, emphasizing how it interferes with prospecting.

Probable Origin—Where a self-limiting behavior comes from; divided between heredity and learning.

Outlook—Likelihood of improvement for each call reluctance type, assuming accurate diagnosis is made and appropriate corrective procedures are used.

CareerStyle—Most characteristic behaviors associated with each type of call reluctance; serves as reference point for behavioral observation and diagnosis.

Self-Assessment—Questions you should ask yourself and answer as honestly as you can. They could reveal which particular type of call reluctance is limiting your career.

Objective Assessments—Pertinent information obtained from formally developed assessment scales such as the Call Reluctance Scale, the Potentia CareerStyles Inventory™ (PCSI), the Sixteen Personality Factors Questionnaire (16PF), and the Motivation Analysis Test.

> ***Selling Styles Profile Analysis***™ —The type or style of sales presentation an individual naturally prefers or gravitates to. The six selling styles are based on Dudley and Goodson's factor analytic research with formal personality tests such as the 16PF and the PCSI.

> ***Call Reluctance Scale***—A highly specialized, computer-scored research questionnaire first introduced in 1982 and improved many times since. Used daily by sales organizations in many countries, it is the only test available specifically designed to measure all aspects of sales call reluctance, including the call reluctance impostors. *(See appendix)*

>> ***Brake and Accelerator Scores***—These measures are provided to guide users of the Call Reluctance Scale. They are two of the most important scores derived from the scale. Using the analogy of an automobile, the Accelerator score gauges the total motivation currently invested in propelling a salesperson forward into the community to initiate contact with prospective buyers. The Brake score estimates the total amount of motivation currently being short-circuited into coping behaviors that inhibit prospecting. Call reluctance is indicated when the Brake score is *higher* than the Accelerator score. Call reluctance is not present, at least in toxic amounts, when the Brake score is *lower* than the Accelerator score.

Frequency of Occurrence—Frequency with which a particular type of call reluctance is observed.

Most Effective Countermeasures—Procedures found in the Prescriptions (Rx) section of this book designed for each type of call reluctance.

Equipped with these preliminary terms and concepts, you can explore each of the twelve forms of call reluctance in greater depth. Hopefully, you will be able to identify some of the attitudes and behaviors that could be interfering with your own prospecting efforts. Identifying the type of call reluctance you're struggling with is the first and most important step you can take to correct it.

Call Reluctance Types
(as measured by the Call Reluctance Scale)

Doomsayer

Characterized by energy being diverted away from contact with prospective buyers into over-vigilant preparation for low probability catastrophes. Habitual worrying about the worst case scenario.

Over-Preparation

Characterized by energy being over-invested in analyzing at the expense of prospecting. Preparation for making calls is out of control. Salesperson is an encyclopedia of technical information with no one to make presentations to.

Hyper-Pro

Characterized by energy being lost due to over-investment in the mannerisms and appearances of success. Energy is expended at the expense of goal-supporting behaviors such as prospecting, which is viewed as "demeaning" and "unprofessional." Often accompanied by over-stylized use of professional jargon, name-dropping, and a reflexive need to appear better informed and more sophisticated than the "average" salesperson.

Stage Fright

Characterized by avoiding or bypassing opportunities to prospect through group presentations due to emotional discomfort. Highly targeted form of fear. Other forms of prospecting may be completely unaffected.

Role Rejection

Intricate type of call reluctance characterized by energy being lost due to unexpressed and unresolved guilt and shame associated

continues

Call Reluctance Types *continued*

with being in sales. Highly contagious. Recognized by the absence of objectivity and the rigid insistence upon appearing positive at all times, which has the effect of doubling the energy lost.

Yielder

Characterized by hesitating to prospect for new business due to a reflexive fear of being considered selfish, intrusive or pushy. Salesperson may compensate by developing over-stylized, rigid adherence to consultative selling skills which can exaggerate the importance of relationship building at the expense of clientele building.

Social Self-Consciousness

Characterized by emotional hesitation to initiate contact with up-market prospective buyers. Habitually intimidated by persons of wealth, prestige or power. This reaction may be camouflaged by a verbalized, over-cavalier disregard for status. Highly targeted fear. Other forms of prospecting may remain unaffected.

Separationist

Characterized by emotional resistance to mixing business interests with friendships. Salesperson usually finds it difficult to prospect for sales among personal friends or even to ask them for referrals. Can have adverse consequences even in sales settings where it is not necessary or appropriate to call on friends.

Emotionally Unemancipated

Characterized by emotional resistance to mixing business and family. Salesperson experiences difficulty prospecting for new business among accessible family members or even asking them for referrals. Can have adverse consequences even in sales settings where it is not necessary or appropriate to call on family members, or when family members are not accessible due to death or geographic distance.

Referral Aversion

Characterized by emotional discomfort associated with asking existing clients for referrals. Salesperson may experience little or no distress actually initiating contacts or closing sales.

continues

Call Reluctance Types *continued*

Telephobia

Characterized by fear when trying to use the telephone for prospecting purposes. Highly targeted. Face-to-face forms of prospecting may be completely unimpaired.

Oppositional Reflex

Hard-edged type of call reluctance characterized by high approval needs and low self-esteem. Result is ambivalent need for continuous feedback which is then criticized and rejected as invalid. Compulsive need to argue, make excuses, and blame others. These salespeople are emotionally unable to allow themselves to be coached, advised, managed or trained. Many low producers remain low producers because of this form of call reluctance.

Types of Call Reluctance Impostors (as measured by the Call Reluctance Scale)

Motivation

Total motivational energy available to support career-related behaviors. The more the better, although 70-90% may reflect the optimum zone. Low scores indicate the Low Motivation Impostor discussed in Chapter 2.

Goal Level

Degree of focus on career-related objectives. The more the better, although 70-90% may reflect the realistic optimum. A low score indicates the Low Goal Impostor described in Chapter 2.

Goal Diffusion

Number of clear goals simultaneously competing for energy and attention. The lower the better. High scores are common in organizations with unclear direction, regular reorganizations, or constantly changing plans. A high score suggests the Goal Diffusion Impostor outlined in Chapter 2.

THE TWELVE TYPES
OF CALL RELUCTANCE

According to the Book of Genesis, naming all the creatures, to gain dominion over them, was among man's very first tasks. Though less lofty an enterprise, our first task must also be to name the twelve types of call reluctance so we can gain dominion over them. This chart should help. It provides a concise, preliminary overview of the twelve types of call reluctance along with a key characteristic associated with each. Following the chart is a more detailed description of each call reluctance type.

Call Reluctance Types	"Marker" Behaviors
Doomsayer	Worries, will not take social risks
Over-Preparation	Over-analyzes, under-acts
Hyper-Pro	Obsessed with image
Stage Fright	Fears group presentations
Role Rejection	Ashamed of sales career
Yielder	Fear of intruding on others
Social Self-Consciousness	Intimidated by up-market clientele
Separationist	Fears loss of friends
Emotionally Unemancipated	Fears loss of family approval
Referral Aversion	Fears disturbing existing business or client relationships
Telephobia	Fears using the telephone for prospecting or self-promotional purposes
Oppositional Reflex	Rebuffs attempts to be coached

DOOMSAYER

Technical Name **Threat Sensitivity**

TS

Capsule Summary:

Doomsayer Call Reluctance occurs when salespeople remain preoccupied with worst-case prospecting possibilities. To cope with the fictional dangers they dwell upon, they maintain an unnecessarily high degree of emergency preparedness. Their continued vigilance drains away emotional and physical energy. They are left with insufficient stamina to initiate contacts with prospective buyers on a regular basis.

Probable Origin:

Popular studies are now beginning to confirm what some scholars and researchers have suspected for many years. Certain *personality*-based behaviors, like Doomsayer Call Reluctance, reflect both a learning and a hereditary influence. Some Doomsayers extend their fear beyond initiating contact with prospective buyers. They are also borderline agoraphobics (abnormal fear of open spaces). A recent news article about agoraphobics stated, "Evidence is mounting that vulnerability to agoraphobia is *inherited*. If one identical twin has the disorder, the second twin has a 40% chance of developing it." [our emphasis]

Some Doomsayers experience panic attacks. A June 1986 article in *American Health* magazine noted that "...many researchers now believe they [the panic attacks] aren't a psychological trouble at root, but part of a biological disorder involving the nervous system."

Outlook:

Since Doomsayer Call Reluctance is a personality trait influenced by unknown physical, chemical and learning agents, it can only be arrested. It is very difficult to "cure."

CareerStyle:

- Overly alert to low probability problems
- May be prone to panic attacks

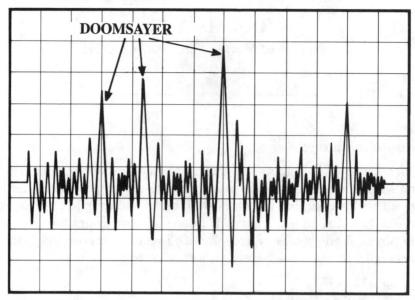

When Doomsayers are connected to a physiological monitoring device like a polygraph and asked threatening questions about prospecting, the polygraph printout displays large, rapid physical changes and takes more time to return to normal (baseline) levels.

- Appears friendly but enjoys only limited social involvement
- Low social or emotional risk-taking
- Visibly distressed if required to make cold calls in person or on the telephone
- Highly self-controlled; may appear rigid
- May tend to measure success by the absence of failure
- Prepares by memorizing a small number of fully scripted presentations
- Blind-sided and momentarily disoriented when a prospect deviates from the classical sales training scenario that the salesperson was taught
- Paralyzed by spontaneity
- Unrelated to intelligence, dedication or self-discipline

Self-Assessment:

How do you see prospecting in terms of social or emotional risk-taking? *Look for an imbalance of perceived danger over perceived opportunity.*

How many total social, civic, fraternal or religious organizations are you presently active in?
Look for low social involvement.

How much do you tend to rely on memorized sales scripts?
Look for heavy reliance upon scripted sales presentations and canned rebuttals to sales objections.

How many total prospecting contacts do you initiate daily?
Look for low total number.

When you daydream, do you see yourself involved in reckless, devil-may-care risks and adventures?
Doomsayers coping with too much self-imposed fear and emotional congestion may try to compensate by creating an imaginary world where they behave just the opposite.

Objective Assessments:

Call Reluctance Scale—A high prospecting Brake score plus a high Doomsayer score suggest that Doomsayer Call Reluctance is limiting prospecting performance now.

A low prospecting Brake score plus a high Doomsayer score indicate a predisposition to Doomsayer Call Reluctance, although it is probably not interfering with prospecting at the present time.

Selling Styles Profile Analysis—Doomsayers tend to prefer Product-Oriented or Need-Oriented presentation styles.

Frequency of Occurrence:

Relative to the other types, Doomsayer Call Reluctance is uncommon in salespeople. It is much more frequent in non-salespeople.

Most Effective Countermeasures:

- Threat Desensitization

- Thought Zapping

- Sensory Injection (Therapeutic Massage conditioned to relaxation cues)

- Yellow Dot

- Target Reversal

- Thought Realignment

- Biofeedback

- Physical check-up by qualified physician; evaluate for inner ear disturbances

- Hot Water Bottle

OVER-PREPARATION
Technical Name **Desurgency**
DSY

Capsule Summary:

Over-Preparation Call Reluctance occurs in sensitive salespeople who become anxiously concerned about being swept away by the intensity of their own feelings. To cope, they force their emotions underground, developing interests in highly technical or artistic matters. Over-Preparers manage their feelings by keeping them locked up and out of sight. Interactions with others are conducted through emotionally safe, information-bound channels. In sales, they tend to spend too much time preparing what to say and how to say it, while spending too little time prospecting for people to give their presentations to. Stressing technical specifications and product information, they often surge into lifeless presentations, neglecting to establish rapport with prospective buyers. Psychologist Patrick Vann would include Over-Preparers among the people he says are searching for safety in repetition and ritual. According to Vann, "...their preference is for methodical and meticulous tasks." (*American Way*, Oct. 1987)

Probable Origin:

Over-Preparation Call Reluctance is believed to be influenced by both heredity and early learning experiences. Most practitioners would probably still characterize Over-Preparation as an entirely learned behavior problem. Mounting physical evidence, however, is beginning to weaken the link to learning, suggesting that some forms of Over-Preparation may be due to chemical assaults on the cortex of the brain.

Over-Preparers: Closing by the Book

Both authors of this book are Doomsayers and Over-Preparers. Trained in experimental design, personality theory, and psychological testing, our first-hand attempts to sell were colorful, but not profitable.

In preparing for his first sales opportunity, Dudley spent days practicing his only sales presentation, one he fashioned after attending a sales training workshop. About 90 minutes long, it featured facts, figures, charts, statistics, one unreliable joke, two feeble anecdotes, three marginally literate endorsement letters, and four obligatory "benefit" statements. Following this, as instructed, was the close.

Among the things we aspired to sell with this strategy were specialized computer reports based on the highly regarded Sixteen Personality Factors Questionnaire (16PF).

We arrived for one particular sales presentation exactly on time, as was our custom. Fully armed with a box of textbooks containing advanced technical support, several reports, various brochures, and an assortment of other inconvenient details, we were ready for the hunt. After a brief exchange of courtesies, Dudley catapulted right into his well-rehearsed presentation. Early on, there were subtle indications that the customer was ready to buy—including a few weakly veiled requests.

"What do I have to do to get started using some of these today? Who do I write the check out to?" the stout, honest-faced prospect said congenially, looking somewhat bemused.

Dudley seemed unaware. Instead of going for the early close, he plodded through more charts, more graphs, more statistics. The luminously smiling prospect courteously followed the presentation, but after a while his eyes seemed to glaze over and become vacant as if watching a motion picture from a great distance. Exactly 20 minutes into the presentation, a short break was scheduled. (Five minute breaks were *always* scheduled 20 minutes into Dudley's presentations.)

"Didn't you hear him?" Goodson said sternly but discreetly, projecting only a polite ghost of a smile and speaking just loud

continues

Over-Preparers *continued*

enough for Dudley to hear. "He wants to place an order. *Now!*"

"That's impossible," Dudley said matter-of-factly, casually dismissing the issue with a know-it-all sidelong smile.

Eyebrows raised in disbelief, Goodson pressed further. "Why? Why is it *impossible?*" she asked, exaggerating each syllable of "impossible" for emphasis.

"Because we haven't gotten to the close yet!" Dudley snapped, growing more agitated.

Exasperated by Dudley's devotion to his neatly codified and exhaustively detailed presentation, Goodson approached the problem from another perspective, sarcasm. "Isn't it conceivable," she asked with the wiliness of an experienced lawyer cross-examining a witness, "that some people *could* be ready to buy before your sales presentation reaches the close? And isn't it possible," she implored, "that if we don't let this guy buy right now we might lose the sale?"

"Look!" Dudley grimaced, emotionally stiffening for a fight. "I spent 14 hours learning this presentation and this guy is *going* to hear it."

Some Over-Preparers may have borderline obsessive-compulsive personalities. A June 1990 *Discover* magazine article claims that "obsessive-compulsive behavior disorders are caused by a serotonin-dopamine interaction gone wrong." Serotonin and dopamine are two natural substances manufactured by the brain which aid the transmission of nerve impulses. A new drug, clomipramine, has been found to modify the balance of these chemicals thereby reducing the ritualistic behavior found in obsessive-compulsive people. "The evidence of [the] disorder's biological roots has prompted researchers to search for a genetic basis," the article concluded. Nevertheless, we believe most Over-Preparers in sales *acquire* their call reluctance from sales managers and trainers.

Outlook:

Most cases of Over-Preparation Call Reluctance, given sufficient time, an accurate diagnosis, and proper training, are preventable and correctable. Prevention, however, is more cost effective.

CareerStyle:

- May seem cold, distant and emotionally unresponsive to casual observers
- Tends to over-analyze and underact
- Reserved and emotionally self-restrained
- Preoccupied with being *absolutely* prepared for each sales call
- Sales presentations tend to stress information while neglecting emotion

The Best Sales Managers

Sales Management Superstars. What traits set them apart from the also-rans? Little is known. True, books and presentations on the subject vibrate with esoteric offerings about ethics, sensitivity, self-discipline, nurturing, empathy, ego strength, optimism and internal locus of control. But these are psycho-buzzwords, jargonistic superstars, momentarily strutting about until they are discarded and forgotten, like stale beer. Each may contain a kernel of truth. In our judgment, however, the issue, despite sensationalistic claims to the contrary, remains unresolved.

No one, including us, has reliably itemized all the psychic forces at work in super sales managers. In our case, we used various methods and rigorously explored the minds of superior sales managers for many years. In the end, all we had to show for our efforts were a couple of publishable scientific articles. We found no trustworthy trait differences, and only one commonplace, but dependable, behavioral difference: Superior sales managers can be identified *by the tools they use.*

Like professionals in every career, high level sales managers acquire the things they need to support *growth*—in themselves and their salespeople—with or without home office consent or financial participation. In other words, *they invest in themselves.*

Also-rans, on the other hand, are more inclined to be custodians. Instead of trying to facilitate growth in every way they can, they direct their best managerial efforts toward enforcing *compliance* with corporate policies, procedures and practices. To summarize: *Growth-oriented sales managers ask, "What's new?" Custodial managers ask for home office permission.*

- Likes meetings (planning, reorganization, market "roll outs")
- Workshop participation limited to reporting typos on handouts
- Places high value upon realism and objectivity
- Over-Preparers who write about failure in sales are inclined to see the problem as a lack of organization ("When salespeople fall short of their potential, it's almost always attributed to *lack of organization.*" *Boardroom Reports*, May, 1988)
- Very difficult to impress (similar in this respect to Oppositional Reflex but for different reasons)
- Tends to excel in one-on-one sales situations
- Considers motivational/inspirational management techniques unprofessional, superficial and demotivating
- Tends to have encyclopedic product knowledge
- Reflective and contemplative
- Considered very private person
- Refuses to self-disclose; then feels alienated from others and misunderstood
- Slow to take action
- Does not like to be physically touched in public
- Tends to be comfortable with computers, systems and procedures
- Incorrectly considered to be unmotivated
- Smothers sales calls with too much sales support material
- Cynical about the value of interpersonal or rapport-building sales training procedures
- Does not visibly show excitement for new products or programs
- Hesitates (or refuses) to ask for help when it is needed
- Suspects the motives of people who "smile too much"
- Threatened by sales training that involves role-playing
- Becomes Custodial Sales Manager
- Demotivated by inspirational pep talks
- Exaggerates the role of organization and planning to such a point that they become limiting

Self-Assessment:

Do you tend to censor yourself from expressing what you really feel and how much you feel it?

Over-Preparers tend to be painfully aware of how much and how frequently they censor their feelings.

Do you think public displays of emotion are often signs of character weakness, lack of self-control, or insincerity?

Over-Preparers are suspicious when too much emotion is expressed too easily.

Do you have a ready, exuberant sense of humor?

Over-Preparers usually don't. They consider hair-trigger humor awkward, insincere, superficial and socially improper.

Do you tend to touch the people you talk to?

Over-Preparers consider touching intimate, and regard people who touch during conversation to be forward, impulsive and socially improper.

Do you ever discuss sex, religion or politics with people shortly after meeting them?

Over-Preparers consider these subjects personal. They wait five years.

Do you ever daydream about being in emotionally charged situations where you are swept away by the intensity of the moment without regard for what is proper or expected?

Over-Preparers compensate for their rigid emotional self-control by allowing their feelings to express themselves without constraint in their fantasies.

Objective Assessments:

Call Reluctance Scale—A high prospecting Brake score plus a high Over-Preparation score suggests that Over-Preparation Call Reluctance is probably limiting your prospecting performance now.

A low prospecting Brake score plus a high Over-Preparation score indicates a predisposition to Over-Preparation Call Reluctance although it is probably not limiting your prospecting performance at the present time.

Selling Styles Profile Analysis—Over-Preparers tend to prefer Product-Oriented sales presentations.

Frequency of Occurrence:

Over-Preparation Call Reluctance is the most frequent form of call reluctance found in technical salespeople. It is the second most frequently observed type overall.

Most Effective Countermeasures:

- Thought Zapping
- Sensory Injection (Fragrance)
- Negative Image Projection
- Thought Realignment
- Target Reversal

HYPER-PRO
Technical Name Protension

Capsule Summary:

Hyper-Pro Call Reluctance erupts in salespeople who are trying to compensate for secret doubts they have about their worth and acceptability. To plead their case, that they are worth knowing and valuing, they affect the *appearances* and *mannerisms* of successful, accomplished people. Ostentatiously flashing the *symbols* of success, the motto of the Hyper-Pro is: "If you can't love *me*, maybe you can love the Mercedes Benz I rode here in." Trying to look like they have already arrived, but never even getting up to speed, Hyper-Pros stand out in stark relief, like a coquettish, yuppie bride frantically trying to change a flat tire in her wedding gown—without getting dirty. Salespeople with Hyper-Pro Call Reluctance are impaled on their own image.

Most reasonable people agree that dressing for success and active image management can contribute to success in sales. But for salespeople with Hyper-Pro Call Reluctance, image management ceases being instrumental and starts to interfere. It drains energy earmarked for prospecting and becomes an end in itself.

CALL RELUCTANCE UP CLOSE

Confessions of a Hyper-Pro

Jennifer Daniels, a veteran Oklahoma City real estate agent, confronted her Hyper-Pro Call Reluctance—head on. Motivated, genial and cooperative, she candidly recalls her eccentric ritual of getting out of bed every day at 5AM to prepare for her daily wake-up walk and workout. Robotically, she spent the first 30 minutes transfixed—packaging herself, carefully coordinating her wardrobe. She selected from an assortment of designer sweats during the cool months, expensive shorts and halter tops for the warm ones. Then, of course, there were accessories, freshly hand-picked each morning from her vast and expanding collection of sparkling attention-getters.

It had not occurred to her, prior to her confrontation with her Hyper-Pro Call Reluctance, that her carefully staged morning commencement rites might be unnoticed. "I know this sounds ridiculous, but it was usually dark. In three years I don't remember seeing three people!" she said, raising her voice and grinning in disbelief as she spoke.

After returning from her morning promenade, she turned her attention to more important matters. Her car. She washed and dried it every morning in her garage (which she had custom-fitted with a floor drain). Then she drove to work. By then, most people had already parked their cars. Jennifer decorously positioned hers like a wheeled billboard where everyone could see it. There it would sit in shiny repose each day until 5:30 when she returned home.

Her company was not concerned because Jennifer's production met their loose-fitting, laid back criteria for success. But when Jennifer, a dynamic lady, realized how much more she could be earning, she was unsettled. Her production might have been sufficient for her company, but it was unsatisfactory to her. Impatient with mediocrity in anyone, including herself, Jennifer Daniels struck back at her call reluctance. She now boasts a new image. Motivated, revitalized and self-reliant, she has more time, more energy, and a dramatic increase in personal income.

"The way you dress," wrote survey-taker Srully Blotnick in *Forbes*, "does reveal something about your chances for success, but not what the fashion peddlers would like you to believe. People who tend to dress well naturally are often—but not always—play-it-safe types, concerned about how they look to others. We found that they are inclined to take the low risk route both privately and professionally. They rarely become entrepreneurs."

For Hyper-Pros, projecting a successful image is just step one. Once contrived, their image must be defended. To do so, Hyper-Pros assume a constant emotional readiness to snuff out any real or imagined threats to their self-merchandised petition for dignity and respect. To them, most prospecting, for example, is inconsistent with the image they project, so it is emotionally impossible. Prospecting, as practiced by most sales-people, is just hustling. Hustling is demeaning, undignified and well beneath someone of the Hyper-Pro's projected character, aspirations and social graces. Ordinary prospecting, for a Hyper-Pro, would be like wearing ultra expensive designer clothes with bargain basement shoes. So they *don't* prospect (in the ordinary sense of the word). Instead, they concentrate almost exclusively on one or two low-probability, large (or prestigious) cases. Exotic, unproven prospecting methods are relied upon, methods they insist are more compatible to their temperament and professional image. Talented, they remain immobile. Motivated, they remain inert.

Unless it is confronted and resolved, Hyper-Pro Call Reluctance will decompose a once promising sales career, leaving behind only a putrid concoction of eloquent excuses and dead-end results.

We know of a famous personality who retires to bed each night dressed in hand-picked designer clothes, the attire she wishes to be buried in should she die in her sleep. Similarly, salespeople with Hyper-Pro Call Reluctance are certain to *look* accomplished as large blocks of business go to their competitors and their sales careers expire because of neglect.

Probable Origin:

Protension is the technical term for an important aspect of Hyper-Pro Call Reluctance. It comes from a mathematically sophisticated, internationally respected personality test called the *Sixteen Personality Factors Questionnaire* (16PF). In 16PF studies, Protension is abbreviated with the letter "L" to reflect the order in which the factor was originally discovered. (We have adhered to this convention so 16PF users can trace the nativity of Hyper-Pro Call Reluctance from our earlier work with Protension.) The word "protension" is formed by combining two other words, "projection" (a psychological defense mechanism) and "inner-tension" (emotional agitation). Thus, the word technically means the projection of inner-tension onto the outside world.

Hyper-Pro Call Reluctance was first identified by observing, then refining, the measurement of prospecting avoidance behavior in salespeople who had high Protension scores on the 16PF. It is considered one of the more resistant forms of call reluctance due to the difficulty some Hyper-Pros have admitting they have a performance-limiting problem. A 1984 article illustrates the point. The article appeared in an industry magazine for sales managers. Six sales managers were asked which measures, if any, they took to help their salespeople cope with the public's negative perception of them. All six managers denied the problem existed. The industry was life insurance. (Subsequent studies confirmed that Hyper-Pro Call Reluctance is rampant throughout the management hierarchies of that industry.)

Researchers claim the protensive personality, as measured by the 16PF, may have a modest hereditary connection. Accordingly, since there is some relationship between the protensive personality and Hyper-Pro Call Reluctance, some salespeople may be generally predisposed by hereditary influences (as yet unspecified) to this prospecting difficulty. Yet, many protensive salespeople never develop Hyper-Pro Call Reluctance. When the problem does erupt, like an unwanted pimple, it's usually quickened by learning. Someone had to show you how to be a Hyper-Pro. Find them. Sue them.

Outlook:

Is your image more important than your career? The outlook for Hyper-Pro Call Reluctance depends entirely upon self-responsibility. If you are able to admit to yourself that you have call reluctance, then the outlook is bright indeed. The outlook is not so optimistic if you are unable to admit the presence of performance-limiting blemishes, like Hyper-Pro Call Reluctance. Nevertheless, the prescriptions in this book could be just what your career needs. Keep reading. Give them a try.

CareerStyle:

- Over-concerned about making strong, favorable first impressions
- Women tend to wear designer clothes and flash—not just wear—pretentious jewelry
- Men tend to wear monogrammed shirts, designer suits and maintain a neat, fussy appearance

Emergence of a New Call Reluctance Type

Our original work with Hyper-Pro Call Reluctance owes much to the scholars who had originally charted the boundaries of personality while constructing the 16PF. However, after testing many thousands of salespeople with the 16PF and the Call Reluctance Scale, we were troubled by an inexplicable phenomenon. In some ways, Hyper-Pros behaved exactly as predicted. For example, most devoted entirely too much energy to image enhancement. But in other important areas, they appeared to vary erratically from the behavior their scores predicted. Some were jealous of the accomplishments of others; some were not. Some argued and made excuses; some did not. Some spent endless hours preening in front of mirrors trying to earn the attention of their managers; others spent endless hours trying to avoid attention, hiding in the shadows, taking potshots, trying to undermine their managers.

This suggested that the issue was still not settled, the measure not yet refined. More research was indicated. Additional research funds required. (In layman's terms, that means we were probably wrong and we knew it, but we hoped somebody else would pay for it.) The search ended three years later with the discovery of the twelfth type of call reluctance, the Oppositional Reflex, which is covered separately later in this chapter.

- Never seen in public with messed-up hair (a mystery to rival the Trinity)
- Dapper decorum, dingy production
- Enjoys discussing factoids and fine points of movies, cars, clothes, cameras, computers, cuisine and wines
- Confuses "packaging" with prospecting
- Writes a highly flourished, exaggerated signature
- Self-absorbed in matters of appearance
- Preening when should be prospecting
- Owns a color coordinated library
- Probably reads *Dress for Success* and corporate image books
- May be pretentious and affect cultured mannerisms

- Becomes overextended in professional or industry organizations granting titles like "Chairman of the Sub-committee on Committees"

- Goes by an affected name, like "E. Michael Smith" instead of "E.M. Smith" or "Ernest M. Smith" (never call him Ernie)

- Overstates, overpositions and name-drops to impress

- Threatened by psychological tests which could expose imperfections or, worse yet, result in an *average* score (Note: Unlike Oppositional Reflex, Hyper-Pros cooperate, follow instructions, and complete tests)

- Needs to be perceived as competent and respectable

- Searching for dignity and respect

- Articulate: Actually enjoys being interviewed

- Perfectionist; very difficult to impress (like Over-Preparers but for different reasons)

- Exclusively works on big dollar, low probability prospective sales ("big case-itis")

- Intensely concerned about professional image

- Pretentiously decorates office with plaques, certificates, awards and other status-declarative references to achievement and character

- Compulsive name-dropper

- Drives (or aspires to drive) an expensive automobile to make an impression, not for enjoyment

- Orders special license tag reading "Ms. No 1" or "Stud"

- Makes exceptionally strong first impression

- When shown a group photo, always searches for himself or herself first

- Tends to have large vocabulary

- Considers ordinary prospecting demeaning and unprofessional

- Emotionally unable to work if the new rug in the next office is brighter or larger

- Often feels slighted, insulted, unappreciated or taken for granted

Self Assessment:

Are you always on the lookout for different, more professional ways to prospect instead of using proven, traditional methods?

Hyper-Pros spend prospecting time searching for alternative ways to prospect.

Do you tend to react emotionally when someone doubts your competency or your integrity?

Usually rational, composed, and well presented, Hyper-Pros come unglued and feel hurt, but, unless Oppositional, they do not attack.

Do you tend to buy expensive things that do not satisfy you for very long?

Hyper-Pros do. They invest in clothes, jewelry, cars and academic degrees, expecting them to permanently remedy the interior questions they have about their worth. Acquisitions of this sort do not insulate or satisfy them for long. When the same feelings surface again, Hyper-Pros go shopping—again.

How important is appearance to a salesperson's success?

Hyper-Pros believe it is the *determining factor.*

Do you spend a lot of time in front of mirrors adjusting your clothes, brushing your hair, checking your appearance?

Hyper-Pros check everything closely, regularly. One reformed Hyper-Pro changed her underwear twice a day in case she had an automobile accident and wound up in the hospital. Learning to drive safely had not occurred to her.

Objective Assessments:

Call Reluctance Scale—A high prospecting Brake score plus a high Hyper-Pro score indicates that Hyper-Pro Call Reluctance is probably limiting your prospecting activity now.

A low prospecting Brake score plus a high Hyper-Pro score indicates a predisposition to Hyper-Pro Call Reluctance although it is probably not limiting your prospecting performance at the present time.

Selling Styles Profile Analysis—Hyper-Pros tend to have Image-Oriented sales presentation styles which stress who they are and what they know over the merits of the product or service they represent.

Frequency of Occurrence:

Hyper-Pro Call Reluctance is the fifth most frequently occurring type of call reluctance in salespeople. It is found much more frequently in sales managers and most frequently in consultants.

Most Effective Countermeasures:

- Fear Inversion (Secondary procedure only)
- Thought Zapping
- Sensory Injection
- Thought Realignment (See Parable of the Eldorado)
- Target Reversal

STAGE FRIGHT

Technical Name **Groups**

GPS

Capsule Summary:

Fear of speaking before a group is a form of call reluctance which occurs in salespeople who are over anxious about their appearance. They may be comfortable and effective prospecting one-on-one but nervous and incoherent in front of groups. Some of these salespeople are able to handle small groups but not large ones. Others are uncomfortable in front of small groups but not large ones. Some are distressed making presentations to groups of *any* size.

CALL RELUCTANCE UP CLOSE

A Personal Case of Stage Fright

Gina L. was a lean, wiry, ambitious district sales representative for a large cosmetics company. Gesturing theatrically as she spoke, Gina usually smiled and never scowled. She was of Italian descent. To those close to her, she could have been the embodiment of physical gracefulness—except for a nearsighted squint which she was too vain to fix with eyeglasses.

Attractive and well-presented, Gina easily attracted and recruited good quality salespeople. They were expected to move the company's cosmetic line primarily through in-home party sales

continues

A Personal Case of Stage Fright *continued*

arrangements. Full of promise, Gina's salespeople were always adequate, but never superior.

When Gina had to speak to a group—even her own salespeople—her voice betrayed an anxious discomfort which blemished her otherwise attractive, business-like physical appearance. Leaking nervous agitation, her words of encouragement seemed insincere, her caring concern for her salespeople became suspect, her commitment seemed doubtful.

Gina knew she had a problem, and the problem had her career. She never denied it. She rightly attributed her distress to making group presentations but wrongly tried to cope by complete avoidance. For example, she rarely accompanied her salespeople into the field where she could coach and teach them in actual group sales situations. Instead, she spent her time trying to find alternative ways to sell her products. Mailouts were tried. Radio advertising. Free gifts. Contests.

Not surprisingly, our assessment revealed that she had Stage Fright Call Reluctance. Supplemental measures found that she was not afraid of people in general, unsure of what to say, or concerned about a poor delivery style. She had a pleasant speaking voice and she knew it. Her fear was linked to her physical appearance.

Though not essential, we questioned her before prescribing two countermeasures: A new form of Fear Inversion and Negative Thought Zapping. She was cooperative and willingly shared with us some revelations which were instructive and helpful.

Initially, she could not remember the first time she experienced the fear she now associates with speaking in front of groups. After some reflection, further questions and discussion, it came to her. She remembered.

When she was 12 years old she had to present a verbal report for her history class. Already unsettled by the raging hormonal transformations of adolescence, Gina handled the project well. But the careless remarks made by some of her friends and classmates were another matter. Indiscreetly sexualizing everything as only adolescents can do, they gave her mysterious sidelong glances and told her they "could see there was more to her than history." But with tight-lipped, conspiratorial resolve, they wouldn't say what it

continues

A Personal Case of Stage Fright *continued*

was or how they knew. Having just recently begun to discover her own sexuality, Gina anxiously searched within herself for answers and troubled herself with questions. Was there something different about her now? Can people tell? Confused, frightened and intensely embarrased—but unsure why—Gina's 12-year-old mind reasoned that the safest way to avoid exposing whatever it was she was exposing would be to avoid speaking in front of groups. It worked but at a cost.

Throughout the remainder of her high school years she managed to miss school on days when verbal presentations were scheduled. During her university years, Gina instantly dropped any course which required her to give a verbal report or presentation. As an adult, the brief success she enjoyed in cosmetics sales extracted a profound emotional tariff. So she escaped into sales management where her natural gifts as a sales trainer and a coach were constrained and unable to develop.

By now she had acquired another perspective on her problem. She knew what it was, where it came from, and why the general procedures which had worked for so many other salespeople failed to work for her. Motivated, goal focused, and impatient to get on with her career, Gina was ready to counter-attack. She did, applying Thought Zapping and Sensory Injection, two countermeasures best suited for neutralizing Stage Fright Call Reluctance. Today, she is equally comfortable working with people one-on-one or speaking to vast convention audiences in her industry. She proudly manages a super-productive sales organization, spotlighting several extraordinarily high-level salespeople. It's a tribute to her and a model for her industry. But it's not an accident. To reach her stride, Gina had to tenaciously pursue her fear of group presentations beyond the traditional definition of Stage Fright. She found it hiding, like a coward, behind an adolescent fear of physical exposure. The "search" portion of her mission was over. Now it was time to "destroy" the fear which had been sabotaging her career for years. She did. Showing no mercy, Gina won her fight with herself. Her salespeople won, too.

Stage Fright Call Reluctance has no noticeable impact on sales performance in industries where prospecting is traditionally done through non-group channels. In industries where "seminar" or "party" selling is encouraged or required, Stage Fright Call Reluctance can be catastrophic.

Probable Origin:

Stage Fright Call Reluctance appears to be entirely learned. It may come from inexperience as a group speaker or from an early traumatic experience associated with making a group presentation. The Fear of Physical Exposure subtype (see Research Appendix) may be associated with a poor or incomplete body image and may be due to awkward or unsuccessful experiences making group presentations during heightened developmental periods such as puberty.

There is some sketchy evidence that the "fight or flight" impulse which is experienced by salespeople with the General Apprehension Syndrome variant of Stage Fright Call Reluctance (see Research Appendix) may be due to body chemistry. Some researchers claim that the prescription drug Propanolol may be able to block these distressful feelings at their chemical source. The drug does have a few noteworthy side effects, however, including, but not limited to, possible death.

Outlook:

Depending on the subtype, Stage Fright Call Reluctance can be among the easiest forms of call reluctance to correct, assuming it has been properly assessed and the proper training supports are used.

CareerStyle:

- Just *thinking* about giving a group presentation can be distressful

- Obsessively fidgets and inspects clothing to assure everything is arranged properly and nothing untoward is exposed ("Did I forget to zip my fly?" syndrome)

- Starts preparing and worrying weeks before giving a group presentation

- Dissatisfied with voice, inflection, tone, pace, vocabulary

- Avoids opportunities for group presentations when possible

- Reads *safe* self-help books about making presentations that don't require making presentations as part of the cure

- Exits early from remedial programs and activities that require speaking before groups

- May overprepare notes, scripts, dialogues—even for short, informal situations like introductions or spontaneous remarks in a group setting

- Dreads "ice-breaking" activities (so do Doomsayers and Over-Preparers but for different reasons)

- Permits markets best worked by seminar selling or in-home party sales to wither away or, worse yet, default to competitors

- Reads notes verbatim when forced into a group presentation

- Some dread role-playing in sales training circumstances (so do Doomsayers and Over-Preparers but for different reasons)

- Some cope by trying to be too cavalier when giving group presentations resulting in mechanistic, rigidly overpracticed Mr. Cool/Ms. Bubbly Personality performances

- Intellectually blocked, "can't think of anything to say" (fear of verbal incompetence)

Self-Assessment:

Do you actively *seek* out opportunities to appear before groups of various sizes to promote yourself?

Salespeople with Stage Fright Call Reluctance don't. They try to avoid such situations.

Are you inclined to be extremely self-critical when you hear yourself on audio tape or see yourself on video?

Salespeople with Stage Fright Call Reluctance are mercilessly self-critical. Some don't like what they see. Others don't like what they hear. A few can't stand to watch or listen to themselves; they are certain they would be mortified if they did.

Do you secretly rehearse your "spontaneous" words and gestures prior to speaking before a group?

Actors and salespeople with Stage Fright Call Reluctance do.

Do you believe most of the speakers you hear are more gifted, better orators than you could ever be—no matter how hard you try to improve?

Salespeople with Stage Fright Call Reluctance have persuaded themselves that they could never be comfortable or effective making speeches and group presentations.

Do you ever daydream about giving powerful religious or political orations, acting in films or the theater?

Salespeople with Stage Fright compensate for their real-life fears by fantasizing an alternative reality in which they dazzle their audiences with persuasive, spellbinding speeches and performances.

Objective Assessments:

Call Reluctance Scale—A high prospecting Brake score plus a high Stage Fright score indicates that Stage Fright could be limiting your prospecting performance at the present time, if appropriate prospecting channels include seminar or group presentations.

A low prospecting Brake score plus a high Stage Fright score indicates a predisposition to Stage Fright although it is probably not limiting prospecting performance at the present time.

Selling Styles Profile Analysis—Salespeople with Stage Fright Call Reluctance have a slight tendency to be Service-Oriented in their sales presentation style.

Frequency of Occurrence:

Stage Fright Call Reluctance is the sixth most frequently observed type found in salespeople. It occurs much more frequently in non-salespeople.

Most Effective Countermeasures:

- Threat Desensitization
- Thought Zapping
- Sensory Injection (Fragrance and/or Massage Therapy)
- Hot Water Bottle
- Yellow Dot
- Thought Realignment

ROLE REJECTION
ROL

Capsule Summary:

Role Rejection Call Reluctance occurs when a salesperson is intellectually willing, but emotionally unable, to accept a career in sales. In some respects, salespeople with Role Rejection Call Reluctance look like heart transplant patients showing the first signs of organ rejection while insisting they feel great.

Role Rejection is tricky to diagnose accurately because the afflicted salesperson may be unaware of the problem, save for the nagging feeling that he or she should be considering a career change. Motivated and goal-directed, salespeople with Role Rejection Call Reluctance heroically strive to *appear* upbeat and optimistic, denying their doubts, making diagnosis more difficult. But their efforts to appear upbeat and happy when they feel doubtful and discouraged are usually fouled. Malevolent whisperings from deeply entombed negative beliefs shadow every move: every salesperson is just a peddler; every sales career is inherently dishonorable, perhaps evil; their sales careers are grim disappointments to their parents, friends and spouses.

Note to Plagiarists

A helpful note to those plagiarists whose single, remaining brain cell has been fully dedicated to copying our work and claiming it as their own: The old concept of Protensive Call Reluctance has been radically altered. To keep your articles and presentations accurate and up-to-date, you must reference these new changes in our thinking. Please study the changes carefully and make whatever modifications are necessary to your plagiarizations of our work. We regret the inconvenience.

—*The Authors*

P.S.: This caution is especially intended for the artful dodgers who publicly "Thank Dudley for his pioneering research and Goodson for her valuable discussions" (which, translated, means "Dudley had to do the work and Goodson had to explain it to me").

Role Rejecting salespeople, at best, only tolerate their sales careers. They suffer perpetual labor pains, trying to be emotionally reborn as someone they're not.

In Role Rejection Call Reluctance, a seditious residue of guilt and shame blocks salespeople from ever fully integrating into their sales careers. Although they may understand the opportunities available in sales, deeply ingrained negative stereotypes about selling cause them to *feel* like failures. Regardless of motivation or ability, they're destined to remain outcasts, on the outside looking in. They are emotionally forbidden from integrating into their sales careers and banned from feeling real pride in their sales accomplishments. Left to their own devices, they pretend.

The savage stereotype which has displaced their pride uncritically asserts the belief that sales is an inherently dishonorable profession. Salespeople who succeed in a dishonorable profession are probably inherently dishonorable, too. How else could they succeed? They *should* fail, the stereotype imputes. They *deserve* to fail.

Obligingly, too many *do* fail, but not instantly, not all at once.

Role Rejection starts to neutralize positive qualities by deadening any genuine identification with the sales profession. It progresses in small, unnoticeable increments, depositing trite slogans and cynical parodies of success as it advances. Anxiously, slowly at first, Role Rejecting sales-

---

CALL RELUCTANCE UP CLOSE

An Intimate Look at Role Rejection

A lush, tropical location had been chosen. The annual convention was scheduled. Dudley and Goodson were the keynote speakers. Our presentation: The New Psychology of Call Reluctance. As usual, a senior executive from the sponsoring organization personally met us at the airport and escorted us to our hotel suites. After the exchange of social amenities, the conversation (predictably) changed to how his company's "ecology" differed from others. Then the tall, proud figure politely but firmly warned us not to call his salespeople "salespeople." His concept of management was nearly feudal, his representatives were "relationship managers." Besides, he confessed, he was wary of our being there in the first place. It was clearly not his idea. "The subject is too

continues

An Intimate Look at Role Rejection *continued*

negative," he said gravely. His prohibitions continued for quite some time. They were grim, but genial, branching out and thickening like a dark, foreboding forest. The convention audience consisted of 2,000 of his company's top sales producers. "I know you'll do a good job," he wished aloud, as he ceremoniously stood to leave. We exchanged glances out of the corners of our eyes but did not speak until he left. We didn't need to. We've heard all this before.

The next morning we gave our presentation. The audience was polite and enthusiastic, somewhat overanimated by a rich vein of Role Rejecting veteran producers. They loudly laughed on cue at jokes they had heard before and, with only slight nudging, were the first to verbally pledge their loyalty to the company and the product line (while probably contemplating leaving). Determined to provide a memorable, if not exactly entertaining, presentation, we shifted our emphasis, putting the accent on Role Rejection Call Reluctance. The room quickly silenced, except for our amplified voices and the droll, efficient hum of a slide projector's motor. Their thoughts turned inward as we started first to coax, then to challenge them. Get out of the sales recycling business, we exhorted them. Stop turning over the same old accounts. Start prospecting for new ones. Earn what you're really worth this year. Learn how to really enjoy doing it. It turned out to be one of our most successful—and satisfying—presentations ever.

Afterward, the executive who had greeted us at the airport and familiarized us with his company's customs insisted on visiting with us before we left. We met in a remote corner of the lobby. What was the purpose of the meeting? His trim, polished figure revealed no clues as we approached the table where he waited. Were we going to be offered a job, or sued?

"My mother cried the day I went into sales," he began in soft accents, his eyes cocked shrewdly sideways as he spoke. "She said my father and her were awfully disappointed...wasted all their money...sending me to the university and then on to law school." Several times he had to pause, his face congested with emotion, battling to hold back tears. Then he continued, sometimes uttering fragments interpretable only to himself. This was the first time he had ever disclosed this part of his personal history to anyone.

continues

An Intimate Look at Role Rejection *continued*

"You know," he said, his eyes fixed on some distant memory, "they got over it. But I'm not sure I ever did. I got mad at myself and mad at the world...and stayed that way for a long time. Maybe I still am," he said sharply but shakily. We said very little.

"You're wrong in one respect," he said with the explosive lightness of a long-lost traveler catching the first glimpse of a familiar landmark.

"My Role Rejection didn't get me down. At first, I was a real go-getter in sales...I remember," he said, like Scrooge learning he had a second chance. "I hated my competitors and I despised people who were negative. Of course, negative meant anybody who disagreed with me," he laughed, unearthing his own insights as he went along. "I would bury 'em every chance I had...made a lot of money... much more than I would have made as an attorney. But I still felt like a failure."

For two hours he discharged his conscience and his emotions. Then he explained how he moved into management. "The whole time I was a top sales producer I had a dread that the whole thing was going to come crashing down at any time, so I got out. Took a job in management." Soon he became an ascending star in his company's management constellation, building on his reputation for hard-headed business decisions and absolute intolerance for negative attitudes and negative people.

"At first, they [negative attitudes] must have reminded me about what I was trying to forget, what I was really feeling," he offered. "Somehow," he chuckled, "negative just evolved...came to mean...any idea I didn't agree with or just didn't want to hear."

"You know," he pondered further, stroking his chin in thought, "during all my years in sales I never once called myself a salesman. I still don't. We've—I've," he corrected himself, "got this policy that nobody calls our salespeople salespeople. Relationship managers. That's what we call them," he emphasized solemnly. "That's what I told you to call them, too, isn't it?" he said, feigning anger. "Thanks for caring enough about us to do your job. From now on we are a sales company. We have salespeople who happen to manage relationships. It's part of their jobs. But first and foremost we sell things, and I want them to feel good about that."

people (and managers) strive to stuff the holes in their souls with platitudes. Doubts and concerns are frozen out and plastered over with luminous, rigid smiles.

This takes effort. Effort takes energy. Energy earmarked to smother unresolved guilt is no longer available for prospecting. With less and less energy available to fund prospecting, clientele-building activities narrow down and compress inward. Through raw determination, some Role Rejection salespeople manage to sustain respectable production levels. But none approach their true abilities and few feel good—for long—about what they do accomplish. With emotional agitation on the increase and production on the decrease, Role Rejection enters the final phase, actual resignation or psychological termination (where the decision to quit precedes actual resignation—by months or even years). The career collapses from the weight of unresolved guilt and shame, like an impressive structure rushed to completion on a foundation which had never hardened. The cycle complete, many could-have-been sales superstars leave, without ever having given their sales careers an even chance.

Probable Origin:

Role Rejection Call Reluctance is learned. The seeds for future outbreaks are usually sown early, long before a salesperson enters the career. Susceptibility to Role Rejection is stowed away among the traits, habits and predispositions salespeople bring with them to their sales careers. Already primed, all they need is a triggering device. That's supplied upon arrival. Unrealistic production quotas, unethical or shallow sales managers, negative stereotypes held by sales support personnel, and traumatic early sales training experiences can all summon Role Rejection Call Reluctance into malevolent commotion.

Many salespeople—especially those with advanced educational degrees—have difficulty accepting a career in sales because they have been taught that sales is an unacceptable career. Yet few books, articles or presentations directly make such an assertion. So where does the negativity come from? It usually comes from well disguised, often highly respected, sources outside the sales profession. Incredibly, it thrives inside the sales profession, too.

Most negative stereotypes about the sales career are communicated indirectly. The damage is inflicted subtly, but efficiently, by repetition.

- "Steve Wageman was three years out of college when he signed on with Merrill Lynch," the posh Sunday supplement article said. "A quiet, handsome man with a solid background in sales and management,

Wageman, too, seemed like a prime candidate for broker stardom. Sixteen months after he joined the firm, he was asked to leave. 'I wouldn't get in it again, probably, knowing what I know now,'" warns the article.

- A 1989 Louis Rukeyser article had a different slant. "Let's add another, similar peeve: the jerks who choose the dinner hour, just when we're settling in after a long, hard day, to make unsolicited marketing calls on our home telephones."

- An advertisement from Concord Financial Corporation cast aspersion on the character of commissioned salespeople. "Salesman or Advisor?" the eye-catching headline read. "A financial advisor's means of compensation often determines whether he can always act in his client's best interest. Being paid on commission from investment

---

The QWS Syndrome in Veteran Producers

The QWS syndrome is found in productive, veteran salespeople who unexpectedly abandon their sales careers. It happens when Role Rejection is ignored, neglected and left unchallenged.

The "QWS" designation refers to the unexpectedly high number of experienced producers who quit or intend to *quit while they are succeeding* (Quits While Succeeding).

In the past, we thought call reluctance was limited to inexperienced salespeople. Veterans either did not complain or complained so loud and so often that their genuine appeals for assistance were masked. Many QWS veterans enjoyed very high annual incomes. Some were the top producers in their companies. Some were the most productive salespeople in their industries. All were presumed by their managers and companies to be immune to annoying clientele-building problems like call reluctance. After all, weren't they the pillars of productivity? When a problem was suspected, it was quickly abstracted into esoteric, lighter-than-air marketing slogans like "mid-life crisis," "burnout," "fear of success," or "stress."

Armed with an array of formally developed tests, some sophisticated laboratory research instruments, and (uncharacteristically for us) even an interview or two, we methodically set out to track the problem to its source.

continues

The QWS Syndrome *continued*

We found four common behavioral themes. One was *denial*. Very few people—sales managers, close friends, colleagues or even family members—knew call reluctance was still a problem for QWS veteran producers until they unexpectedly resigned.

The second theme which emerged was *compensatory prospecting*. Here, prospecting efforts were shifted away from emotional hot spots to paths of less resistance. One group of QWS veterans we observed tried to cope by selling and reselling their existing clients. New accounts significantly declined. In compensatory prospecting, important market segments are bypassed for purely emotional reasons and then fogged over with impotent excuses posing as rational explanations.

The third theme was *career abandonment*. After psychologically disassociating from the career, veteran QWS producers, unexpectedly and without warning, stepped completely out of character and resigned. Left. Quit. To others, they seemed to impulsively quit the business many of them sincerely loved. Often they vanished, dropped completely out of sight.

In dogged pursuit, we asked some of them to help us understand why. Their common explanation, the fourth theme, was eloquent in its simplicity: *"The financial return could no longer justify the emotional investment."*

Call reluctant as neophytes, they learned how to prospect but never learned how to prospect *comfortably*. Instead, these veteran producers had only been taught how to smother the problem by pretending to be positive, zealous and certain. So they took what they knew and amplified it. Many became success pamphleteers. Writing tracts on commitment, serving as speech-giving cheerleaders, challenging conventioneers to action, they were true believers, desperate positivists. It was all theater, an act, the spastic twitchings of a body already dead. They had allowed Role Rejection Call Reluctance to transform them into emotional frauds.

Among all the debris that call reluctance leaves in its wake, the QWS Syndrome in veteran producers is the most damaging. It is also the most unnecessary. With a bit more sensitivity to the needs of experienced salespeople, this form of call reluctance could be eliminated.

product sales may cause an inherent conflict of interest and raises the question: Is he an advisor or just a salesman?"

- A very unflattering 1988 article by Mike Royko for the *Chicago Tribune* characterized some telemarketers as "Phone Phonies." "Shell-Shocked on the Battlefield of Selling," screamed the banner headline.

- From a perspective formed of foreboding case studies, a July 1990 article devised to accurately portray the difficulties experienced by many salespeople. It appeared in a publication called *Sales and Marketing Management*.

Negative stereotypes like these etch deeper with each repetition into the psyche of salespeople disposed to Role Rejection. Attitudes are slanted, biases are cast, productivity is diminished, career satisfaction is disallowed, tenure is destroyed.

We conducted a study several years ago to assess the kinds and degrees of motivation found in terminating male life insurance agents (back then the overwhelming majority of life insurance agents in the U.S. were male).

Each terminating agent had failed to complete his first year of tenure under contract. An astonishing number, however, quit while performing at highly successful production levels. They were not production failures. The loss of these salesmen was perplexing.

Motivation Analysis Test results showed that a significant number of the terminating agents had a considerable amount of emotional "unfinished business" with their parents. Informal exit interviewing corroborated this finding and added a remarkable insight. Many of them terminated because they felt pressured to "find a more prestigious career," to "make something of themselves." When asked, many attributed the source of this pressure to their parents. In some cases, their parents had been dead for over a decade.

Outlook:

Role Rejection is difficult to diagnose. (It is not diagnosed accurately—or at all—by most sales assessment techniques.) However, once it has been accurately detected and measured, it is among the easiest and fastest forms of call reluctance to correct.

Note: Chronic, high levels of Role Rejection in a sales force convey more about the depth, character and caring of the sales organization than about the human flaws of its salespeople.

Inspirational Speakers:
Are They As Positive As They Seem?

Sales and sales management professionals with Role Rejection Call Reluctance cannot derive genuine satisfaction from the sales career. Unable to artfully cover the signs of their malaise any longer, and faced with declining productivity, some alter their roles. They seek and find cover teaching *other* salespeople how to be positive, how to become successful. Some turn to writing sales pamphlets. Others turn to giving speeches—fiery, fidgety, *inspirational* speeches.

The new role has a function. It disguises the ambivalence they really feel about their sales careers and allows them to hide their concerns behind a perpetually smiling, happy face. Roaring with overstylized, missionary zeal—like a tent evangelist on a hot summer night—they exhort their colleagues to transform their listless careers into vibrant crusades, their rambling confusions into monolithic commitments.

It's an archaic mind-management rite, complete with its own litany: Don't be objective, they say, imagine yourself *already* successful, eliminate all negative information to the contrary and you are sure to radiate passion, purpose, success and sanity. Right? Maybe not. It could be a scam. How can you tell? It could be in the smile.

According to University of California psychologist Paul Ekman, some people use smiles to shape and manipulate the attitudes of others. But there are subtle differences between the smiles of people who are truthful and those using smiles to deceive.

Smiles reflecting unconflicted, genuine enjoyment tend to cause some wrinkling of skin around the eyes. Smiling liars, on the other hand, often try to promote their interests by manipulating the muscles around their lips, but not their eyes—like the televangelists who promise unlimited financial riches to those willing to contribute generous donations to them.

To be prudent, that's not always enough to detect the presence of a negatively driven positive attitude in a speaker with Role Rejection Call Reluctance. Many other aspects of behavior, like body motion, word formation, and subtle changes in voice modulation are used by skilled observers to uncover fabricated attitudes.

continues

> ### Inspirational Speakers *continued*
> (To hedge our bets, we also enlist the aid of sophisticated laboratory instruments, polygraphs, and computers.)
>
> But many sales professionals don't, and won't, use clues such as these to determine who is positively joyful and who is positively lying. To them, the myth is more important than the fact. Sensibly managed positive attitudes can be inspiring and helpful. But don't confuse exaggerated outward *appearances* of a positive attitude with hopeful anticipations and positive inner strength. It could be Role Rejection Call Reluctance. A child walking on stilts, British author G.K. Chesterton said, can't be thought of as *well developed*. Neither can a Role Rejecting salesperson, manager, trainer, or consultant.

CareerStyle:

If you have Role Rejection Call Reluctance, some or all of the following will be true for you:

- Copes by being either too cautious or too cavalier

- Experiences periodic episodes of career-related depression

- Tries to conceal real feelings by *pretending* to be very positive

- A library of vapid self-help clichés

- Copes by using a deflected identity; "It is company policy here," a Role Rejecting sales vice-president told us, "to refer to our salespeople as marketing associates. It makes them feel professional."

  Note: *Insistence* upon nondescript terms like "territorial representative" and "product consultant" for people who are *primarily responsible for selling* is one way corporations institutionalize Role Rejection and pass it on to their sales force.

- Has trouble emotionally taking ownership for career choice

- Unable to fully integrate into sales career, although on the surface appears to be a zealous advocate

- Fears loss of approval from significant others (usually family members or close friends)

- Rarely feels genuine pride in sales accomplishments

- Hesitates to disclose sales role during opportune occasions such as civic, social, religious and fraternal gatherings where such information could facilitate prospecting efforts

- Luminously positive outside, dimmed inside, like a well-lighted office building after hours

- Fragile optimism: Can't tolerate negative people or objective information; exuberant but misguided, given to rigidly reason that anything not positive *must* be negative; emotionally evicted, rational objectivity is given no quarter

- Emotionally unable to affirm the validity or worth of a sales career for anyone

- Internalizes damaging stereotypes about selling, often without realizing it

- Presumes that society holds salespeople in *justifiable* low esteem, even contempt

- Pretending to be positive depletes energy which can lead to burnout

- Compensates for negative feelings by writing attitude-lifting books and giving inspiring speeches about the importance of a positive attitude

- Rhetorically advocates the validity of the sales career for everyone

- Threatened by objective psychological tests capable of poking through the veneer of positive certainty (one very well-known attitude marketeer was threatened by the Call Reluctance Scale and, offered the opportunity, he refused to complete the questionnaire. "Nothing good can come from it," he oozed, enjoying the sound of his own words, "only bad.")

Self-Assessment:

Do you tend to be self-deprecating when you talk to other people about your sales career?

Salespeople with Role Rejection Call Reluctance assume their career is inferior to other people's and react either deferentially or defensively.

Do you tend to be rigidly positive when you are around your sales colleagues?

Salespeople with Role Rejection tend to compensate for their own ambivalence by exaggeration. They appear to be the most positive, the most zealous, and the most committed salespeople in the business. They're not.

Are you *really* positive or is your positive attitude a contrivance?

Salespeople with Role Rejection Call Reluctance are not naturally positive. They must force themselves to act as if they were. Look closely. It shows.

Does your mood about your sales career tend to vacillate from very high to very low?

Some salespeople with Role Rejection Call Reluctance have consistently inconsistent attitudes towards their sales career. Emotionally psyching themselves up to the summit then plunging to the depths, they're like rickety old roller coasters. They span the heights, dive through the valleys, careen around corners—tossing about waiting for the ride to end, only to have it start all over again. When ready, most eventually stop the cycle without assistance. A few need help from competent mental health practitioners.

Do you try to find verbal replacements for "salesperson" when you describe your career to others?

Salespeople with Role Rejection Call Reluctance presume that "salesperson" is unacceptable and try to replace it with terms that dilute

---

Beware of Consultants With Role Rejection

Watch who you let near your mind. Role Rejection Call Reluctance is extremely contagious. Be wary of consultants selling sales training programs who are unable to accept the fact that they, too, are in sales. Implicit negative sanctions inadvertently leaked through their training materials, presentations and behaviors can quickly poison you or your entire sales force with radioactive doses of Role Rejection Call Reluctance. Sales producers can degenerate into "visitors," prospectors into "plodders," proud salespeople into "product advisors." Protect yourself.

How? The logic is simple. You use an umbrella when it rains, a coat screens you from the cold, and tanning lotion insulates you from damaging sun rays. Another quick procedure can protect you from contagious consultants with Role Rejection. Here's how.

Ask your prospective consultant: "Are *you* a good salesperson?" Don't get sidetracked by the subjective definition of "good." That's a tactical evasion. If they say anything that indicates an emotional denial of their sales role, like, "Oh no, I'm a psychologist, not a salesperson," open the door and close your mind—fast.

the sales function, such as "financial planner," "account representative," or "territorial representative."

Do you have to call prospecting something else before it's acceptable to you?

Salespeople with Role Rejection tend to divine alternate names for prospecting, such as "clientele building."

Have you impulsively changed company affiliations for reasons other than production?

Salespeople with Role Rejection tend to keep on the move. Like medieval communicants avoiding the plague, they search. They look for a place where they can, and will, feel good about their sales careers. The quest can send them to, and through, many sales organizations because companies are not empowered to confer what they are looking for—a feeling of respect.

Do you tend to fantasize about being in an important position where everyone likes you and approves of what you do?

Salespeople with Role Rejection Call Reluctance like fantasies. After all, their Role Rejection is founded on stories: the negative stereotypes they heard about sales. To cope, they cast off on imaginary trips to alternative careers. Browsing the jobs listed in the daily newspaper, their daydreams carry them to pretentious professions and alternative careers where the grass is greener, the flowers fresher, the sun brighter.

Have you ever impulsively changed your appearance or moved to another city?

Some Role Rejection salespeople have. Others will. They externally act out their internal restlessness by making spur-of-the-moment changes in their appearance, lifestyle, or address. Makeover after makeover, they search, looking for an alternative version of themselves.

Do you think a career change would help you win approval from others, feel better about yourself, and make you more popular at parties?

Salespeople with Role Rejection Call Reluctance think so. But they also think there's a pot of gold at the end of the rainbow, abominable snow-persons in the Himalayas, and extraterrestrials in flying saucers eavesdropping on their conversations.

Are you a self-help junkie? Do you go on psycho-binges, hitching rides on trendy pop psych reveries, fantasies and inventions?

Salespeople with Role Rejection Call Reluctance make other people wealthy. They gullibly shop for quick-fix answers to their emotional puzzlement. In the process, they've read more books (like this one!), attended more workshops, listened to more cassettes, endured more con-

fidence courses, paced more conversations, meditated more mantras, and studied at the feet of more self-quoting masters of success than the other forms of call reluctance combined. *Unbelievably, they still somehow fail to grasp the most overpowering lesson to be learned: People who successfully enrich their wallets by selling the secret of success to others,* all *self-promote without shame and prospect without hesitation.*

Objective Assessments:

Call Reluctance Scale—A high prospecting Brake score plus a high Role Rejection score indicates that Role Rejection Call Reluctance is probably limiting your prospecting performance at the present time.

A low prospecting Brake score plus a high Role Rejection score indicates a predisposition to Role Rejection Call Reluctance although it is probably not limiting prospecting performance at the present time.

Selling Styles Profile Analysis—No significant relationships exist between this type of call reluctance and the six selling styles.

Frequency of Occurrence:

Role Rejection Call Reluctance is the third most frequently observed type found in salespeople. Some industries, and subpopulations, however, have much higher observed frequencies. Attorneys in sales or sales support roles, for example, often show toxic levels of Role Rejection Call Reluctance. The banking industry has the highest rate of Role Rejection, especially among salespeople who were not originally hired to sell.

Most Effective Countermeasures:

- Thought Zapping
- Sensory Injection
- Negative Image Projection (for inspirational junkies)
- Thought Realignment

YIELDER

Technical Name: **Disruption Sensitivity**
                    DS

Capsule Summary:

Every automobile driver encounters Yielders. They're the twitching tip-toers who are incapable of merging onto busy motorways with the flow of traffic. Instead, they brake to a complete stop at the end of the entrance ramp, forcing the traffic behind them to an unexpected halt. Frozen in place, screeching brakes and avenging horn blasts behind them, Yielders sit and wait, nervously twitch, then wait some more. Why are they holding up traffic? What are they waiting for? No one knows for sure. But we have a working hypothesis: Yielders belong to a radical religious sect (like the Flat Earth Society) which requires motorways to be *absolutely* clear of traffic prior to merging. High priests of indecision, they endure the abuse of angry, motoring infidels, perhaps even gaining resolve from their ordeals. (Rumors persist that some anthropologists have spotted bands of Yielder extremists practicing their exotic rite at the entrance to escalators.)

New Call Reluctance Assessment Technologies

The Call Reluctance Scale has provided a wealth of information and insight into some of the issues related to assessing adults at work. Work on several new applications is progressing. Some of the most interesting include:

Goal Profile Analysis (GPA): a short, easy to take ranking assessment of the terminal outcomes an individual hopes to get from work. Useful for evaluating goal-structure.

Recruiting Preferences Measure (RPM/A): A specialized upgrade of the Call Reluctance Scale designed exclusively to evaluate the contact initiation profile of sales managers, trainers and others who are accountable for recruiting high-quality new agents for the insurance industry. A highly specific application, and the only instrument of its type.

continues

Assessment Technologies *continued*

RPM/P: Another specialized adaptation of the Call Reluctance Scale, this one to be used by international human resources/placement firms to measure the contact initiation profile of prospective recruiters.

RPM/R: A specialized adaptation of the Call Reluctance Scale to be used by international recruitment firms to evaluate management-level personnel accountable for hiring people who must recruit.

CareerStyles Inventory™ (CSI): A state-of-the-art multi-dimensional assessment of personality-like influences on the behavior of people at work. Extremely comprehensive, the CSI was "real-world" calibrated on the assumption that many people tested in industry do not necessarily wish to be tested and therefore can be expected to be less than fully cooperative when completing tests. Two versions are available: a longer report for psychologists and a shorter one for human resources and training practitioners.

SPQ*Assist™: An add-on module for the Call Reluctance Scale. Scores from all 12 diagnostic scales are statistically synthesized into three sales performance summary projections: *How much? How soon? What cost?* (See p. 366 for more information)

SPQ*SELECTRON™: A statistical add-on package for the Call Reluctance Scale, SELECTRON™ is an ultra-sophisticated computer application designed specifically to forecast sales performance. Beyond and free from the statistical limitations of simple correlational procedures, it is a neural network application which was designed to learn the way people learn—by trial and error. The technology was originally developed as part of the Strategic Defense Initiative ("Star Wars") and is currently used by NASA and by medical scientists to detect cancer cells. SELECTRON™ is the first application specifically utilizing this technology to forecast sales performance. The first generation was presented with sales results and Call Reluctance Scale scores from 206 salespeople representing the very highest and very lowest producers in eleven industries. After "learning" the 206 cases, SELECTRON™ hummed and whirred until it had decoded the complex patterns which distinguish very low from very high producers. Additional experimental applications are now being explored for use with other sales support assessments.

In sales, Yielders have difficulty asserting themselves, particularly when it comes to prospecting. Afraid to incite conflict or risk losing approval, Yielders become pathetically polite. Always tentative, never decisive, they whisper through their prospecting chores, hiding like pheasants in the undergrowth.

Prospecting is contact initiation; it *is* an assertive act. It follows then that prospecting is troublesome for Yielders. Unwilling to *appear* pushy or to *seem* intrusive, they sacrifice their career interests to the interests of others. Afraid to bother the busy, disturb the indisposed, or interrupt the otherwise engaged, they become obstinately inactive, waiting for the "right" time, the "right" circumstances—the restoration of Eden.

Probable Origin:

Yielder Call Reluctance appears to result from a combination of hereditary influences and past experiences. The exact proportion contributed by each is still controversial. It surfaces when individuals with low dominance (a general personality trait) enter the sales profession and try to prospect. Prospecting activity is almost immediately impaired by their reluctance to assert. It is worsened when they are exposed to sales trainers or sales training materials that are contaminated with Yielder Call Reluctance. As Yielders experience discomfort prospecting, a loose collection of coping strategies form. Once formed, they harden each time prospecting discomfort is experienced. After a short time, the loose collection of coping strategies mature into Yielder Call Reluctance.

Curiously, Yielders are *not* the opposite, as people often presume, of the exaggerated, over-aggressive individual. Overstated assertiveness is usually just theater, a cover; ineffective behavior displayed by some Yielders trying to *appear* aggressive. Their tough guy talk is tedious, often socially embarrassing, and rarely, if ever, convincing.

Outlook:

Yielder Call Reluctance often contains a hereditary component, so it is not easily eliminated. Nevertheless, the outlook is still very positive. When it is properly assessed and the appropriate training procedures are used, it can be quickly contained and prospecting performance can be markedly improved. Most Yielders are very cooperative, willingly follow instructions and are easy to work with. That makes the outlook for improvement even better.

CareerStyle:

- Hesitates to express needs and interests
- Very self-critical for allowing others to "walk all over me all the time"
- Easy to indoctrinate
- Easy to persuade
- Sometimes gullible, too quick to accept clients' objections
- Indecisive
- Politely laughs at jokes and social pleasantries which are neither funny nor pleasant
- Vulnerable to close reluctance
- May use deception to avoid conflict
- Overemphasizes the rapport-building, relationship elements of the sales process at the expense of assertive prospecting and closing
- Rigidly refuses to be more aggressive; becomes indignant at the suggestion
- Considers aggressive salespeople and managers to be unprofessional
- Has difficulty expressing anger, so it builds up inside
- Defers to the needs of others, bankrupts own interests
- Engages in gossip about office politics, intrigues and power plays
- Tends to be sociable but not necessarily outgoing
- Manipulates others through non-confrontational means such as gossiping, strategic complaining and pouting
- Yielder men seem to prefer Hyper-Pro, Oppositional women; Yielder women prefer Hyper-Pro, Oppositional men. Expectedly, the mixture is highly combustible, contributing to the celestial phenomena known as exploding Hyper-Pros.
- Strives to be more emphatic and assertive but hesitates to follow through behaviorally

Self-Assessment:

Do you often feel people take advantage of you?
Yielders persuade themselves that they have been singled out for abuse.

When you realize people are taking advantage of you, do you *still* find it difficult to do anything about it? Do you assertively confront them?

Salespeople struggling with Yielder Call Reluctance complain loudly and often—to themselves. Anything else would be impolite.

Do you have trouble speaking when you are angry?

Yielders are so concerned about managing their anger—which can often border on rage—and keeping it locked away inside that they can hardly talk to the people who upset them. They could kill them. They just can't talk to them.

As a child, were you taught to never be too forward; that being forward was synonymous with being selfish?

Yielders confuse asserting their interests with being forward, and being forward with being bad.

Do you consider yourself a gentle person?

Yielders tend to be gentle, frustrated people.

How difficult would it be for you to handle a prospective client who called you "pushy and rude"?

Yielders would require two weeks of hospitalization.

Is using the telephone to prospect more difficult than face-to-face prospecting?

Yielders don't like telephone prospecting. They need rigorous visual and verbal assurance that they are not coming on too strong or doing anything wrong.

Have you ever called yourself a wimp?

Salespeople with Yielder Call Reluctance have called themselves worse things than that.

Do you have "command and control" daydreams in which you fantasize yourself in a position to issue orders and take decisive actions?

Many Yielders enjoy this pastime. Some become ruthless tyrants, others despotic monarchs. But not without cost. Many Yielders feel compelled to apologize for having overbearing daydreams.

When you talk to people you are comfortable with, do you tend to exaggerate how you handle conflict, stand up for yourself, and issue ultimatums?

Yielders often tell tall tales of assertive victories which never happened—except in their dreams.

Objective Assessments:

Call Reluctance Scale—A high prospecting Brake score plus high Yielder score indicates that Yielder Call Reluctance could be limiting your prospecting performance at the present time.

A low prospecting Brake score plus a high Yielder score indicates a predisposition to Yielder Call Reluctance although it is probably not limiting your prospecting performance at the present time.

Selling Styles Profile Analysis—Yielders have a strong preference for Rapport-Oriented selling. They consider their approach consultative and emphasize the interpersonal elements of the sales process over image, product, needs or the close. (Rapport-Oriented salespeople often claim that when proper relationships are established, the close is not necessary.)

Frequency of Occurrence:

The Yielder is the most frequently observed type of call reluctance, regardless of industry or sales setting. According to pop-psych pamphleteers, speaking before groups is the most common fear. We have no data to refute this claim for adults in general, but compared to the number of Yielders found among salespeople, Stage Fright is a distant also-ran. We have found some languishing sales organizations comprised almost entirely of Yielders.

Most Effective Countermeasures:

- Assertion Training—Assertion Training is a general grouping of procedures which are not contained in this book because they are readily available elsewhere. One of the best is an inexpensive book entitled *Your Perfect Right* by Alberti and Emmons. Although it does not deal directly with call reluctance, it is an excellent introduction to the problems associated with low assertiveness.

- Thought Zapping

- Sensory Injection

- Negative Image Projection

- Thought Realignment

- Threat Desensitization (for resistant cases only)

SOCIAL SELF-CONSCIOUSNESS
Technical Name   **Social Differential**
SD

Capsule Summary:

Social Self-Consciousness is a highly concentrated form of call reluctance. Devotees practice the inverse of target marketing: target *avoidance*.

Some Socially Self-Conscious salespeople complicate matters by insisting they are not call reluctant. According to them, they can initiate contact with *anyone*—unless, of course, their prospect fits into a group they have emotionally targeted to exclude from their market. Typically, Socially Self-Conscious salespeople shun prospects with wealth, prestige, power, education, or social standing.

Actually, Socially Self-Conscious salespeople are closet snobs. They belabor a rigid, self-imposed, psychological caste system which elevates people with education, position, or wealth to rarefied heights of superiority and influence.

CALL RELUCTANCE UP CLOSE

The Socially Self-Conscious Hatchet Job

Robert M. "Hatchet" Hatcher is proud to be a real estate agent. A busy, preoccupied man, "the Hatchet" has considerable talent but only average production to show for his three years of activity. To date, his pride is unequaled by his achievements.

Recently, Bob held an open house for one of his properties. Throughout the day prospective buyers casually stopped by, looked around, took free printed information about the house, and left. Around 4:30 that afternoon, a married couple, the Barringtons, arrived to inspect the house. They were courteous but obviously tired. They had been looking at new homes all day. Bob skillfully introduced himself, managing to tease some information from them as he gently asked questions and offered his services. They checked each room, quickly deciding that this was not the home

continues

The Socially Self-Conscious Hatchet Job *continued*

for them. The bedrooms were too small, the color scheme was too harsh, and the design of the house was unsatisfactory, they noted almost apologetically.

Hatchet had talent, skill and experience. He had been well trained. He knew how to handle the situation. So he set his course, gently asking questions and searching for preferences, like a warm-handed physician softly and purposefully probing and poking about for a diagnosis.

Hatchet busily wrote notes while the Barringtons answered his questions. Dividing a piece of scrap paper down the middle, they exchanged phone numbers.

Hatchet said he would go immediately to his office to run a computer search for listed homes that might fit the Barringtons' specifications. He did, laboring intensely for 2½ hours on the computer, scanning listings and generating an impressive number of homes for the Barringtons to inspect. As he left for home, he passed the hallway mirror, noticing his eyes. They were strained and reddened. He was tired but happy. He had a good feeling about this one.

Hatchet had agreed to call Mr. Barrington the next morning. At 9 o'clock sharp, he picked up the phone and dialed the number Barrington had given him. After two rings, Barrington's phone was answered. "Doctor Barrington's office," said the cool, officious voice. For a few awkward seconds Hatchet made no reply. He was stunned, frozen in place. Then, at the blink of an eye, he hung up.

Hatchet never called the Barringtons back. To this day he claims it was a matter of personal preference. "I just don't like doing business with that type," he angrily snaps every time the subject is discussed. Unready to admit he has call reluctance, Hatchet still (proudly) excludes educated professionals from his market. Relying totally on sporadic, internal training, Hatchet's manager remains blissfully ignorant. He doesn't realize that Social Self-Consciousness Call Reluctance has blunted Hatchet's blade. What about the Barringtons? Within two weeks they purchased their new home. They enlisted the services of another real estate agent to help out—one who would work with "their type." The home they bought sold for $350,000.

Shackled by self-inflicted emotional boundaries, Socially Self-Conscious salespeople prohibit themselves from prospecting throughout the entire social range. Overly concerned with their own social standing, sometimes defensive, always easily intimidated, they excessively admire influential people. When they are in their presence, they characteristically regress to affected, childlike, ingratiating behaviors.

Socially Self-Conscious salespeople favor coping through abstinence. They ritualistically excise wealthy, educated prospects from their markets.

Probable Origin:

No one is born with Social Self-Consciousness Call Reluctance. Virulent, it is highly contagious and easily acquired, usually through passive learning. Typically, it is carried by sales managers, trainers, consultants, or implicit attitude-shaping messages embedded within the sales training process itself. Often it is confused with low self-esteem and low assertiveness which are more related to other forms of call reluctance.

Top Secret: Covert Operations

We had an unusually difficult time gathering coherent call reluctance data from one U.S. industry that we knew had more than its fair share of Social Self-Conscious Call Reluctance—insurance sales management. These managers were hard to pin down. We tried. But they were a moving target. Defensive. Disinterested. Had to "get home office permission." Too busy. Project not important enough. "Best sales training anywhere. No call reluctance in this company." Salespeople from that industry, however, assured us that was not the case.

We explained our problem to a few sympathetic insurance sales managers who were familiar with our work. Each gave us similar advice. If they won't cooperate, go underground. Gather your observations covertly. Interesting idea. But how?

Determined to collect our observations, we discarded our usual ingenuity for making practical things unbearably theoretical and actually developed a successful plan. We purchased materials to construct a makeshift display booth, selected a call reluctance product to market and transformed ourselves into commercial

continues

Top Secret: Covert Operations *continued*

exhibitors at their national trade convention. Posing as vendors, we used high quality, hidden Berodyne microphones and NADY model 501 wireless transmitters to broadcast our interactions to a concealed Marantz 221 tape recorder for later analysis.

We were never a competitive threat to the highly skilled and experienced professional exhibitors there. But we were adequate. The guise worked. We collected our behavioral samples and made our observations.

We knew that some Socially Self-Conscious sales managers compensate for feeling socially inferior by shamelessly ingratiating themselves to people they admire. But we didn't know that their admiration contains a dark side, an element of conflict and frustration.

Socially Self-Conscious sales managers admire the influential but they are also intimidated by them. It's a confused mixture of conflict and awe. Because of this, we presumed they would be unusually courteous and sensitive in their dealings with service personnel and others assigned to lower positions. We were wrong. We observed several instances where managers rudely and un-necessarily intimidated people they perceived to be beneath them. In a position of temporary influence, they were acting the way they thought they were treated by people who had influence and power over them—their prospects. It was fascinating. In this respect, Social Self-Consciousness in sales managers and trainers seems to closely parallel the cycle of emotional abuse in pathological families. Emotionally abused as children, they become emotional abusers as adults.

Outlook:

Social Self-Consciousness Call Reluctance can be extremely limiting. When a company shifts its marketing emphasis to up-market clients, or when purchasing decisions for a product or service are made at high organizational levels, or when educated, professional people constitute the prime market for a product or service, Social Self-Consciousness Call Reluctance can be lethal to a sales career. If it is detected early, however, and the proper training is provided, it is a relatively easy form of call reluctance to correct.

CareerStyle:

- Most common in veteran salespeople

- Confines experienced salespeople to production plateaus, often for extended periods of time

- Restricts prospecting activity to equal or lower socio-economic groups

- Changes sales organizations frequently to escape up-market sales and marketing campaigns

- Prospects without difficulty in all areas except up-market and professional sectors

- When asked for an explanation, just says, "I don't call on (physicians, professors, community leaders, etc.)!"

- Gives effective sales presentations to non-decision makers; right ammunition, wrong targets

- Assumes submissive, ingratiating, childlike behaviors in the presence of people *perceived to be* powerful or authoritative (which to them is the same as "parental")

- Often misdiagnosed as low motivation or poor goal direction by the uninitiated

- Emotionally dependent on esteem-building self-help books, cassettes, workshops

- Many come from blue collar backgrounds

- Some are sensitive about lacking formal education and compensate by surrounding themselves with books and attending various commercial workshops to obtain certificates

- Some, ingratiating to superiors, tend to be abusive, impatient, tyrannical and intimidating to people they perceive to be *lower* on the caste system than themselves, such as secretaries and maintenance personnel

- Embellishes and exaggerates the power, fame and money of the people who intimidate him/her when discussing them with friends, family and co-workers

- Often plans to make more up-market contacts during goal-setting sessions but never gets around to translating promises into consistent up-market prospecting practices

Self-Assessment:

Does your behavior tend to be childlike when you're in the presence of certain people, such as physicians, clergymen and senior corporate officials?

Salespeople with Social Self-Consciousness Call Reluctance tend to regress to childlike behavior when they are in the presence of influential people.

Are you ever rude, abrupt, or do you pretend to be too busy, when you interact with commercial exhibitors at conventions? What about other salespeople? How do you treat them when they make sales calls on you?

Some salespeople with Social Self-Consciousness Call Reluctance have a blind spot and a short memory. They habitually intimidate other salespeople when they are in a position to do so; and they do so to the same degree and in the same way they feel people in power and control have intimidated them.

How important is it to you for other people to think you are powerful and influential?

To Socially Self-Conscious salespeople it is either very important or so extremely important that they act entirely disinterested.

How many up-market professional people do you know, or know of, whom you could contact but haven't?

If you're Socially Self-Conscious, you probably know many, but to them you're invisible and mute.

Do you get angry with yourself for being easy to intimidate?

Salespeople with Social Self-Consciousness Call Reluctance know they tend to get intimidated easily. Some bother themselves so much and cope so rigorously that they even become hostages to the possibility. They are intimidated by intimidation.

Do you daydream about being chairperson of a prestigious organization or the head of a large corporation where you have uncontested power and influence?

Socially Self-Conscious salespeople dream of worlds where they hold the wealth, prestige and power.

Objective Assessments:

Call Reluctance Scale—A high prospecting Brake score plus a high Social Self-Consciousness score indicates that Social Self-Consciousness Call Reluctance is probably crippling your prospecting performance at the present time.

A low prospecting Brake score plus a high Social Self-Consciousness score indicates a predisposition to Social Self-Consciousness Call Reluctance although it is probably not limiting your prospecting performance at the present time.

Selling Styles Profile Analysis—Socially Self-Conscious salespeople tend to prefer Competition-Oriented or Service-Oriented presentation styles.

Frequency of Occurrence:

Social Self-Consciousness is the ninth most frequently observed type of call reluctance. However, it only limits sales performance in industries where calling on up-market clientele is required. It is only infrequently found in neophyte salespeople who have not had enough time to acquire it from their sales manager or trainer. We found one sales organization with a disproportionate number of Socially Self-Conscious *new* salespeople. Due to some embedded technical errors, their sales selection test actually *recommended* hiring this form of call reluctance! It was extremely difficult working with this organization. It seems they were even intimidated by us.

Most Effective Countermeasures:

- Thought Zapping
- Sensory Injection
- Thought Realignment
- Logical Problem Solving—A general procedure, based on appeals to reason, which is not provided in this book because it is readily available in sales training materials elsewhere. Logical Problem Solving is ineffective when Social Self-Consciousness is accompanied by the Oppositional Reflex.

SEPARATIONIST
FRN

Capsule Summary:

Separationist Call Reluctance occurs when salespeople negatively anticipate how their friends would react if they were to make a sales call on them, *or ask them for referrals*. An October 1989 Richmond, Virginia, *Times-Dispatch* article described the experiences of a failed securities broker. "Friends are crucial to building a client base," the article said, "but Alexander felt so awkward that he didn't call a single person he knew. Mrs. Alexander (also a failed broker) phoned only a few."

Separationism is a natural emotional reaction to doubts that some salespeople have about the depth, quality and durability of their friendships. They presume their friends would be offended, or feel exploited, if they made a sales presentation to them or asked them for referrals. So to prevent conflict and to protect their friendships, salespeople with Separationist Call Reluctance emotionally exile (*separate*) discussions of business and career interests from their contacts with friends. To them, making sales calls on friends is emotionally prohibited and asking for referrals is a threat to the relationship. Regrettably, their competitors do not recognize and will not honor the arbitrary emotional boundaries Separationists set for themselves.

Probable Origin:

Separationist Call Reluctance is learned. It can be passively acquired through exposure to negative stereotypes about selling. Or it can be picked up from direct contact with friends who had negative experiences with salespeople, sales trainers who are undiagnosed Separationists, or even from respected sales role models who carry the virus, unintentionally spreading it to others. According to reports from securities salespeople, some of the commercial sales training and telemarketing programs used in their industry actually endorse and actively teach Separationist Call Reluctance.

Separationist Call Reluctance has only a mild relationship to Emotionally Unemancipated Call Reluctance (a structurally similar form of call reluctance which places the family emotionally off limits). A correlational analysis of 1,830 salespeople demonstrated only a 33% overlap between the two call reluctance types. This means that the two measures are psychologically separate and distinct. A salesperson with Separationist Call Reluctance (Friends) is no more or less likely to have Emotionally Unemancipated Call Reluctance (Family) than any other type.

CALL RELUCTANCE UP CLOSE

Separationist Illusions

Some salespeople overcome their call reluctance quickly. Others take longer. Some bounce aimlessly from short-lived, self-help fads to slick, varnished self-help frauds, toting their prospecting fears along with them.

But not Tom Ravenscroft, a 56-year-old residential real estate agent in Phoenix, Arizona. He was tested for call reluctance but didn't need to see the results. He knew. Listening with careful attention, nodding in perfect agreement with the instructor, Tom learned the name for what he already knew. He had call reluctance. He was a Separationist.

For Tom, sharpening the outline of his call reluctance and giving it a name was all it took. Ready to put the countermeasures to immediate use, he grew agitated and impatient. It was time to start prospecting.

First on his list were the Whitmyers. They were longtime friends of his, members of the same church. He had not called on them before because he didn't want to "crisscross business and friendships."

"Hi, Sandy, how are you," Tom said, his voice animated with a rich, renewed mixture of excitement and purpose. "Are you still thinking about putting your house on the market?"

"Well, Tom, we'd just about given up on you," Sandy said playfully but truthfully. "We've been thinking about putting our house up for almost a year now. We kind of wanted you to help us, but we didn't think you wanted to. So we just let it slide...hoping you'd ask. Sure took you long enough!"

Tom listed the Whitmyers' house for $285,000. It sold quickly for $265,000. Tom Ravenscroft, reformed Separationist, made almost $5,000. "It was the easiest sale I ever made," Tom said with disbelief, still unable to comprehend how he could have excluded his own friends from his market for so long.

Parenthetically, Separationist Call Reluctance may actually be more functionally related to Role Rejection, another form of call reluctance, which feeds on unexpressed guilt and shame associated with being in a sales career. A salesperson with both Role Rejection *and* Separationist Call Reluctance reacts to his friends as if they hold his sales career in the same low esteem that he does.

Outlook:

Separationist Call Reluctance is easy to correct if it is properly detected and the appropriate training procedures are used. The earlier it is detected, the easier it is to overcome.

CareerStyle:

- Does not refer to business when around friends

- Tries to convince other salespeople that calling on friends is *always* unethical, unprofessional and unnecessary

- Takes longer to develop a stable prospect base (because of failure to make use of one of the fastest and most potent sources of referrals available—friends)

- May have no problem calling on family members or asking them for referrals

- Considers salespeople who make sales calls on their friends, or even ask them for referrals, to be unethical and unprofessional

- May get belligerent when management requests a rational justification for his/her position

- "Never mix business and friendship"

- Hesitates to give names of friends to other salespeople for referrals

Self-Assessment:

Do you ever feel you have to protect your friends from your managers or other salespeople in your organization?

Without realizing it, Separationists often act as if they have to protect their friends from their sales associates and their sales managers, too.

Do your friends *know* you have been valiantly protecting them from *you*?

Separationists usually decide to protect their friends from their sales presentations without first asking them if they want or need protection. Is it conceivable that some of your friends might want to hear your sales presentation?

Do you try to keep your friendships and your business interests absolutely separate?

Separationists don't just try, they succeed. The two remain separate.

When you talk about your job with your friends, do you purposefully use euphemisms and deemphasize prospecting?

Separationists verbally disguise what they do, rarely discussing their prospecting activities with their friends.

Note: On this, salespeople with Role Rejection Call Reluctance have clearly outclassed Separationists. They have stretched the creative usage of alternative titles for the sales function into a new literary genre. Separationists, however, only resort to such eloquence when discussing their careers with friends. Salespeople with Role Rejection Call Reluctance attempt to downplay or disguise what they do to everyone—their friends, family, enemies, prospects, God.

Have any of your friends ever tried to sell *you* anything? How did you feel? Exploited? Manipulated? Did you immediately sever the friendship?

Most Separationists have succumbed to a double standard. While allowing friends to sell them things like cosmetics, burglar alarms, investments, insurance and real estate, they refuse to grant themselves the emotional freedom to do the same.

Objective Assessments:

Call Reluctance Scale—A high prospecting Brake score plus a high Separationist score indicates that Separationist Call Reluctance could be limiting prospecting performance at the present time.

A low prospecting Brake score plus a high Separationist score indicates a predisposition to Separationist Call Reluctance although it is probably not limiting your prospecting performance at the present time.

Selling Styles Profile Analysis—Separationists do not have a characteristic selling style.

Frequency of Occurrence:

Separationists are the fourth most frequently observed call reluctance type. In some organizations, most notably in the securities industry, it is pathologically high.

Most Effective Countermeasures:

- Thought Zapping

- Sensory Injection

- Thought Realignment

- Logical Persuasion (a general support procedure that is not included in this book because many versions are available elsewhere)

EMOTIONALLY UNEMANCIPATED
FAM

Capsule Summary:

Salespeople with Emotionally Unemancipated Call Reluctance share an important feature with one of the more cutting intellects of our time, *Psycho*'s Norman Bates: They are not yet completely emancipated from their parents. Gratefully, the salespeople with Emotionally Unemancipated Call Reluctance we have met were more stable and less tangled than Norman. Though articulate, talented and able, they could not make sales calls on members of their own family—or, perhaps more important, they couldn't even ask for referrals or request help networking.

Adult-like in most other respects, when they interact with their parents or close relatives they regress to the perceptions, emotions and behaviors they experienced as children. Around family and relatives, they *are* still children. They claim that prospecting or asking for referrals among the members of their own family won't work. It would involve risking parental rejection and disapproval. Their kin would be justifiably offended and feel exploited. Worst of all, no family member would ever take a presentation seriously if given by a salesperson they knew as a runny-nosed child and a fumbling adolescent.

Probable Origin:

Emotionally Unemancipated Call Reluctance is acquired through active and passive learning. The predisposition to it is usually set into motion long before entry into the sales career. Typically, this may include repeated exposure to negative stereotypes about salespeople held by members of the immediate family. Later, it is unintentionally worsened by sales management (at all levels) and the sales training process.

Curiously, Emotionally Unemancipated Call Reluctance has only a modest relationship to Separationist Call Reluctance (a structurally similar form of call reluctance which places friends emotionally off limits). Repeated statistical studies have shown that the correlation between the two is considerably less than common sense would suspect. That means that these two forms of call reluctance are psychologically separate and distinct entities. An Emotionally Unemancipated salesperson is no more, or less, likely to be a Separationist than a Yielder, Hyper-Pro or any other type of call reluctance.

Outlook:

Emotionally Unemancipated Call Reluctance is easy to correct once it has been properly detected and appropriate training procedures are used.

CareerStyle:

- Considers family members totally off limits

- Hesitates to even ask relatives for referrals

- Maintains that calling on family members is *always* unprofessional and unethical

- May experience no difficulty calling on personal friends

- Takes longer than necessary to develop a client base

- Becomes unnecessarily emotional (angry or belligerent) when asked for rational justification for not calling on family or asking them for referrals

- Considers salespeople who do prospect and ask their family for referrals exploitative and unprofessional

- Believes business and family interests should never mix

- Refuses to give other salespeople the names of family members to use as referrals

- More volatile (emotionally) than usual when in the presence of family members

- Feels the need to insulate family members from the sales career

- Doubts family members can accept them as competent, well-intended sales professionals

  Note: The fault here lies with the emotional *feeling* about the career, not the career itself. Salespeople prone to Emotionally Unemancipated Call Reluctance would probably feel this way about *any* career or profession they chose, not just sales.

Self-Assessment:

Do you ever feel you have to insulate members of your own family from your manager or other salespeople in your organization?

Salespeople with Emotionally Unemancipated Call Reluctance go to great lengths to protect the members of their family from their mercenary colleagues. We can only speculate about the kooky, disjointed complexion which might characterize a salesperson with Emotionally Unemancipated Call Reluctance who worked for a sales organization owned by his or her family.

Do the members of your family know you have been insulating them?

Salespeople with Emotionally Unemancipated Call Reluctance rarely discuss this, or any significant aspect of their sales career, with family members.

Has a member of your family ever tried to sell you anything? If so, how did you feel?

Salespeople with Emotionally Unemancipated Call Reluctance live a double standard. They allow members of their family to sell them insurance, real estate, investments, cosmetics, vitamins, and burglar alarms, but they won't confer the same freedom upon themselves.

In general, do you keep a lot of secrets from your immediate family?

Salespeople with Emotionally Unemancipated Call Reluctance play two roles, live two lifestyles. One, the adult lifestyle, is lived away from the family. It's invisible and largely unknown to them. The other is emotional dependence, a childlike lifestyle that is familiar to, expected, and sometimes encouraged by family members.

How difficult would it be for you to give your sales presentation to the members of your family—*even if they requested it?*

Salespeople with Emotionally Unemancipated Call Reluctance would mentally seize up, smoke and flame out like a transmission starving for oil. They would slur and stammer over the familiar words of their presentation, nervously fidget about, probably have to pause for frequent toilet breaks, and demonstrate to the family in various ways that they are not, as the family already suspects, ready for autonomous adulthood.

Do you ever entertain yourself with fantasies where you feature yourself as an emotionally free spirit able to do things that would never be accepted or understood by the members of your family?

Salespeople with Emotionally Unemancipated Call Reluctance perform in such imaginary features. They invent in their dreams and fantasies the adult-like emotional independence they lack.

Objective Assessments:

Call Reluctance Scale—A high prospecting Brake score plus a high Emotionally Unemancipated score indicates that Emotionally Unemancipated Call Reluctance could be limiting prospecting performance at the present time.

A low prospecting Brake score plus a high Emotionally Unemancipated score indicates a predisposition to Emotionally Unemancipated Call Reluctance although it is probably not limiting your prospecting performance at the present time.

Selling Styles Profile Analysis—Salespeople with Emotionally Unemancipated Call Reluctance do not have a single, characteristic selling style.

Frequency of Occurrence:

Emotionally Unemancipated Call Reluctance is often observed in salespeople. It is most concentrated in sales environments that don't use or don't encourage the use of family members as prospects or as sources for referrals. (Actually, some of our early, now discarded, data suggests that some salespeople in these organizations are probably refugees from sales positions that did encourage or require contacting family members.) Unexpectedly, statistical studies of this call reluctance type nominate it for "most robust." It tends to have a significant (negative) statistical relationship to sales success—even in settings where family members don't make up the market or function as necessary sources for referrals!

In the U.S., Emotionally Unemancipated Call Reluctance is highest (by far) in the securities industry. There are unverified reports that some sales training organizations in that industry actually teach young brokers to exclude family members.

Most Effective Countermeasures:

- Thought Zapping
- Sensory Injection
- Threat Desensitization (for very resistant cases)
- Thought Realignment
- Logical Persuasion (a general procedure not provided in this book but readily available elsewhere)

REFERRAL AVERSION
RA

Capsule Summary:

Referrals are names of potential customers you don't know that you get from people you do know. Most sales trainers agree that referrals are the fastest, most direct route to increased sales and earnings. They can be obtained before the sale, during your presentation, after the close, when the order is delivered, and any time after delivery. But you have to ask.

Most satisfied customers are willing to provide you with the names of other people to call on. Many will actively endorse you and your product if given the chance. With few exceptions, most people expect to be asked for referrals. Some would be offended if they were not.

For most salespeople, asking for referrals is appropriate and easy. For a call reluctant minority, however, it is difficult and distressful. They think that asking for referrals will threaten a just-closed sale, damage delicate rapport with their current customers, or appear grasping and exploitive. They cope by hesitating, putting off the request for referrals as long as they can, or avoiding the situation altogether by never asking. Although the manner of coping may differ, the result is always the same. Failing to follow through with the entire sales process, including asking for referrals, they *default on the bridge to their next sale*.

Probable Origin:

We did not finish excavating this type of call reluctance until 1987. We knew from our statistical research that other forms of call reluctance remained to be isolated and identified. We had even been told that some salespeople had difficulty asking for referrals, but it never occurred to us that asking for referrals could be so distressful that it could develop into a mature call reluctance type. To us, it didn't make sense. All the other types of call reluctance obstruct the initiation of contact with prospective clients. Referral Aversion does not obstruct initial contact, nor does it interfere with giving powerfully persuasive presentations or even resolv-

---

The Insidious Seed of Referral Aversion

Calvin Hunt was a highly respected, experienced life insurance agent. But despite numerous sales awards and perennial membership in his industry's top performance group, Calvin's reach for success was still not complete. Uncomfortable asking for referrals, his otherwise exemplary sales skills cloaked a major flaw—Referral Aversion Call Reluctance.

For Calvin, the matter had its nativity in his formative years in sales, when foundational skills are laid, attitudes are formed, and limits are set. He had just wrapped up his first major sale. Dutifully, as instructed, he immediately asked for referrals. "You can't even wait for the ink to dry, can you?" his new client said angrily, ripping his order to shreds as he spoke. "You're just like all the others." Reeling from shock, Calvin steadied himself and tried to regain his composure—a process that was to take him years.

"I haven't asked for a referral in 17 years," he confessed. "I just never ask. That one time was enough for me."

Excited, open-minded, and resolved, Calvin learned quickly about Referral Aversion Call Reluctance, what it was, how it worked, and what to do about it. He was determined to forcefully evict his Referral Aversion. He wanted control of the total range of prospecting opportunities—even referrals. Then maybe he would start asking for referrals again. Maybe he wouldn't. Whichever, it would be his choice, not the ominous echo of an event that occurred years ago.

Calvin Hunt applied the countermeasures for Referral Aversion Call Reluctance. They worked for him. Shortly thereafter, he posted a commissions increase of $30,000—a pay boost he awarded himself by asking for referrals.

---

ing the close. Instead, it disables the bridge to the next sale. For many salespeople, this subtle but devastating form of call reluctance is all that stands between them and the super production levels they aspire and deserve to attain.

No one is born with Referral Aversion Call Reluctance. It is always learned—sometimes in only one trial or experience. Initial learning typically occurs when salespeople ask for a referral and get scorched by an unexpected rude or discourteous reply. The flood of heightened psychological, chemical and behavioral reactions which follow are impressed into memory. If the original experience was sufficiently intense, it is generalized to all potential referrals. When asking for referrals is attempted again, or even just contemplated, the past unfortunate experience is summoned up and superimposed on the current opportunity where it sets off a hazardous behavior alert. With each repetition, this sequence gets reinforced and etched deeper into the behavioral repertoire until it becomes mindlessly automatic. To the wincing Referral Aversive salesperson about to ask for a referral, it now feels like asking for referrals *causes* their distress. It doesn't.

For some Referral Aversive salespeople, their discomfort is only virile enough to make them hesitate. For others, it's consuming and results in complete avoidance. But one thing is certain: Every time a Referral Aversive salesperson hesitates or withdraws from the opportunity to ask for a referral, the associative bond between asking for referrals and the original unpleasant sensations gets stronger and generalizes further. A cruel, self-destructive habit is born.

Referral Aversive sales trainers discreetly model the discomfort they associate with asking for referrals in one of three ways: 1) through alternative prospecting methods they wholeheartedly endorse, 2) through prospecting methods they dispute with unnecessary passion, and 3) most often, by the prospecting methods they simply ignore—like asking for referrals.

Outlook:

Armed with appropriate training aids, Referral Aversion Call Reluctance is easy to prevent, diagnose and correct.

CareerStyle:

- Initial contact with prospective buyers may be unimpaired

- Distress increases as the time to ask for referrals draws nearer

- May be more comfortable making anonymous contacts (cold calls) than asking existing clients for referrals

- Considers asking new clients for referrals to be exploitative, untoward or tasteless.

- May also be uncomfortable letting colleagues or trainers ask his or her clients for referrals

- Thinks asking for referrals might jeopardize existing relationship with clients

- Thinks extraordinary service after the sale will prompt clients to volunteer referrals on their own

Self-Assessment:

Do you ask for referrals as often as you know you could?
Salespeople with Referral Aversion Call Reluctance knowingly pass over opportunities to ask for referrals, yet only rarely miss opportunities to offer excuses.

How do you see asking for referrals in terms of social risk-taking?
Salespeople with Referral Aversion Call Reluctance see more risk than opportunity.

To you, is there an optimum, appropriate time to ask for referrals?
Salespeople with Referral Aversion use time and circumstances as excuses for not asking for referrals as often as they could. They claim there are appropriate times and places for requesting referrals, but like the Big Bang and the Harmonic Convergence, scholars have had difficulty observing those circumstances.

How much do you rely on canned techniques and scripted sales approaches when you ask for referrals?
Uncomfortable with the enterprise, salespeople with Referral Aversion tend to lean heavily on stiff, mechancial scripts when they ask for referrals. Paradoxically, for some salespeople these rote, lifeless methods probably contribute to the unpleasant experiences they associate with asking for referrals.

Do you fantasize about engaging in intimate, private conversations with friends and acquaintances?
Some salespeople with Referral Aversion Call Reluctance do, in wide-screen color. They're afraid to jeopardize existing client relationships with requests. So they tend to compensate by imagining themselves as an unconditionally trusted professional—like a physician or mental health

practitioner—whose intimate and possibly threatening questions are an appropriate part of the professional relationship.

Objective Assessments:

Call Reluctance Scale—A high prospecting Brake score plus a high Referral Aversion score suggests that Referral Aversion Call Reluctance could be limiting your sales production now.

A low prospecting Brake score plus a high Referral Aversion score indicates a predisposition to Referral Aversion Call Reluctance although it is probably not interfering with your production at the present time.

Selling Styles Profile Analysis—Salespeople with Referral Aversion Call Reluctance are somewhat more likely to be Product-Oriented or Service-Oriented sellers, but the relationship is weak and unsteady.

Frequency of Occurrence:

Referral Aversion occurs less frequently than most of the other types of call reluctance. Statistically, less than 5% of all salespeople will experience Referral Aversion Call Reluctance. In organizations where it is more common than that, it is usually due to contaminated sales managers, toxic sales training practices, or both.

Most Effective Countermeasures:

- Thought Zapping
- Sensory Injection (Fragrance)
- Yellow Dot
- Thought Realignment (to consolidate gains only)

TELEPHOBIA
TEL

Capsule Summary:

Telephobia Call Reluctance is a highly selective impairment. It is found only in salespeople who become distressed when they try to use a telephone as a prospecting tool. It has absolutely no effect on those same salespeople using the same telephone for non-self-promotion purposes. They don't report distress when they use the telephone to call a friend, order a pizza, or to make an appointment with a hair dresser. Their discomfort is reserved entirely for those times when the telephone is to be used as a prospecting device.

Some Telephobic salespeople claim to have driven 100 miles or more to follow-up dubious leads because they were unable to prospect by phone. A Telephobic computer salesman summed it up this way: "The telephone is an annoyance and a hindrance to all mankind. I wish Alexander Graham Bell had been shot or never been born." A half-hearted participant in a recent basic telemarketing course, this salesman *knew* what to say and how to say it on the phone. He did not know how to do so comfortably.

Probable Origin:

Like fine wines and good cigars, Telephobia Call Reluctance is an acquired taste. It has to be learned. Most cases contain highly fermented elements from one or more past events when the use of the telephone became connected to intense feelings of alarm or threat. In other cases, in which a flood of anxiety is instantly triggered when *any* phone unexpectedly rings, the trouble can usually be traced to having received a tragic message by telephone.

Telephobia Call Reluctance is parented and sustained by our native ability to mindlessly overgeneralize and then repeat those generalizations as if they were true. A single, long forgotten attempt to use the phone for prospecting purposes is usually enough. That isolated negative event is all that's needed to stigmatize your telephone, transforming it into a ponderous and threatening aberration. Years later, the unpleasant sensations you experienced with *that* phone call can still be superimposed on *all* phones you try to use for prospecting purposes. That's what happened to one of the authors.

After approximately 13 years on this earth, young men are hormonally commandeered into the mindless pursuit of young women. Curious, physically awkward, and psychologically incomplete, the moment arrives when it is time for them to ask for a date—the first date. For some young men that's easy. For most young men it's not. For shy young men it's iron-bound difficult.

Shy by temperament and slight of physique, it took two weeks of dedicated rehearsal before 13-year-old George Dudley could muster the transcendent courage required to pick up the phone, put it to his ear, dial, and then speak.

"Hello, Brittany?" he carefully modulated while trying to project a confidence he didn't feel.

"This is George."

There was no reply, no words of greeting, not even elementary telephone courtesy.

"You know," he hurriedly reminded her, grimacing as he painstakingly formed his petition, "I sit next to you in history class."

But there was still no reply. Inferring from this that the event was not going to unfold according to plan, he decided to abandon all the small talk he had rehearsed and strike with apocalyptic resolve.

"Do you think you'd like to go to a movie with me Friday night...?"

"No, I don't think so. Are ya kidding?" Brittany asked with the egotistical self-absorption of a gum-chewing, world-wise 13-year-old stripper. "I only date football players, ya know," she hastily added, packaging each of her words with all the tenderness and sincerity of a superficial, self-quoting politician. Then she hung up. Slam. Dial tone. Telephobia.

That was the prologue to Dudley's Telephobia Call Reluctance, and it's representative of how it originates in salespeople as well. In Dudley's case, the present reverberations of an old, ego-busting catastrophe can be concealed and circumvented by clever avoidance. How? By simply delegating all self-promotional phone calls to other people. But for most Telephobic salespeople, especially those in telemarketing, that's not a realistic or feasible option. For them, Telephobia gets resolved or the career gets dissolved.

To sales-driven companies, the financial losses incurred from large numbers of Telephobics in the sales force probably stretch to billions of dollars of unrealized income each year. Yet some of the sales management executives at the head of these companies (who are often, it turns out, Telephobic themselves) resolutely press on, looking for quick and dirty solutions and finding only convenient scapegoats in their sales managers, trainers, or sales training departments.

Outlook:

Telephobia Call Reluctance is usually easy to diagnose and correct once a serious commitment is made and serious measures are used. If left unmanaged, especially in large organizations, it can promptly expand to epidemic proportions. Left undiagnosed in sales managers, trainers or senior sales executives, the prognosis is corporate self-destruction.

CareerStyle:

- Makes fewer number of prospecting phone calls per unit of time relative to other salespeople in same organization

- Compensates by emphasis on alternate prospecting methods which don't require using the phone

- May suffer from (undiagnosed) hearing problems which could translate into discomfort using the telephone

- Inadequate phone follow-up of leads acquired from other sources

- Gullible, vulnerable to expensive, silver bullet solutions like automatic telephone prospecting machines

- Slow to get started making prospecting phone calls each day

- Takes too many unscheduled breaks from scheduled telephone prospecting sessions

- Psychs up to get started; instantly deflated by turn-downs, put-downs and rejections

- Presence of sales trainer, manager or supervisor increases distress when teleprospecting

- Repeated attempts at reassurance and confidence boosting don't work and don't last

- May resort to psychological distancing techniques like frequent joke telling, nervous laughing and visiting during teleprospecting sessions to cover distress

- Practices the Excremental Theory of Nervous Energy; when teleprospecting, may *insist* on rigidly exercising body movement techniques like standing, pacing, or facing a mirror to camouflage discomfort and help discharge built-up nervous tension

    (This drill is based on a once popular belief that nervous energy, when stored, builds up until it explodes unless it is discharged first. In this context, body movement is like a bowel movement. By standing up and moving around when you're under stress, like when teleprospecting, you're helping your body discharge nervous waste. Unappealing but true, the principle behind the practice holds that you're lending your body an assist as it surrenders nervous excrement. What fun. Next time someone invites you to stand up and move around while you try to prospect on the telephone, think first, think carefully. Do you really need a behavioral laxative?)

- Harsh, self-protective practices like hanging up on prospective buyers before they can reject your offer reveals porous self-confidence and fragile Telephobia management skills (not to mention the bad image it creates for your company)

Self-Assessment:

Have you ever received unexpected, tragic news by telephone?

Some Telephobics, especially those who are easily startled by unexpected calls, may have received tragic news by phone. The memory is vivid, the feelings lucid, even though the event may have occurred years ago. Non-Telephobics may have also experienced similar situations but, unlike Telephobics, they have worked through the emotions and kept them from tainting the telephone.

When the telephone rings, do you maintain a relaxed state while reaching to answer?

Telephobics—even those who are not startled by the ring—tend to experience a sudden rush of intensity which remains until the phone call is answered.

How many total sales or sales appointments do you typically originate by telephone?

Telephobics usually originate far less than average and less than they are otherwise capable of initiating.

Do you daydream about reestablishing contact by phone with past romantic involvements or being called with unexpected good news?

Most people occasionally fantasize about these things. But Telephobics feature the phone, not the good news, in the starring role.

Objective Assessments:

Call Reluctance Scale—A high prospecting Brake score plus a high Telephobia score suggests that Telephobia Call Reluctance could be limiting your earnings now.

A low prospecting Brake score plus a high Telephobia score indicates a predisposition to Telephobia although there are probably no current overt symptoms and it is not interfering with telephone prospecting at the present time.

Selling Styles Profile Analysis—Salespeople with Telephobia Call Reluctance do not have a single, characteristic selling style.

Frequency of Occurrence:

Telephobia Call Reluctance is frequently found in salespeople. It tends to be more common in managers and trainers. It tends to be *much* more common in sales training consultants. It tends to be even more common in senior sales management executives.

Most Effective Countermeasures:

- Threat Desensitization
- Yellow Dot
- Thought Zapping
- Sensory Injection (Fragrance)
- Hot Water Bottle
- Target Reversal
- Thought Realignment

OPPOSITIONAL REFLEX
OR

Capsule Summary:

"I noticed the insulting remarks about motivational speakers in your book," the hot-tempered caller snorted. His sharp-edged words conveyed the intellectual force of a self-righteous moral crusader opposed to all vice that isn't profitable. (That description will probably earn us another call.) Claiming to be a motivational speaker of some repute himself, he concluded his irate critique of our book: "Well let me tell you something. Your book is the *worst* book ever written for salespeople. I'm going to *personally* see to it that nobody reads it," he blustered malevolently.

...It only took ten minutes. Then, the marginally effective sales manager shot straight up out of his seat, like a jet pilot ejecting from the cockpit. Storming from the room, he ripped his Call Reluctance Scale questionnaire booklet into jagged little pieces, theatrically tossing them into the air as he left. "Tests like this are a trivialization of the human experience!" he barked, dramatically slamming the door behind him.

...Her eyes grew small and fierce as the smartly dressed, under-achieving saleswoman interrupted her trainer loudly and self-confidently, "Yes, but in my former company we *always* used the *other* version." With near-perfect timing, she always interrupted her sales trainer. Every time he gave a suggestion or offered her advice she would add to it, subtract from it, modify it, or correct it.

What do these three salespeople have in common? Oppositional Reflex Call Reluctance.

Oppositional Reflex is the twelfth and most recently discovered form of call reluctance. Like a small child accidentally trapped in a dark closet, salespeople with Oppositional Reflex Call Reluctance are wildly banging and kicking at the door, shouting frightened, angry outrages for everyone to hear. "I'm somebody!" they're shrieking. "And you better know it!"

Despite strutting about with know-it-all, pretentious self-certainty, Oppositional Reflex Call Reluctance actually guards a bruised, embattled psyche which probably decided—perhaps years ago—that no one can be trusted and the only option left is to fight. Like slightly built macho men trying to outrun the Small Man Syndrome, Oppositionals mindlessly brawl, wildly striking at real and imaginary affronts to their pride. Dedicated to appearing independent, self-reliant, and complete, Opposi-tionals usually do the *exact opposite* of what they are asked to do. Repeatedly doing so, they diminish the independence they try to project to a noisy, transparent self-contradiction. Claiming to be psychologically stronger, more resourceful, and better informed, Oppositional salespeople reflexively speak when they should be listening, instruct when they should be learning, criticize when they should be commending, reject when they should be accepting. When Oppositional Call Reluctance possesses sales-people, it causes them to perform an angry burlesque, tediously boasting of their refinements while discrediting the methods, contributions, and achievements of everybody else.

Victimized by a reflexive emotional twitch, Oppositional salespeople are unable to allow themselves to be coached, advised, instructed, man-aged, or trained. Ignoring their talents, discarding their dreams, they soon swell the ranks of malcontented, underachieving salespeople, humorless, grasping bureaucrats, and garish, gold-chained consultants.

Unable to be taught, they never learn how to prospect successfully, manage their sales career, or control their frustrations. Bursting with promise but bound to their righteous indignation, salespeople with Oppositional Reflex Call Reluctance rarely reach their goals or realize their potential.

Unable to excel in sales, some migrate to high visibility, low accountability home office management positions. Once there, they fade into high-sounding, low-payoff projects and successive interoffice political intrigues. When they successfully scheme their way into influential positions over management training, sales training, or sales selection, profitability becomes the bridesmaid to insatiable power needs, and departmental creativity degrades to compliance. Always seeking ways to enlarge their territories, departments under their control become bloated with unnecessary manpower, operating costs rise, profits stagnate, and senior management can't figure out why. Unreformed Oppositionals are clever, committed, and covert. When they infiltrate key home office sales support functions, the result is increased you-can't-tell-me-anything-I-don't-already-know management coupled with slow, painful corporate decay.

Sadly, writing about Oppositional Reflex Call Reluctance is like preaching to the choir. Most of the people for whom this section was written will never read it. Those who try will be immediately challenged by a corrosive emotional undercurrent determined to intellectually paralyze them with mind-numbing criticisms, clever critiques, and caustic comments.

If you're a salesperson with Oppositional Reflex Call Reluctance, you've already been finding fault, denying *you* have call reluctance, making excuses, and rebuffing our efforts to try to help you. But take heart. This time could be different. *You're still reading.* Is a small part of you ready to consider making some big, positive changes? Pause for a moment. Listen to yourself—carefully. Then lay down your weapons. Lighten up. Keep reading. Join the choir.

Probable Origin:

Like Adam and Eve's other descendants, salespeople with Oppositional Reflex Call Reluctance have built-in emotional on/off switches. But they can't seem to locate their emotional volume controls. To them, all frustrations are prospective catastrophes, disagreements are rebellions, suggestions are ultimatums.

Interestingly, their *capacity* to agitate quickly, intensely and frequently is probably due to hereditary factors. But hereditary tendencies don't necessarily translate into full-blown Oppositional Reflex Call Reluctance. That has to be learned, practiced and refined.

Oppositional salespeople typically bear personal histories of traumatic disappointment, misplaced trust, or unrequited affection. Striking back and resisting was how they chose to save face and cope. Repeated countless times since then, in countless circumstances, resisting has been honed and polished into an overpowering behavioral theme. Sovereign and autonomous, it now controls them.

Oppositional Reflex Call Reluctance Is Not Dominance

Managers and consultants typically mistake the Oppositional Reflex for high dominance. That's because salespeople with Oppositional Reflex Call Reluctance usually score "high dominant" on simplistic grid-type sales assessment scales.

Companies using these devices learn the hard way: High dominance and Oppositionality are not the same. They're not even from the same behavioral constellation. Yet, when viewed through seriously flawed lenses they look the same.

Inferior sales assessment instruments obscure the critical differences between dominance and Oppositionality, like a bargain basement telescope unable to distinguish the sun from the moon.

Salespeople with Oppositional Reflex Call Reluctance easily outwit the efforts of good assessment procedures—from assessment centers to sophisticated tests—to detect them. Superficial, grid-type assessment tests offend their ingenuity. Able to successfully hoodwink them, Oppositionals register high marks on dominance on these sales selection tests—effortlessly, almost at will.

Dominance and Oppositionality do share enough characteristics to make accurate assessment very difficult and extremely hazardous. (Only vain managers, dishonest test marketeers, and ignorant users think it's easy.) But numerous behavioral "markers" exist for each benign similarity. These attributes help distinguish Oppositionality from dominance.

Dominance, when properly measured, is personality-based *forcefulness*. Oppositionality is *recoil*. If you're a dominant salesperson, you struggle up the mountainside whistling, "Mama, don't let your babies grow up to be cowboys," *because the sensation of the challenge is exhilarating*. If you're Oppositional, however, the climb is tougher and more threatening.

First, you never let them see you perspire (Oppositionals don't sweat, they perspire). It's important to try to look cool and maintain composure at all times. Secondly, while scheming your way to the top, you whistle Mozart and look for hidden shortcuts while frequently glancing back over

Consultative Oppositionality?

Oppositional salespeople deploy intimidation, exaggeration, veiled threats, and occasionally, when necessary, direct confrontation to win consent. Surprisingly, though, Oppositionals verbally endorse—even promote—consultative, participatory, or negotiating sales procedures. The effect can be discordant.

One self-help guru, for example, currently selling his sales training program on television, goes to extraordinary lengths to forcefully posture himself as the embodiment of sincerity, the personification of success. He achieved success, the announcer implores us, because he faithfully applied the breakthrough principles of communication featured in the cassette training program he sells. Acting the role of the self- sacrificing altruist, Mr. Success got what he wanted only by helping other people get what they wanted. Now, God help us, he wants to help us.

Looking straight into the camera, his smiles are frequent but false; his sales pitch is smoothly modulated and well-practiced, like a news anchor reciting the news. "I like people. I just want to help them," he says, aggressively baring his teeth as he speaks, like a hungry animal who has spotted his prey.

Is every sale a negotiation? Can everybody be a winner? Comer, Ardis and Price, in their book, *Big Lies in Business*, don't think so. "Our views are more cynical," they write, "than those held by many of the negotiation gurus who appear to believe that by the end of the day, techniques that result in mutual gain for all parties are almost bound to succeed." We have seen Yielders consultatively selling (when they should have been closing). We have seen Hyper-Pros direct long, complicated sales negotiations when a brief presentation of product particulars would have probably done just as well. But consultative Oppositionals? That's a self-contradiction. Perhaps, somewhere, there are salespeople who are both consultative in their approach to sales and Oppositional in their approach to call reluctance. But if there are, we have never seen them. But we have never seen a four-sided triangle, either.

I Am *Not* Oppositional, You S.O.B.!

A few years ago, one of the authors had an opportunity to review Call Reluctance Scale results with a talented, capable, motivated salesperson for a hospital supply company. A tall man with a striking, professional appearance, he was not meeting his perform-ance quota. He had been in several sales positions since graduating from college, the current one for almost a year.

Early indications were positive. He had talent, ability, product knowledge, and training. According to other tests he had taken, he was a clear-cut candidate for sales superstardom. But by the tenth week his trainers complained that he was difficult to manage and impossible to train. He was uncooperative, disturbed other members of the sales force, and deflected his lack of productivity to poor economic conditions, unsellable products, uncaring senior management, incompetent sales managers, and a plethora of other failings—none of which were his fault.

Sent to us for evaluation, his first accusing words were: "What is this test? What does it measure?" Then he wanted to know who designed it and if it was legal. Next he asked, "Who else has to take it?" Finally he grumbled, "Who's gonna see the results?"

He was comfortable participating in face-to-face discussions because he felt he was in control. He proudly boasted as an aside that he could easily outwit psychologists' interviews (and he probably could.)

He had heard of the Call Reluctance Scale from another mar-ginally producing salesperson, and he didn't like what he heard. So, tentative and unsure, he went on the offensive. But after several verbal skirmishes he agreed to complete the questionnaire. About forty minutes later he was finished. His results were computer-scored, analyzed, and ready for evaluation in minutes.

Most of his scores were exemplary, suggesting someone who could, and should, have been producing far more than he was. His motivation was high. His capacity to set and manage goals was high. But his Oppositional Reflex score was 38. A score of eight to thirteen is considered average. High producers average less than 1 percent. (Studies repeatedly show that the tendency to blame,

continues

I Am *Not* Oppositional, You S.O.B.! *continued*

make excuses, and find fault increases with the Oppositional Reflex score, while sales production takes a nosedive.)

"John," the author warmly facilitated, "you scored a 38 on Oppositional Reflex. That's a little higher than we usually see...maybe that's why you are not doing as well as your managers expected. What do you think?"

"I'll tell you what I think," John said angrily. "I don't care what your silly test says, you little bastard. I'm not hostile!"

John resigned his sales position shortly thereafter to assume a sales training position with another company in another industry. At last report, sales figures for that company were beginning to trend downward.

your shoulder to see who's gaining on you. Third, you make excuses every time you stumble, snarl at the people trying to help you, and threaten anything that gets in your way with a lawsuit. That's Oppositionality.

Win or lose, dominant salespeople try to do the best they can because they enjoy overcoming obstacles. They delight in the struggle. Oppositional salespeople are involved in another enterprise altogether. They believe they *must* get to the top, be the best, and annihilate their competitors. If they don't, they might become dependent on other people who might hurt or disappoint them. Oppositionals think they're fighting for survival.

Dominants derive satisfaction from the challenge itself; Oppositionals cope with fictional, self-imposed pressures, dreading the humiliation of failure. To unskilled observers and simplistic grid scales, both appear to be just climbing the mountain.

Outlook:

Is winning senseless arguments more important to you than accomplishing your goals? Is it more important than earning what you are worth?

The outlook for Oppositional Reflex Call Reluctance depends upon your answers. If you can admit to yourself (and others) that you probably have Oppositional Reflex Call Reluctance, then you've already taken the first, and most difficult, step. For you, the outlook is promising and bright. Change should come quickly. The outlook is overcast if you can't—or won't.

Even so, if you're growing restless with meaningless arguments, transparent excuses, casting blame and denying responsibility, the countermeasures in the next section of this book could be just what your career needs. Why not give them a chance?

CareerStyle:

- Usually unaware of being Oppositional until after the fact (when he/she feels guilty due to inability to control anger)

- Oppositional episodes may be accompanied by remorse

- Distorted perception of knowledge and ability (verified by instantaneous critiques—usually without access to complete, detailed information about the subject being critiqued)

- Self-celebrating, multifaceted conversationalist (considered by others a puffed-up bore)

- Belligerently resists verifying mastery of product knowledge or presentation content to sales trainers or management observers

- Says "no" more frequently than "yes"

- Quarrelsome

- Wastes time searching for policy loopholes which would confer an advantage instead of concentrating on improving sales performance

- Quick to find fault, slow to show approval

- Copes with shortcomings by blaming and denial

- Gossips and schemes

- Intensely dislikes making joint sales calls with managers or sales trainers

- Oppositional men may posture themselves in neatly trimmed beards, pretentiously displayed jewelry (Rolex watches?), and if they are smokers, imported cigars or affected pipes (Interestingly, scientists, such as Oxford psychologist Peter Marsh, claim that wearing a beard projects "overtones of hostility and aggression.")

- Has much to say about the quality of movies, cars, clothes, cameras, computers, theology, wines, the company's products, executive management, and the competence of the sales training staff

- Defensive; argumentative

- Facial gesturing: Tends to *snarl* when offended or disagrees

- May appear rigidly gentle, easygoing and overcaring on the surface; conflicted and angry just beneath

- Some may be prone to substance abuse; have problem controlling smoking or drinking (at this time, this is only a speculative hypothesis based on informal observations)

- May speak with a soft, exaggerated gentleness to conceal impatient, demanding nature

- Holds grudges over *long* periods of time

- Motivated by anger and vengeance ("No one can tell me I can't do something and get away with it. I'll show them!")

- Mortified by dependence on others and fears of powerlessness

- Uses intimidation to emotionally manipulate and control others

- May use volatile emotionality to manipulate and control others ("If you don't do what I want you to do right now, I'll lose my temper and cause a scene here in front of all these people.")

- Refuses to be considered average, in anything

- Self-postures as the smartest, most refined, most perceptive, with the best judgment; then expects deferential treatment

- Enjoys faking through simplistic, grid-type assessment scales which measure values, optimism, etc; very threatened by more sophisticated, multi-dimensional, objective tests

- Expert interview-taker; actually *enjoys* manipulating interviews and interviewers
    (**Note:** Oppositionals enjoy exploiting self-deluded depth interviewers the most)

- Criticizes more than compliments

- Very difficult to impress (like Over-Preparers, but for different reasons)

- Has trouble *honestly* self-disclosing (fears people would not like him/her and would use what they learned to power over and control, making him/her dependent)

- Obsessed with credibility and respect

- Quick to blame management, training, the company and its products, advertising, sales supports, and general economic conditions for personal lack of verifiable sales performance

A Workshop's Worst Nightmare

Since discovering Oppositional Reflex Call Reluctance, we have observed and analyzed many thousands of salespeople with it. Many of our observations and analyses have occurred in workshop surroundings.

In the workshop setting, many forms of call reluctance surface. Salespeople with Stage Fright are reluctant to participate in exercises involving group presentations. Over-Preparers compulsively check for spelling errors and don't like to participate in role plays. Doomsayers, if they show up at all, try to avoid being singled out or called upon—for anything. Oppositionals don't, and won't, follow instructions.

Salespeople with Oppositional Reflex Call Reluctance follow an alternate, but extremely predictable pattern. As if spellbound by a witch's curse, they inflexibly do the opposite of what they are asked to do. But that's not all. Experienced workshop instructors and seminar leaders will also recognize other endearing traits. Do you recognize some in yourself?

- Falls asleep during meetings

    (Low Motivation Impostors also fall asleep during meetings because they are tired, disinterested, or both. Oppositionals use the appearance of being asleep to signal their resistance to the meeting, its content, the instructor, or the method of presentation. Many trainers, intimidated by this behavior, hasten to make adjustments in their content, structure, method of presentation, or style. Don't. *It won't make any difference to salespeople with Oppositional Reflex Call Reluctance.*)

- Needs to be the focus of attention; the bride at every wedding, the corpse at every funeral; acts accordingly, trying to wrestle attention away from the instructional center of the room

- Promptly questions the instructor's credentials, credibility

- The Assistance Dilemma: Demands more "meaningful support" while simultaneously resisting help

- Postures for attention by staging late arrivals, distracting the group, disrupting progress, and sending a signal to other

continues

A Workshop's Worst Nightmare *continued*

participants that the workshop/seminar is *not* as important for him/her as it is for the others

- Postures for attention by staging early exits

- Starts complaining about inferior "instructional design" (another area of professed expertise) during or before *the first morning break*

- Postures for attention by making frequent phone calls, frequently receiving hand-delivered "important messages," to demonstrate how busy and successful he/she is

  (An Oppositional sales manager attending one of our presentations arranged to have a hotel staff member hand deliver a very important message from *herself*!)

- Becomes more agitated and more critical as the subject matter becomes more applicable, making deflection and denial more difficult

  ("Excuse me!" the voice from the rear of the room inconsiderately shouted. "I don't see how you can expect us to move into the call reluctance types when you haven't even proved we exist yet!")

- Attempts to sabotage group dynamics by telling jokes, writing scathing notes and creating doubt about the instructor's credibility *during breaks*

- Attempts to preemptively discredit the assessment tests they fear, but must complete, by disputing the way the questions are asked, the multiple choice answers provided, the relevancy of the test to their personal situation, and other similar deflections; failing that, writes angry notes on the answer sheet, refuses to comply with instructions by leaving threatening questions unanswered, threatening legal action, or destroying the answer sheet in an uncontrolled rage

- Attempts to polarize the group into cliques

- Tries to evade direct measures of accountability; the "What I do is not really measurable" syndrome

continues

A Workshop's Worst Nightmare *continued*

Seminar instructors should try to avoid being intimidated or frustrated by salespeople or managers with Oppositional Reflex Call Reluctance. That can be difficult but it's not impossible. We train managers and instructors how to use a workshop management process called "unplugging." It was developed to control Oppositional Reflex Call Reluctance by *preemptively* neutralizing it with paradoxical information, declarations and instructions. Paradoxical statements are carefully fashioned remarks which remove the oppositional alternative. According to the theory, you can't be Oppositional if you can't oppose; and you can't oppose if all the options available to you result in compliance. It's a paradox.

Unexpected paradoxes befuddle Oppositionals. They knock them off center. Momentarily confused, they don't know how to behave if they can't find a clear-cut way to oppose. So they quietly sit, momentarily disoriented, like a deer stunned by headlights. That gives us time to penetrate their defenses and follow-up with the full force of our training.

Unplugging works like a disinfectant. It's one of the reasons we have been so successful with Oppositional dropouts and alumni from other sales training programs.

- Secretly jealous and envious of the success earned by coworkers; Some resort to sabotage, others pout

- Company sniper; constantly tries to undermine management, plans rebellions, sows discontent among other salespeople

- Won't let anyone train, teach, instruct, advise or counsel him/her (leaving few management options)

- Issues ultimatums, even for the smallest disagreements (Some Oppositionals have jettisoned once highly productive associations due to their inability to control this aspect of their behavior)

- Over opinionated, under informed

- Does not hold meetings, holds court when assigned to home office management

- Applies the Doctrine of Immaculate Perception when assigned to sales selection/assessment department: All psychological tests, rating scales, and means of assessment but one, *me*, contain error

- Unable to find lasting satisfaction in people, things or career

- *Passionately* disagrees with many of the company's training policies, practices and procedures (unlike constructive, rational disagreements which do not rely upon or need intense emotionality)

- *Must* inflict the last word; reflexively adds to, subtracts from, modifies, alters, or amends *all* statements of fact, description, or opinion made by others (Oppositionals are secretly terrified by fears of their own powerlessness. They leak signs of this fear by even refusing others the benefit of a complete thought or an unaided opinion. It's a feeble, symbolic attempt to make other people intellectually dependent on them.)

Self Assessment:

Do you tend to use prospecting techniques which are the opposite of those used by your coworkers?

If you have Oppositional Reflex Call Reluctance you do. Too much of your time is probably squandered criticizing and rejecting your company's field-tested methods. Instead of prospecting, you try to assemble your own prospecting techniques, highlighting in the process your complete independence and self-reliance. Now, honestly, what do you have to show for it?

Do you usually add something, subtract something, amend, alter or modify what other people say to you?

Oppositionals are fast, but rarely substantive. They begin to form their comeback quips before the statement they're reacting to has even been completed. If, from this, you reason that salespeople with Oppositional Reflex Call Reluctance probably don't listen well, you're right.

When attending a workshop or seminar, do you find yourself immediately questioning the value of the material, the credibility of the instructor, the method of presentation, the validity of the information?

Oppositionals have exalted fault-finding to an esoteric art form. Their skills are so extraordinarily extended that, unlike lesser people, they don't even need the context or assurance of complete understanding to formulate instant conclusions.

Do you tend to overreact with righteous indignation when someone doubts your competence or integrity?

No one likes to have their integrity questioned. But most people realize that it's necessary to ask the right questions in today's world. Assumptions can be dangerous. Verification is a modern survival tactic. In certain circumstances, such as a sales presentation, questions about corporate and personal integrity are justifiable and bound to occur. Most salespeople take questions about integrity in stride, responding to them calmly and rationally. Salespeople with Oppositional Reflex Call Reluctance don't. They immediately heat up and boil over. Instead of answering the prospect's questions, they react to their own feelings about being questioned. With melodramatic resentment, they alternately fume and fuss, act hurt, then grievously offended, all while accusing the prospect of not trusting them (a manipulative attempt to make the prospect feel guilty for questioning their integrity in the first place)

Do you get all worked up and excited when you make a major, expensive purchase only to find out that it doesn't satisfy you for long?

Salespeople with Oppositional Reflex Call Reluctance are inclined to romantically elevate new people and things (like cars and careers) to unrealistic heights. Then, after a few, disappointing real-life experiences, they denigrate these same people and things to the depths of worthlessness. What then? When Oppositionals get involved, they get frustrated; when they get frustrated, they go shopping. It starts all over again.

When asked to complete objective assessment tests, do you try to discredit the test, scribbling unsolicited commentary (usually negative) on the test booklet or answer sheet, ignoring questions you don't agree with (despite instructions to answer every question), or just refuse to complete the test?

Oppositional salespeople can't contain their impulse to criticize and critique. This becomes particularly noticeable in their test-taking behavior. They volunteer self-protecting, unsolicited, critical comments about the test or certain test questions, or in some rare cases refuse to complete the test altogether. Ironically, their test-taking behavior clearly reveals the Oppositional temperament the test's scores might have missed.

Do you have a cynical, sarcastic or cutting sense of humor?

Salespeople with Oppositional Reflex Call Reluctance often enlist humor to strike at the people and situations that frustrate them.

How often do you get sidetracked, trying to win essentially useless, unimportant arguments?

Oppositional salespeople and their opinionated, temperamental kin, Oppositional attorneys, are drawn to nonproductive arguments like flies to a dung heap. Needing to be right (even when they are obviously wrong), these tiresome verbal combatants squander their energy, poison their outlook and undermine their social acceptablilty. (A series of recent sociometric studies we completed show that salespeople with Oppositional

Reflex Call Reluctance don't know how they are perceived by others. While rating themselves high on style and ability, their competence is questioned by their peers and they are judged least popular—especially in groups they try to dominate and control.)

Do you approach a sale as if it were a debate you have to win?

That's how salespeople with Oppositional Reflex Call Reluctance tend to see the sales process. But because they don't prospect as effectively as they could, they have relatively few sales to approach—regardless of mindset.

Are you inclined to be ruthlessly self-critical?

Oppositionals are hard-edged under-performers. Their criticisms and critiques, fussing and fault-finding corrode their relationships with managers, spouses, colleagues, and friends. But Oppositionals are most dissatisfied with themselves. Finding little good and much bad, they silently beat up on themselves, wanting desparately to stop and not knowing how.

Do you ever fantasize about being a tyrant with absolute power?

Salespeople with Oppositional Reflex Call Reluctance daydream about running the company, the country, and the cosmos with absolute power. Rebellion is impossible and obedience is obligatory; fear and frustration are unknown.

Are *you* Oppositional?

If you angrily insist you're not, you probably are. If you admit that you probably are, you probably aren't because you have already taken the first critical step to becoming a reformed Oppositional.

Objective Assessments:

Call Reluctance Scale—A high Brake score plus a high Oppositional Reflex score suggest that Oppositional Reflex Call Reluctance is probably limiting your prospecting performance now.

A low Brake score plus a high Oppositional Reflex score indicate a predisposition to Oppositional Reflex Call Reluctance which could be interfering with your social life but probably not your prospecting at the present time. (It could also mean that Oppositionality might be present, but only in low or high but transitory doses which do not necessarily impair prospecting.)

Selling Styles Profile Analysis—Most salespeople with Oppositional Reflex Call Reluctance tend to prefer Competition or Close-Oriented presentation styles. These styles place emphasis upon the close or outcome more than the product, service, image, or discovery of need. Some Oppositionals, however, take exception to this conclusion (no surprise). They claim they don't *sell* anything. That's what other salespeople do. In practice, however, they artfully apply highly manipulative perversions of the nondirective philosophy formulated by psychologist Carl Rogers during the early 1950's. They jargonistically tag their approach "consultative" and claim it results in "a win-win situation for everybody."

Frequency of Occurrence:

Oppositional Reflex Call Reluctance tends to occur in pockets. Within industries, there are only faint patterns. It tends to be high in stressed-out securities salespeople and insecure organizational development practitioners. It is commonly found in marginal sales managers and in congested companies headed by marginal, Oppositional senior sales managers. It is higher in snarling psychologists, psychiatrists and sales trainers wearing Freudian beards and moustaches. It is even higher in consultants and inspirational speakers. It is the highest in mean-spirited attorneys.

Most Effective Treatment:

- Fear Inversion (must be applied first)
- Thought Zapping
- Sensory Injection (Therapeutic Massage)
- Threat Desensitization
- Yellow Dot
- Thought Realignment
- Hot Water Bottle

Why "Type" is Important to You

Determining the type of call reluctance you have, or could be predisposed to, is extremely important. The countermeasures which follow are all assigned according to type. Experience has proven that mindlessly applying the wrong corrective procedure to a particular type of call reluctance could easily make the problem worse.

Let's review our opening case examples: We now know that Nancy has Doomsayer Call Reluctance. Four procedures, Threat Desensitization, Sensory Injection, the Hot Water Bottle, and possibly Biofeedback Training—would be recommended for her. Other procedures, such as Assertion Training or Fear Inversion, could make her problem worse.

Bob has both Emotional Unemancipation (family) and Separationist (friends) Call Reluctance. Both of these are relatively easy to correct if Bob uses two special procedures—Thought Realignment and Thought Zapping. A third, general procedure, Logical Persuasion, could also be used by Bob's manager as a supplement but not as a replacement.

Larry, the computer salesman, has Social Self-Consciousness Call Reluctance, a condition which usually responds quickly to Thought Zapping, Thought Realignment, and Negative Image Projection. Logical Persuasion could also be used by Larry's managers as a fourth, supplemental procedure once the primary procedures have a chance to work.

The next section of this book consists of detailed, step-by-step instructions for correcting call reluctance. You can apply them yourself, although your chances of success substantially increase if you persuade a sales manager, colleague, friend, or spouse to help you.

To apply the prescriptions effectively, you have to do certain things in order. First, candidly evaluate your prospecting activity. Is it consistent with your desire to succeed, your talent, and the potential of your market? If it is, you could still have a problem, but it's not due to prospecting or call reluctance. That would be a self- contradiction. If not, first review the impostors. Do you *really* have the motivation and goals necessary to have authentic call reluctance? If you don't, you're an impostor. Consider using some of the resources outlined at the end of Chapter 2. If you answered "yes," then you have prospecting problems and you have ruled out the impostors. So you probably have authentic call reluctance. But which *type*(s) do you have? Review the twelve types to determine which seem to fit your experience best. (Rarely does a salesperson have more than two or three types at one time.)

If you have more than one type, choose the most bothersome one to begin with. Then turn directly to the Most Effective Treatments listed at the end of the description for that type. If there is more than one procedure listed, go through them *in the order they are listed*. The rest is straightforward. Simply read through the prescriptions and try to follow the instructions. Good luck! Remember, we did it. So have thousands of other call-reluctant salespeople who are now enjoying more personal and financial success. Now it's your turn.

2

THE
PRESCRIPTIONS

The techniques we have included in the following pages were selected because they have been successfully field tested. They work.

Chapter Four

INTRODUCTION TO THE PRESCRIPTIONS

CALL RELUCTANCE COUNTERMEASURES IN PERSPECTIVE

I t's odd, isn't it? There's just one law of gravity and one Heaven. Oxygen has one chemical structure. One system of technological knowledge, principles and practices builds bridges and erects skyscrapers—with little regard for cultural differences or individual taste and preference. Yet, there is a profusion of so-called "laws of success." Problems like sales call reluctance attract mobs of self-helpers, each savagely swinging a different conceptual axe. According to one count, there are more than 250 systems available to help you pull your life and your career together (*Science* magazine, June 1986). How can we distinguish genuine help from overstated hyperbole? It's not easy.

Iridescent how-to-live experts are everywhere. There are gurus to advise, exalteds to dazzle, speakers to incite. Their voices clamor for your attention, their hands hungrily claw at your wallet. You can consume the *One Minute Manager* by Ken Blanchard (as a single book or multiple cassette series), or you can read the *Fifty-Nine Second Employee: How to Stay One Second Ahead of Your One-Minute Manager* by Rae Andre, Ph.D., and Peter Ward, J.D. You can chase a brain buzz in one of W. Clement Stone's you-can-have-it-if-you-can-think-it books. Then you can sober up with *How to Cure Yourself of Positive Thinking*, by Donald G. Smith. The choices are endless and bewildering.

"No matter how you're now living, you're not living right," the change-your-life ideologues say as they prowl about like hunting dogs searching for a scent. Each promises a "dramatic, breakthrough technique, guaranteed to alter the course of your life"—like a calendar changing from BC to AD. Look about. You can see them on TV, hear them on the radio, and in some cases even find them hustling their secular philosophies in church where their very presence can be taken to imply celestial endorsement.

Perched out there high above us like grinning, jeering gargoyles, you'll find the rational behavior trainers, psychodramatists, Gestalt practitioners, reality therapists, right-brain/left-brain/no-brainers, bioenergetics, cognitive therapists, marriage and family counselors, subliminal tapes (pounding you with verbal affirmations you can't hear), transcendental meditators (muttering mantras), transactional analysts (now mostly unemployed), ex-Est instructors (found in unemployment lines with the transactional analysts), hypnotherapists (breathing comfortably and deeply...), psychoanalysts (a resilient, if not particularly stable breed), thinking-feeling-sensing-knowing Jungians, Adlerians (birth order), Rogerians (trying to avoid confrontation), rational emotive therapists (looking for a fight), sensitivity trainers/team-builders (better communication through more trust), psycholinguists, indefatigable primal screamers, rat-running behavioral therapists, some astrologers, amateur hypnotists, Presbyterians, and, recently, neurolinguistic programmers (anxiously trying to keep pace with your breath rate). They *all* have the answer, or so they claim.

Call Reluctance: The Orthodox View

Formally trained mental health practitioners tend to approach problems of living, like call reluctance, from five basic directions. Unlike many of the methods catalogued elsewhere in this chapter, these five approaches reflect accepted, scientific orthodoxy.

To *Cognitive Practitioners*, it's all in the words we use. According to their system, you're call reluctant because someone once may have called you call reluctant or taught you to mindlessly repeat call reluctance baiting messages to yourself. That "someone" was probably you! Change the way you label your behavior, the Cognitive Practitioners say, and you'll change your behavior.

Personality Trait Theorists believe that some salespeople are just born to raise hell. Others are born to be call reluctant. They contend that call reluctance could be strongly influenced by heredity, like height, weight and intelligence. Since your propensity for call reluctance was probably hard-wired into your system at birth, you can't reasonably expect it to yield significantly to training. Like a permanently gimpy leg, you can only adapt to your psychic limitations and develop compensatory methods of going around it.

continues

Call Reluctance: The Orthodox View *continued*

Psychoanalysts insist that call reluctance is just the surface manifestation (read "symptom") of a much deeper, more intricate unconscious conflict. To them, your call reluctance is the exterior rumbling of a war between your Id, Ego and Superego which you don't want to deal with head on. So you repress it, squeezing it into some dark corner of your unconscious mind. They like to free associate and interpret dreams—especially sex dreams. Their cures also take a long time and they charge high fees.

To *Behaviorists*, your call reluctance is due to botched learning. Somehow, probably through no fault of your own, you formed distressful associations between making sales calls and feeling bad. Rejecting nebulous terms like "unconscious mind," they communicate in more straightforward prose with terms like "instrumental conditioning" and "variable ratio interval."

Sociologically Oriented Practitioners say call reluctance comes from exposure to individuals and groups practicing maladaptive, call-reluctant prospecting behaviors. Studying varieties of strange and wonderful cultures, like commercial real estate religious rites, they look for call-reluctant patterns in your colleagues, managers, trainers, consultants and priest-experts who have the problem themselves. You just innocently picked it up. (Who then, was the *first* call-reluctant person? Adam? Some unnamed aborigine?)

Major variations occur within each of the five approaches listed above, making it impossible and probably unfair to encapsulate them into a paragraph. Hopefully, our snapshots will not be mistaken for portraits and will not offend the sensitivities of the faithful within each group. If we have offended, we apologize. If we have unbearably offended, let us know. We shall be happy to refer you to a competent mental health practitioner in your area.

To overcome call reluctance in yourself or others, you need special knowledge. Attaining it requires specialized training. Most of the techniques named above have been, in our judgment, baked in a quick oven. Puffed up, pretentious and over-promoted, they are inappropriate for serious call reluctance training.

The techniques we have included in the following pages were selected because they have been successfully field tested. They work. But our research is not complete, so they cannot be uncritically accepted as the last—or even best—word. Stripped of their pretenses, they are merely self-help tools chosen on the basis of the *probability* that they can help you. They will not help everyone equally, and taken together, they do not even form a complete rational system like behavior modification (instrumental learning theory) or psychoanalysis. Instead, they reflect a vital, changing process which simply and honestly represents our progress as we try to help salespeople and their managers abolish call reluctance.

Which countermeasures should you learn? Which should you use? That depends entirely upon which type(s) of call reluctance you have. *You don't have to apply them all and you don't even have to read about them all.* (However, you should browse through the research chapter at the end. It boasts new and exotic call reluctance factoids you won't find anywhere else. Besides, it took a long time to write it!)

Four Simple Steps

Mathematically, the number of call reluctance types and counter-measure combinations is enormous. Yet, regardless of the particular combination of countermeasures you use, there are only four steps to overcoming call reluctance.

First, you must *admit* you have call reluctance and that your call reluctance is keeping you from earning what you're worth. For some call-reluctant salespeople and sales managers, that will be difficult but not impossible. Second, you must *diagnose*, find out which particular type or types of call reluctance you have. To do that, use the rating scales we have provided or take the appropriate psychological tests. Ask your friends, managers or trainers. They can all be helpful. Third, *match* your call reluctance type to the step-by-step countermeasures we have developed. A summary chart will help. Then read the procedures and do precisely what they say. Don't argue with them and don't confuse your natural desire to understand them with your real objective: increasing your prospecting activity. Last, *follow up*. Make calls. Don't confuse a change in your outlook with a change in the number of contacts you initiate with prospective buyers. A poor attitude in a good producer may not be desirable, but it is tolerable. A good attitude in a non-producer may be endearing, but fatal. It can cost you your sales career.

THE COUNTERMEASURES

This book arms you with five primary countermeasures and several supplemental techniques. The countermeasures fall into two groups: *word-based* procedures and *mechanical* procedures.

Word-Based Procedures

Word-based procedures depend primarily upon words to *explain*, *excite* or *extort* (threaten). Most popular self-help techniques are word-based.

Explain. At one time or another, each of us has intuitively used words to carry new information which in turn was supposed to facilitate new understanding. Practitioners who use word-based procedures expect that new information will establish a new perspective. An improved perspective, they surmise, spearheads improved performance. This line of reasoning finds its champions in popular self-help works like David Burns' *The New Mood Therapy*, Wayne Dyer's *Pull Your Own Strings*, and a series of books on the subject by Albert Ellis, including his bona fide classic, *Guide to Rational Living*.

A 1986 article written by a sales trainer illustrates how words can be used this way. The subject of the article was "overcoming stage fright." "View each person in the audience," the author explained, "as if he or she were worth $100,000 to you." A 1989 article on "handling rejection," which appeared in an Australian sales magazine, approached the problem similarly: "Every time you're rejected in any way, tell yourself: I never see failure as failing, but only as a learning experience." Our own original approach to call reluctance depended heavily upon this approach for over a decade. (The Call Reluctance Clinic, 1978.) The 1986 edition of *The Psychology of Call Reluctance*, however, leaked the first signs of our declining confidence in word-based procedures.

Excite. Words can also be used to agitate and inflame the emotions. Used by gifted orators, the right words can transform a career into a crusade. A 1989 assembly of more than 700 salespeople in Singapore was galvanized by the motivational theme, "Yes, I can!" Each speaker carefully maneuvered words to challenge, provoke and inspire participants to record levels of production.

Extort. Words can sing; but words can also sting. Frustrated sales managers often try to use poison-tipped words to shock their call-reluctant salespeople into activity. With all the subtlety of a 155mm howitzer, they fire their directives: "Hit the phone, or hit the road!" The method has little noticeable effect except perhaps to swell the ranks of embittered ex-salespeople.

Mechanical Procedures

Some techniques rely on words only secondarily or not at all. We call these techniques "mechanical procedures" because they don't depend on words. They can work whether you understand them or not. They can work whether you agree with them or not. They do require patience and vigilant compliance with their instructions, but given sufficient motivation and goal focus they can produce lasting improvement. Fast.

Here's an overview of the principal methods covered in this book.

PRIMARY COUNTERMEASURES

Word-based:

- Thought Realignment
- Fear Inversion

Mechanical:

- Threat Desensitization
- Negative Image Projection
- Negative Thought Zapping

SUPPLEMENTAL/EXPERIMENTAL COUNTERMEASURES

Word-Based:

- Assertion Training

Mechanical:

- Biofeedback
- Physician prescribed drugs
- Sensory Injection—Smell (Fragrance)
- Sensory Injection—Temperature (Hot Water Bottle)
- Sensory Injection—Visual (Yellow Dot)
- Target Reversal (best for Doomsayers)
- Massage Therapy (a form of Sensory Injection)
- Nutritional supplements

OTHERS

- Hypnosis
- NLP (Neurolinguistic Programming)

- Subliminal Messages
- Positive Mental Imagery/Attitudes

Each countermeasure leaves its own mark. Each works best with certain types of call reluctance and not with others.

Suggested Strategy

Which countermeasures work best with each type of call reluctance? We have tried to constrain our answer to a chart. But neatly tabled solutions to complex human problems like call reluctance don't always work. Our chart is no exception. At best, it's only a recommended strategy.

Why? There are simply too many rules and considerations to condense into one chart and still remain within the size constraints of this book. For example, some types of call reluctance *always* take precedence over others when assigning countermeasures. If you have Oppositional Reflex Call Reluctance, you must attend to that *first*. If you don't, you probably won't be able to comply with the instructions accompanying the others, and, rushing to criticize, it will look to you like they don't work. Then there are the assumptions we must make about your motivation and goals. Are you an impostor? If so, the countermeasures for call reluctance won't work. Last, no information about important *combinations* of call reluctance, called "call reluctance configurations," could be included. That will have to wait for a future platform presentation, magazine article, or book. But for now, we suggest you simply match the call reluctance type(s) you think you have to the countermeasures we recommend in the chart below. It's a start. For most of you, it's all you will need.

The following chart provides an overview of the countermeasures and their suggested match-ups with the call reluctance types. *The countermeasures for each type are listed in the order in which they should be applied.* If you have Role Rejection Call Reluctance, you should try Thought Zapping first, then Negative Image Projection.

Call Reluctance Type	Suggested Prescriptions
Doomsayer	Threat Desensitization
	Thought Zapping
	Sensory Injection (Massage Therapy)
	Yellow Dot
	Target Reversal
	Thought Realignment
	Biofeedback
	Physician prescribed medications if necessary
	Hot Water Bottle
Over-Preparation	Thought Zapping
	Sensory Injection (Fragrance)
	Negative Image Projection

	Thought Realignment
	Target Reversal
Hyper-Pro	Fear Inversion (secondary procedure only)
	Thought Zapping
	Sensory Injection
	Thought Realignment (See Parable of the Eldorado)
	Target Reversal
Stage Fright	Threat Desensitization
	Thought Zapping
	Sensory Injection (Fragrance and/or Massage Therapy)
	Hot Water Bottle
	Yellow Dot
	Thought Realignment
Role Rejection	Thought Zapping
	Sensory Injection
	Negative Image Projection
	Thought Realignment
Yielder	Thought Zapping
	Sensory Injection
	Assertion Training
	Negative Image Projection
	Thought Realignment
	Threat Desensitization
Social Self-Consciousness	Thought Zapping
	Sensory Injection (Fragrance)
	Thought Realignment
	Logical Persuasion
Separationist	Thought Zapping
	Sensory Injection
	Thought Realignment
Emotionally Unemancipated	Thought Zapping
	Sensory Injection
	Threat Desensitization
	Thought Realignment

Referral Aversion	Thought Zapping
	Sensory Injection (Fragrance)
	Yellow Dot
	Thought Realignment
Telephobia	Threat Desensitization
	Thought Zapping
	Sensory Injection (Fragrance and/or
	Massage Therapy)
	Hot Water Bottle
	Yellow Dot
	Target Reversal
	Thought Realignment
Oppositional Reflex	Fear Inversion
	Thought Zapping
	Sensory Injection (Massage Therapy)
	Threat Desensitization
	Yellow Dot
	Thought Realignment
	Hot Water Bottle

You need not read or learn about all of these unless you are just curious. But first read through the countermeasures you need most to improve your prospecting activity. Satisfy your curiosity later.

Procrastination

Like species of birds and insects, human behavior has many variations. Yet in one respect human behavior can be distilled to a single option: to contract our muscles or release them.

As infants, driven by impulse, our repertoire is rather limited. We can squeeze or we can let go; we can grasp or we can push away. But by the time we reach early adulthood, most of us discover a third alternative: We can procrastinate!

Procrastination sounds worse than it is. For all of its five (count 'em) pretentious syllables, procrastination is not some anti-social act or a taboo sexual practice. It is simply an acquired taste some of us have developed for deferring to another time things that need to be done now. For Scarlett O'Hara and Little Orphan Annie, there's always tomorrow.

continues

Procrastination *continued*

Procrastination is like paying the interest on a loan, never the principal. A short-sighted tactic, sooner or later the note must be paid off. Nevertheless, procrastinators favor waiting out storms and unpleasant obligations. They prefer instead to occupy themselves with other things (like taking a nap) until their problems resolve themselves, offensive tasks finish themselves, or both just go away.

Our interest in procrastination is peripheral. We are only concerned about significant areas of behavioral encroachment as it affects the 12 call reluctance types. (Some day we may take a closer look at procrastination, but we prefer not dealing with it right now.)

Indecisive Yielders procrastinate. Compulsive Over-Preparers procrastinate. *All* call-reluctant salespeople procrastinate. But procrastination is their symptom, not their problem. Procrastination is one of the agents they use to deal with the real problem—call reluctance. They fear one or more of the activities necessary to initiate contact with sufficient numbers of prospective buyers. So they put off these activities as often and as creatively as necessary. In that sense, they procrastinate. But the resolution of their problem is not likely to come from zapping them every time they sneeze. It is much more likely to come about when they remove the *root* cause, the virus causing their head cold—in our case, call reluctance.

The countermeasures in this book will not overcome all cases of procrastination. They were not designed for that purpose. But they can simultaneously reduce procrastination in call-reluctant salespeople who are diligently working to rescue themselves from the constraints of their fears.

What you say to yourself about prospecting has a powerful impact upon what you feel when prospecting. What you feel when prospecting has a powerful impact on what you do about prospecting.

Chapter Five

R_X One
THOUGHT REALIGNMENT

> **PRIMARILY AFFECTS:**
>
> ✓ **Thoughts**
>
>   Feelings
>
>   Actions
>
> **PRESCRIBED FOR:**
>
> ✓ **Doomsayer**
> ✓ **Over-Preparation**
> ✓ **Hyper-Pro (when not Oppositional)**
> ✓ **Stage Fright**
> ✓ **Role Rejection**
> ✓ **Yielder**
> ✓ **Social Self-Consciousness**
> ✓ **Separationist**
> ✓ **Emotionally Unemancipated**
> ✓ **Referral Aversion**
> ✓ **Telephobia**
> ✓ **Oppositional Reflex**

A BRIEF OVERVIEW

Thought Realignment is a word-based procedure. It is a special adaptation of the self-talk techniques introduced by ancient philosophers, popularized in our time by psychologists Aaron Beck and Albert Ellis, and recently sensationalized as a modern breakthrough. It's not.

The technique, and the philosophical basis from which it grew, is not new. It has a long and distinguished heritage. It asserts that most, if not all, of our distressful feelings are caused by the view we take of things and situations in life, not the things and situations themselves.

Greek philosopher Epictetus: "Man is disturbed not by things but by the view he takes of them."

Roman philosopher Marcus Aurelius: "If you are pained by an external thing, it is not the thing that disturbs you, but your own judgment about it."

English playwright William Shakespeare: "There is nothing either good or bad but thinking makes it so."

Philosopher Spinoza: "I saw that all the things I feared, and which feared me, had nothing good or bad in them insofar as the mind was affected by them."

Poet John Milton: "The mind is its own place, and in itself can make a heaven of Hell and a hell of Heaven."

Philosopher Immanuel Kant: "The only feature common to all mental disorders is the loss of common sense and the compensatory development of a unique private sense of reasoning."

W.E.B. DuBois: "If we wish to change the sentiments it is necessary before all to modify the idea which produced them."

Psychologist Alfred Adler: "It is very obvious that we are influenced not by facts but by our interpretations of facts."

No Silver Bullet

If you read the first edition of this book you will recall that we, too, once heavily endorsed using this approach for all types of call reluctance. Our enthusiasm was misplaced. We were wrong. The technique did help some, not others, and certainly not everyone. Perhaps our experience with this procedure can be summarized in the words of a veteran call-reluctant sales manager who tried mightily to teach a salesman how to apply Thought Realignment to himself. "I made absolutely *no* progress at all," the salesman said. "I tried for about a week, but I guess I didn't really understand what self-chatter...self-talk you called it, was supposed to be. I did try though. I listened to myself...and I listened to myself some more...but I didn't hear a word. I even told myself a couple of jokes and I still didn't hear anything!"

We know now that self-talk based techniques can be useful for some types of call reluctance, but they don't work for everyone. If they don't work for you, don't get discouraged. Just move on to the mechanical procedures.

Thought Realignment is an easy-to-learn, three-step procedure. First, you will learn to identify counter-productive messages hidden in the way you describe prospecting to yourself. You will then learn to control feelings that interfere with prospecting by changing how you describe what it means to prospect. And finally, you will apply what you have learned by intentionally putting yourself into emotionally difficult prospecting situations while you practice emotional self-management skills that support your career goals.

Guiding Principles Behind Thought Realignment

1. *You are motivated* to improve.

2. *Your motivation is directed* specifically towards reducing unwanted distressful feelings associated with self-promotion in order to improve your prospecting activity.

3. Your feelings can either *enhance* or *impede* the flow of motivation into goal-directed behavior.

4. What you *think* about something influences how you *feel* about it.

5. Thinking (reasoning) is based on the selection and use of words.

6. Thoughts can be fallacious and disabling.

7. The counterproductive feelings which accompany prospecting are *learned* and *reinforced* with each use. They can be *unlearned* and *extinguished* by non-use.

Sighting the Target

Thought Realignment is useful for the forms of call reluctance indicated in the chart at the beginning of this chapter.

Estimated Completion Time

Learning to identify how your thoughts and feelings can limit your prospecting performance takes most salespeople only a few hours. Developing new automatic mental management skills takes longer, perhaps a few days of attention and practice. Detraumatizing call-reluctant feelings takes about two weeks of application and practice *in actual prospecting situations which tend to be emotionally difficult.*

Some salespeople using this procedure make substantial gains in the first few hours. Others take a little longer for the information to sink in and become "real" for them.

PART ONE:
THE UNALIGNED SALESPERSON

Every car runs more smoothly when its wheel alignment is inspected periodically and adjusted when necessary. The purpose of a wheel alignment is to make sure that all the wheels point in exactly the same direction. When the steering wheel is in a position to drive straight ahead, the road wheels should be pointed in that direction. When they are not, you experience energy-robbing bumps and vibrations which feel like they are coming from the road. But they are not. They are coming from a steering wheel aimed in one direction and road wheels trying to go in another. If misalignment is not corrected, wear and tear on the car will be accelerated. Major damage eventually results when symptoms of misalignment are ignored.

Motivated, goal-directed salespeople are like cars. Sometimes their motivation tries to steer them straight ahead towards their goals, while a few renegade thoughts exert a counter force which tries to pull them off the road. When that happens, it is experienced in the form of goal-disruptive feelings, or call reluctance. Wear and tear results. If misalignment is not corrected, serious damage to the career can be expected.

Tales of Terror

Consider the following prospecting situations taken from actual call reluctance files.

Real Estate: The Hour of Doom

It's 6:55 on Wednesday evening. Each of the agents in the Jack L. Smith Real Estate Agency knows that in five minutes it will be time to start using the phone to prospect for new listings. One agent, the newest, becomes progressively more frightened as the time draws nearer. Another, a veteran agent, shows predictable signs of anger. A third begins to look deflated and depressed. A fourth projects a practiced, knowing, cynical half-smile.

Insurance: The Haunting

Times are changing. Larry G., a veteran insurance agent for a high visibility agency in the Northeast, is preparing for his first prospecting seminar. He knows the product, has years of experience under his belt, and is highly motivated to come away from the experience with several new clients. But as the hour approaches, he becomes more and more distressed. There's more. In his industry, he is well-known as one of the "most dynamic advocates" of a positive mental outlook. Recently, when he spoke at an industry convention, he strongly argued, "If you can conceive it, you can have it." But now Larry's up against the wall. His hands are clammy, his pupils dilated, and his knees are shaking. Call reluctance is making a mockery of everything he values and stands for. He's beginning to wonder if the whole enterprise might be a mistake.

Office Equipment: Spirits in the Boardroom

Phyllis K. is a seasoned sales veteran. She has sold computer software, encyclopedias, and now copying machines. She knows her product. She knows how to sell it. She recently presented her product to a personnel manager who wants it, and to the company's purchasing manager who has tentatively approved its purchase. There is only one hurdle left. Now, because of the large dollar amount of the sale, she must give her presentation to four senior officers—in the boardroom. For Phyllis, the whole thing takes on a different look. As she approaches the boardroom, she senses a vague internal struggle to retain her characteristic self-confidence. But the closer she gets, the harder it is to keep it all together. Finally, when she enters the room it becomes obvious to everyone that she is coping, not selling. She has successfully gone through this process a hundred times with owners of small and moderate-sized businesses. The opportunity to close a really big sale approaches, but the presentation switches to a boardroom and the prospects are executive officers of a large organization. That changes the complexion for Phyllis. She knows she's trying too hard. Talking too much. She overstates. Cuts the competition. Seems boastful and over-confident. Even defensive. Ultimately, she will lose this sale. She will lose it because she was unable to manage herself in an up-market sales situation.

What happened? Why did these salespeople sabotage their opportunities to move closer to their production goals? Let's find out.

The Role of Feelings

We assign meanings to each person, place, situation or thing we perceive. Research scientists have been trying for a long time to discover exactly how we do this. To date, they have learned much. But more remains to be learned. So where do we venture from here? And how do we get there?

One way to begin piecing together an understanding of the meanings behind our feelings is to use a speculative license called a conceptual model. Models are helpful because they allow theoreticians and practitioners to proceed from a point of ignorance as if they know something they really don't. At present, there are several good models aspiring to explain where feelings come from. Each has its own strengths and weaknesses. Our version approaches the problem from the unique perspective of call reluctance.

When a Rose is Not a Rose

If you were a perfect computer, you would process information by carrying out the steps you were programmed to perform, and you would do it the same way every time. Nothing added. Nothing taken away. You would execute commands you recognized from your programmed experience. You would ignore or refuse to ponder commands you did *not* recognize. Simple. Elegant. But not human.

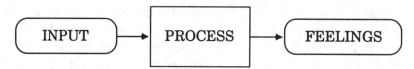

As a human being, when you get a parcel of information from inside or outside yourself, you respond similar to a computer and you rush to process it. But here you part company with computers. You do not dash straight ahead in objective, predictable order. Instead, you hang a screeching hard left turn at the first intersection and proceed down Subjective Avenue to the Personal Meaning Check-In Station. There, all incoming information is frisked and subjected to three filters. Based on the results, you begin the process of selecting 1) how you will feel and 2) how much you will feel it.

One of the filters waiting to process incoming traffic is *past experience*. It compares incoming information with prior records. A horsewhip might cast a smile on your face if you pleasantly recall from your childhood the sounds and sights of crisp autumn horse-and-buggy rides. But what if your parents used a horsewhip for disciplinary purposes when you were a child?

Present needs is another filter. It tilts our perceptions towards the things we need at the moment. You might not even notice a restaurant as you drive by if you have just finished a hearty meal. But what if it's been two days since you last ate?

The last filter consists of your *values*. This one has to do with what you consider to be right and wrong, good and bad. You might see an offer of brandy as a kindly warm-up for a cold winter's night. But how would you respond if you strongly believed that alcohol consumption was inherently evil and spiritually corrupting?

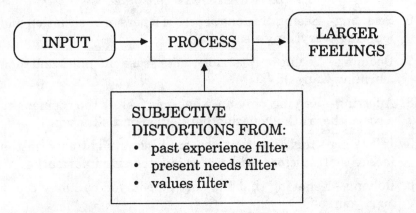

A now classic research study illustrates our model. Ten-year-olds from rich and poor backgrounds were asked to estimate the size of a coin which they held in their hands. According to the study, "When the results for rich and poor children were looked at separately, it was found that the poor children overestimated the size of the coin more than the rich children." Why? Can the "perceptual filtering" model you have just learned help explain these results?

---

17 Mindbenders

Here are 17 ways you can distort your perceptions and bend your frame of mind.

1. Reading Minds—Believing that you are particularly perceptive about other people and that you know what they are really up to.

2. Blaming—Trying to hold other people, places and situations responsible for your current behavior.

3. Ruling—Trying to impose rigid, inflexible regimentation on yourself and others.

4. Weighing—Believing you can impose legalistic balance and fairness on your relationships with other people.

5. Deferring—Deferring too many present enjoyments to some distant time when everything is just right.

continues

---

17 Mindbenders *continued*

6. Selecting—Seeing only one aspect of a person or situation and ignoring everything else.

7. Dooming—Seeing only terrible, worst-case outcomes and then alarming yourself.

8. Affecting—Relying only on what you feel at the moment to discern the truth about another person or a situation.

9. Informing—Insisting that you are always right even in the face of contradictory evidence or inconclusive information.

10. Relying—Believing that the only person you can ever count on is yourself.

11. Charming—Believing that other people will never act in your interest unless you first charm and manipulate them.

12. Name Calling—Inflicting people with global names, labels and stereotypes which may contain a morsel of truth but are based only on a single observation or incident.

13. Defaulting—Feeling helpless because you believe other people and circumstances have control over what you can and cannot do.

14. Overgeneralizing—Forcing big conclusions from little observations.

15. Personalizing—Believing that everything that occurs is related significantly to you.

16. Controlling—Assuming you have omnipotent power and control, and that you are responsible for everything and everybody.

17. Polarizing—Seeing everything that happens in either/or extremes.

Call Reluctance

Call reluctance occurs when goal-disruptive feelings accompany distorted perceptions of prospecting. These distortions can occur when perceptions are processed by your past experience, present needs, and valuing filters. But be careful. The story does not end here. Your feelings are not the problem. They only serve as messengers to alert you to the presence of a problem which has been created by your filters.

Your feelings are always in exact proportion to their *actual* cause. In the case of call reluctance, feelings become suspect because they are always found at the scene. There, they become innocent victims of circumstantial evidence and mistaken identity while the actual guilty party remains free to strike again.

Your filters exert their influence through mind chatter, the ongoing process of describing the world to yourself. You continuously carry on an internal dialogue about what you think you see and hear. Since this dialogue is a by-product of your filters, its appraisal of a particular prospecting situation is highly subjective. Prospecting situations do not contain meaning in and of themselves. You appraise prospecting outcomes as good or bad, painful or pleasant. You predict whether your next prospecting efforts will be emotionally dangerous or emotionally safe. Then, based on your conclusions, positive emotions move you towards prospecting activities, while negative emotions prepare you to avoid a danger you told yourself lies ahead.

The Role of Self-Talk

The labels you pin on things and the judgments you make about them are fashioned from an unending dialogue you have with yourself. Albert Ellis, whose psychotherapeutic model is based on changing behavior by changing internal dialogue, calls your internal chatter "self-talk." Aaron Beck has had an equal, if not greater, impact on the practice of psychotherapy. He calls internal dialogue "automatic thought." Our work has been focused upon call reluctance. We have chosen the label "self-pressurization" to describe the mental chatter associated with the feelings that impair prospecting in goal-directed, motivated salespeople.

Charity Begins at Home

We talk to other people differently than we talk to ourselves. We are usually more sensitive, kind, honest, generous and attentive when we converse with others. When we talk to ourselves, privately, about the world as we see it, we often get tangled up in petty childlike habits of thought and emotion. Without realizing it, we color some of the meanings a deep blood red. In the case of call reluctance, neutral prospects, things and circumstances are inflicted with the residue of our childish fears, adolescent demands for attention and approval, and insistence upon perfect performance in everything we do all the time. Here's an actual example.

A Career Can Hold Only So Much Pressure

One high-producing computer salesman for a very well-known computer hardware firm attended a workshop a few years ago with a growing dread of prospecting. He was the company's number one salesman, yet the better he got, the more distressed he became when he tried to prospect. He coped successfully by himself for a number of years because he didn't know what else to do. His sales managers were too busy maintaining the company's first-rate reputation as a sales organization to be perceptive enough to know that behind their best producer's bravado was a growing, festering, unresolved problem—call reluctance. After a few years of peak performance, his production began to show dangerous signs before inevitably tapering off. He began recycling his business by reselling his current clients. He was not developing new sources of sales. The competition, a younger, leaner, more agile company, was.

"What nobody ever knew," he confessed to other workshop participants, "was the horrifying things I was telling myself about prospecting from the very beginning. Things I never realized, like if I don't get more appointments than anybody else tonight, then I won't be the best, and if I'm not the best, then I'm a failure, and if I'm a failure, then I can't provide for my family, and if I don't provide for my family, people will ridicule me, and if people ridiculed me, I would just die."

This salesman enjoyed pointing out two things about his struggle with call reluctance to other salespeople who were also struggling with the problem. First, the things he was telling himself were not true. Second, they had absolutely nothing to do with prospecting. His distress was the result of daily doses of self-inflicted verbal poison. But no matter how reckless his self-statements might have been, he accepted them as true at the time he said them to himself. He then acted as if they were true by always being alert to fictional prospecting dangers and being prepared to do battle with the evil Mr. Prospect. Since coping took energy away from meaningful performance, and Mr. Prospect was never the problem in the first place, the real problem got worse, not better. After a while, he found himself lost in the middle of his career and almost out of gas.

What you say to yourself about prospecting has a powerful impact upon what you feel when prospecting. What you feel when prospecting has a powerful impact on what you do about prospecting.

Pulling the Plug On Career-Limiting Self-Talk

How can you find out if your self-talk is prospecting poison? If you find that it is, what can you do about it? Other salespeople, veteran and neophyte alike, have found that they can regain control over their emotional response to prospecting by learning four simple steps: 1) Slow Down, 2) Listen In, 3) Replace, and 4) Apply. Let's pause for an overview of each step before starting through the entire Thought Realignment procedure.

First: Slow Down

The insults and offenses you hurl at yourself only need an instant to do their work. Before you can hear the poison-tipped words and phrases, and see the horrible visual images which attend them, you must first slow them down.

If you're like the authors, you get annoyed with self-help experts who say you can move a mountain but fail to tell you where to get mountain moving equipment. It is not unusual for a self-help program to advise you to slow down. But how?

You can slow down the rate of your internal dialogue by a simple procedure called Thought-Deceleration. Here's how it works.

First, just talk to yourself. Don't talk out loud. Talk the way you normally do when you talk to yourself. Then listen. Notice how your imaginary voice sounds, then answer the following questions. How loud is it? What is the tone like? How would other people describe your internal voice if they could hear it? If you have trouble hearing your voice, just pretend you hear it, but answer the questions. Perhaps when you read you sub-vocalize (actually say the words to yourself that you are reading). If so, then use your "reading" voice.

Second, continue to talk to yourself, but purposefully lower your voice one octave. Imagine your voice is coming from deep down inside your chest when you talk. Again, if you have trouble, just pretend to lower your voice. Three things should now happen. The pace of your self-talk automatically slows down when you lower your voice. Your imaginary voice pronounces things more clearly. And it becomes easier to hear the words and phrases, and see the pictures you associate with them.

Here's a third, optional step. Whenever you thought-decelerate, lightly bite your tongue and say out loud: "This is my thought-deceleration cue. Whenever and wherever I do this I will immediately slow down the pace of my self-talk."

What you have just learned is an automatic method for slowing down the pace of internal self-talk. If you will practice it for five minutes, three times a day for three days, something even more interesting will happen. By just lightly biting your tongue, you will start speaking to yourself in a slower, clearer, more manageable pace. Slowing down enough to take a census of the messages bouncing around inside your head is the first step to cleaning house.

Second: Listen In

Now that you have slowed things down, you can start listening for content. Most of what you see and hear will be about as absorbing as Saturday morning cartoons. But if you are call reluctant, the next time you are prospecting (or about to prospect), turn down the pace and listen in. Soon you will hear your Self-Propaganda Channel broadcasting daily career-busting messages at full strength. Pay attention. You will be introduced to the phantoms that lie beneath the surface of your call reluctance.

Twelve Career-Damaging Themes

The things you say to yourself that inhibit your ability to prospect will, if left unchallenged, result in one or more of the twelve known types of call reluctance. We have listed below the most common self-talk themes associated with each of the twelve types.

Doomsayer
"I must always be vigilant and careful to avoid anything the least bit fearful or unpredictable."

Over-Preparation
"I must always be perfectly prepared before I have the right to initiate contact with any prospective buyer."

Hyper-Pro
"If I don't look distinguished and professional, people won't like me."

Stage Fright
"In order to be an effective speaker, I must absolutely dazzle everyone in the room with my charm, wit, and mastery of the subject."

Role Rejection
"All salespeople are just peddlers, and since I am in sales, all the people who expected me to aspire to a dignified occupation must be thoroughly disappointed."

Yielder
"I must never interfere or intrude upon other people for any reason, ever."

Social Self-Consciousness
"All wealthy, educated, positioned people are better than me. I must always remember to keep my place and never presume to be their equal."

Separationist
"I must never do anything that would ever lead any of my friends to think I was trying to exploit them."

Emotionally Unemancipated
"I must never seek to advise any member of my own family in any business matter because it is always unethical and they will never take me seriously anyway."

Referral Aversion
"My prospect didn't really buy it. I sold it. So I better get the order and get out of here. Asking for referrals slows things down. Slowing things down would give my customer too much time to rethink. If they thought about it, they might cancel their order."

Telephobia
"People always hate to be called by salespeople on the phone. If I use the phone to make calls, they would hate me. I could not stand it if anyone disliked me. I better not use the phone."

Oppositional Reflex
"I must never appear like I need to rely on anyone for anything. That would make me dependent, and people who depend on others for anything always get hurt in the end."

The Play-By-Play Approach

Sometimes slowing down is not enough to allow you to survey the impact that negative self-talk has on your prospecting. When it's not, try this thought experiment adapted from one of the Gestalt routines popular in the 50's and 60's:

Think of an actual prospecting situation which is particularly difficult for you. Now imagine you are listening to a sportscaster's play-by-play description of the things you are saying to yourself while watching the accompanying visual images on the screen of an imaginary television set. When the sportscaster describes a careless thought or reckless bit of self-talk that you would like to observe more closely, request an instant replay. Back the scene up several frames. Then let it move forward slowly, frame-by-frame. Give the sportscaster editorial freedom to elaborate on what you are saying to yourself. Zoom in on the pictures you see on the screen. Move in as close as you can. Look at the pictures. Listen to what your sportscaster has to say.

Gil T., a stockbroker from Connecticut, had trouble slowing things down. Thought-deceleration worked but it did not slow things down enough. So he let sportscaster Howard Cosell help by providing the play-by-play. It worked. Here is how he did it:

> *"Here comes Gil T., a talented newcomer who is not playing at his potential. There he goes reaching for the phone. His determination shows, but here comes the old habits back again. Look at his forehead perspire! Listen to what he is saying to himself: 'Getting real scared...don't know why...can't use the phone...too scared.' Look at that man squirm in his chair! This has happened before folks. He starts to fidget and perspire every time he starts to use the phone; then he starts to tell himself how scared he is."*

Gil learned that whenever he reached for the phone he was telling himself how scared he was. Simultaneously, he was calling up a mental snapshot of himself *looking* panicked. Then he perspired. Squirmed. Fidgeted. Predictably, within seconds he panicked. He actually heard himself telling himself, "I'm scared. Can't dial the phone because something bad will happen to me. I have got to stay away from things that scare me because if I don't, I'll get hurt. People would see how weak I am and nobody will like me because I'm a weakling who's always getting hurt."

Gil learned much about what he was telling himself about prospecting (in his case about using the phone to prospect). Once he slowed things down enough to get in touch with what was happening, he was able to see what he was doing to himself. He could even remember the first time he said those things and had those feelings.

According to Gil, it all began one day at school when he was 11 years old. Ever since, he has been vigilantly trying to avoid "peril" as seen through the eyes of an 11-year-old version of himself. Eleven-year-old Gil was doing one hell of a job protecting the adult Gil from his childhood fears. But Gil's prospecting activity was in shambles.

Third: Replace

Call reluctance occurs when we allow ourselves to mindlessly recite career-limiting messages and experience the distressful feelings they produce. Thus, the next step is to disconnect the career-limiting thought from the distressing fear it produces. How? By thoughtfully replacing career-limiting chatter with goal-supporting self-statements. Here's a brief exercise which illustrates the logic behind the strategy.

Before you next use the phone to prospect, recite the following statement three times: "I must make everybody like me or I am nothing." How does reciting this statement influence how you perceive the phone? How does it influence the way you feel about using the phone to prospect?

Feelings are an important part of our survival instincts. They do not like being placed in situations that could result in annihilation. Annihilation? Who said anything about annihilation? You did. That is how your feelings interpret a situation when you say, "...or I am nothing." The only information your feelings have about an upcoming prospecting situation is: 1) You are about to use the phone to call people who may not appreciate being called. 2) You must make everybody like you. 3) If anyone does not like or approve of you, you will cease to exist. 4) Therefore, you are about to place yourself in a situation that threatens your very survival. What fun.

So how do you change this scenario? You replace your fear-producing self-statements with non-fear-producing self-statements.

To illustrate, let's return to the career-limiting self-statement you recited before using the phone. Imagine you are in the exact same prospecting situation. You are about to use the telephone. However, this time recite the following amended version of the previous self-statement three times: "I would like to be liked by everyone because I enjoy being liked for a lot of good reasons." Consider how you feel now as you reach for the phone. Notice the difference in the role your feelings play. In the first example, they were told a potential disaster might occur if you dialed the phone. In the current example, you substituted a preference for a nonverifiable requirement. The first version rang an alarm; the second did not because none was needed. The first statement was fear-soliciting; the second was not because there was nothing to fear. One projected the threat of annihilation, the other projected an opportunity. Of the two, which statement is more true? Which is goal-supporting? Which takes more energy?

Fourth: Apply

Thought Realignment would fall woefully short of the mark if all it did was to help you know yourself better or feel better about yourself. These are commendable goals, but they are better left to pep-talkers on motivational cassettes. Insight is not our primary objective. Increased prospecting is.

In keeping with that aim, the next step in Thought Realignment is to translate what you learn into more phone calls and more seen calls. Nothing more. Nothing less. If, for example, you hesitate to call on educated, professional people, then your action objective is to initiate contact with more educated, professional people more often.

Thought Realignment: A Permanent Solution

How does Thought Realignment differ from attitude-changing appeals you can readily hear on a cassette or in a one-hour pep-talk by A. Dynamic Motivator, Ph.D.? Consider the following differences:

1. *The objectives are different.* This method is designed to help you acquire new and better control of your emotions, particularly those that interfere with prospecting.

2. *This method is a system*, and as such it draws from an integrated set of procedures, each of which contributes to the overall objective.

3. *The time-frame is different.* This approach teaches a discipline. It takes time, practice and attention. It is not an entertainment.

4. *Applied correctly*, Thought Realignment has proven to be *more lasting and durable* than inspirational quick-fixes. If you are a typical salesperson, you may tend to experience cyclic feelings. Early in the day you may be high, expecting nothing but more highs only to find that at the end of the day you are down, expecting nothing but more downs. Inspirational speakers are masters at exploiting this situation. After a few hours of podium-pounding, they get salespeople who are on a high to be momentarily higher, and salespeople who are on a low to believe they are high for up to an hour. But the effect doesn't last for either group, and often damages both.

Don't Blame Your Feelings!

Some ill-fated approaches to managing call reluctance are too centered on the way fear feels. But how you happen to feel when you attempt to prospect is not the total picture. Your feelings just form one of the symptoms of the problem, another being insufficient prospecting.

The real culprit is mismanaged emotional energy. Think about it. If every time you have the opportunity to initiate contact with a prospective buyer you silently shout to yourself, "RED ALERT!...DANGER AHEAD!...ESCAPE IMMEDIATELY!" what do you expect to experience? Feelings of peace? Joy? Serenity?

Feelings are not thoughts. They do not evaluate or discern. They mobilize to action. Think of them as your obedient servants down in the engine room who follow, without question or argument, whatever directives you, the pilot, issue. If you have the nasty habit of telling them to prepare for a life-threatening emergency every time you reach for the phone, open the door to your prospect's office, or greet your prospect's receptionist, then you can be assured that your feelings will respond to the alert by preparing your body to survive a life-threatening emergency.

So, while it may appear that your feelings have gone berserk, don't jump to conclusions. Don't rush to blame your feelings for doing what they are supposed to be doing. And don't let other people play mind games with your emotions.

Some would-be hypnotic games, for example, try to put a quick fix on call reluctance. They try to get you to delude yourself into thinking that you are not feeling fear in situations when you are feeling fear. This approach may be harmless in most situations, but in the case of call reluctance it can compound the problem into one that is much more difficult to deal with for everyone concerned. Be careful!

Positive mental attitude games, on the other hand, do not try to hypnotize you. Instead, they attempt to get you to deny your feelings. That could be helpful in some situations, but in the case of call reluctance it could be psychologically brutal and extremely damaging. Be careful!

Don't get seduced by drug games played with lightning fast prescription pens. Under close supervision, Valium and other

continues

> ### Don't Blame Your Feelings! *continued*
>
> mood anesthetics can be necessary in certain situations. Used imprudently, however, they can cause problems far more severe than an honest dose of call reluctance. And that goes for alcohol and other consumer chemicals. They might anesthetize painful feelings, but they never offer a solution to the problem. Be careful!

PART TWO
THOUGHT REALIGNMENT STEP-BY-STEP

Up to now you have surveyed the basics of Thought Realignment. But how can you apply it to your day-to-day prospecting activities? Thought Realignment consists of well-defined steps which are interesting and easy to learn. Salespeople who have used this procedure have seen significant and lasting improvements, some in record time. But how much and how soon you benefit from Thought Realignment depends upon which type of call reluctance you have, how long you have had it, and whether you have been victimized by ill-advised quick fixes which may have strengthened the habits you are now trying to break.

Step One:
General Feeling Consequences I (GFC's)

Take out a piece of paper and write down a list of words which, in your judgment, describe what call reluctance feels like. Title your list "GFC's" for General Feeling Consequences. ACTION BREAK

The feeling consequences you just listed are some of the ways that call reluctance signals its presence. These signals work the same as warning lights on the dashboard of your car. Their job is to signal the presence of a problem. They themselves are not the problem.

The Difference Between Label and Content

In today's over-psychologized society, we are losing the ability to accurately describe our own problems in terms we can meaningfully deal with. We constantly get sidestepped into using fashionable scientific names to describe our distress. Then, when we attempt to do something about our problems, we find that the names evaporate into words without substance or utility.

Let's look closer by taking a brief mind trip. Imagine you are standing naked in the middle of a snowstorm. Got it? Now pause. Take a few seconds and try to describe what is happening. Then take out a piece of paper and write down your observations as accurately as you can. ACTION BREAK

Most salespeople who have taken this curious trip say things like, "I get cold." Some say, "I'm uncomfortable." At least one always says, "I'm embarrassed." Occasionally, there are individuals who are unable or unwilling to fantasize the situation at all.

Consider this. When you say you are cold, you are correct in the figurative sense. But that is not particularly instructive. Cold is not what is happening to you. Cold is the label you attach to the variety of sensations you are experiencing.

Let's look at it from another perspective. Imagine you have gone to a convenience store to buy a bottle of ketchup. You place your order with the clerk. He reaches up and grabs a bottle with a label that reads "ketchup." So far, so good. That's what you wanted. But then he takes a razor from a nearby drawer and scrapes off the label. He hands you the label and says, "That will be $1.25 please." More than just a little miffed, you do not let the situation pass by uncontested. You demand the contents of the bottle. That's what you are entitled to. And so you are.

Now return to the snowstorm. You are still standing there naked. But this time when you are asked what is happening, instead of just saying you are cold, ask yourself what cold stands for. What does it mean? Demand the contents. What exactly is happening to you that causes you to assign the label "cold?"

By this time, most salespeople say, "Well, I'm turning blue!" "I'm shivering!" Interestingly, what one individual calls "cold" may not be what another experiences as cold.

The MAD Test

When you check out a label, use the MAD test. MAD is an acronym which stands for "Make Any Difference?" Does it make any difference to use this word or that label to describe what is happening? Does it point you in a helpful direction? Does it provide a solution? Does it provide meaningful guidance? Labels like "stress," "esteem," "secondary call reluctance," and "fear of rejection" are word games. They sound sophisticated but fail the MAD test. They do not reveal, direct, change, enlighten or instruct in any way that makes a difference. Listen to the following advice taken from an insurance industry publication:

Sales anxiety (a label for what?) is a normal occurrence in this business, but too often the occasional day or two of call reluctance turns into weeks and months of poor production. When the early symptoms are ignored, the problem can have a snowball effect: fear of failure (another label!) can cause poor performance, resulting in greater fear of failure (still another label!) causing worse performance...

The next time a consultant tells you that your sales career is burdened down by the "fear of rejection," apply the MAD test. Ask if that information alone is supposed to cure you, or if something more instructive is going to follow.

Descriptors like "goose bumps," "turning blue," and "shivering" can be objectively verified by your senses. They are your body's way of communicating to you that your temperature is lowering to potentially dangerous levels and you need to seek warmth. Note that you would not die from exposure to the cold immediately. There are hints, signs and symptoms all along the way. What are they? "Goose bumps," "turning blue," and "shivering." Notice that in our example, shivering serves two purposes. First, it signals that something is amiss. Second, by starting your body in motion, it directs you to get moving.

The Case of Positive Paul

Some salespeople, like Positive Paul, will not accept information on this level. They are perpetually tuned in to pop-psych chit-chat and will not listen to anything that does not ring of modern mental mysticism. With ears plugged up with confusing jargon, they ignore their body's simple but elegant way of informing them that something needs serious attention, now. There he is, Positive Paul, standing there naked in the middle of a snowstorm with a frozen grin on his face trying to convince himself that he is soaking up sunshine on the warm, sunny beaches of Hawaii.

A Matter of Priorities

If you were driving down the street and your oil pressure gauge glowed a bright red, what would you do? Most people would take that as an apocalyptic sign to immediately pull the vehicle over and check the problem. They would not complain about the color (red), and they certainly would not try to pretend that it was a bright green.

Would you ignore the signal and keep on driving? Would you pat your car reassuringly on the dashboard and say, "You must be upset. We don't need any negativism here, now do we? So let's compose ourselves and listen to Dr. Moonbeam's brand new motivational cassette series, 'Turning Panic into Profit.'"

If you are like most people, you would not treat your car that way. You should not treat yourself that way either. When you are prospecting and your "warning lights" glow bright red, pull over, lift the hood, and take an honest look.

The Experience of Call Reluctance Revisited

So far, two things have been clarified. First, we cleaned up our understanding of what the actual experience of call reluctance feels like from the perspective of our sensations. Second, we found out how many salespeople and their managers spend energy and money chasing after, and trying to correct, labels for call reluctance instead of the problem itself.

Step Two:
General Feeling Consequences II (GFC's)

Take out another sheet of paper and try again to list what you think call reluctance feels like. But this time no labels, please. Just contents. Title your chart GFC's II for General Feeling Consequences, Version Two. Concentrate on what actually happens, what is being experienced. Remember, if you can't think of anything, just pretend, but do the exercise anyway. Here's an example to help you get started. It is a list of three things call reluctance actually felt like to the authors.

Heart pounding

Dry mouth

Nervous stomach

Now it's your turn. ACTION BREAK.

Inventory of Call Reluctance Experiences

How did you do? Did you permit labels to infiltrate your list? Here are some of the most common experiences other call-reluctant salespeople have listed through the years.

Sensations Reported	Percent Experiencing
Butterflies in stomach	28%
Perspiring more than usual	34%
Fidget, can't keep still	7%
Breath faster, shallower	10%
Hyperventilation	2%
Get very thirsty	3%
Have to go to the bathroom often	16%
Cry	1%
Heart pounding	42%
Voice rises to higher pitch	13%
Mind goes blank	7%
Get the shakes	6%
Stammer and stutter	18%
Talk louder and/or faster	43%
Pupils dilate	5%
Chest feels tight	21%

Total does not equal 100% due to some respondents reporting multiple sensations.

When call reluctance is examined from the perspective of what is actually happening, it can be seen for what it is, a menacing, energy-sapping parasite. Labels like "fear of rejection" or "fear of success" are more sophisticated and respectable than admitting that you have to go to the bathroom whenever you try to prospect. But are they more useful? Clouding the natural behavioral indicators of call reluctance with non-specific terms can—and often does—conceal the problem, allowing it to grow worse. It gets glossed over, intellectualized, discussed and theorized. It does not get corrected. Recall. Have you ever actually met one call-reluctant salesperson whose low prospecting activity and physical call-reluctance indicators were eliminated by enhancing his or her "self-image?"

To us, physical signs of distress, like those inventoried above, *are* the problem. They keep you from devoting full energy to prospecting. They will remain the problem regardless of the label you attach, until you can reach for the phone, open doors, and ask for referrals without showing signs of distress. The battle lines are drawn.

Step Three:
Personal Feeling Consequences (PFC's)

Take out another piece of paper and compile your own personal inventory of call reluctance experiences. Begin by referring to the last list you constructed (GFC's II) and the Inventory of Call Reluctance Experiences we provided. List all the sensations you actually feel when you try to prospect. Be sure to include all the experiences you feel even if they do not appear on the other two lists. Watch out for labels! ACTION BREAK.

Step Four:
General Activating Events (GAE's)

So far, you have listed some specific "feeling consequences" of call reluctance for salespeople in general. You then made a personal list of what call reluctance feels like to you. Now we will proceed one step closer to the origin of call-reluctant feelings. You do not feel your "PFC's" everywhere or all the time. So, the next step is to identify when you do experience them and under what conditions.

Take out another piece of paper. Set it up as shown in the example below. Then, based on your experience and knowledge of prospecting in general, list as many call reluctance "where's" and "what's" as you can. If you don't know any, or can't think of any, then just pretend, but do the exercise.

<u>Where</u>	<u>What</u>
When I'm sitting at my desk (*Where* I am)	Getting ready to cold call (Exactly *what* I am doing)

Now it's your turn. ACTION BREAK.

How many different situations did you list? Salespeople attending our presentations usually come up with long and enlightening lists. Let's see how yours compares to theirs. Here is a sample of some of the more common situations call-reluctant salespeople and their managers have listed over the years.

- When I realize that it is about time to ask for a referral.

- When I look at my watch and notice that in about five minutes I'm supposed to be on the phone prospecting.

- When I am driving in my car and pull up in the parking lot for my first call on someone.

- When I get to the building and see my prospect's name, title or educational degrees on the building directory.

- When I am about to place a prospecting call on the phone and notice that I only have a few prospect cards left and wonder where my next ones will come from.

- When I dial the phone and a secretary answers.

- When I dial the phone and the prospect answers.

- When I get right outside the door of my prospect's office and reach to open it.

- When I'm in the waiting room mentally rehearsing what I'm going to say.

Can you identify with any of these situations? We call them GAE's for General Activating Events. (Psychologist Albert Ellis calls them Activating Events.) They may be familiar to you, but as you can see, they are by no means unique to you.

Step Five:
Personal Activating Events (PAE's)

Review the list you have just constructed. Then take out another piece of paper. Set it up the same as you did in Step Four. This time, however, list only those situations which apply specifically to you. These will be your PAE's for Personal Activating Events. Be certain to include on your list any that are applicable to you even if they did not appear in your general list or the list we provided. ACTION BREAK.

Step Six:
Putting It Together

Now let's consolidate what we have learned so far. Set up a new piece of paper like the example below. Then, under the first column, copy your Personal Activating Events (PAE's). Under the second column, copy the specific emotional reactions you listed on the other form you completed called Personal Inventory of Call Reluctance Experiences (PFC's II). ACTION BREAK.

Where I Am/What I'm Doing	My Emotional Reaction
(PAE's)	(PFC's)
"Prospect answers phone"	"My mind goes blank"
"Arrive at prospect's office"	"Heart starts pounding"

How did you do? Were you able to bring into sharper focus exactly what feelings you have in specific prospecting situations?

For some salespeople, the problem seems to become more manageable once they are able to break it down, diagram it, and plot it out. The scale becomes smaller. The problem consists of smaller, more clearly defined components.

Now our job must be directed to the next step, the search for the missing link which connects your PAE's to your PFC's. In other words, we now begin searching for the wires which connect your feelings to the prospecting situation.

Step Seven:
The Search for the Missing Link

If you are like most call-reluctant salespeople, trainers, consultants and managers, the last exercise resulted in a mirage. It appears that what you feel (PFC's) is connected to where you are and what you are doing (PAE's). Right? Wrong. When it comes to call reluctance, that "common sense" inference can be lethal. To gullibly accept it as true can actually generate call-reluctant behavior and maintain it once it has formed.

Since it appears that the prospect's voice on the other end of the phone is what makes my mind go blank, I incorrectly conclude that if I stop or reduce my telephone prospecting then my mind will not go blank. Since it appears that my tight stomach is caused by my arrival at the prospect's office, I wrongly conclude that if I do not go to his office, or go to the address but don't actually enter the building (null calls), then my stomach will not get tight.

Many well-intentioned but seriously flawed solutions for call reluctance are based upon the presumption that the setting is somehow linked to your emotional reactions. But take a closer look at the consolidation exercise (Step Six) you just completed. Your reactions are physically real.

They are not imaginations. They exert an authentic, negative pressure on your ability to prospect. But is there any actual, *physical* connection between them and prospecting? Are there any wires that connect your head to the telephone which could explain the negative psychic shock you get whenever you try to dial? The answer is no.

The presumption that where we are (PAE's) causes what we feel (PFC's) is part of the problem, not the solution. Misleading explanations which reinforce the fictional connection between the two tend only to strengthen the problem. They do not reduce it. Furthermore, if events (PAE's) did cause feelings (PFC's) then our prospects actually could terrorize us. That would give us a valid, objective reason to fear them. But in most cases, prospects are feared before they are met.

The following are actual examples of misleading advice which subtly presumes that prospecting events (PAE's) are the cause of goal-disruptive feelings (PFC's). Uncritical acceptance of advice like this can further complicate an already existing problem.

> *"The primary way to cope with call reluctance is to experience a series of successful calls. The key to that is to remain active."*

> *"To sidestep rejection...we phone for appointments. But we are different here (than other sales organizations) in that we identify ourselves as survey takers, not salespeople."*

Using the MAD test as a barometer, let's examine the above statements more closely. According to the MAD test, when you isolate the real cause, you should be able to do three things. First, you should be able to prove that every salesperson who has been exposed to the call reluctance toxin should be sick. In other words, every salesperson who experiences a series of unsuccessful sales calls should develop call reluctance. Second, they should be sickened in direct proportion to their degree of exposure. The greater the exposure, the greater the severity of the symptoms you should observe. Third, you should be able to find a toxin that, when removed, causes the symptoms to disappear.

The advice in the first quote is based upon the presumption that unsuccessful calls mysteriously make a salesperson call reluctant. But does every salesperson become call-reluctant after one unsuccessful sales call? If it takes more than one unsuccessful call, then exactly how many are required? Two? Three? Five? Ten? If only some salespeople become call-reluctant after one or more unsuccessful calls, then do they become reluctant to the exact same degree? If not, why not?

The second bit of advice presumes that the role of a salesperson, in other words being a salesperson, inherently causes call reluctance. But does it? Do all salespeople have call reluctance? Since the quote presumes that it originates from a single common source, just being a salesperson, then do salespeople who have call reluctance have it to the exact same degree? Of course not. The real cause is yet to be discovered.

Private Meanings Revisited

An intermediate step exists between the instant we assign meaning to an experience and our emotional reaction to that meaning (not the experience). So far, we have referred to this step as "self-chatter" or "self-talk."

Experience does not come to us prepackaged. It comes in the form of raw, unprocessed sensory data. How we process the data of our experience varies with each individual. During the processing phase, we assign meaning to our life experiences. We then react to the meanings we assigned, not to the experience itself.

There are two basic types of meanings which can be generated from our self-talk: self-enhancing and self-diminishing. Self-enhancing self-talk is more consistent with the actual data of our experience and results in constructive emotional responses. It has the following general characteristics:

1. It is *flexible*.

2. It permits a *positive assault* against real life problems.

3. It helps you feel *in control*.

4. It allows you to objectively consider *options*.

Self-diminishing self-talk, however, is different. It explodes and amplifies emotional responses beyond the level required by the actual data of the experience. It inflicts unnecessary, surplus feelings which can easily become unmanageable and overwhelming. Its general characteristics are:

1. It *rigidly* results in the same reaction regardless of differences in the situation.

2. It is always *defensive*.

3. It *takes control*. You just go along for the ride.

4. It implies that you have *no opinion* and *no options*.

You can easily spot self-diminishing self-talk by simply observing what it does to your prospecting behavior. Intense feelings are aroused when they are not wanted or needed. Self-pressurizing words invade your mental vocabulary. Once there, they distort your running narration of the prospecting situation and steal energy which would have been allocated to support your prospecting objectives. Here are a few examples:

Instead of saying...

"I would *like* to land three sales appointments,"

you say...

"I *have* to land three sales appointments, or else."

Instead of saying...

"I would *prefer* to be the best sales prospector around,"

you say...

"I *must* be the best sales prospector around, or else."

Self-Inflicted Ghosts and Goblins

The authors are often privileged to speak before very large and influential audiences. We know that if we do well in our presentations, other speaking engagements will surely follow and additional sources of income will result. (Did you know that authors also have to prospect and sell? We have to promote the books we write or bookstores won't stock them. If bookstores don't stock them, people can't readily buy them. If people don't buy them, we don't get paid. Royalties on books sold is a form of straight commissions. If we do not sell what we create, we starve.) Assuming we are motivated, and our motivation is focused on making good presentations, what goal-supporting behaviors should follow?

- Would we prepare?

- How would we handle questions?

- What would be our attitude towards the people in the audience?

On the other hand, what would happen if we constantly told ourselves that we *had* to deliver the very *best* presentation those people ever heard?

- The intensity of our emotions would probably interfere with our ability to prepare.

- Improperly prepared, we would probably cover by trying to rigidly act like we were experts in absolutely everything.

- We would seem preoccupied and relate mechanically to our audience.

- We would blame the intensity of our feelings on the audience and call it "stage fright."

But wait. Was the audience the cause of our stage fright? Did they plot together just to find a way to cause us to experience counterproductive feelings? Or was it something we did to ourselves? Was it how we allowed ourselves to interpret the situation we found ourselves in?

We intended to tell ourselves to prepare for an opportunity which could move us closer to our goals. Instead, we wound up saying that it was imperative (not just desirable) to do a good job, that we had to dazzle everybody there (an impossible task), and then we implied that if we failed to do these things, something absolutely terrible would happen to us (which would not). So instead of performing well, we had to cope with self-inflicted ghosts and goblins which we conjured up from within ourselves and projected onto the audience!

Some Good Reasons for Talking Straight to Yourself

There are several techniques you can use to distinguish goal-supporting self-talk from the twisted, contorted self-talk we have described. Here are a few.

Goal-supporting self-talk is...

1. VERIFIABLE. It should be obvious (to motivated, goal-focused people) why anybody prefers to perform well as opposed to poorly. On the other hand, the belief that you *must* perform well is totally unverifiable. Test it out. You will find several good reasons to support the case for good performance. But these reasons only serve to further justify why you should *desire* certain outcomes, not why you *must* have them.

2. LOGICALLY CONSISTENT. It moves you closer to, not farther away from, the things you want.

3. UPLIFTING. It permits you to have more pleasant feelings, more often.

4. OBJECTIVE. It helps you to form more accurate assessments of situations, choose from available alternatives, and realistically estimate the probable consequences of your actions.

5. RELEASING. It contributes to the solution of problems, not the strengthening of them.

6. ENLIGHTENING. It allows you to learn from your good and bad experiences, reducing the likelihood that the same problems will needlessly occur again.

When these criteria are applied to internal call reluctance dialogue, it becomes apparent that some of the things you are saying to yourself are not goal-supporting. They are goal-denying.

Altered States

Can you think of a song that brings to mind the face of a special person? Does the thought of a math or science test make you shudder? Is there a perfume or an aftershave lotion that automatically invokes the memory of a special past experience? Certain cues, like a particular piece of music, a certain smell, a touch, a vague internal sensation, or even certain words, can cause you to vividly reexperience highly charged past experiences. Career-damaging self-talk works the same way. A cue which has become associated with a distressful event from the past starts the wheels in motion. Then we relive the experience, as if it were happening again—now.

Cues can also be embedded in prospecting situations. When prospecting, some salespeople actually check out momentarily and go into an altered state of consciousness. For that moment they are oblivious to what is going on around them. Has that ever happened to you? If so, you could be hypnotizing yourself into call reluctance behavior every time you process a particular cue.

One salesperson, Rachael Z., told the authors how she experienced distressful feelings associated with prospecting whenever she saw a computer printout. It seems that her first and last day in magazine subscription sales was particularly traumatic. She was seated in a booth with a phone, a sales script, and a huge computer list of names and telephone numbers. She started out high on confidence but low on training and mental preparation. It didn't take more than a couple of hours for the printout to become indelibly associated with feelings of despair and distress. The telephone ceased to be an instrument of opportunity and instead became associated with unpleasant sensations. Even the blue color of her cubicle became part of a negative memory imprint. Now, whenever she sees a computer printout, an office telephone, or a blue cubicle, she remembers her experience and relives how she felt.

The Negative Power of Words

Negative self-talk consists of highly charged word cues that can cut and hurt. When used, these words will automatically invoke sensations associated with distressful past experiences. Words which typically work in this way include, "it would be terrible," "awful," "horrible," "couldn't stand it," "tragedy," and "catastrophe if." Not infrequently, a single careless or incidental event in the course of sales training can be enough to set the process in motion.

During her training as a chemical salesperson, Barbara T. was insensitively corrected in front of her prospect by her young, ambitious sales trainer. Following a minor error in her presentation sequence, she remembers him smiling condescendingly at her and pointing out to her prospect that she was "new in the business." Following that incident, whenever anyone smiled at her in the same manner and asked, "How long have you been in the business?" she replayed the earlier event. Her self-talk immediately took over and amplified the situation as follows: "Since this smile is like that smile, this person must be like that person, and no person is ever going to treat me that way again, ever!" Needless to say, Barbara T. acquired a reputation for being hostile and uncoachable. Bright, young, motivated sales trainers report having the most trouble with her.

Counterfeit Messages

No matter how peculiar, bizarre or unbelievable it may seem to others, negative self-talk is uncritically accepted as truth by call-reluctant salespeople. Left untested, it has the same truth value as any other source of information, even immediate sensory experience. For example, whenever Sid G., a financial planner, saw Marty receive a sales performance award, he would automatically launch an internal assault. He would say, "He's got it made. He has a lot of advantages I don't have and he doesn't care for anybody but himself!" To Sid, the conclusions he drew while talking to himself in this way were true. This type of self-propaganda tends to camouflage the real issue. Instead of concentrating on why he was not performing at a level equal to his ability, Sid became preoccupied with the production of other people who were. His self-poisoning thoughts became more real each time they were repeated. And he repeated them every time Marty or anyone else was recognized for outstanding sales performance. Only when Sid learned that his self-talk was not objectively true was he able to see that he was wasting his energy and sacrificing his sales career in the process. Up until that time, he had never tested, verified, challenged or evaluated his internal dialogue, nor had he considered its consequences.

You were not born with career-damning self-talk. It was acquired in most cases without your even knowing it. Perhaps it was the result of an ill-advised sales training program or a well-intentioned but poorly trained sales manager. Where it came from is not important. The fact that you learned it is very important. With a determined will and the right methods, you can begin to unlearn it—now.

How You Can Make Prospecting Distressful

- Never try to hear what you are telling yourself prospecting *means* to you.

- Always presume that your fears about prospecting are based upon undisputable *fact*.

- Exclusively associate with non-performers.

- When you are distressed by prospecting, always fix your attention on how you feel. Then trust your feelings to guide you quickly out of the situation and exclude any reasonable information that does not agree with the awful things you are telling yourself.

- Always concentrate on self-limiting themes such as your failures, inabilities, imperfections and lost opportunities. And by all means, dwell incessantly on a bleak outlook for the future.

- Never try to change. If you do, do it half-heartedly.

Twelve Themes of Traumatic Prospecting

Through the years, we have noticed that the self-talk which interferes with prospecting can be reduced to twelve common themes. These themes correspond to the twelve known forms of call reluctance. They are listed below.

Doomsayer
"It's a fact. I must be absolutely careful not to put myself in any danger of any type, because I could not handle it and that would be the end of me."

Over-Preparation
"It's a fact. I must be absolutely prepared before I initiate any contact with prospective buyers, because any one of them could ask me a question I couldn't answer. Then they would think I was stupid and superficial and I could never handle that."

Hyper-Pro
"It's a fact. I must always look polished, professional and refined even if I'm not. If I didn't, people would not respect me. And if they didn't respect me I couldn't handle it."

How Rational Should You Be?

Should you be gray, pin-striped rational all the time? Some adherents of Thought Realignment apparently think you should. But is that self-enhancing? We don't think it is. We see this as a self-contradiction. It is not reasonable to be rational all the time. The object of Thought Realignment is to help you recover the ability to choose from among various behavioral alternatives, not to replace one form of self-limitation with another, even if the other is based in rationality. We prefer having a choice. We want you to be free to act mature or immature, caring or petty, optimistic or depressed, and even call-reluctant if you want to. We would like for you to have those choices. We do not want you to exchange one set of constraints for another.

Stage Fright
"It's a fact. Every presentation must be dynamite. I must never screw up in front of a group. If I did, they would all think I was crazy or incompetent and I know I could never survive that."

Separationist
"It's a fact. I must never bring up my business concerns with my friends because they might think I was trying to exploit them and I could never bear the thought that even one of my friends would ever think that way about me."

Emotionally Unemancipated
"It's a fact. I could never talk to my relatives about my business concerns because I know they would never take me seriously, and if any of them should ever fail to take me seriously I could not handle it."

Yielder
"It's a fact. I must have the love and approval of everyone, everywhere, all the time. If I called on people who are not expecting a call, they might think I was pushy and intrusive. I could never deal with that."

Role Rejection
"It's a fact. I must never fail to meet the expectations of other people. I know everybody looks down on salespeople. They think they are selfish and dishonest. I could not stand it if anyone ever thought that

way about me. So I'll say I'm a customer relations consultant and just happen to be in the neighborhood taking a survey."

Social Self-Consciousness

"It's a fact. I know I should never step out of my place and presume to be good enough to call on people who are better educated or wealthier than I am, because they would quickly discover that I am not as classy as they are and I could never handle being reminded of that."

Referral Aversion

"It's a fact. I must never risk appearing grasping or ungrateful. Asking someone who just bought something from me for a referral always appears ungrateful. Therefore, I must always wait for an appropriate amount of time to pass before I ask."

Telephobia

"It's a fact. I have to have everyone's affection and approval or I would shrivel up and die. Every time I make a prospecting phone call without first asking permission, I risk losing affection and approval. Therefore, I risk annihilation, so I better avoid telephone prospecting as much as I can."

Oppositional Reflex

"It's a fact. I could not withstand being hurt or disappointed again. Only intimidating and powerful people survive and prosper. Everyone else is cheated, exploited, and pushed around. So I must look imposing, sound professional and strike first to hide my vulnerabilities and protect myself from being taken advantage of."

These general themes, when inserted between your prospecting situation (PAE's) and your emotional reaction to that situation (PFC's), fit like the parts of a perfectly formed puzzle. In the case of call reluctance, one always fits better than the others. When that theme is discovered, you will have found the *real* connection between the prospecting situation and why you react to that situation the way you do.

Once you have reviewed the Twelve Themes of Traumatic Prospecting listed previously, take out the last form you completed in Step Six (Putting It Together). As you read through your list, write down the themes that best fit between your Personal Activating Events (PAE's) and your Personal Feeling Consequences (PFC's). Following is an example from the author's experience to get you started.

Where I Am/What I'm Doing	My Emotional Reaction
(PAE)	(PFC)
About to make a prospecting phone call	Hyperventilating

Self-Talk Theme

(STT)

"It's a fact. I have to have everyone's affection and approval or I would shrivel up and die. Every time I make a prospecting phone call without first asking permission, I risk losing affection and approval. Therefore, I risk annihilation, so I better avoid telephone prospecting as much as I can."

Making a phone call (PAE) does not in and of itself sufficiently explain the presence of the author's hyperventilation. However, when the self-talk themes were inserted one at a time, Telephobia fit better than the others forming a logical connection between the author's PAE and PFC. Notice that the author was not saying that he did not want affection and approval. What he was really doing was *demanding* that nobody *ever* see him doing anything (including prospecting by phone) which could cause the loss of affection and approval. If anyone ever did, he believed it would be absolutely *catastrophic*.

Now it's your turn. ACTION BREAK.

THOUGHT REALIGNMENT IN THE REAL WORLD

"Wow, Mr. Science, now that I know all this, am I cured?" No. Call reluctance is not a problem of knowing. It is a problem of doing. In order to claim a victory, you must move closer to your real world prospecting goals. You must apply what you have just learned to actual prospecting situations.

Clearing Questions:
How to Unplug Performance-Limiting Self-Talk

We always have at least two choices when we are faced with distressful prospecting situations. We can try to change the situation or we can accept it as it is and change how we feel about it. In the case of call reluctance, the greatest difficulty is experienced when the situation is unchangeable and we are forced to deal directly with our feelings about prospecting.

As you recall from earlier in this chapter, it is imperative that you first identify the alarming things you tell yourself about prospecting. Once this is accomplished, you must interrupt these self-limiting belief statements and replace them with ones that are goal-supporting. To actively challenge old beliefs and the poisonous self-talk which attends them, you may find it useful to use the following three "clearing" questions.

Clearing Question #1

When you feel a debilitating negative emotion when prospecting, chances are you are reciting a self-pressurizing belief without realizing it. When this happens, immediately listen in on your internal dialogue, identify the belief that is detonating your fear response, and forcefully pounce on it. Begin by asking the first clearing question: "Where's the *proof* that this *has* to be a frightening prospecting situation?" Or you can ask, "Where's the connection between my fear in this prospecting situation and what is supposed to be scaring me? Show it to me!"

The first clearing question, in its various forms, is a direct attack on your reasoning. It is a demand for evidence. *If no convincing evidence is forthcoming, you will have discovered that you can continue to feel fear if you want to, but there are no compelling reasons for doing so.* Blaming the fear on the prospecting situation is unreasonable.

Richard A., trust officer for a major northeastern bank, suffered from Over-Preparation Call Reluctance. He spent far too much time organizing and planning and much too little time prospecting for new business. He learned to identify and control the fear he associated with prospecting by demanding proof. "What's the connection?" he insisted of himself. "How does the possibility of someone asking me a question I can't answer *force* me to feel fear?" By challenging the belief for evidence, it became apparent

---

Are You Dependent on Cures?

Some salespeople are true believers. They believe they can change only if they attend an emotionally charged workshop, listen to a melodramatic, motivational cassette, or read a self-help book like this one. For true believers, can the cure become part of the problem? Is your career being held hostage by books, cassettes and workshops?

to Richard that no one could cause him to feel anything he did not first tell himself to feel. So, what was he telling himself to feel?

Richard traced the real source of his feelings to the tyrannical belief he held that if he ever made a mistake, people would not take him so seriously, and if people did not take him seriously, it would be catastrophic. While in an actual prospecting situation, he snared the belief as it flew by and demanded, "Wait a minute! Where's the evidence that I would not be taken seriously if I ever made a mistake? Who wouldn't take me seriously? Maybe they wouldn't take me seriously regardless of whether I made a mistake or not, so why am I holding up my career for them?" Being technical and somewhat analytical, all Richard needed was to see the illogic of what he was believing about himself. That was enough for him. He simply shut off his fear by pulling the offending belief rug right out from under it. But for some salespeople, one clearing question is not enough.

Clearing Question #2

You may have difficulty snagging these goal-sabotaging self-belief missiles as they sail by on their destructive missions. So a second clearing question has been positioned to help in these situations: "Do I *have* to feel the fear I am feeling right now in this prospecting situation? Does the prospecting situation *require* me to feel this way?"

If you find yourself saying, "No, the situation cannot really force me to feel this way," then you have discovered something very important: You have a choice about what you feel in any prospecting situation. You do not have to automatically be afraid; therefore, you do not have to act afraid.

If you are like some salespeople, however, the insight that weakens the illusory bond between prospecting fears and actual prospecting situations still remains elusive. Your reply to clearing question number two may be, "Yes, of course I have to feel the way I'm feeling. I can tell you have never been call-reluctant or you wouldn't ask such stupid questions!" So another clearing question is available for a third line of attack.

Clearing Question #3

The first two clearing questions are rational attacks on the kinds of feelings you have when you prospect. The third clearing question is an attack on the degree: "Even if I believe that I have to feel the fear I am feeling (clearing question number one), and even if I cannot feel any other way (clearing question number two), then do I have to feel my fear as *much* as I am feeling it now? Could I amplify it and feel it more if I wanted to? Could I diminish it and feel it less? Do I *have* to stay so upset that I *cannot* make calls while I am feeling this way?"

Newton R., a young sales manager for a midwestern sales training company, was having trouble recruiting new consultant-trainers. His limitation was found to be Yielder Call Reluctance. He was not initiating contact with centers-of-influence and other important contacts in his community because he didn't want to be intrusive. The first two clearing questions failed to neutralize the beliefs which produced his negative self-talk, which then neutralized him. So Newt got to the third clearing question and something happened. He found that although he could not easily shake his fear, he could control how *much* fear he felt while recruiting. Newton learned that being afraid was not enough to keep him from recruiting. He discovered the volume control and turned his fear level down. That was a legitimate beginning. Soon thereafter he found the on-off switch.

The clearing questions begin the process of pulling the plug on call reluctance. A few salespeople never get that far. They refuse to honestly evaluate the product of their own reasoning. They have trouble admitting mistakes—even to themselves. If you are one of them, where does that leave you?

If your answer to all the clearing questions is, "Yes, I can prove that prospecting scares me, and that I have to feel fear when I prospect, and I cannot prospect when I feel fear," then congratulations! You have assumed a non-negotiable, flat-world perspective. Based on your beliefs, prospecting will always be a fearful, edge-of-the-world experience. Why? Because you accept the belief that prospecting situations directly cause your feelings and even determine exactly how much fear you experience.

Are you angry with us for boxing you into a logical corner? Good! Prove us wrong. Transform a small ounce of your anger into five sales calls you would not have made otherwise.

Bernard G., ChFc, CFP, CLU, is a financial planner in the northwest. He has all the right credentials, belongs to all the right organizations, and considers himself a professional among professionals. But he does not have many clients. Bernard refuses to promote himself. He considers it unnecessary and unprofessional. Bernard does suspect that something is wrong, but hesitates to call it fear or to ask for help. His Call Reluctance Scale scores showed a career-lethal dose of both Hyper-Pro and Oppositional Reflex Call Reluctance. His body showed up at a call reluctance workshop but his mind held out. He insisted that prospecting, not thoughts about prospecting, cause his "fear of rejection." In response to the first clearing question, he cited four experts from his industry and

Dealing With the Source Makes the Difference

Doesn't forging ahead and making prospecting calls despite how you feel just reinforce the old, automatic fear responses? No. By using Thought Realignment you actively *sell* yourself on the truth about the situation while you are prospecting. You do this by reminding yourself 1)that there is no reason to be afraid, or 2)that you can be afraid and still make calls anyway. Then, you immediately put your best self-persuasive efforts to work by acting as if you are not afraid.

It is the combination of first dealing with the source of the feeling and then practicing new goal-supporting behaviors which separate Thought Realignment from the "just make calls anyway" school of sales management.

The old approach does not deal effectively with the actual source of your feelings (self-talk). Therefore, instead of helping, it strengthens the implied connection between making calls and distressful feelings, thus making the problem worse instead of better. Failure to neutralize the underlying beliefs while making calls leads only to self-brutalization. It works for a few but it kills sales careers as often as it cures. You probably know someone who tried it. You may have tried it yourself. If it and other folk cures actually worked, then call reluctance would not still be the social disease of the direct sales profession.

Remember: To effectively reduce or eliminate call reluctance, you must precede the right actions with the right thoughts. Do not do one without the other.

played two taped presentations he had recorded at an annual convention for insurance sales managers. The more we pointed out the logical futility of his position, the more defensive he became. The second clearing question did not dislodge him either. It confused him. He could not allow himself to grasp and take responsibility for the feelings he was internally generating when he tried to prospect. The third clearing question produced a monologue of pseudo-psychological jargon which, to the untrained, might have seemed impressive. Bernard's position was fixed and his message was clear. To him the world of prospecting is a hostile and frightening place. For Bernard, it is destined by his own choice to stay that way. He is his own jailer.

If you agree with Bernard, your unquestioning belief in a cause-effect connection between external situations and internal feelings precludes anyone or anything from helping you, so long as you continue to hold, recite and protect this belief. Holding this position permanently places you in a perpetual *loop of self-victimization* where you will remain, toil and spin until either centrifugal force or a life trauma mercifully jars you loose from your delusional orbit.

Installing New Prospecting Habits

The clearing questions are the first part of a two part process. They cleared the way for the cultivation of new behaviors which are more consistent with your prospecting goals. The second part of the process is to act consistent with your prospecting goals while continuously applying the clearing questions. The combination of active challenging and behavioral defiance can knock out entrenched call-reluctant habits that have withstood the efforts of battalions of consultants and trainers alike.

THE PARABLE OF THE ELDORADO

A story in two parts for Yielder, Hyper-Pro, Social Self-Consciousness, Role Rejection and Referral Aversion Call Reluctance

Part 1

The Failure

Imagine for a moment that the authors have persuaded you to believe the following about yourself: To convince us that you are a person of worth and ability—a person worth knowing and being with—we first prefer to see you driving a new Cadillac Eldorado and nothing else. With this in mind, say to yourself out loud, "In order for Dudley and Goodson to see people as having worth, they prefer to first see them driving a new Eldorado and nothing else. That means if I want them to see me as worthwhile and accomplished, then they would prefer to see me driving a new Eldorado, too."

It's a mild Tuesday afternoon in your city. It has just rained and you are out driving around on business. There is a rainbow in the eastern sky. You pull up to a red light. There, in the next lane, you see Dudley and Goodson. Like you, we are waiting for the light to change. We are looking straight through you with a punishing moral squint as you, in an old beat-up Volkswagen bus, wait for the light to change to green. Looking over at us, as we obviously are looking at you, how do you feel? Upset? Small? Insignificant? Embarrassed? Depressed?

A Chance to Atone

Being generous and charitable, we condescendingly smile and give you an opportunity to atone for disappointing us. We offer to forgive you if you will sign over to us all you now own or ever will own. Furthermore, you must terminate your present job and gain some other employment more to our satisfaction. To us, based on the vehicle you are presently driving, you would probably be especially suited to late night street cleaning. Do you find this offer acceptable?

Or do you catch yourself saying, "No way! I may not feel proud, but I don't feel that bad!" Do you become indignant? Do you hear yourself tell us off in no uncertain terms? Do you even feel a little anger?

If you do, join up and close ranks. Most salespeople insist, some passionately, that it's not *that* important what Dudley and Goodson think. They are genuinely sorry they disappointed us, but they quickly point out that they have their own lives and careers to live, and that we can come along for the ride if we can be supportive. If not, the light has turned green and they have things to do and places to go.

If you are like most other salespeople you probably drew the line on how much distress you would allow yourself to feel in this situation, and how much you would allow that feeling to interfere with your life and your career. We agree. We would do the same.

Part 2

The Failure

What if we modified two simple elements in this story. Instead of Dudley and Goodson telling you how we would personally prefer to see you, we represent a well-intentioned mother, father, sister, brother, friend or spouse who influences you to believe that it is *imperative* to be seen in a new Eldorado if you are to be a person of worth and accomplishment. Silently recite this self-belief: "I *must* be seen in an Eldorado if I am to be seen as a person of worth and accomplishment." Remember, this time you tell yourself it is a *requirement* to be seen in an Eldorado in order to be a person of worth and accomplishment.

It's the same mild Tuesday afternoon in your city. It has just rained and you are out driving around on business. You pull up to a red light. There, in the next lane, you see Dudley and Goodson. There we are waiting for the light to change. We are looking straight through you with our punishing moral squint as you, in an old beat-up Volkswagen bus, wait for the light to change. Looking back at us, as we obviously are looking at you, how do you feel? Upset? Small? Insignificant? Embarrassed? Depressed?

The Atonement

Most salespeople agree that they feel upset, angry, afraid or depressed. When preference becomes "must," they become grateful when atonement is charitably offered. Why? Because in this situation, it makes sense to feel psychologically bottomed-out if you believe that you *must* be seen in an Eldorado, and nothing else, in order to be a person of worth. You set yourself up by holding the belief.

The belief implies that you are somebody if you have an Eldorado and are nothing if you do not. Emotionally, you have a perfect right to become melodramatic when you put yourself in such an all-or-nothing live-or-die situation. Emotions prepare your body to defend against its own demise, and that is what you allowed yourself to believe was at stake.

Of course, the whole scenario is preposterous. Nobody would actually hold such beliefs, especially motivated, goal-directed salespeople. But they do. We do. You do.

What You Said You'd Never Do

The Car

How salespeople cope with the effects of such beliefs is even more peculiar. Some think it's the car which is at fault, not their beliefs about the car. So they spend a lot of time trying to get their Volkswagen bus to pass for a Cadillac Eldorado. The result can be bizarre.

The Intersection

Some blame the place. They cope by continuing to drive but avoid the intersection. In that way, they hope to escape discovery. Could that be why salespeople with Social Self-Consciousness Call Reluctance avoid up-market clientele?

Driving

Others give up driving altogether. They never venture out. They cope by killing off some of their options. In that way, they are assured that they will never have to deal with any intersection. Could that be like call-reluctant salespeople who won't even try to prospect? They've incorrectly convinced themselves that the intersection is responsible for their distress. So to avoid being distressed, they avoid the intersection.

See Me?

One group of salespeople stretch the parable to even greater lethal lengths. They become approval-seeking addicts. With chest-pounding bravado, Hyper-Pros struggle to actually buy the Eldorado they believe they must have in order to have worth as a person. They anxiously wait to be seen by the Dudleys and Goodsons at intersections in cities everywhere. They *want* us to see them. They *need* us to see them. They dutifully wait to be wreathed in praise and repeatedly told that they are good and worthy people. But life is not necessarily fair. So seeing them, Dudley and Goodson dispassionately acknowledge their presence and apologetically say, "So sorry. You must have missed our last memo on personal worth and accomplishment. You see, this is Lincoln Continental week."

Dismayed, but not disheartened, these salespeople are resolved to do what is needed to win the approval of the Dudleys and Goodsons of the world. They are true believers. They accept as true the misconception that they must have the approval of others in order to be people of worth and accomplishment. Without it, they believe they are nothing.

Time passes. Once again they appear at the intersection adorned in the latest Lincoln Continental. "Am I somebody yet?" their approval-seeking behavior silently queries each passerby. After a while, Dudley and Goodson show up. Anxiously we are asked, "Am I somebody of worth now?"

"You would have been, five minutes ago," one of us answers politely, "but Lincoln Continental week just expired. Now if you want us to see you as a person of worth and accomplishment, you must purchase a new Mercedes-Benz. This is German car week." Still aspiring to please, they rush off without thought or reflection. They just kick up dust and go. Little do they know that we have been reading about two top-of-the-line Japanese automobiles, Lexus and Infiniti....

The futility of believing that feelings of self-worth can be based on anyone else's expectations is a popular misconception that is easier to see in others than in ourselves. It is a never-ending treadmill.

Your worth as a person is not something that you win or are ever really in danger of losing. It is asserted by God, not conferred by men. True, the concept of self-worth may occupy the imperfect attention of imperfect men and provide matter for their idle speculations. But as an act of sacred will, not profane transaction, it is never in doubt. It never has been. Some of us just tend to forget.

It is nice to meet the expectations of others. It is even nice, for a number of objective reasons, to be able to enjoy the ownership of a Cadillac Eldorado. But that ownership does not confer acceptability, credibility or worth—it's just a nice car. If you believe it is an instrument that can buy the lasting approval of others, you limit it and you limit yourself. You limit the Cadillac because to you it ceases to be a car. Instead, it has become the currency of self-worth and must be vigilantly monitored, managed and seen. That leaves little room for enjoyment. You limit yourself by believing you must meet other people's expectations before you can allow yourself to feel worthwhile.

In actuality, your worth is a God-given constant. It needs to be recognized, not discovered. So why not do what you insisted you would do when we began this parable. Say, "I see the light has turned green. If you can be supportive of who I am and what I do, then come along for the ride. If you cannot, I'm sorry I disappointed you but I must be off now. I have a life to live and a career to enjoy."

One Final Word

There are always going to be people who aspire to judge your worth. They're out there, somewhere, waiting at the intersections of your life. Poised. Watching. And this could be Batmobile week.

RECORD YOUR PROGRESS

Most salespeople have found it useful to maintain a daily contact initiation diary. Whenever you experience a goal-limiting feeling when you are prospecting, stop and write in your log: (1) where you are and what you are doing, (2) what you are feeling, (3) how you would have coped with that feeling in the past, (4) any underlying belief(s), accompanying self-talk, pictures, or other alarming sensations that are present, (5) things you could do or say to yourself to challenge the validity of those things, (6) what behavioral steps you could take, (7) the steps you actually did take. Set yours up like the one below.

Contact Initiation Log

Where I am and what I am doing (PAE): _____

_____

_____

What I am *feeling* (PFC): _____

_____

How I *coped* in the past: _____

_____

Active *beliefs*, pictures, self-talk (STT): _____

_____

Things I can say to *challenge* validity: _____

_____

Things I *could* do: _____

_____

What I actually *did do*: _____

_____

Keep your Contact Initiation Log for at least three weeks. It does take time and it does mean more paperwork, but it can also really help. So carry it with you and review it at the end of each work day.

ONE FINAL CHECK

Let's see if we can identify some of the self-limiting beliefs embedded in actual statements we have heard from call-reluctant salespeople and their managers over the years. Read each statement carefully. Then decide whether you think the statement is goal-supporting or goal-obstructing. Be careful. Some are tricky. Try to read between the lines. Look for underlying sources of self-pressurization.

Example:

1. "To be a success in this business you have got to have a positive mental attitude." Sounds like common sense. But is it goal-enhancing? Or, is it goal-obstructing?

Answer: Goal-Obstructing. It would be nice to have a positive outlook. Reasonable people prefer one over a negative, gloomy outlook. But the statement above is goal-obstructing for two reasons. First, it is simply not true. There are many top producers in every industry who are anything but positive. Some are morose! Just talking to them is like entering a dark mausoleum. Their level of financial success and their outlook on life are clearly unrelated. Their outlook does not necessarily help nor does it hinder their performance. Even so, we would still rather be positive than negative. But it's our choice, not a requirement.

Secondly, in the statement above, attitude has become more important than production. Some salespeople believe they cannot prospect or work unless and until they have a positive mental attitude. In that sense, the belief statement takes a desirable attribute, a positive mental attitude and stretches it until it becomes career-obstructive.

Now it's your turn. See what you can find in the following self-statements. Decide for yourself if they contain the seeds of self-growth or self-defeat. The answers are at the end of the exercise. Additionally, if you have the time, alone or with a group of your colleagues, determine what you would say to each of these people if you were their sales manager. How would you help them discover what they are really saying to themselves? How would you help them to see the effect that the statement has on their ability to prospect? ACTION BREAK.

2. "The last call I made got me so mad I can't call anybody else. But I'll get even. I'll call that miserable scum every hour on the hour till dawn!"

3. "I can't make calls until I get organized!"

4. "I'd like to learn as much as I can as fast as I can, but I've only been in this business for six months now and reasonable people won't expect me to know everything."

5. "How can you expect me to prospect right now? Can't you see I'm not in the mood? You lied to me about this career, about the hours I'd have to keep, and about how much money I'd make. God will get you for that!"

6. "When I make the Top Performers Club I'll have it made. I'll be up there with the big hitters. Then I'll feel more confident because people won't be doubting my ability anymore."

7. "Sure, I would like to have the respect of all the people I try to call on. But I know that I don't have to have it to do a good job."

8. "Eureka! I've finally landed on my feet. I just know this manager is gonna treat me right. Now I can prospect because I have finally found a sales organization that is going to make me happy!"

9. "I feel so terrible I can't work. Bob, one of my good friends who I influenced to come into this business, is doing very badly. I'm really upset."

10. "I can't really cut myself loose and begin to prospect until I know that this is really the right career for me."

Answers:

Goal-Supporting: 4,7
Goal-Obstructing: 2,3,5,6,8,9,10

What Next?

Now, turn to the next Rx section prescribed for the particular type of call reluctance you are working on.

The principle behind this process is simple but elegant. As you lower your fear response to that which you fear least about prospecting, your greater fears about prospecting will automatically be lowered by the same degree.

Chapter Six

R_X Two
THREAT DESENSITIZATION

PRIMARILY AFFECTS:	PRESCRIBED FOR:
Thoughts	✓ **Doomsayer**
	Over-Preparation
✓ **Feelings**	Hyper-Pro
	✓ **Stage Fright**
✓ **Actions**	Role Rejection
	✓ **Yielder**
	Social Self-Consciousness
	Separationist
	✓ **Emotionally Unemancipated**
	Referral Aversion
	✓ **Telephobia**
	✓ **Oppositional Reflex**

BRIEF OVERVIEW

Threat Desensitization consists of a small group of procedures you can use to cope with people and situations which threaten your daily prospecting performance and, for one reason or another, are resistant to word-based procedures.

How Does Threat Desensitization Work?

Threat Desensitization is a simple, four-step process. By seriously applying yourself to each of the steps you can significantly reduce the emotional effort it takes to initiate sales calls. The four steps are:

1. *Learning to relax* on cue
2. *Composing a list* of the things you associate with prospecting which trigger your fear response
3. *Ranking* the items on your list from most fearful to least fearful
4. *Learning to move through* the items on your list without experiencing immobilizing fear

Guiding Principles Behind
Threat Desensitization

1. *You are motivated* to really learn more effective means of coping with threat-sensitive call reluctance. You don't just want to talk about it or discuss it.
2. *Your motivation is goal-targeted.* You desire to overcome Doomsayer Call Reluctance so you can improve your prospecting efficiency.
3. Doomsayer Call Reluctance is primarily the product of inborn fight/flight mechanisms combined with learned reactions to perceived threats.
4. Your call-reluctant response to specific things, people and situations was *learned* and, therefore, can be *unlearned*.
5. Two contradictory feelings cannot be present at the same time; therefore, an individual cannot be simultaneously threatened and relaxed.
6. You can learn to tolerate, cope with, and even become accustomed to most prospecting circumstances regardless of the degree of the perceived threat.

Sighting the Target

Threat Desensitization is a makeover of Joseph Wolpe's Systematic Desensitization—tailored to the special needs of call-reluctant salespeople.

The technique can be described, as it usually is, with austere terms like Conditioned Stimulus, Unconditioned Response, Reciprocal Inhibition, Classical Conditioning, and Experimental Paradigm. Fortunately, there are other ways to describe the process.

Want to eat an elephant? Don't try to swallow it whole. Nibble on it, one small piece at a time. That's how Threat Desensitization works, one step at a time. First, you just explore your fear for awhile, reducing it to smaller pieces to nibble on. Then you rank your fears from least to worst on a subjective fear scale you construct. You then stage a mock confrontation, in your imagination, with each fear starting with the least fearful. You tentatively approach each one until you can successfully substitute the previously learned feeling of relaxation for the apprehension you now associate with the situation. Last, you transfer the skills you practiced in your imagination to real-life prospecting situations. You are now certain to be dazzled by the apparent migration of your newfound emotional management skills. It's called the Spread of Effect, or Stimulus Generalization. It works. Confused? Then think of it as the opposite of tactical seduction. Do we have your attention?

Most men already think in Threat Desensitization terms. They just don't know it. When in tenacious sexual pursuit, they talk of "first base," "second base," "home plate," and the always disappointing "strike out." These terms, uprooted from American baseball, have been used by generations of men to describe their dating progress. Though lacking concrete proof, we strongly suspect that women have their dating progress hierarchies, too.

Threat Desensitization works like strategic dating hierarchies. But instead of carefully building *up* to something positive in small, calculated moves, Threat Desensitization seeks to *remove* distress. It extracts the psychic stinger from call-reluctant situations in small, exact moves.

Threat Desensitization works best with specific, chronic fears such as making presentations to groups (Stage Fright) or distress associated with using the telephone to prospect. It is not recommended for more generalized fears such as "sense of dread," "low self-esteem," "poor self-confidence," or the "fear of failure."

Estimated Completion Time

The preparatory relaxation sequence and development of a *Perceived Prospecting Threat Inventory*: 5-6 days

Ability to visualize threatening prospecting situations without triggering a fear reaction: 1-2 weeks

Ability to approach actual prospecting situations without triggering a fear response: 2-3 weeks

HOW TO APPLY THREAT DESENSITIZATION

Step One: Learning to Relax

Learning to relax is the cornerstone upon which Threat Desensitization rests. Some salespeople are inclined to ridicule relaxation procedures like this one. If you are one of these, we need your patience and momentary cooperation, for this skill is a vital step in neutralizing your automatic fear reactions to specific prospecting situations.

You are going to learn how to relax your body muscle groups by tensing and releasing them while you recite a relaxation cue. This cue will then become paired with the sensation of relaxation that you experience when you release muscle tension.

To begin, find a quiet, nondistracting place and make yourself comfortable. You can either lie down or sit in a comfortable chair. You may wish to read the following relaxation dialogue into a tape recorder which you can then play back whenever you want to practice the exercise.

If you have recorded the instructions, turn the recorder on and close your eyes.

Relaxation Dialogue

Begin by clenching your right fist tightly. Notice how you can allow yourself to feel the other parts of your body as you feel the pressure in your right hand. Visualize your right hand clenched into a fist. Now let yourself become momentarily aware of how you are breathing and how you can feel the tension growing in your hand and up your forearm as you see your clenched fist grow tighter. Now imagine that you are looking at your fist through a large pair of binoculars. The binoculars have a special button on top of the lens near the front. Can you allow yourself to see it? Don't press it yet, but when you do it will flash a large multi-colored sign in front of your eyes that says "SET." The message "SET" is designed to automatically stay on for only two seconds. Then it automatically turns itself off until you press it again. If you can't allow yourself to see the word "SET," then just pretend you see it and continue.

As you feel your tightened right fist, take a deep breath and hold it for five seconds...now allow yourself to slowly exhale. At the moment you begin to exhale, depress the imaginary button one time. As you see yourself pressing the button, you can also see the word "SET," and as you do, slowly begin to relax your right hand. When it is relaxed, touch your left index finger to your thumb and say to yourself, "RELAX." Pause for thirty seconds. Now clench your right hand again, take another deep breath and hold it for five seconds...exhale, then press the imaginary button so you again see the word "SET" as you are exhaling and slowly releasing the pressure from your right hand.

When your hand is relaxed, again touch your left index finger to your left thumb and say, "RELAX." Pause for another thirty seconds, then continue the sequence one more time: Clench, deep breath, hold for five, press the button, see the word "SET," exhale and continue to slowly release the pressure from your hand until it is totally limp. Then, again touch your left index finger to your left thumb and say the word "RELAX." Now, just pause. Don't do anything for five minutes except to breathe deeply. Don't even try to notice how different your hand now feels compared to how it felt when it was clenched.

An Effective Short Cut to Relaxation

Most practitioners of relaxation techniques begin by relaxing a toe or a hand. They then move through every part of the body step-by-step. The method taught here, however, is a short cut. We have learned from experience that for our limited purposes we can achieve the same results with much less effort and in much less time. How? By teaching you a *code word* (SET) which prepares you to relax by first focusing your attention on relaxation. The word is not the process of relaxation itself. It merely *signals* you to focus your attention upon the process so that your relaxation response can then be easily triggered by the *cue word* (RELAX). Since you cannot relax and be tense at the same time, it logically follows that the relaxation response should spread throughout the body. With practice, your relaxation response can be called upon at will. When you find yourself in a potentially threatening situation, you can call up your relaxation response by saying your code word (SET) followed by your cue word (RELAX) and your body will reexperience the entire relaxation sequence. Practice it. Give it a try.

The ability to enlist your automatic relaxation response at will is the key to many stress reduction programs. It also plays an important part in other procedures in this book. Hence, it is important that you do not skim through the procedure. If you have Doomsayer Call Reluctance, and want to correct it, the battle starts right here, right now.

Step Two: Developing
Your Prospecting Threat Inventory

When we say that prospecting threatens us, what we really mean is that certain *aspects* of prospecting set off automatic fear responses which vary from person to person. What aspects of prospecting set off your automatic fear responses? What aspects of prospecting do you see as threatening? Take a few minutes to compile a list of all the people, situations and things associated with prospecting that you avoid or fear because you perceive them as potential threats.

Here is a partial list completed by Tom L., an experienced stockbroker, during one of our workshop sessions:

Prospecting Threat Inventory

1. *Preparing* to make a cold call
2. *Making* a cold call
3. Just *thinking* about making a cold call
4. *Showing up late* for the first sales appointment
5. *Being unprepared* for questions I might be asked
6. *Being watched* by my sales trainer as I give a prospecting presentation
7. *Not knowing* who will answer the phone
8. *Contacting someone who just had a bad experience* with the last salesman that contacted him
9. *Getting sick* while I'm there
10. *Calling someone who is already mad* for some other reason
11. Trying to psych myself up for the call, then *having a bad experience on the phone* and getting depressed
12. *Being ridiculed* or made a fool of

13. *Dropping my sales script* in the middle of a phone presentation

14. *Being forced by my trainer to make a call* before I say I'm ready

As you can see, Tom's list (which was actually much longer) contains several *themes*. The most obvious is cold-calling on the telephone. Now take a few minutes and construct your own Prospecting Threat Inventory. It can be as long or as short as you like. But be sure to list all the threatening things which come to mind about prospecting. Then look for the themes that are present in your inventory. If you cannot think of anything, then *just pretend, but go through the exercise*. It's important. ACTION BREAK.

The Self-Interview Approach

What themes emerge from your list? Cold calling? Using the phone? Asking for referrals? Being found unprepared? Sometimes it is hard to take a candid and objective look at ourselves. But the success of this procedure rests in part upon your having done that. So let's take a moment to play a mind game. Pretend you are a highly paid training consultant hired to review a very special case—yours. Interview yourself from the consultant's objective perspective. In front of a mirror, ask yourself aloud what prospecting situations frighten you the most. Check if anything should have been included on the list that was omitted. If so, go ahead and add it to your list. Some Doomsayers and Over-Preparers have taken several days to complete a *thorough* list. So give yourself all the time you need. But be careful! *Do not let the part of you which is call reluctant sabotage your efforts by insisting on a perfect list. That's a decoy tactic to keep you from completing your inventory. Don't fall for it!*

Step Three: Threat Ranking

Select any one of the themes from your inventory. On a separate piece of paper, copy everything from your list that relates to that theme. Then ask yourself, "Which one do I fear the most?" and assign it 100 prospecting distress points. It's important that you really get into the situation and make it as real as your imagination will allow. Try to observe as much detail as you can about the people, places, events and sensations associated with the situation. Then do the same thing with the least threatening item on your list and assign it ten prospecting distress points. Now all you need to do is fill in the middle ground between least and most threatening. The following is an example of an actual list. Look it over and then complete your own. ACTION BREAK.

Tom L. Stockbroker
Theme from Prospecting Threat Inventory:
Using the phone to prospect

Threatening Situations	Prospecting Distress Points
Getting into an argument with a prospect on the phone	50
Picking up the phone	85
Dialing the phone	60
Hearing the phone ring on the other end	40
Hearing the individual on the other end say "Hello"	100
Having a secretary answer the phone	70
Having the secretary ask me what the call "is in regards to"	75
Looking at the clock and realizing in 5 minutes I'm supposed to be on the phone prospecting	30
Hearing Bob and John talk about how many calls they just finished making	20
Seeing the number of phone calls my trainer listed for my daily objective	15

Notice that the *most* threatening item on Tom's list (100 distress points) is dialing the phone and hearing someone on the other end say "Hello." The *least* threatening item (15 distress points) is seeing the number of calls his trainer assigned for the day.

Step Four: Moving Through the Ranks

So far we have done the following: 1) Learned to relax on cue, 2) taken an inventory of those things about prospecting that threaten us, 3) identified distressful theme areas in our inventory, and 4) selected one theme and assigned prospecting distress points to each individual part.

What you have done so far has been in preparation for what comes next. You are about to imagine that you are in your *least* threatening situation. With the help of the following procedure, try to hold this image until you no longer experience the distress that you normally feel in that situation.

The principle behind this process is simple but elegant. As you lower your fear response to the least threatening element on your list, *the other elements will automatically be lowered by the same degree.* Some people get used to the water at the beach this way. They slowly immerse themselves a little at a time until they are completely wet. Though the water may seem cold at first, once completely wet, they find it hard, in retrospect, to imagine that the water ever was cold enough to be uncomfortable. It was certainly not cold enough to keep them out of the water! *If you closely follow the steps below*, you will see that Threat Desensitization works exactly the same way. Good swimming!

1. Find a place where you can be alone and will not be distracted for several minutes. Have the threat ranking exercise you just completed handy.

2. Assume a comfortable position. Use your code word (SET) and your cue word (RELAX) to allow yourself to become more relaxed.

3. Preferably with your eyes closed, allow your mind to visualize the least threatening item on your threat ranking list. Once you can see it, pretend to make it *as real as possible.* Notice any sensations you would experience if you were actually in that situation. Pretend to hear what you would actually hear if you were in that situation. Pretend to see the things you would see and smell the things you would smell.

4. Be alert for any sign of distress—regardless of how subtle it may be. Once you feel distress, take a deep breath. Then use your code word to focus your attention and your cue word to relax.

5. Notice any difference in how you allow yourself to feel? If you like the difference, nail it down by saying to yourself, "I can see myself in this situation, but now I can allow myself to be more relaxed."

6. Pause. Turn the scene off for a moment. Try to think only of the color gray, or just allow your mind to drift, but do not become too relaxed. Try not to fall asleep.

7. Repeat steps one through six again. Can you visualize the same scene again? Is it any clearer? What changes in the scene do you allow yourself to notice this time?

8. Once you have been able to go through steps one through six *three times in a row* while experiencing as little distress as you will allow, you can then proceed to repeat the process with the next higher item on your Prospecting Threat Inventory.

Walking Through the Process with Tom L.

Let's see how Tom, our stockbroker, did with the process. Tom had difficulty allowing other people to know how he was actually feeling. He even had trouble admitting that he needed help with his prospecting. Thus, since this procedure is self-administered, it was especially suitable for him.

He followed instructions by first removing himself from the ebb and flow of human enterprise. He practiced at home just before bedtime or in an empty office during his lunch hour. At first it was difficult for him to visualize a threatening scene from his inventory. So, thinking that he had found a loophole in the exercise, he compliantly *pretended* to visualize the situation as instructed. This is how he related his experience to a support group of other call-reluctant salespeople:

"After a few minutes, something funny happened. I forgot I was pretending and the whole scene began to play just like I was really there. When I realized I wasn't pretending anymore, it kind of hit me like one of those insights you get about yourself from time to time. And along with that insight came another one. I realized that I could visualize anything I wanted to, including the things that scare me about prospecting. I guess I just didn't want to see them, and I didn't particularly like the idea of other people telling me to picture something I didn't want to see."

Tom proceeded to use his code and cue.

"Earlier they had taught me how to do the code and cue thing, but for the life of me I couldn't see what good it was going to do for me."

He was soon to find out.

"As the scene got real to me, I did begin to feel some of the things I feel when I'm really sitting there listening to Steve, my trainer, tell me how many calls I'm supposed to make before the day is over. I could feel myself begin to fidget and tighten up all over. It became so real for me that I began to see and hear myself do what I always do, begin to make an excuse or change the subject or something. But then I remembered I was supposed to use the code and cue thing they taught me. I took a few quick deep breaths and then said SET and RELAX. It was fabulous. Almost immediately I could feel myself loosening up all over my body, just like my fist felt when I stopped clenching it. It was great. Once I could see what was happening, I practiced until I could get all the way through seeing my trainer giving me phone calling objectives for the day without feeling any [negative] reaction. It took me four times to get through it, but once I got up to speed I moved through the rest of the list fast. Hearing the prospect answer the phone used to scare the hell out of me. I can honestly say that I got to where [prospects] could say anything they wanted to and it wouldn't bother me."

You may be more or less successful than Tom. If the process comes easy, try moving through three or four items on your list in one sitting. Remember, however, to go through each item as many times as necessary until you can visualize the scene with as little distress as possible. Be sure to stop for the day if you feel bored, annoyed or overly distressed.

APPLICATION IN REAL LIFE PROSPECTING

So far, the procedure has only been applied in your head. But what happens when you face these prospecting threats in the real world? To your mind, there is very little difference between what you have rehearsed during this process and an actual prospecting situation; your mind does not qualitatively distinguish between the two. Your reaction to many of the events which once were threatening will now be markedly reduced or eliminated. This is because you have reengineered your mind to handle these situations, *real or imagined.*

Tom never learned to enjoy using the phone to prospect, but he did learn to stop fearing it. Today he uses it, along with other prospecting tools, to further his already successful career as a stockbroker.

"I didn't think much of [the procedure] on paper. But lucky for me I gave it a try. I won't say that it will work for everybody. But it worked for me, and if it could work for somebody like me, it ought to be able to work for damn near everybody."

DEBRIEFING AND PROGRESS MAINTENANCE

Debriefing has two purposes. The first is to help you determine what worked best for you so you can apply the procedure more effectively in the future if you should need a booster shot. The second is to find out what went wrong if you did not benefit from the procedure as much as you would like.

Your debriefing may be more effective if you have a friend interview you about your struggle with call reluctance and your recent experience with Threat Desensitization. If that is not possible, then interview yourself. Ask yourself the following questions and record your answers into a tape recorder for later review.

Debriefing Questions

- Did you apply this procedure alone, in a group, with a professional counselor, or with the help of a friend?

- Tell me about the use of the code and cue words. What are they and how do they work?

- What are the prospecting-related situations, people and things that formerly distressed you?

- Can you describe what it was like when distressful feelings blocked your career?

- What was the purpose of threat ranking?

- How did you go about threat ranking?

- How many times did you use your code and cue words with your least threatening item before you would allow yourself to feel less distressed?

- Did learning to *visualize* yourself prospecting with less distress result in less distress in the real life prospecting situation?

- Overall, do you think your experience with Threat Desensitization was a positive one?

- How closely did you follow the instructions?

- Do you have any other thoughts or feelings about your experience with Threat Desensitization?

Repeat the debriefing section if you think you need a booster shot. If you catch yourself regressing to the old response habits, repeat the entire procedure. Over the years, we have found that some call-reluctant sales-people, like Doomsayers, need to use this procedure once or twice a year—every year. For others, like the authors who are not naturally outgoing personalities and who are naturally predisposed to being Doomsayers, an inoculation of this procedure is required at least quarterly. For most call-reluctant salespeople, however, one shot properly administered will probably last your entire career.

Additional Reading

Would you like to read more about Threat Desensitization? There are several sources. Here is a representative, but not exhaustive, list of books which explain or apply the principles behind Threat Desensitization. Warning: These books range from pop-psych trivialities to narcissistic, pretentious textbooks.

Psychotechniques, by Dr. Salvatore V. Didato

Behaviour Therapy, by Australian psychologist Aubrey J. Yates

Behavior Therapy, by Rathus and Nevid

The Practice of Behavior Therapy, by Joseph Wolpe

Julia was addicted to the pleasures of escaping from any prospecting situation she feared. She was an avoidance junkie. Whereas some people get hooked on alcohol or sugar, others get hooked on the momentary pleasures associated with a successful escape.

Chapter Seven

R_X Three
NEGATIVE IMAGE PROJECTION

PRIMARILY AFFECTS:	PRESCRIBED FOR:
✓ **Thoughts**	Doomsayer
	✓ **Over-Preparation**
✓ **Feelings**	Hyper-Pro
	Stage Fright
Actions	✓ **Role Rejection**
	✓ **Yielder**
	Social Self-Consciousness
	Separationist
	Emotionally Unemancipated
	Referral Aversion
	Telephobia
	Oppositional Reflex

A BRIEF OVERVIEW

One of the chief characteristics of any self-crippling habit is the short-term *relief, gain* or *pleasure* it produces. This is why negative habits persist. Certain forms of call reluctance work the same way. For example, Over-Preparation, Yielder, and Role Rejection Call Reluctance all feature evasions which provide momentary escape and relief.

The Case of Julia Z.—Avoidance Junkie

Julia Z. was a salesperson with Yielder Call Reluctance. She tried to initiate contact with owners and managers of large organizations to sell her company's line of mini-computers. But Julia was afraid she would appear pushy or intrusive, so she procrastinated, waiting for the *right time* to make her calls. She experienced short-term relief when her cluttered social life interfered with her scheduled prospecting activities. Curiously, distracting social activities managed to surface almost every afternoon. Julia thought she was disorganized, scatterbrained or possibly suffering from signs of early senility. But a closer look at her avoidance behavior revealed a very organized and highly disciplined commitment. Her manager, in an attempt to help, sent her to two different time management and goal setting courses. They failed to make a difference, though not through any fault of their own.

Julia was psychologically *addicted* to the pleasures of escaping from prospecting situations she feared. She was an *avoidance junkie*. Some people get hooked on alcohol, some on sugar, others on the momentary pleasures associated with a successful escape. Paradoxically, salespeople like Julia experience a rush of relief when they successfully *avoid* having to prospect. But the escape exacts a heavy toll. In the case of Julia, it made prospecting even more difficult and emotionally charged; she fell behind in her prospecting activity and ran out of people to sell to. Julia's sales career fell apart, imploded. Worst of all, her failure might have been avoided had she learned how to apply Negative Image Projection.

How Does Negative Image Projection Work?

Negative Image Projection is a mental process you can apply to yourself. It is based on the understanding that self-limiting habits become strengthened (reinforced) *by repetition and association with sensations of immediate relief*. Therefore, the key to eliminating these habits is to disconnect them from the momentary gain that accompanies them, even if the gain is only a feeling of relief. This is done by *repeatedly* associating the habit with obnoxious (negative) mental imagery. After some repetition, the old habit will no longer be bonded to its pleasant sensations. Instead, it will be linked by habit to disgusting, noxious, repulsive images. Under these circumstances, *prospecting becomes the more desirable choice*!

Guiding Principles
Behind Negative Image Projection

1. *You are motivated* to overcome call-reluctant reactions to prospecting.

2. To improve your prospecting activity, *your motivation is directed* specifically towards reducing unwanted distressful feelings associated with prospecting.

3. Feelings can enhance or impede the flow of motivation towards goal-directed behaviors.

4. Habits of escape result in momentary feelings of relief.

5. Relief from having to prospect feels good and reinforces whatever method you used to evade prospecting.

6. Pairing your evasive behavior with a pleasant sensation (relief) increases the likelihood that you will use that behavior again.

7. Repeated evasions become *habits* which, like all habits, grow stronger when repeated and reinforced.

8. Habits can be eliminated if the link between them and the pleasant sensations they evoke is broken.

Sighting the Target

Negative Image Projection is particularly suited to call-reluctant habits which result in predictable patterns of escape and avoidance. The Over-Preparer escapes by reading another book or journal article. The Yielder visits and drinks more coffee. The salesperson with Role Rejection listens to another inspirational cassette. This technique is easy to learn and many salespeople have even enjoyed using it—although we cannot discern how.

Estimated Completion Time

Meaningful results will usually take about a week, though some salespeople have reported lasting results within a few days.

POSITIVE ATTITUDE VS. NEGATIVE IMAGES

If you survey the many available self-help books, cassettes and articles on this subject, you will find that most of them accent self-confidence and a positive mental attitude as the essential foundations for a successful career in sales. There are some courageous exceptions, like Paul Buckner's article, "The Negative Side of Positive Thinking." But optimistic positivism represents the majority viewpoint. Thus, we are somewhat reluctant to introduce a skill for using negative images to correct certain forms of call reluctance which are popularly believed to come from negative attitudes in the first place. Nevertheless, try to suspend judgment and we will explain why we think you will find this to be among the preferred procedures for correcting the three call reluctance types mentioned previously.

Lunch With Kevin and Brian

Brian T., a young consultant for a prominent sales training firm, is still enjoying a lunch which started at 11:30. It's now 1:15. Brian realizes that one of his responsibilities as a trainer-consultant is to generate new business. This requires him to spend time in the office on the telephone, something he should be doing now. But he and Kevin, one of his co-workers, feel obligated to order another vodka and tonic to soften the afternoon's phone calls. Brian knows better but, as usual, offers no resistance as he lifts his glass toward the waitress and says, "How about a refill?"

Both Brian and Kevin are motivated, goal-directed sales training consultants. Neither, however, is generating new business at a satisfactory level. Harold "Bubba" Kline, their managing director, is growing weary of having to repeatedly point out to them that they spend too much time at lunch and on breaks and not enough time calling on prospective clients. Their production shows it.

Neither is an alcoholic, so why don't they stop? The next round of drinks will waste more valuable prospecting time. Plus, when they *do* return to the office, their productivity will be low. And by three or four in the afternoon, they will experience episodes of energy-sapping stress as they struggle to catch up.

Let's view this situation under a microscope. As Brian and Kevin sit and discuss the afternoon's prospecting, multiple images pass in mental review, images of calling on prospective clients. Locked in step with the images are negative memories and sensations they associate with the images. So when another drink is suggested as an alternative to prospecting, both Brian and Kevin flash to a new set of mental images paired to a glass of crystal clear liquid anesthetic. Unlike prospecting, these images are potent and beguilingly pleasant.

This ritual occurs whenever Brian and Kevin have lunch together prior to an afternoon of prospecting. And since they lunch together every day, this scene is replayed every day, and the escape route is strengthened *every day, day after day after day after day...*

A Few Other Pleasant Escapes

The same thing happens when you shuffle through your presentation notes instead of contacting people whom you know might be interested in your product or service. But wouldn't they question your competence if you were unable to answer their questions? If you have Over-Preparation Call Reluctance, your answer is "yes," but it doesn't stop there. You actually *project* the images and feel the sensations you think your prospects would experience if they were to consider you incompetent and uninformed. By contrast, your presentation notes feel better than making the call, so you momentarily escape by shuffling and reshuffling the notes.

The same thing happens when you refuse to contact a person who needs your company's services (Yielder Call Reluctance). Instead of making the call, you feel compelled to escape from sinister images of yourself being accused of being too aggressive or intrusive and the feelings of loss of approval which accompany them. To cope, you search for a more pleasant image. You see yourself gossiping with your friends in the company cafeteria; feeling the comforting warmth of coffee in your mouth, sliding down your throat, warming the bottom of your stomach. Prospecting cannot successfully compete with such escapist imagery. Bali Hai is calling, you are answering and your sales career is paying the price.

BREAKING THE BOND

Disconnecting pleasurable habits associated with escaping from things we wish to *avoid* is different than eliminating habits like smoking, nail biting or nervous tics. Why? Because most people consider nail biting and nervous tics undesirable and want to be rid of them. Call reluctance habits, however, provide immediate positive gain in the form of escape. The momentary relief call-reluctant salespeople get when they successfully evade having to prospect *feels good.* So how do you break a habit which produces a feeling you like as opposed to dislike? By transforming the outcome from a positive to a negative, from relief to repulsion, from psychic pleasure to psychic pain.

Step One: Relax on Command

The first step in using Negative Image Projection is learning how to allow yourself to relax on command. You can do this by referring to "Step One: Learning to Relax" in the chapter on Threat Desensitization.

Step Two: Examine Your Escape Route

Next, think about the escape route you use to escape from prospecting. Do you pretend to be sick? Do you lie to your manager? Do you shuffle prospect cards? Do you extend your coffee breaks longer than you should? Do you go on endless searches for *more* information? What exactly do you do? Localize the event. Where are you located when you first feel the need to escape? What are you doing? Who are you with, if anyone? For Brian, when lunch approaches, can prospecting be far away? His thoughts seek out a more tolerable theme.

Step Three: Fill in the Details

Now relax. Fill in the details of your prospecting escape route. List *in sequence* all the pleasurable things you associate with your escape route. Be detailed. Be graphic. Be explicit.

Fifteen minutes prior to lunch, Brian begins to see flashing *images* of himself entering the restaurant, reviewing the menu, placing the order with the waitress, holding the glass of vodka and tonic, and having an enjoyable conversation with Kevin. He mentally rehearses his escape before he actually arrives at lunch.

As you imagine going through your escape route, it would be helpful to number each step along the way for later use.

Step Four: List Your Repulsers

The next step is to compile a list of things which immediately repulse you whenever you think of them. Everybody has some. To make the job easier, we have listed some suggestions below. Take out a piece of paper and copy those items from our list which are especially repulsive to you. Feel free to add any of your own.

The Repulser Sampler

- Fingernails screeching across a blackboard
- Painful injection by needle directly into your stomach
- Kissing the face of a dead person whose eyes are open and looking directly at you
- Your dentist deep-drilling your teeth
- Open, infected, running wounds
- Standing several stories up and looking straight down with nothing to hang onto
- Stench of dead, decaying animals on a hot day
- Having blood drawn directly from an artery in your neck
- Sinking neck-deep into a pit of slimy, slithering snakes
- Insects crawling into your mouth while you are sound asleep
- Vomiting uncontrollably in a restaurant
- Unknowingly stepping on a live rat
- Absentmindedly saying a sexual obscenity while making a presentation to an auditorium full of family members
- Knowing a spider has dropped down your shirt (or blouse) during an important presentation and not being able to scream or get it out
- Unknowingly squashing live worms underfoot as you walk into a dark room

Select as many items from the list of repulsers as there are steps in your escape route. Choose only those items which turn you off the most. (If any of the above items turn you on, there are other books you should be reading.) The items you choose should produce distinct sensory impressions which result in clear physical sensations. Don't play safe. These choices are important. The procedure will only work if your selections cause you to be grossed out.

Step Five: Applying Your Repulsers

This step depends upon your success with the previous two steps (breaking down the pleasurable components in your escape route and selecting your repulsers). Connect each step of your escape route to one of your repulsers, creating narrative pairs similar to this: "As the time to prospect draws near, I start to shuffle my prospect cards. The more I fondle them, the more I...can smell the stench of dead, decaying animals on a hot summer's day."

Here is how Brian broke the habit of social drinking in lieu of telephone prospecting. He started by mentally rehearsing the escape scene. He remembered and imagined each good sensation he felt while escaping. *Then, when he had the first item of his escape route in mind, and felt the pleasant sensations which accompanied it, he inserted one of the repulsers which immediately and dramatically changed his reaction from pleasure to disgust.*

"I saw myself getting ready to order the next drink. Looking into her (the waitress's) face. Hearing Kevin ask me to order one more. Placing the order. *Then I saw this guy who always sat in a nearby booth. He was unremarkable in every respect but one: He had the ugliest open running wounds I have ever seen covering both arms. He was a real gross-out. I wanted to leave right then and there.*

"Next, I saw myself enjoying the drink. Feeling the glass. Tasting it. Feeling the warmth as it slid down my throat. Listening to Kevin complain about his boss, his job, life in general. *As he spoke, I saw myself being drawn down neck-deep into a pit of slippery, wet snakes. I wanted to get out of there real bad. Then I smelled the stench of dead and decaying animals which I discovered were under our table. The smell was gagging. I thought I was going to vomit all over the restaurant table. I told Kevin I had to leave and immediately got out of there. I remember thinking, 'I would rather prospect than stay there.'* Heading back to the office, the air felt refreshing. I felt relief, like I had escaped from something. I was ready to get back to work. I was ready to prospect."

Make sure that you turn off your repulsers as soon as you make your escape. Then allow yourself to feel relief and relaxation.

Now you are ready to apply the relaxation skill you learned in step one. After you have paired repulsers with each of the pleasure traps in your escape route, relax and close your eyes. Dwell on the first escape item. Fix it clearly in your mind. Pretend to be there. Hear the sounds. Smell the odors. Feel the textures. Taste the flavors. Then, when you have the scene in mind, go *immediately* to the paired repulser. Once you have the repulser in mind, stay with it for at least a few seconds or until you have displaced any pleasurable sensations associated with the first escape item. Progress through each item on your escape route until you have successfully experienced pairing all of them with a repulser.

Step Six: Disengaging the Repulsers

Relive your escape scenario again. But this time avoid the repulsers by imagining yourself sidestepping the once pleasurable escape route and making your calls instead.

As soon as you feel the need to fondle your prospect cards, as opposed to using them one at a time to make calls, you will begin to smell the stench of death and decay. But you can make it go away by going directly to the telephone and making calls. Repeat the sequence several times, pairing the prospect cards with immediate use of the telephone. You will soon learn that it is easier to make calls than to remain totally grossed out.

A REVIEW AND FINAL STEP

Let's review the essential steps:

1. Build a detailed description of your escape route.

2. Just as you begin to enjoy the pleasures of escaping, introduce a repulser.

3. Continue to pair repulsers to the escape route until you permit yourself to sidestep the escape route in favor of making calls. At that time, and only at that time, stop using the repulsers.

You have learned how to make the pleasure of escape disgusting. But by doing so, you have not made prospecting any more enjoyable. To do that, whenever you successfully make a call as opposed to avoiding it, list three things you are moved closer to realizing or obtaining because you made the call. Do that immediately after you make each call regardless of its outcome.

Watch out for understanding. The compulsion to understand everything about call reluctance can get you into serious trouble. Dance around it. It's a booby trap.

Chapter Eight

R$_X$ Four
FEAR INVERSION

PRIMARILY AFFECTS:	PRESCRIBED FOR:
Thoughts	Doomsayer
	Over-Preparation
Feelings	✓ **Hyper-Pro**
	Stage Fright
✓ **Actions**	Role Rejection
	Yielder
	Social Self-Consciousness
	Separationist
	Emotionally Unemancipated
	Referral Aversion
	Telephobia
	✓ **Oppositional Reflex**

A BRIEF OVERVIEW

Motivation empowers us. As it surges through us, it provides the energy necessary for accomplishing our goals. But sometimes our motivation gets misdirected or interrupted. Wires get crossed. Sparks arc across conflicting intentions. Our energy is pirated away to other purposes. The result is a motivational short circuit. In complex behaviors like Oppositional Reflex Call Reluctance, the flow of motivational energy gets reversed. Positive becomes negative, negative becomes positive. Instead of energizing us on to greater achievement, it turns angrily back on itself. Our options become limited to a few rigid counterproductive parodies of our true talent and ability.

Of all the known procedures for dealing with Oppositional Reflex Call Reluctance, Fear Inversion is the one found to be the most helpful. But unlike the other procedures in this book, Fear Inversion is a blind application. It must be applied without an explanation of what it is, or how it works.

Guiding Principles Behind Fear Inversion

1. You *acknowledge* that Oppositional Reflex Call Reluctance is a problem which limits your prospecting.

2. *You are motivated* to improve.

3. You, like all salespeople, have *choices*.

4. Much of what you are today, and will be tomorrow, is due to choices you make.

5. Although your behavior has been influenced by instinct, inheritance, predisposition, and your sales environment, you can still exercise the freedom to choose within those preconditions.

6. *You already have the knowledge, motivation and discipline* you need in order to change. They have just been misdirected.

7. In dealing with Oppositional Reflex Call Reluctance, the pursuit of understanding and self-knowledge is wasteful and usually futile.

8. *Taking responsibility* for what you do, rather than what you know, is the essential building block.

9. You have at least a minimal *imagination*.

10. You have at least a minimal *sense of humor*.

11. You have at least a minimal *ability to tolerate ambiguity and follow instructions*.

Sighting the Target

Fear Inversion is based on your inclination to act in opposites. It will not change your life, only your prospecting behavior. It is fast and very powerful. It can be particularly helpful to Oppositional salespeople (or managers) who may be coping with problems like "anxiety attacks," social embarrassment, fear of being exposed (for who you "really" are), or loss of self-control. It works quickly and sometimes very dramatically because it does not rely on *understanding*. It targets the way you ineffectively cope. In addition to Oppositionality, it may also be effective with Hyper-Pro Call

Reluctance. It is not particularly suited for any other types. It makes sense to the people who need it and makes no sense whatsoever to those who do not.

Estimated Completion Time

Used correctly, Fear Inversion is one of the fastest and most mysterious procedures in the entire arsenal of behavior change techniques. *The key is to use it correctly. The instructions must be followed in the order given.*

Side Effects

This procedure, unlike others in this book, may have side effects on some readers. A few salespeople (more managers, most consultants, every attorney) will strongly react to the procedure by insisting that it is comically shallow, boring, beneath them, theoretically confused, and won't work for *them*. If that happens to you, don't be dismayed. It's a predictable side effect. It's proof that the medicine is having an effect on your call reluctance.

Failure Rate

Success does not come easy to salespeople with Oppositional Reflex Call Reluctance, even when Fear Inversion is used. The reason is straightforward. Oppositional Reflex Call Reluctance is much more complex than the other forms of call reluctance and requires more complex countermeasures. Arguably, procedures like Fear Inversion should be used only by professionals with specialized call reluctance training. But go ahead and try it. You could be among the important exceptions. And even if you are not, you may still derive some benefit from the experience.

THE PROCESS BEGINS

Oppositional Reflex Call Reluctance actually consists of two basic processes, anticipation and covering. Together, they combine to form one of the most vicious forms of call reluctance identified so far. Highly motivated, intelligent and creative salespeople who are coping with an *unrealistically low impression of themselves* are the most vulnerable to this form of call reluctance. It is among the most stubborn types to overcome because its victims often become unwitting co-conspirators, using highly intelligent, creative and circuitous means to cope.

Psychologist Michael Nichols claims that inadequate self-respect primarily originates from unresolved shame. He seems to agree that self-talk techniques are of limited utility: "Overcoming insecurity is the theme of countless self-help books, and the popularity of these books attests to the universality of the wish for greater self-esteem. Their continuing flow proves that self-doubt doesn't go away easily. Most of the usual advice boils down to trying to talk yourself out of being insecure. Some authors advise identifying your 'critical inner voices' and then talking back to them. Dale Carnegie called the technique 'the power of positive thinking'...The trouble with reassurance is that it doesn't last. You can turn from one book to another and go from friend to friend for pep talks and inspiration, but none of this encouragement will have a lasting effect...You can't create self-respect by...talking yourself into it." (*No Place to Hide*, Michael P. Nichols, Ph.D.).

Anticipation

Oppositional salespeople fearfully *anticipate* certain people, prospecting events, or situations. In so doing, they set themselves up for a complete emotional wipeout. If and when the event actually does occur, they are overwhelmed by the fear they anticipated. Then the distressing encounter is used as additional justification to fearfully anticipate the event happening again! So Oppositionality is actually a part of a fear cycle. The anticipation phase can be so self-restricting that some salespeople do not even want to know *what* is frightening them because they fear they would be emotionally overwhelmed if they ever found out. The plot thickens.

Covering

Salespeople with Oppositional Reflex Call Reluctance are almost always highly motivated perfectionists who are mercilessly self-critical. They tolerate some imperfection in others but refuse to allow themselves to be less than perfect in every respect. They are concerned about even *appearing* less than perfect, an awkward objective for someone who is call reluctant. And since they are afraid of being seen as weak, immature or out of control, they go to considerable lengths to hide blemishes such as their call reluctance. Afraid of being afraid, they seek relative safety behind a facade of superior taste, intellectual ability, and the appearance of internal strength. With the passage of time, they may begin to gradually believe and then passionately defend their cover while feeling fragmented and unsure of how and when it all began. The weaker an Oppositional salesperson believes he or she is, the more he or she is likely to feel the need for a cover. Thus, the amount of motivation lost to covering a perceived deficiency is proportionate to the perceived need to compensate for being just the *opposite*. For example, an Oppositional consultant who thinks that people might hold his advice in low esteem covers by growing a Freudian beard and liberally sprinkling his conversation with psychobabble. Another who believes her competence might be suspect attempts to cover by papering her office with ego-inflating degrees, awards, plaques, certificates and French provincial furniture. Yet another who thinks his worth is suspect may costume himself in designer clothes, join a country club, and endlessly drop the names of influential people he knows or just knows of. Sound familiar?

Prospecting Charades

If you are a Hyper-Pro or have Oppositional Reflex Call Reluctance, you are probably investing too much energy in your image and not enough in fundamentals like prospecting. Like Hyper-Pros, Oppositional salespeople allow image enhancements to become exaggerated and distorted into complete lifestyles. Enhancements such as appearance, name dropping, cars, cameras and watches become ends in themselves. By emphatically displaying the symbols of success, Hyper-Pros and Oppositional salespeople become immersed in the charade of accomplishment. But the similarity ends there. Hyper-Pros are usually able to recognize and acknowledge their image-oriented lifestyles. Many even find some humor in it. Able to accept their call reluctance, Hyper-Pros have the readiness to do something about it, which means countermeasures prescribed to reduce the over-importance they place on appearance can immediately be applied.

Oppositional salespeople are another matter altogether. To point out, criticize or ignore any element of their charade is likely to be interpreted as a personal *attack*. Thus, simply offering advice can be seen as an attempt to scratch their veneer of accomplishment. Oppositionals have difficulty acknowledging their call reluctance, so a countermeasure engineered to help them lighten up and take responsibility for what they are doing to themselves must be inserted first. Does this describe you?

Above Average?

Oppositional salespeople are driven to seek out new ways to distance themselves from other salespeople, a race they consider to be inferior and sometimes hold in secret contempt. To them, other salespeople hustle; *they* "market." Other salespeople have been indoctrinated; *they* have been educated. Others prospect for new business; *they* hold out for quality rather than quantity. Consequently, *they* characteristically initiate fewer numbers of contacts with prospective buyers (often alarmingly few), a practice which they defend with allusions to large, pie-in-the-sky cases that are always just around the proverbial corner.

As a matter of personal principle, some insist on trying to circumvent prospecting altogether. To them, prospecting is a demeaning and un-professional activity that is only done by lesser salespeople. Thus, some spend the majority of their prospecting time trying to find ways to get prospective clients to come to *them*. Others cover by investing their time, energy and money in the ceremonial dance of professionalism: Instead of initiating contact with prospective clients on a consistent, daily basis, they join professional organizations, climb the political ranks, and conduct themselves with the solemnity of a valedictorian at a high school gradua-tion. Some write books. Others climb onto the speakers circuit. Few prospect. Fewer can readily admit to being call reluctant. None earn what they are worth.

Critical Reflexes

If you have Oppositional Reflex Call Reluctance, you probably try to avoid objective self-evaluation and may have a history of discrediting the people and procedures that could offer help.

Are you a master dabbler in the enlightenments of our time? Are you fluent in the latest pop psych jargon? Do you find yourself reciting running commentaries on behavior change techniques in lieu of seriously trying to apply them to yourself?

If you answered "yes" to any of the above questions, you have probably tried them all: role playing, mind control, biofeedback, sensitivity train-ing, Est, Neurolinguistic Programming, Transactional Analysis, and all the other attempts to explain the irony and complexity of the human experience. Your exposure to these programs probably followed a predict-able pattern. First, you took small doses over a very short time. Second, you failed to adhere to instructions or complete assignments. Third, you concluded that the program was not effective and reduced it to just another disappointment. Right? The procedure was shallow, or the practitioner was misguided, or the time was just not right for you to change. It never is. So, predictably, you dropped out, unenlightened and unchanged. Again.

Exit Ramp Number One

The ritual above is common to Oppositionals; it's one of the ways they cope—unsuccessfully. Are you Oppositional? If you are, maybe this time will be different, maybe it won't. But if you are going to drop out again, read no further. Do it now. It's your choice.

On Being Right

Congratulations! Since you're still reading, we assume you have decided to fight toe-to-toe with the urge to drop out. Most Oppositional salespeople can't make the choice you just made. Regrettably, most don't get any further than the last part of the last paragraph. Here's why.

Salespeople with Oppositional Reflex Call Reluctance listen and read on two levels simultaneously. One level is fueled by curiosity plus a genuine desire to perform at peak levels. This quality has brought you to this point.

Operating at a second, more subtle level is the part of you that fears prospecting and probably a lot of other things as well. It works to keep you at an intellectual-only, safe distance from the content and purpose of books like this one. It will entrap you in petty, nitpicking, fault-finding and involuntary critical commentary about what you read *while you are reading it*. Then it will try to discredit the content and persuade you against taking it seriously. Since the content is deemed unacceptable, you are relieved from any practical obligation to try it. Winning another speechless debate, you lose the opportunity to change.

If you will candidly observe yourself for a moment, you may notice that you have been evaluating what you have been reading. You are probably doing it right now. But grant us the use of one platitude: In the battle with Oppositional Reflex Call Reluctance, *being right is the booby prize*.

Risking

The tendency to deflect personal responsibility for call reluctance is the primary reason that your corrective efforts usually fail regardless of which procedure is being used or who is trying to help you. So the first step to overcome Oppositional Reflex Call Reluctance is to take a risk. If your prospecting activity is below what you know your ability to be, then you must assume personal responsibility for not performing at your actual level and resolve to do something meaningful about it. Now.

True. It's a risk. You may succeed or you may fail. But the act of trying will level the first deafening blow to your call reluctance by reaffirming your ability to allow yourself to try. Risking growth is an act of personal strength that defies the infantile part of you which has successfully asserted up to now that you could never be afraid and prospect, never be afraid and survive. You can. Give it a try.

Exit Ramp Number Two

The process of Fear Inversion begins with four agreements you make with yourself. Each should be considered carefully.

Agreement Number One: Do you agree to acknowledge that your prospecting activity is not consistent with your level of ability? Yes or no?

Agreement Number Two: Do you agree to temporarily suspend your tendency to blame, criticize or make excuses for your call-reluctant behavior? Yes or no?

Agreement Number Three: Will you honestly make an effort to do something significant about your call reluctance other than just thinking about it or talking about it? Yes or no?

Agreement Number Four: Do you agree to follow our instructions completely and in the order they are given without demanding any explanations? Yes or no?

Can you allow yourself to agree? If you can accept these terms, you are ready to proceed with a mysterious but effective process you should find helpful. If you cannot or will not agree to the terms, then stop reading at this point and turn instead to a less-demanding self-help book, cassette or video program, one which is less threatening. (Be careful here. Your decision will be made by choice or by default. One or the other. Continuing to read or skim beyond this point without agreeing or responding to the terms above psychologically invalidates this procedure for you because it interprets your answers to be "no.")

FEAR INVERSION DAY-BY-DAY

Days One and Two

The first two days of Fear Inversion are devoted to learning to follow instructions. This will be done by unplugging your critical reflex circuit. You will use a simplified form of Thought Zapping. Begin by placing a rubber band on your left wrist. Whenever you find yourself about to criticize, add to, modify or amend in any way what you read or what people say to you sting your wrist while imagining yourself yelling "Stop it!" as loud as you can. Unless you derive pleasure from pain, your reflexive criticality is about to enter the last two days of its life.

Does this mean you should never criticize? No, it just means you will not do it as a lifestyle, automatically, all the time. Actually, your criticisms will become more authentic since they will be made from choice, not mindless reflex.

Day Three

Watch out for understanding. The compulsion to understand more about Oppositional Reflex Call Reluctance can get you into deep trouble. Dance around it. It's a booby trap. Though the path to greater understanding looks productive, interesting and worthwhile, be forewarned. It already boasts a very high body count. Yours would make a nice addition. You do not have to understand everything about your automobile to drive it. You don't have to know everything about your call reluctance to change it. You probably already know if you have it, and you probably already know why. Your success depends on doing something about it.

Begin this day's activities by examining your Fear Cycle. Concentrate on what you actually do in reaction to your fears about prospecting. But think about what you do simply as an inefficient action. Try not to think of it as a symptom, problem or imperfection. It's not. It's just what you do under certain circumstances. Describe it to yourself non-judgmentally. Think about what you do, though it won't be easy. But don't fight it. Allow the part of you that fears (humiliation, exposure or whatever) the right to control your answer. When it senses the time is right, the recollection of what you do when you are afraid will float to the surface of your consciousness. When it does, copy it on a piece of paper. Here's an example:

"When I try to prospect...I guess I get a little defensive and hostile."

Now rewrite your answer in terms of your behavior. For example, "I get defensive and hostile" really means:

"I get belligerent with my trainer and argue that prospecting is unprofessional."

Day Four

We have provided a list of short questions for you to answer during today's activities. The questions are all about prospecting. When you are alone at home or in your office, stand in front of a full length mirror.

Verbally ask the questions *one at a time* to your image in the mirror. Then answer each one as completely and honestly as you can. Spend at least five minutes, preferably more, answering each question. As you answer each question, allow the critic in you to take complete control. Notice your image in the mirror. How are you standing? How does your voice sound? How do you look? Are your answers really honest? Are they logically sound? Make yourself find fault with what you see and hear and verbally criticize as much as you can as long as you can.

This activity can be even more effective if it is videotaped. If you videotape the activity, first record your spontaneous answers to the questions *without* criticism. Then play the tape back and make yourself criticize what you see and hear yourself saying.

Questions to Ask Yourself:

- Where are you when you experience call reluctance?

- What exactly are you doing when your call reluctance begins?

- How long do you tend to continue behaving this way once it begins?

- What do you feel?

- Could you make yourself feel this way more on Tuesdays than on Thursdays?

- Does your call reluctance feel the same when you are dressed in a blue shirt or blouse as it does when you are dressed in a white shirt or blouse?

- What mental images do you see?

- What are the usual reasons you give for behaving this way (fear of rejection, etc.)?

- Do you really want to change this behavior? Yes or no?

If you answered the last question "yes," you are probably being too uncritical. If you answered "no," you have taken a risk by being very forthright with yourself and have clearly demonstrated that you are prepared to continue to the next section.

Day Five

Why are you reading this book? Most people give very general reasons for wanting to improve or correct something within themselves. But we would like you to be as focused as possible on the payoffs you desire for yourself. You need to state your goal in your own language and in terms that are meaningful to you and which you can dedicate yourself to. For example, instead of just saying, "I want to stop being call reluctant," you could say, "I want to stop feeling so demeaned when I try to make prospecting phone calls." Or you could say that you wanted to stop critically jumping on people and discrediting what they say before they finish saying it. As a general rule, your objective should be stated in terms of a *behavior* as opposed to a principle, idea, concept or virtue such as "be a better salesperson."

So take a look at the examples below and decide what you would consider a successful goal for you.

- To never fear prospecting again

- To reduce the frequency of call reluctance episodes

- To lower the intensity of call reluctance episodes when they do occur

- To recognize that call reluctance episodes may occur, but learn to tolerate them better

- To be call reluctant only if and when *I want to be*

- To decrease the duration of call reluctance episodes

Based on the information above, decide what conditions must be met for you to consider this process a success. The process cannot continue indefinitely, so be sure to include a cutoff date. For example, "If by the end of six days I have at least improved based on the conditions I established above, then I consider the enterprise to have been successful." The termination date can be any reasonable length of time, but it should be no less than six days.

Day Six

Spend the sixth day reviewing what you have done in the past to cope with your call reluctance. Some salespeople forget their sales script to avoid having to recite it. Some become passive and overly apologetic when initiating contact with prospective buyers. Others conceal their fear by defensively lashing out with face-saving arguments. Some feel faint. Some protect themselves by imposing a cynical and sarcastic wall between them and their prospecting duties. What do you do? (Subtle hint: The answer is probably embedded somewhere in the critical conversation you had with yourself on the fourth day.)

Day Seven

Devote the seventh day to total and absolute resistance. Let your mind wander (do not force it) to as many excuses as you can possibly think of for *dropping out now and refusing to seriously continue this procedure.* It's not necessary to write down all your excuses but it would be very helpful. It is necessary, however, to keep a running total of *how many* excuses come to mind during the course of the seventh day. Begin your list by selecting at least two excuses from the list below. This should help you get started. Then if you wish to, write down all the excuses you can think of during the day on a small piece of paper. If you don't want to write your excuses down, then just keep a running total of how many excuses come to mind on a piece of paper folded into the approximate size of a dollar bill.

Carry the dollar-sized piece of paper you use to record your excuses (and running total) in your wallet where you normally keep your paper money. Keep it with you for the entire seventh day.

Examples to Get You Started (Select at Least Two):

- This is superficial. It's not helping me.

- The authors have never sold anything *themselves*.

- The authors have never *really* had call reluctance.

- Everybody else has call reluctance, so why shouldn't I?

- Having call reluctance is my prerogative.

- It won't work anyway, nothing will.

- Even if it does work, it won't last.

- I'll look like a stupid fool if I try this procedure.

- It will destroy my positive attitude.

Now it's your turn.

Day Eight

The prescription for the eighth day may strike you as preposterous, but remember: You agreed to follow our instructions. Refer back to day six. Review what you allowed yourself to learn carefully. What did your fears let you discover? How do you cope with your call reluctance? Forgetting? Feeling faint? Arguing? Cynicism? Denial?

Today, just relax and be yourself—sort of. At *every* appropriate opportunity, you are to *mimic and exaggerate* the way(s) you have typically coped with your call reluctance in the past. Overact. Be melodramatic. Really ham it up. Get into it. Make it real.

If you feel demeaned by having to make prospecting phone calls, then make several intensely demeaning phone calls. Feel really demeaned.

If you tend to lash out at and argue with your managers, then today do so intentionally. Try to create arguments. Be contentious. Combative. Dispute everything. Try to keep a straight face while being intensely hostile.

If you tend to be uncoachable, create situations in which you can act like you already know everything. Find as many opportunities as you can where you can refuse to be advised, coached, managed or trained. Act haughty. Know it all.

Day Nine

On the ninth day, tell at least one person *you do not particularly like or trust* that you have been reading this book and trying out one of the procedures. Use as many of the following negative points as possible to explain to them that the *procedure does not work and the book is not worth reading.* Be as convincing as possible. (You can explain your actions later if you wish to, after you have completed all of your activities.)

Negative Points List

- You have already tried all the procedures in this book. None work.

- You have *never really been* call reluctant.

- Call reluctance can't penetrate *your* positive attitude.

- You are pretending to be call reluctant just to be able to try a procedure in this book.

- Actually, you are just evaluating this book for your home office, local manager or a friend to see if it has possibilities. It doesn't. It's no good.

Optional Day Ten

We typically encourage individuals we work with personally to contact us at the end of the ninth day to get special instructions for the tenth day. The tenth day is entirely optional, but useful. It helps assure complete follow-through, like continuing to take a prescribed antibiotic long after your symptoms have vanished.

It's difficult for us to assign your tenth day follow-through task without the benefit of firsthand observation. But we are willing to try. If you have successfully completed the ninth day and want to get instructions for your tenth day's activity, here's how:

Near the end of the ninth day, complete the form below.

Fax your form to: Fear Inversion c/o the publisher at (972) 243-6349. There is no cost for this service except for the cost of faxing your form.

Depending on when your fax is received, you should have your instructions back within 24 hours.

Fear Inversion™: Request for Tenth Day Instructions

CAUTION: You must successfully complete the first nine days first!

Name_____Phone_____

Address_____

Country_____

Date_____

Company_____

Position/Title_____

FAX NUMBER_____

Type of Call Reluctance you are working on_____

Specific behavior(s) you exaggerated during day eight_____

_____

_____

Please remember: The tenth day may be useful but it is entirely optional. It is not necessary to the success of the procedure.

As you can see by now, this procedure is definitely not intended for everyone or every form of call reluctance. It takes a certain amount of imagination and high motivation to make it work. But if you have honored the agreements you made with yourself and followed the instructions as given, at least some results should be evident by now.

Negative thought habits which produce distressful feelings during prospecting can be eliminated if they can be stopped in their course. And they can.

Chapter Nine

R_X Five
THOUGHT ZAPPING

PRIMARILY AFFECTS:	PRESCRIBED FOR:
Thoughts	✓ **Doomsayer**
	✓ **Over-Preparation**
✓ **Feelings**	✓ **Hyper-Pro**
	✓ **Stage Fright**
Actions	✓ **Role Rejection**
	✓ **Yielder**
	✓ **Social Self-Consciousness**
	✓ **Separationist**
	✓ **Emotionally Unemancipated**
	✓ **Referral Aversion**
	✓ **Telephobia**
	✓ **Oppositional Reflex**

A BRIEF OVERVIEW

Each day, when you first look at yourself in the mirror, you make a fundamental choice: "Will I allow myself to be satisfied or dissatisfied with what I see?" The choice made by self-limiting people reflects mindless, negative thought habits that totally ignore the objective image in the mirror. Some call-reluctant salespeople are unable to prospect for much the same reason. Their prospecting efforts are consistently blocked by mindless negative concerns which must be forced aside each time they approach certain prospecting situations. That takes effort. Effort takes energy. Energy used to *enforce* prospecting is energy not available *for* prospecting. Is that you? If it is, then perhaps Thought Zapping can help.

Thought Zapping (Negative Thought Zapping to be exact) is fast, effective and easy to apply. It works by severing the vulnerable linkage between negative thoughts which *precede* prospecting and the unpleasant feelings they summon by habit to accompany them. With sledgehammer subtlety, Thought Zapping launches behavioral guided missiles to disrupt, disorient and disengage undesirable thought-habit combinations. Once weakened, they can be replaced with more career-supporting attitudes about prospecting.

Guiding Principles Behind Thought Zapping

1. *You are motivated* to overcome call-reluctant reactions to prospecting.

2. *Your motivation is directed* specifically toward reducing unwanted distressful feelings associated with call reluctance in order to improve your prospecting activity.

3. Feelings can enhance or impede the flow of motivation into goal-directed behavior.

4. All habits, good and bad, are strengthened by uninterrupted repetition.

5. All habits, good and bad, are weakened by interruption and behavioral substitution.

Sighting the Target

Thought Zapping is useful for correcting certain types of call reluctance. It is also useful for many other forms of call reluctance, but as a secondary procedure.

Doomsayer, Over-Preparation, Hyper-Pro, Stage Fright, Social Self-Consciousness and Telephobia are excellent candidates for Thought Zapping. Role Rejection, Emotionally Unemancipated, Separationist and Referral Aversion Call Reluctance are helped by Thought Zapping, but not by itself. Oppositional Reflex Call Reluctance does not usually benefit from Thought Zapping as a primary countermeasure. It can, however, be useful in *conjunction* with Fear Inversion.

Estimated Completion Time

Weakening the habit connection between unwanted thoughts and feelings can usually be accomplished within about five days. For highly motivated, goal-directed salespeople, however, Thought Zapping can work within two days of conscientious use.

THE ROLE OF HABITS

Habits play important supporting roles in our lives. They help make complex and repetitive acts such as driving, walking and various social courtesies possible without having to constantly stop and think about them. Habits make our lives more enjoyable.

But some habits can make our lives miserable. Unpleasant, renegade habits of thought and feeling which combine to form certain types of call reluctance frustrate, perplex and annoy us. They also keep us from earning what we are worth.

Have you ever driven a car with a manual transmission and then tried to drive an automatic? Making the switch can be awkward at best. By habit, your leg muscles try to push down on the clutch pedal only to find the brake instead. In the meantime, your hand reaches for a nonexistent stick shift. Retraining ourselves to adjust to an automatic transmission once we have become accustomed to a manual one takes practice and purposeful effort. At first, the transition feels awkward. But by suppressing the old habits and repeating, forcibly if necessary, the new behaviors, the old habits soon loosen their iron grip. This method also works with habits of thought and feeling. By repeatedly interrupting yourself whenever an unwanted behavior asserts itself, and substituting—forcefully if necessary—a desired behavior in its place, an old habit dies and a new habit is born. That is how Thought Zapping works.

A Bad Habit's Worst Enemy

Negative thought habits which produce distressful feelings can be eliminated if they can be stopped amidst their destructive course. And they can, as the following exercise demonstrates.

Get a clock radio and tune to the most annoying station you can find. Turn the volume up loud. Now set it to go off in three minutes. Find a comfortable place to sit in a quiet room and place the radio nearby. Sit down. Close your eyes. Allow yourself to reflect upon the most fearful situation you can think of which is not related to prospecting. Really try to get into it, and stay with it until the radio signals that your three minutes are up. ACTION BREAK.

What happened? If you are like most salespeople, several interesting things occurred. We ambiguously asked you to "reflect upon the most fearful situation you could think of." So how did you carry out the instructions? How do you "reflect upon?" What did you actually do? You probably "thought about" the most fearful thing you could recall which was not related to prospecting. But how did you do that?

Everyone can recall a distressful event. But most salespeople do not *immediately* recall the distressful feelings associated with that memory. That takes a split second longer and requires a separate step. Instead of recalling both the remembered image and the corresponding feelings at the same time, the image, the feelings and connecting the two together is a construction which requires three separate steps. Exactly how this is accomplished is an enigmatic scientific riddle which has captured the attention of some of the most gifted neuroscientists of our time.

What Is Memory, Anyway?

Human memory. What is it? Where is it located? How does it work?

Except for some sophomore psychology majors and most neurolinguistic programmers, human memory is still an unsolved mystery. Like UFO's, heavy metal music, and ethical politicians, human memory is a complex puzzle waiting to be solved.

Author Richard Bolles (*Remembering and Forgetting*) claims that we intuitively think memory is a vast storehouse of experiences located somewhere in the brain. But nobody really knows how memory works. The storage metaphor is just an explanation we deduced from our experience. We say, for example, that an image is "burned into our brain," or "preserved in wax." We "carve them in stone." To us, memories are inscribed with pencil and paper, then "filed away." Some people, we say, even have "photographic memories."

But memory may not be so simple. Our storage metaphor may be wrong. It's certainly incomplete. A little thought experiment may show why. Answer the following question as quickly as you can: Who was the *second* successor to your country's president (or prime minister) during the first world war? In other words, count two presidents or prime ministers forward from the first world war. Who was it?

continues

What Is Memory, Anyway? *continued*

Some of you are probably already replying (with more than a little pride) that you *know* the answer *even before you can figure it out or recall it.* Congratulations, but you have just created a paradox for yourself and a terrible problem for the storage metaphor of how memory works.

Most of us presume that during the pause between acquiring a memory problem and finding the answer to it, our brain busily rummages through its file cabinets looking for the answer. But the paradox comes from your apparent foreknowledge of the answer. *How did you know you knew the answer unless you had already checked your memory and found that you knew the answer? There's more. If in fact you knew the answer why didn't you just come out with it?*

This dilemma occurs every time we recognize that we are not recalling something correctly. How do we know we're incorrect, unless we already know the correct answer? *If we know it, why can't we just remember it?* It's a paradox. We don't have the answer. Not even neurolinguistic programmers have the answer. But we do know this: The foreknowledge paradox spells trouble ahead for the "storage" metaphor of memory.

We can deduce, however, that some change in our internal or external state, which has something—no matter how incidental—to do with prospecting, signals us to scan our remembered experiences about prospecting to see if we can construct a memory of an event or series of events about prospecting. At this point our interrogation is just a generalized response to some "cue," and prospecting is just some kind of memory cipher—perhaps a tiny blob of protein deposited in the cerebral cortex, or a microscopic rock-like formation of trace minerals arranged along some nerve pathway like a stone age residential address.

The pattern we recognize as the directive to "prospect" launches a full-scale multi-dimensional, multi-directional search through our recollections for a picture (image), smell or sound "marker" which got connected by habit to our memory about prospecting. Once the link to a distressful feeling has been encoded and strengthened by repetition, whenever the marker is sensed, and prospecting is summoned from memory, the feeling also surfaces and is reexperienced just as it was when the original event occurred.

Sales scripts shouldn't frighten salespeople. And they don't. But sales scripts coupled to phone books coupled to a telephone to be used for cold calling as instructed by an overheated young trainer in horn-rimmed glasses might very easily activate apprehension in others, apprehension which could easily continue for the remainder of their sales career. If the event is intense enough or repeated often enough, any young trainer in horn-rimmed glasses may produce the same distress. A sales script and the word "prospect" might do the same. When the causative agents become strong and generalized, just the word "prospecting"—said or just thought—is strong enough to activate overwhelming apprehension.

How Do We Know When To Be Afraid?

We have not seen very many full-featured sales training programs. General sales training is not our area of expertise. But the few we have seen all rest upon a basic model. Most seem to have been taken from the same book and share the same structural defects. From "blackbox" models relying on notions like "the unconscious mind" to simple variations of stimulus-response themes, the sales training programs we have seen rest their techniques upon a limited understanding of how humans come to interact with their environment. Like it or not, much has been learned since the two basic conjectural models mentioned above were popularized. Modern brain science is leading the way. Scientists like Bernard L. Strehler ("Where Is the Self? A Neuroanatomical Theory of Consciousness", *Synapse*, Vol. 7, 1991) outline a more complete, up-to-date understanding of how we use sensory input and stored memories to fashion our behavior.

Imitating a Socratic catechism, our brain continuously asks a series of questions. Like a microcomputer keyboard, it is continuously querying itself to determine if a key has been depressed. Then, in a split second, some response is fashioned based on further information received.

1. Is something happening? (Experts call this extremely important topic "signal detection." If we don't detect a cue or change of some type, we have no need to respond. Are the hidden messages on subliminal audio cassettes really detectable?)

2. Where is it? (If we have detected something, where is it located? This involves all the ways the brain uses both eyes,
continues

How Do We Know When To Be Afraid? *continued*

both ears, and other sensory inputs and internal decision methods to find out where the thing we have detected is. We can't react to something if we don't know where it is.)

3. Is it moving? (Have we detected something that is in motion, or is it standing still. Your nervous system comes equipped with highly dedicated groups of receptors whose only purpose in life is to answer questions like this. Your eyes, for example, have bureaucratic receptors which will only fire if they detect something moving from the upper right to the lower left of your vision. They ignore everything else. It's not their job.)

4. Which direction? (If the something is moving, what direction is it moving in? Is it moving *towards* me or *away* from me? In a fraction of a second this brain-based process calculates enough sophisticated trajectory predictions to embarrass our best manmade computers.)

5. What is it? (Up to now, everything has been reflexive and mechanical. But a qualitative change is required for the calculation at this stage, which is called "Pattern" or "Feature Recognition." This is where we make our first attempt to figure out what the something we first detected is. To do that, we need information from memory.

6. Is this something I have experienced before? (Here, we are asking what the thing we have recognized is like. No two experiences are exactly similar so our brain has to approximate a match between what we now recognize and what is contained in memory.)

7. Is this unlike anything experienced so far? (If it is, is there something in my memory that is somehow related to some *aspect* of the current experience?)

8. What did I do in the past when I perceived something like I am perceiving now? (This could be considered a search for advice. We're looking to our past remembered experiences for guidance.)

9. Which of the things I did was most *beneficial*? Which were most *harmful*? (Once I recall the moves I made in a similar
continues

How Do We Know When To Be Afraid? *continued*

situation, I make a sophisticated risk-benefit analysis before I determine what I am going to do in this situation.)

10. What do I have to do to implement the response? (Now that I have selected the best course of action to take, what do I have to do to start the ball rolling? Particularly, what muscle groups have to be moved, in what ways, in what sequences? This is not as simple as it seems. Before anything can be done, the muscle groups to be deployed must first each be queried to determine their current status and position. Then calculations have to be made fixing the beginning and end-points for each muscle to be moved.)

After each response, further questions remain to be asked. Is the action complete? Was the physical or emotional result of my action important (or need-satisfying) enough to warrant remembering this sequence for future reference?

If all this seems mind boggling rest assured. It's not. Your brain does this for you all the time. It's doing it for you right now.

The connection between what we recall and how we emotionally react to what we recall is essentially one of habit. The habit is strengthened because each time we recall a particular event we immediately summon the same feeling. Through repetition, the connection between the two becomes formidable until they are experienced as one. The bond is strong, but is it unbreakable? No.

Think about the behavioral experiment you just conducted. What happened as you sat with your eyes closed, got into your disturbing event, and felt the distressful feelings which accompanied it? Three minutes passed and the radio came on. As it did, the bond uniting your memory to your feelings was momentarily interrupted. A new experience was introduced (hearing the radio) which *interfered* with the previous connection between the thought you were remembering and the feeling you were experiencing. Think about what happened to you. Were you momentarily startled when the radio came on? Did you shift your attention, for a second, *to* the sound of the radio and *away from* the distressful feelings you were reexperiencing? If you did, then Thought Zapping will work for you.

You cannot attend to an external interference and sustain an intense memory at the same time. The survival of a habit of thought or feeling is maintained by a thin thread of *uninterrupted* repetition. A purposeful interruption is a bad habit's worst enemy.

Listing Your Negative Intruders

What negative habits of thought and feeling interfere with your ability to prospect comfortably? The following activity will help you find out. Take out a piece of paper and divide it into two columns. Title the top of the page "Inventory of Negative Intruders." Title the first column "Negative Thoughts" and the second column "Emotional Reactions." Carry your Inventory of Negative Intruders with you for at least one work day, preferably two or three. Every time you prepare to prospect (or are in the process of prospecting) list all the negative thoughts and accompanying emotional reactions you experience. These are your Negative Intruders—the habit residue of unwanted thoughts and feelings which continue to happen because they happened once and have been reinforced since that time through uninterrupted repetition.

Here are some examples of Negative Intruders the authors had to contend with prior to appearing on radio and television.

Inventory of Negative Intruders

Negative Thoughts	Emotional Reactions
Worry about gathering all possible documentation in support of presentation	Muscle tension
Worry about the questions which might be asked	Dread
Worry about being late for an appearance or presentation	Agitation
Worry about on-camera appearance	Compulsive shopping for new clothes
Worry about running out of time or over allotted time	Hurried

These are just some of the things we habitually worried about. Our worrying amounted to ineffective coping which sapped energy from our goals without returning a single ounce of profit or relief. Then we got smart. We applied Thought Zapping to ourselves and it worked. If it can work for us it can work for you too.

Recording the Negative Intruders

The next step is important and should be performed *right after you have completed your inventory*. You will need a lined tablet. Title the first page, "Frequency of Intrusion Chart: Pre." Under the title, list any one of the intruding negative thoughts from your inventory. We recommend that you begin with one of the least distressful thoughts. Then set up the remainder of the page as shown below. What you should have when you finish is an intrusive negative thought you wish to zap, the date your measurement is taken, the time span the measurement covers, and a place for the total number of times the negative thought occurs during the measurement period.

Frequency of Intrusion Chart: Pre

Intruding Negative Thought (From Inventory of Negative Thought Intruders): "Worry about the questions which might be asked" _____

_____

_____

Date: <u>11/5/93</u>   Measurement Period: <u>8 hours</u>

Occurrence During Measurement Period: <u>11 times</u>

To get your total, simply keep track of the number of times the negative thought comes to mind (intrudes) during the time period you have selected. Then simply total it and copy it onto a form set up like the one above.

Zapping the Intruder

Now that you have discovered how often the negative thought intrudes, you are ready to do something about it.

One: Begin by placing a rubber band around your left wrist. It should be large enough to fit loosely.

Two: Sit in a comfortable chair and close your eyes.

Three: Think about the intruder you selected. Every time you become aware of the negative thought, do the following:

• Imagine the whole sky turning into a huge stop sign.

- As you see the stop sign, imagine yourself shouting, "Stop it!" as loud as you can.

- Simultaneously snap the rubber band and sting your wrist. Yes, it hurts, but once you begin this program *it is imperative to sting yourself every time you have the negative thought. Wherever you are. Whatever you are doing.*

- *Immediately* after snapping the rubber band, think of a positive mental picture of yourself. For example, you might recall a time when you did well in a similar situation and felt good about yourself afterwards. Remember that event and allow yourself to reexperience some of those good feelings. If you can't think of anything, then try to allow yourself to pretend.

- Now, while reexperiencing these pleasant sensations, momentarily place yourself mentally back into the negatively intrusive situation you are trying to defang. What happens? Most people have trouble focusing their attention on the intrusive situation. Every time they try, the memory of the rubber band pops to their attention. What about feelings? They start to recall the revised, more positive feelings they borrowed from a past positive event. A new habit of thought and feeling is being born.

Now that you are familiar with Thought Zapping, you will find it easy to transfer to real life situations. Continue to wear your rubber band. Then, every time your old negative thoughts about prospecting try to intrude, zap your wrist and insert your borrowed positive feelings. Monitor the number of times the thought intrudes on your Post Chart (illustrated below). If all goes according to plan, you will notice a significant decline in the frequency with which the negative thought intrudes. When it does try to intrude, it will grow weaker with each zap.

Actually, you may only have to use your rubber band during your treatment of the first negative intruder. After two or three days of practice, it can be removed. Your memory of the rubber band's effect will linger far after its removal, and from this point on the phrase "Stop it!" will have developed its own potency. The authors needed the rubber bands longer than that. As a matter of fact, if you see us on television or speaking before a large group, look closely. You will see we still wear our rubber bands. We wear them with honor next to our newly acquired affected watches and jewelry. Now, however, we rarely ever have to actually sting ourselves. We applied Thought Zapping so faithfully in the beginning that now when one of our old intruders tries to hijack our career, we simply glance down at our left wrists and mutter, "Go ahead, make my day!" It works. (We each wear a *"designer" Thought Zapping Rubber Band*. These rubber bands have "Official Thought Zapper" printed on them. They are presently available *free* from the publisher to anyone sending a stamped, self-addressed envelope.)

Measuring Your Progress

You can monitor your improvement by completing the Frequency of Intrusion Chart: Post (see below) which is set up like the Frequency of Intrusion Chart: Pre. Use it to track the frequency of your intruders once you begin Thought Zapping. By using it, you can observe your daily progress.

Frequency of Intrusion Chart: Post

Intruding Negative Thought (From Inventory Of Negative Thought Intruders: _____

_____

_____

Date: _____ Measurement Period_____

Occurrence During Measurement Period_____

Is Thought Zapping the Same as Positive Thinking?

Isn't Thought Zapping just another form of positive thinking—with a gimmick? That's a reasonable question, especially since you are instructed to insert a positive thought at a certain point. Nevertheless, the answer is no. Thought Zapping has little—if any—overlap with positive thinking.

Positive thinking and its derivative methods underline the importance of positive mental imagery and then rely on sheer repetition to establish new habits of positive *thought*. They assume this process will eventually lead to more positive *behavior*.

Thought Zapping concentrates on eliminating the negative stumbling blocks which keep salespeople from being *able* to think positively about prospecting. The use of positive imagery is incidental to its success.

continues

Is Thought Zapping the Same *continued*

The link between positive images alone and measurable changes in productive behavior has yet to be clearly evidenced except through anecdotal reports.

The link between Thought Zapping and the successful elimination of unwanted behavior can be easily measured by almost anyone willing to apply the procedure correctly and complete the pre and post forms.

Positive thinking is essentially word-based. It relies on the use of words and often appeals to highly subjective concepts such as the "unconscious mind" to explain otherwise unexplainable thoughts and behavior.

Thought Zapping is essentially an objective, mechanical procedure. It disrupts and scrambles the automatic circuitry of undesirable self-limiting habits, thereby decreasing the frequency of their occurrence. In our adaptation, the rubber band activates and utilizes your inborn *startle response* to disrupt and disengage the linkage between an unpleasant experience you recall about prospecting and the undesired feeling state you have linked, by habit, to your thoughts about prospecting.

In theory, this means you can modify the feeling you attach to *any* thought or memory. In practice, people do it all the time, in many ways. Long-term psychoanalysis is one example. Est, popular in the U.S. during the 1960's, is another. The current Rational Behavior Training model is still another. Experiential (Gestalt) psychology and its clones, such as neurolinguistic programming, essentially attempt to effect behavior change by modifying the link between feelings and thoughts or memories. However, for certain forms of call reluctance where measurable improvement must commence almost immediately, Thought Zapping gets the job done—faster, with longer lasting results.

Zapping Stage Fright

Gail B. had already survived beyond the norm for her industry. She had been in direct sales for 36 marginally productive months. Although her training was only minimal and her support from management superficial, she knew she had what was necessary to do extraordinarily well. But she grudgingly admitted to a persistent problem, call reluctance.

During our initial interview with Gail, she told us she was in cosmetics sales with a highly visible company that uses "party" or in-home group gatherings for prospecting and selling. The Call Reluctance Scale (Sales Preference Questionnaire) revealed that Gail had a vulnerability to call reluctance, but only in one form, speaking in front of groups. Having that hesitation made it difficult not only for her to speak in front of her small groups but also impaired her ability to set up the number of parties needed to meet her production objectives.

Gail had previously been exposed to a variety of potential cures, but each had failed. Regrettably but understandably, she became semi-cynical. Yet beneath the cynicism, she still had a stronger desire to improve than to remain inert.

Gail grudgingly consented to try. But against our advice, she only agreed to try Thought Realignment. Due to her cynicism, we had little hope that Thought Realignment by itself would work. As expected, it failed to dazzle her with the immediate results she wanted. But she persevered and agreed to try another countermeasure we had originally asked her to apply first: Thought Zapping.

Expecting another "mental" approach, Gail was very receptive to the mechanical, straightforward nature of Thought Zapping. We demonstrated the procedure by having her close her eyes and concentrate on her problem. Shortly, we startled her by slamming a book down on the table beside her and shouting "Stop it, Gail!" Then we took a few minutes to explain to her what had happened, how Thought Zapping works, and how to put it to use. Convinced this would work for her, she completed her setup charts, listing several intruders.

Gail chose to start with the first intruder on her list: "Having to speak to a group of women makes me feel exposed and vulnerable, I can't concentrate on my presentation." Using her Frequency of Intrusion Chart: Pre, she found that this negative thought intruded every time she tried to use a network or contact to set up an in-house party. During a typical work day, she recorded the intruder each time it occurred and discovered to her amazement that it appeared approximately 17 times per hour!

Next, Gail was given her Official Thought Zapping rubber band. To be sure she knew how to use it correctly, we had her practice the procedure once while we watched. She imagined getting ready to call a contact to set up a party, becoming aware of the intruder and zapping it *before* the negative feeling that usually accompanied it could occur. Then, instead of the usual negative feeling, we had her visualize herself setting up an enjoyable and profitable party. She inserted the enjoyable sensations of accomplishment.

At first Gail reacted with the usual litany, "This hurts!...My wrist will develop welts....I'll look like some kind of hard drug junkie!...Visualizing is phoney....It's not really me....Isn't there some other way?" Without arguing with her, we secured her commitment to continue the procedure.

She went out into her world of prospecting for in-home parties armed with her rubber band and self-monitoring forms. Although her next appointment with us was more than a week away, she called our office just two days later. She no longer needed to actually sting herself with the rubber band and she didn't need to see us again. "It hurt for a while, but it worked," she said. "Fast." She could already prospect without the intrusion of the first negative thought and was working on the next intruder on her list. Thought Zapping worked for Gail. Although we have not seen her since her first visit, we have heard that she has developed into a very powerful prospector and is really enjoying herself in the process.

A Final Remark

Sometimes old habits do not die and remain buried. They sometimes resurface to haunt again, though to a lesser degree. So be prepared. The old habit will probably try to occasionally reassert itself. The phenomenon is called "spontaneous recovery." It's natural. You can expect it. When it happens, don't panic. Just have your Thought Zapping rubber band at-the-ready and give yourself a booster shot.

Thought Zapping is a fast way to modify thoughts and feelings. It's fast, but not instant. Give it the time, attention and patience your particular application deserves and needs.

Research scientists are finding that our senses may influence our moods and behaviors more than we realize.

Some of the techniques in this section are clearly experimental. Some are controversial. But in our judgment, they are forerunners of the next generation of sales training breakthroughs.

Chapter Ten

SUPPLEMENTAL COUNTERMEASURES

Unlike primary countermeasures, none of the supplemental techniques are intended at present to be complete behavior change systems in themselves. They should be used with one or more of the main countermeasures.

Admittedly, some of the techniques in this section are clearly experimental. Some are controversial. But in our judgment, they are forerunners of the next generation of sales training breakthroughs.

SENSORY INJECTION

PRIMARILY AFFECTS:	PRESCRIBED FOR:
Thoughts	✓ Doomsayer
	✓ Over-Preparation
✓ Feelings	✓ Hyper-Pro
	✓ Stage Fright
Actions	✓ Role Rejection
	✓ Yielder
	✓ Social Self-Consciousness
	✓ Separationist
	✓ Emotionally Unemancipated
	✓ Referral Aversion
	✓ Telephobia
	✓ Oppositional Reflex

> *When the dog barks,*
> *When the bee stings,*
> *When I'm feeling sad,*
> *I simply remember my favorite things,*
> *And then I don't feel so sad.*
>   "My Favorite Things" from *The Sound of Music*

What do a small bottle of lake water, a brass ammunition casing, a slap to the back of the neck, a flake of cow manure, a slow, sweaty 1950's rock 'n' roll tune, and a bottle of Windsong perfume have to do with call reluctance? Much. Some successful salespeople use them to manage their call reluctance. Their techniques are called *Sensory Injection*. Their ingredients come from mixing one part traditional learning theory with two parts of its theoretical nemesis, modern brain science.

Sensory Injection techniques are interesting, innovative, practical and easy to apply. Since words are not needed for them to work they are considered "mechanical" procedures, in contrast to "word-based" procedures like Thought Realignment. Sensory Injection techniques are fun and usually effective when used as directed. Although still in development, we think they're authentic precursors of some intriguing new sales training technologies.

We wish we could say Sensory Injection techniques work equally well for everyone, but they don't. They have, however, proven beneficial for many call-reluctant salespeople. The key is to find the one or two techniques that work best for you. At present, there is no simple formula for determining which form will work best for whom. But we have our hunches and we're busy testing, trying to stretch them into educated guesses. So stay tuned.

Guiding Principles Behind Sensory Injection

1. *Your motivation is intentionally directed* toward reducing unwanted distressful feelings you associate with prospecting.

2. You are presently using, or you completed, one or more of the primary countermeasures for the particular form of call reluctance you are trying to eliminate.

3. Intense feelings can be provoked by either internal or external triggers called *cues*.

4. Feelings can enhance or impede the flow of motivation to goal-supporting behaviors.

5. Both good and bad habit sequences (*chains*) are reinforced by uninterrupted repetition.

6. Many call-reluctant episodes are the direct result of habit-based reactions to external cues that you have 1) detected by one or more of your senses, 2) recognized as a call reluctance cue, and 3) reacted to in strict accordance with certain "rules of responding" which you learned in the past for dealing with potentially threatening situations like prospecting.

7. Two contradictory reaction states, such as fearful distress and confident expectation, cannot both be present at the same time, in the same situation, or to the same degree.

8. Positive feeling states can be called up and inserted by force, but to do so, the cues triggering them must meet at least one of two conditions: Either they must be introduced *prior* to exposure to a potential call reluctance cue, or they must be *stronger* than a cue that has already been conditioned to produce a call reluctance reaction.

Too theoretical? Don't worry about it. Just keep reading.

How Sensory Injection Works

Sensory injection is actually a collection of advanced attitude-shaping techniques. Though differing in approach, each works by forcing unwanted thoughts and feelings aside by attacking them at their base, where they are weakest.

Call reluctance never occurs by accident. It is always a carefully orchestrated emotional response to cues you learned to associate with distressful prospecting: telephones, computer prospecting lists, doorknobs, secretaries, large audiences, microphones, television cameras, order forms, quota sheets. For call-reluctant salespeople, these have become reminders, cues, capable of sparking call reluctance explosions. They do so *now* because they have done so *before*. Each time they are permitted to trigger another call reluctance episode, they dramatically increase the odds that they will do so again.

Call reluctance cues consist of much more than just things you see. Innocent smells, like those in a large auditorium, droning sounds like those emitted by air conditioner vents in a boardroom or efficient but impersonal put-downs by a prospect's secretary can be sufficient to ignite a heart pounding attack of call reluctance. Once a call reluctance reaction is experienced in the presence of a previously benign environmental element, that element is a candidate to become a call reluctance cue.

Let's try to approach the subject sideways, with a practical example from your experience. Think of the word "hospital." What comes to mind? Most people immediately visualize health care professionals dressed in sterile white uniforms busily rushing about discharging their duties. But that's just a fragment of what we associate with the word hospital.

Other images include antiseptic smells and busy, disembodied sounds. In one split second, our memory projects a multilevel recollection (a *re*-collection) of what the word hospital has come to mean: sights, sounds, smells, and possibly sensations of physical pain. Taken together, these elements form our memory of hospital. Once we recreate what hospital looks, sounds, smells and feels like, an emotional response is triggered. How do the sights, sounds, and smells you associate with hospital dispose you to feel? Sad? Alarmed? Helpless?

In the above example, you were asked to "think" only of the word hospital. The rest was automatic, compliments of your memory. Sensory Injection puts another twist on the matter of memory. You don't have to visualize a hospital to invoke memory and incite feelings. You also can get there through other sensory doorways. A slight whiff of an antiseptic—*anywhere*—can send impulses racing through your memory to locate pictures and sounds you associate with the smell. Once the smell of an antiseptic is organized into a coherent memory, it may continue to remind you of a painful hospital experience and trigger distress even though you are miles away and years removed from the event you recall.

Electronic bells may remind you of chimes used in hospitals to page physicians. They can jog your memory to recall visual images and antiseptic smells. Regardless of the sensory door through which you enter memory, the result is a composite of remembered experience *set off by a single cue*. All that's needed to complete the memory process are some thoughts and feelings for texture. But which ones? Probably the ones you remember from your first, most recent, or most intense experience in a hospital. Can you remember when that was?

Call reluctance works the same way. The feelings you experience as call reluctance are the result of memory connections that got wired to call reluctance cues (things you see, hear, touch or smell that you associate in memory with distressful prospecting). A *single* traumatic prospecting experience, or a bad experience in general that you associate with prospecting, is enough to create a call reluctance cue within your memory. Nobody knows how. But the *connection* between the call reluctance cue and prospecting is not permanently etched into memory. It can be tricked. That's where Sensory Injection comes into play. The cues which routinely activate *distressful* feelings when you prospect can be smothered by substitute cues which you have previously trained to activate *alternate* feelings.

Kenny, a pimple-faced adolescent, knows it works. He revs up his hypersonic, heavy metal, ear-blasting boom box just so he can watch mild, pleasant people change into crazed, potential killers. "According to me... and my opinion," Kenny said, trying to affect lucidity, "it kind of works best, you know, in a bus [long pause] or the train [another pause] late at night and stuff."

Instead of letting cues in your prospecting environment run their call reluctance course, Sensory Injection encourages you to strike back by striking first. Launch a preemptive, anti-call reluctance surprise attack. Overpower call reluctance cues *before* they command your memory to connect your feelings to distress. Purposefully fire salvos of your own sensory projectiles either before or immediately after a call reluctance cue is detected. This momentarily seizes your attention and steers it away from call reluctance cues, forcefully directing it, instead, to a substitute positive cue. Any sense will do. You can use sight, sound, touch, smell or taste. We have devised Sensory Injection techniques for them all.

Five Kinds of Sensory Injection Techniques:

- Sensory Injection—Sound
- Sensory Injection—Taste
- Sensory Injection—Sight
- Sensory Injection—Touch
- Sensory Injection—Smell

So far, no one has successfully used extrasensory perception to overcome call reluctance. Nevertheless, we doubt that compulsively unorthodox salespeople will be dissuaded from trying.

The organization of countermeasures we developed is called Sensory Injection because a potent inoculation through one of your senses grabs attention away from potential call reluctance cues and focuses it on manufactured cues engineered to activate positive emotional states.

Most salespeople use a form of Sensory Injection every day without knowing it. You practice it intuitively—every time the scent of a perfume inflames vivid romantic memories, a slow, heavy breathing, close dancing rock 'n' roll melody sends you back to your senior prom, or a certain "look" gets your blood boiling, you experience Sensory Injection.

After thirty years, Windsong perfume *still* automatically transports coauthor George Dudley back to his adolescence and a special young lady. Interlude does the same for coauthor Shannon Goodson. Can you think of a fragrance or song that invokes similar memories for you? At last count, Shannon has received 76 gift bottles of Interlude perfume from male admirers intuitively trying to exploit Sensory Injection.

Are you weary of trying to sweet-talk the fear out of prospecting? Why not come to your senses? Literally. Pick a sense. Give it a try.

There is no need to provide detailed, step-by-step instructions for each Sensory Injection technique. They all follow the same sequence, differing only in the sense used.

We suggest working with your sense of smell first. It's portable, fun, and very easy to use. It has already helped several call-reluctant salespeople. Could you, perhaps, be next?

NOTE: Some salespeople with Oppositional Reflex Call Reluctance will experience a critical seizure at this point. But they'll be easy to spot. Their mouths will be frothing rabidly, sensitivities will be outraged, and their intelligence will be convulsing spastically unless we permit them to identify all the major reasons why our suggestion, "try the sense of smell first," might not work.

They are correct. There are important exceptions. If your nose is congested due to the flu, a recent fist fight, allergies, common cold, or, due to some heinous trick of nature, missing altogether, you must be inventive. Experiment. Try one of the other anti-call reluctance missiles in the Sensory Injection arsenal. One is likely to hit the mark.

Why Sensory Injection Works

For Fido, your family dog, the slightest scent of fox (Fido is British) carries with it the memory of food and the exhilaration of the hunt. For Peter Rabbit, the same scent signals imminent danger and means "run for your life!" "When a person glimpses the face of a famous actor, sniffs a favorite food or hears the voice of a friend," writes Walter J. Freeman, "recognition is instant. Within a fraction of a second after the eyes, nose, ears, tongue or skin is stimulated one knows the object is familiar, and whether it is desirable or dangerous." Yet, Freeman notes, "Investigators are only now beginning to suggest how the brain moves beyond the mere extraction of features—how it combines sensory messages with past experiences." ("The Psychology of Perception," *Scientific American*, February 1991)

Research scientists are finding that our senses may influence our moods and behaviors more than we realize. A 1986 article in *Science* magazine reported that each of our senses has neural connections leading directly to the amygdala which functions like a black box made of human tissue. Brain scientist C.A. Dudley says the amygdala "forms part of the limbic system, the brain structure associated with emotionality and the release of certain hormones." (Joseph Alper, "Our Dual Memory," *Science*, July/August, 1986; C.A. Dudley, Department of Physiology, University of Texas Health Science Center, Dallas, Texas, private communication, 1991)

When basic science provokes our imagination with teasers like this, practical applications can't be far behind. And they're not. Susan Schiffman was hired to develop an aroma which could be sprayed in New York City's subways to reduce commuter aggression. The walls of a California jail cell were purposely painted pink to reduce aggressive behavior. Psychologist/composer Steve Halpern produces music which can "seize the nervous system in 15-20 seconds" by imitating the rhythms of the body. ("A Way to a Sound Mind and Body?," *USA Weekend*, July 1-3, 1988) Each of these projects uses one of the senses to directly manipulate mood. Currently, several projects in this research domain are underway. We've been working on call reluctance applications for a number of years.

Using Your Nose to Overcome Call Reluctance

Helen Keller once remarked, "Smell is a potent wizard that transports us across thousands of miles and all the years we have lived." Of all our senses, the sense of smell may be the most powerful mood changer. "Odor is, after all, mediated by the area of the brain that also mediates sexual behavior, survival and appetite," writes Judith Stone. ("Scents and Sensibility," *Discover*, December 1989) In the same article, Arnie Cann of the University of North Carolina reports that fragrance is powerfully linked with memory—whether the smell is good or bad.

Unlike call-reluctant salespeople who are Socially Self-Conscious, the sense of smell does not hesitate to make influential connections in high, neural places.

- Dr. William Cain, a Yale professor doing research on the sense of smell, says it's not unusual to "think smell would be one of the sensory stimuli to reduce stress."

- Arthur Henley, himself a self-cured phobic and author of *Phobias: The Crippling Fears*, writes that "...smells, good and bad, can have psychological effects...Good smells can...have a positive effect on your psyche."

- Experiments in Japan with keypunch operators found that the average number of errors per hour dropped by 21% when office air was scented with lavender, which is claimed to reduce stress. Errors dropped by 33% with jasmine, which induces relaxation, and 54% with lemon— *even when the scent was below the level of conscious awareness.* (Think of it as elevator music for the nose.) According to the same study, chamomile, Japanese cypress, orange peppermint and eucalyptus have a soothing effect on the psyche, while scarlet, sage and rosemary are stimulating.

- Yale professor Gary Schwartz exposed a group of phobics to pleasant scents like apples. The group showed less stress (measured by heart rate, blood pressure, and muscle tension recordings) than a comparable phobic group which had not been exposed.

- Another research project claims the smell of rich chocolate can elevate the spirits of clinically depressed patients.

Scent engineers are quickly gaining the ability to design mood-enhancing fragrances. For the last few years we, too, have been busily exploring call reluctance applications for this new technology. Call-reluctant salespeople, managers, consultants, and others we worked with the last several years were taught how to apply Sensory Injection using their sense of smell. They liked it. We hope you will, too.

SENSORY INJECTION STEP-BY-STEP

To start, you have to make a choice. How would you like to feel when you prospect? More relaxed? More self-confident?

Decreased prospecting pressure and increased self-confidence are not opposite ends of the same scale. The two states represent differences *in kind*, which means they are distinct entities. Your status on one may have no influence whatsoever on the other. So make your choice wisely and don't presume that working on one automatically brings about improvement in the other. It doesn't.

Selecting the relaxation option implies that you probably get "stressed out" when you're in certain prospecting situations. You'd like Sensory Injection to help you calm down so you feel less agitated, more relaxed.

Self-confidence is a different matter altogether. It merges feelings of self-direction with the expectation of positive results. Choosing the self-confidence option means you would like to approach prospecting with a less pessimistic, more affirmative outlook.

Why can't you do both? You can. But not simultaneously. The instructions for these two different Sensory Injection applications are parallel but not identical. There are very important differences. Accordingly, we have provided detailed, step-by-step instructions for both.

Relaxation

Prospecting is not automatically unpleasant. It does not have to be distressful for you. The objective of this section is to teach you a practical countermeasure you can use to depressurize your prospecting.

1. Select a "fragrance cue"

Your fragrance cue can be something you *already* identify with being loved, cared for, nurtured, contented or relaxed. What could it be? Some people must stop and think about that for a while. But not salesman Dave Richardson. He loves to go fishing. So he carries a small vial of lake water from his favorite fishing spot with him. Mark Coffman sells sophisticated infrared monitoring equipment in the northeast area of the United States. A rifle marksman, he has trained himself to utterly relax before squeezing the trigger. When selling, Mark carries a spent brass ammunition cartridge along with him. The scent automatically directs his body to relax before pulling the prospecting trigger. One salesperson we met during our international travels now lives and works in a large cosmopolitan city. After he learned about Sensory Injection he volunteered how, having been raised on a farm, he came to fondly associate barnyard odors with the love and safety he associates with his childhood. You guessed it. He carries a chip of cow manure (hopefully in an airtight box) with him on sales calls. For him, the odor evokes the same pleasant feelings other salespeople get from smelling apple pie and recalling childhood visits to grandmother's house.

If you can't think of a fragrance you associate with contentment or composure, *then select a fragrance you have never smelled before.* Try a new perfume or after-shave. It need not be expensive. It doesn't even have to smell good. It just has to be something you have not used before.

2. Calibrate the desired state, relaxation

What relaxes you the most? Music? Deep breathing? Prayers? Hypnosis? Going fishing? Meditation? Biofeedback? Reading?

Relaxation is a highly individual matter. Certain broad guidelines exist for understanding how people relax, but they are too general to be of any practical use on an individual level. How you relax is up to you. Do whatever works best. If you wish, you can borrow the relaxation procedure described in the Threat Desensitization section of this book. Alternatively, there are many commercially available audio cassette tapes which can help you relax. They feature a variety of sounds. Hypnotic ocean sounds, specially prepared musical selections, tropical rain forests, white noise, thunderstorms. They have all been recorded to help you relax. Used properly, they work.

We teach people who have trouble relaxing a technique they can use while lying in bed listening to their radio. First, get your radio and get in bed. Tune in any non-heavy metal music station—unless you actually enjoy being assaulted by heavy metal music. Pick a station with few voice interruptions if possible. That's important. Lay back, get comfortable, close your eyes, and *turn the volume control so low you have to make an effort to hear the music*. It works. Once you are about to fall asleep, remove the headphones, turn your radio off, and drift off.

Simple modifications of this method may be all you need to help you recover what it feels like to be relaxed. If you don't like music, any simple, boringly repetitive sound will work.

3. Connect the fragrance cue

Laying in bed, on the floor, or just sitting in a comfortable chair, continue to the point where you are distracted, inward and relaxed. Once you have achieved that state, *with as little physical motion as possible*, dab a drop of your fragrance cue onto a piece of cotton and sniff it three times for about one second each time. Then put the cotton aside and continue relaxing for a few more minutes.

4. Fortify with practice

Practice this sequence at least once a day for five days, giving your fragrance cue a proper chance to develop a strong association with the physical sensations of relaxation. Some people may require more than five sessions, some less. Use your own judgment, but we recommend a minimum of at least five. When you have successfully completed your practice sessions, the hard part is over. Now comes the fun.

5. Aromashots: Stun gun for call reluctance

Get a small container such as a pillbox. Treat a small piece of cotton with your fragrance cue, put it inside the box and carry it with you in your pocket or purse. Then, *just before* entering a potentially distressful prospecting situation, get out your cotton ball and smell it three times for about one second each—like you did during relaxation training. You might mentally tell yourself to prepare for distress, but your body is on the receiving end of a stronger, clearer signal: relax. If you followed the instructions carefully, that's exactly what your body will do.

6. Consolidate and reinforce

Now and then give yourself a booster shot. Renew the connection between your fragrance cue and relaxation by repeating steps two and three.

CAUTION: Never use your fragrance cue for any non-call reluctance purpose. Careless misuse, inconsistent use, or mixing fragrance cues can seriously weaken the ability of this method to achieve the results you desire.

The Smell of Success

Joanna Moore sold successfully for seventeen years before buying her own franchise from a Canadian training/consulting company. Now she was a small business owner with three employees, a territory defined and protected by legal contract, and according to a colorful brochure, an "unlimited opportunity for personal and financial growth." Joanna felt she had arrived.

"It's the purest form of straight commissions there is," she said ruefully, her face tightened with caution in a way her friends were not accustomed to. "If my company profits, I get paid. If it doesn't, I don't."

Though not university educated, her ostentatiously displayed sales trophies radiated enough pride to exceed any academic degree. She had been dramatically successful selling cosmetics, precious metals, wholesale jewelry, and real estate. She had sold time management, goal setting, and neurolinguistic programming sales training courses. But equal success in her new venture was not forthcoming. Business was flat, stale and motionless. After four months of trying, Joanna was confused if not bewildered. But ever the sales pro, Joanna knew she needed help more than inspiration and was resolved to get it. So, determined to succeed again, she asked questions, talked to anyone who would listen, and sought advice. Yet she anticipated what the problem was and what the solution would have to be: Her business was not acquiring enough new accounts because she was not prospecting on a consistent daily basis. The problem was her, and she knew it.

"Guess it's time to put down *The Little Engine That Could*. I like listening to that sales training stuff—it gets me going in the morning. They're great," she said, energetically starting to describe her situation while walking to her seat. Her voice and body were constantly in motion, restlessly announcing the value she placed on every minute and encouraging everyone else to do the same. "I think I'm experiencing call reluctance," she said, cutting to the core of the matter while glancing at her watch as if her day was planned to the second. "I need help."

Joanna was hurried but never defensive. We had to repeat ourselves rather often, but that was because she didn't listen well, not because she was oppositional. Her Call Reluctance Scale results indicated that she did, indeed, have Role Rejection Call Reluctance, and a predisposition to two additional types: Networking through her friends (Separationist) and networking through her family (Emotionally Unemancipated).

Typical of all the high-level salespeople we have worked with, Joanna immediately corroborated our diagnosis without argument and proceeded to speculate upon where her call reluctance came from. "Why didn't it bother me before now?" she wondered aloud. "Maybe it did," she answered herself. "I just didn't know it."

Reflecting over her years in sales, she recalled that she began to feel shame early in her career, during the three years she sold cosmetics. Neglecting to soothe, or even recognize, her situation, she decided to outrun it by default. She changed sales careers as often as fashion-conscious yuppies change their "look."

Her failure to work all the contacts accessible through her family and friends never appeared to limit her sales career for two classic reasons: 1) She used compensatory prospecting, making up for threatening leads she didn't work by over-reliance on leads that were less menacing, and 2) she remained a moving target, perpetually changing sales positions long before it became necessary to work all the prospects available to her. Her strategy worked. She never stayed long enough in any sales position to allow her Role Rejection to visibly limit her, and she skillfully danced around her two dormant types of call reluctance, not realizing that one day she would have to confront them. To her sales managers and colleagues, Joanna personified success. But in her own words, "I never was as successful as I could have been—or should have been."

Now fixed in place as owner of her own business, there was no place to hide. Nowhere to run. No alternative forms of prospecting to lean on. She had to start from scratch, tenaciously prospecting every way she could, for every new account she could get. Her company's expenses always seemed to exceed income. The pressure was beginning to cause her moods to fluctuate wildly.

The antidote was simple and sure. She had to make herself and her product line more visible. There were presentations to give, advertisements to write, mail outs to send, press releases to prepare, radio interviews to arrange, and referrals to obtain. Friends and relatives (most of whom lived in her community) had to be queried for contacts and connections. And it all had to be done with pride and determination. It would be difficult. Or would it?

Joanna used Thought Realignment to repair the cracks in her attitude about sales professionals. With speed and dispatch, she mastered the technique in record time. Applying each step in order, exactly as prescribed, she persevered until she read the Parable of the Eldorado. Then it happened. Her over-stylized career dedication lightened up. She looked transformed, like Scrooge on Christmas morning, or a student relieved to find that a difficult examination had been postponed—indefinitely.

Joanna always smiled, though her smile was not always believable. Now she beamed, infecting everyone within her range—even the two authors who are not by nature given to wanton smiling, and not quickly heartened by those who are.

Returning from lunch fifteen minutes early, Joanna sprinted into our office for further instructions, as we had agreed. Gushing in without warning, she grabbed one of us, then the other, and began hugging and kissing us like blood relatives at a family reunion. Like a New Zealand tourist unexpectedly stumbling onto an Australian nude beach, we were not quite certain what one is supposed to do.

Delighted, but unpracticed at communicating with someone in her state of commotion, we proposed using Sensory Injection next. Warily backing away, we spoke very slowly and very loudly, emphasizing each syllable as one would speak to the hearing impaired.

Joanna decided to use baby powder for her fragrance cue. It reminded her of the love and comfort she associated with her early childhood, the same love and safety she wished for her own children.

After selecting her fragrance cue, Joanna struggled mightily to relax, a phenomenon relatively unknown to her before confronting her call reluctance. Yet she claims that after a few unsuccessful attempts, she was finally able to relax.

Once relaxed, she initially paired the smell of her baby powder to the sensation of relaxation as she experienced it. After that, she strengthened the bond by repeating the process twice a day for the prescribed five days.

Preparations accomplished, it was time to see if she could ask a family member or a friend to help connect her with some prospects. With a supply of baby powder in her purse, she ventured out to apply what she had learned.

Firing an aromashot of baby powder immediately before telephoning her best friend, head of public relations for a local defense engineering conglomerate, Joanna paused to see what would happen. "In my mind I was waiting to feel embarrassed or awkward or something. I thought I would. But it didn't happen. I felt fine even though I was about to do something I really don't like doing," she said, stabbing the desk with her index finger to emphasize "don't like doing."

"You know, Richard, my friend?" she asked excitedly. "He gave me seven good referrals!" For Joanna, it was another beginning. Four years later, she is a complete prospector. Tireless. Successful. Still checking her watch.

Her small company grew, and was sold for "an obscene profit." Today, she manages other salespeople. Her career has soared. But she makes sure that her new salespeople get off on the right track. A lonely can of baby powder rests among her prized sales trophies.

Self-Confidence: The Feeling of Competence

This section contains step-by-step instructions for using your sense of smell to help optimize your prospecting performance.

A salesperson recently showed us a self-help book which improperly claimed that if you purged yourself of negative self-talk you'd be happy. We showed him a second book, our own, which if read too hastily could be accused of the same logical misconduct.

Countermeasures like Thought Zapping help quiet negative feelings which accompany distressful prospecting. They do not result in positive feelings about prospecting because dislodging a negative does not deposit a positive in its place. The two conditions are radically different.

This logic is flat-footed and steady. It is foolish to reason that because your call reluctance no longer has you lying down, you must, therefore, be standing up. You could be sitting. A separate application may be necessary to help you to your feet. Sensory Injection, using your sense of smell, can help boost your confidence and raise your spirits. But how high is high enough?

Positive Attitude, Positive Results?

Is an upbeat attitude really a precursor for effective sales performance? If so, under what conditions? To what degree?

The influence of attitude upon performance is hazy. The claims are confusing, the evidence contradictory, and the conclusions unequivocally unclear.

Credible data on the issue is scant, but what there is seems to grudgingly support a *preference* for a positive attitude but not a *necessity*. Attitude probably contributes about as much to actual sales performance as self-esteem, mental rehearsal, and other "soft" training concepts, but not as much as "harder" components such as physical energy, career focus, and disciplined daily prospecting. What do *you* think? Do you know salespeople who are failing to achieve their performance potential even though their attitude is upbeat and optimistic?

Positive people expecting to perform well ought to do better than negative people expecting to fail. Besides, most people, sales and non-salespeople alike, probably agree that optimism feels better than pessimism.

Would you like to fortify your attitude before a potentially distressing prospecting situation? If so, consider using the following technique. It can help you engineer your attitude to an optimum state of positive expectation.

What Is Self-Confidence?

We hold the minority view of self-confidence defined below because we intend to do something with it. We're forced to define it in terms of what it *does*, not what it is. Admittedly, like our definition of motivation, our definition of self-confidence is probably too restrictive for most sales trainers.

To us, self-confidence is: the entire mosaic of *sensations* which correspond to certain known and unknown neurophysiological changes associated with attaining a highly prized or desired end as a result of personal achievement.

Don't despair if that was hard to digest. It's hard for us, too, and it's our definition! So we'll try again: In Texas terms, self-confidence is what you feel when you know you "done good." Using Sensory Injection, you can trigger the same feelings *before* you do good, so hopefully you will do good again.

The following technique can be used successfully even if you have yet to experience success in your sales career. It can even be used if you have never experienced success in anything in your life. The procedure is so promising we think Sensory Injection should be included in preventive call reluctance training for *all* new salespeople. Here's how to use it.

1. Select a Fragrance Cue

Most salespeople don't have a fragrance cue they associate solely with high performance. But there are exceptions.

Kirk Jamison, area sales manager for a large consumer electronics manufacturer, carries a can of leather fragrance. The smell reminds him of his little league baseball years when he regularly experienced "sweat and success." Saleswoman Janet Marshall uses spices and herbs usually associated with Christmas to help her ready her attitude for prospecting.

She says it makes her feel like an eager child at Christmas again. Commercial real estate agent Buzz Lederer has carried an old, worn dollar bill in his wallet for almost four years. He ritualistically takes it out and sniffs it before closing every big sale. "Money has a smell," he says. "That old dollar bill tunes my senses to the opportunity in front of me, not the obstacles around me." Kirk, Janet and Buzz are fortunate. They have working *positive* sensory cues. Most salespeople don't. They just have negative ones. Positive cues must be *crafted*.

To set up the technique, you have to select a "clean" fragrance cue. What is a "clean" fragrance cue? It's a perfume, after shave or some other fragrance that is *free of surplus meaning*. It should be something you have not smelled or used before. Also, it should be one you don't already associate with anyone else.

The fragrance cue you select must be portable so you can carry it with you. Additionally, you will need a small wad of cotton or cloth so you can precisely administer your fragrance cue to your nose.

2. Select Support Person (Optional)

It is not absolutely essential that you work with another person. It's not required for Sensory Injection to work. But it sure makes matters easier. Critical initial training steps are achieved much faster and require less effort. Using a confederate also helps insure that the technique will be as effective as possible. A sales manager, trainer, colleague, friend or spouse all make excellent support persons.

You work alone? In solitude? You don't have a spouse? No friends? No usable contacts at all save for occasional voices? Well, if you answered "yes" to those questions, you're a hard-core mystic, Oppositional, or have some very serious problems. Have you considered dancing lessons?

3. Select a Success Calibration Task

Now you must choose a task. It should be one that stretches you, takes you to the edge of your abilities, and then requires a little bit more. Choose one that is difficult but accomplishable, one that reflects skill, disciplined concentration, and single-minded purpose, not just luck. Here are some examples:

- Target practice with a rifle or pistol
- Throwing a basketball
- Pitching horseshoes
- Throwing darts
- Pitching coins

Whichever you try, *you must try to perform at a distance which is slightly beyond your present level of skill or native ability.* (Failure to do this properly now will assure failure of the technique later on.)

We recommend pitching coins for several good reasons. 1) Most people are unpracticed coin throwers, so they approach the activity without significant emotional "noise." 2) It is logistically the simplest. It can be done in your office or home and requires only a cup and about 30 pennies, a reward cue (discussed next) and your fragrance cue. The instructions that follow presume you will be attempting the coin toss.

4. Select a Reward Cue

What turns you on? (Perhaps the question should be rephrased with more verbal precision.) What represents achievement to you? Money? Recognition? Applause? Candy?

Achievement should be closely followed by reward, even if it is only symbolic. So choose something to reward yourself with each time you pitch one of your pennies into the cup. Your reward cue should be easily accessible, relatively plentiful, and something you value or desire. We suggest gold coins and diamonds but small pieces of candy or dollar bills will work nicely, too.

Each successful performance must be *immediately* followed with a reward. To be effective, rewards must be given quickly and consistently. They must be given *every* time you pitch a coin into the cup and *only* when you deliberately pitch a coin into the cup. You should not, for example, receive a reward for angrily throwing all your remaining coins at the ceiling in frustration, only to have some ricochet off the wall and fall into the cup. No reward should be given for "close calls," "best personality," or "most improvement." They can't substitute for consistent daily prospecting and they don't apply to the coin toss, either.

5. Surrender Your Setup Supplies To Your Confederate

Give your fragrance cue, cotton swabs, and rewards to your support person.

6. "X" Marks the Spot

Using a scrap of paper or some other means, mark the spot on the floor where you will stand while you try to pitch your coins into the cup. Stand there. Ask your support person to place a small cup at a distance that should enable you to pitch coins into the cup with about 25% accuracy. Try to guess the correct distance, but do not verify it by actually pitching coins. Your cup should not be placed so close that achievement is assured or so far that it is impossible. Once you and your support person have negotiated the proper distance, the support person should take the cup and move it about 10% further away. Hitting the target at that distance will require tenacious self-control, persistence, resilience, concentration, patience and practice (just like prospecting). You will probably find hitting the mark difficult, frustrating and infrequent. But when you do, it will be a genuine achievement, a cause for celebration.

Once your cup is in place, your support person should stand aside, at-the-ready with your reward and a cotton swab pretreated with your fragrance cue.

7. Connect Your Fragrance Cue

While standing at your mark, start pitching your coins. Remember, as in prospecting and selling, almost doesn't count. Don't stretch so far forward that you lose your balance, or waste time and effort trying to find clever ways to cheat, reinterpret the instructions, or beat the system. That drains energy that could be put to better use. (Be careful: If you're prone to search for loopholes or find an easy way out, your rewards will be fraudulent and unfairly earned.)

Each time you successfully pitch a coin into the cup, your support person should *immediately* present you with a single reward, closely followed by one or two short whiffs (aromashots) of your fragrance cue. Make certain you do not inadvertently get any on your lip or nose where the scent would linger.

8. Consolidate

Every time you successfully complete a coin-toss/reward/aromashot sequence, feelings of achievement should be augmented by voice and body cues. To do that, amplify the sensations surrounding your accomplishment by verbally confirming *aloud*: "I did it! I feel great!" A heartfelt smile would be a nice touch, too—if it is genuine.

9. Strengthen

Continue pitching coins until you have been through the reward/aromashot sequence at least five times. Ten is better.

Some salespeople will complete the task in less than 30 minutes. Others will take longer. If 30 minutes pass without reward, move the cup 10% closer. If more than 10 rewards are earned in 10 minutes or less, move the cup 10% further away.

10. Fortify

Practice this procedure at least once a day for five days, allowing your fragrance cue to become automatically linked to feelings you associate with achievement. Twice a day for five days is better. The more time you invest in fortifying your fragrance cue before taking it into the "real world," the better your results should be.

11. Fire When Ready!

Now the fun begins. Anxious? Doubtful? Uncertain? Fire an aroma-shot. Apply your fragrance cue *prior to* prospecting situations where you need to feel like you can perform at your optimum. Watch what happens. Out of habit, you may still be aware of looking about for distress cues. But *your body is receiving a salvo of concentrated, unmistakable notifications to expect optimum performance. Go for it!*

You can fire Aromashots preventively by applying your fragrance cue immediately *before* possible exposure to distressful prospecting cues, or correctively by responding covertly with your fragrance cue immediately upon detection of a distressful prospecting cue. Simply excuse yourself for a moment, find a private place, and apply your fragrance cue. Or, try to do so surreptitiously. There are ways: Secretly treat your shirt-sleeve or a handkerchief with your fragrance cue before you prospect—just in case.

If you know you're going to be in an intense prospecting situation, violate one of the guidelines above by dousing your upper lip, under your nose, with your fragrance cue. It will overpower any other cues you are exposed to. Coauthor George Dudley often uses this procedure prior to talking to very large audiences.

12. Renew the Cue

Aromashots can transform your lifeless attitude about prospecting into spirited, positive expectation. But you have to protect your fragrance cue carefully or you could develop a tolerance.

The best way to keep your fragrance cue fresh is to renew it often. While experiencing a rush of exhilaration from highly significant or unexpected successes, get out your fragrance cue and smell it while saying aloud: "I did it! I feel great!"

Some moments are tailor-made for fragrance cue maintenance. Here are some examples:

- After closing an important sale
- Right after you have successfully overcome a formidable prospecting obstacle

- When you successfully outmaneuver a major competitor

- When you successfully overcome a potentially nasty episode of call reluctance, fear or hesitation

CAUTION: *Never* use your fragrance cue for any non-call reluctance purpose. Careless misuse, inconsistent use, or mixing fragrance cues together can seriously impair the ability of this technique to produce the results you want.

Variations on a Theme

Call-reluctant salespeople brew elaborate, creative schemes to avoid prospecting in threatening areas. They show the same ingenuity when selecting fragrance cues. The range is staggering. Here are some examples:

- Menthol inhalers

- Ammonia

- Motor oil

- Vegemite (An incomprehensible Australian breakfast food spread like jam or jelly. Its consistency is not unlike motor oil or axle grease. It actually may be recycled motor oil or axle grease.)

- Floral bouquet

- Window cleaner

- Armpit sweat (Claimed by one saleswoman to be a sexual turn-on. Note: Male armpit sweat does contain tiny amounts of Androstenol, a steroid that is naturally secreted into the armpit area. Some researchers contend that it's a "pheromone," a naturally occurring sexual attractant.)

- Typewriter ribbons

- Soap

- Freshly cut grass

- Camphor

- Cedar

- Mud

- Shampoo

- Eucalyptus

- Sweaty socks

- Herbs

As you can see from the list above, fragrance cues are a highly individual matter. Since we first began teaching Sensory Injection a few years ago, salespeople have confessed to using an extraordinary array of smells, stenches, odors and scents to evict call reluctance. Now it's your turn. Pick a fragrance cue. But be careful. *Use good judgment.* We strongly advise you not to use stinging substances like ammonia or menthol inhalers which could be harmful—if not dangerous. You don't have to slaughter your nose to salvage your wallet. Play it safe. Stick with Vegemite or mud.

Sensory Injection helped us quiet down our fears and fattened our wallets. Aside from that, it's fun! In our opinion, it's one of the most effective emotional management tools you can use. Try it.

If you use an unusual or creative fragrance cue let us know. Your correspondence will reach us if sent in care of the publisher.

The Reemergence of W. Percy Barden

W. Percy Barden was skeptical. He didn't think call reluctance training was very important. It was certainly not applicable to him. But then, Percy was skeptical about most things. He didn't think large corporations—like his—needed to communicate with employees. He was also suspicious of fair employment practices or anything, for that matter, that came from "liberal social scientists." Years ago he had come to doubt the existence of God, but remained open to intellectually deeper questions—such as the existence of UFO's. Yet his faith in his corporate employer never wavered. He was an "organization man" all the way. He carried himself with quiet satisfaction, perhaps even a touch of arrogance. W. Percy Barden was senior vice-president of personnel.

Percy's squinted, austere perspective endowed him with tireless skepticism about the character of others, and hazardous delusions about himself. He walked tall, rode high, and believed he was essential. He was lost in the long, narrow littleness of his life.

No one ever stopped to ask him for advice or to engage in friendly conversation, except for an occasional pin-striped sycophant aspiring to be like him. His heart was empty, his mind was dry, and his soul had blown away. But Percy did his job, and did it well.

He never asked for our help. Carrying his regulation briefcase, he presented himself only as an "observer" for his company—which, he was fond of reminding us, "may or may not be interested in booking you to speak at next year's annual sales convention." He had connections. We were touched.

Like a hard-core chain-smoker losing count of the cigarettes smoked, Percy seemed unaware that he was *no longer employed by "his company."* After 27 years, he was now redundant, obsolete. He had been "outplaced," along with 746 other employees, in a move to make the company appear more profitable during a tough economic downturn. Personnel was now called "Human Resources."

Percy had supervised traumatic discharges before—many times. Most former employees referred to outplacement services had been, like him, loyal. Most had decades of tenure. This time was no different. He terminated the employment of all 746 except for one, himself. That came as a total and unexpected surprise.

Two months passed. Percy was still unable to emotionally accept what had happened, and he still had not found a new position. Mentally and financially, he needed a job. A concerned staff member at the outplacement firm referred him to us.

Percy had not marketed himself since his first job years ago. His company's outplacement firm tried gallantly to help. They offered him first-rate counseling, supplied helpful search advice, and even provided an office for him during the transition. But Percy refused to market himself. He would not self-promote. Though *technically* not a salesperson, he was *call reluctant*. That had to change.

The Call Reluctance Scale, which he completed to "check out, not for himself," showed morbid levels of Over-Preparation and Role Rejection. Percy was a walking personnel manual who could not let his light shine. We found no other major obstacles. But no others were needed. He was shut down and out of touch.

After some gentle but persistent prodding, we finally got him to acknowledge that his company—the place where he had entrusted his career as a youth only to be discarded in his later years—had let him go. It was traumatic. The experience deflated him, but he managed to accept what had happened and, more importantly, assume responsibility for what would, or would not, happen next.

We used the same techniques we use with salespeople who have Over-Preparation and Role Rejection Call Reluctance. He learned and applied them. They worked. Soon he was over his hesitation to self-promote, but he didn't have the spark of confidence necessary to catch the eye of prospective employers. So we taught him how to apply Sensory

Injection using his sense of smell. As expected, the idea was greeted with skepticism which he immediately zapped with his Thought Zapping rubber band!

We set up and calibrated Percy's coin toss and he began. At first, tossing coins at a cup seemed too juvenile. Then he started having fun. Smiling. On a few occasions he even laughed, saying it reminded him of his childhood during the Great Depression. After a few days of practice he was ready. He selected Old Spice after-shave as his fragrance cue. He

Turn Yourself On To Turn Your Fear Off

Aromashots can help control the type, timing and degree of feelings you experience. By smothering your cortex with scents to elicit mood-enhancing states, you can put the squeeze on prospecting worries. Which fragrances work best? That's up to you. Experiment. Be creative. Amaze yourself.

Some call-reluctant salespeople use only trustworthy smells, such as cinnamon, which they associate with reassuring past experiences. Others confess to more playful practices. They use potions and perfumes they associate with heightened sexual experiences.

It works. Would-be call reluctance episodes are checked, fast, because you can't be sexually turned on and call reluctant at the same time.

But before you douse yourself with a sexy scent, consider. Can you really make a serious sales presentation with *that* smile on your face?

All versions of Sensory Injection work the same way. They seize attention and then activate previously learned attitude-enhancing states *before* potential call reluctance triggers can signal the presence of a threat. Using trained sensory cues, you can direct yourself to feel any way you want—confident, sexy, admired, accomplished or relaxed. The possibilities are limitless.

Each version of Sensory Injection follows the same instructional sequence so there is no need for us to repeat every step for each. Instead, we will briefly describe each, highlighting important differences when necessary. You can take it from there, making any other adaptations you might need.

confided that he hadn't used Old Spice since his early "tiger years" with the company. That revelation was a surprise. Percy a tiger?

It took three weeks of hard work and two bitter setbacks, but Percy finally got a job: personnel manager for a medium-sized building materials company. The industry was new to him so he had much to learn. But he had already learned something important. "I hire myself out every day," he said, proud of his new perspective. "I'm no longer for sale."

We're far from certain that his success was due to Sensory Injection. That would be overstating the point. Perhaps it was something in the Old Spice. Or luck. Maybe he would have found a job anyway, even if we had done nothing. We're not sure. But Percy, the reformed skeptic, doesn't share our doubt. He fondly recalls tossing coins and sniffing Old Spice just before his interviews. An approachable man with a contagious smile, he genuinely likes to tell others how he transported himself to a new life and a new career with a pocket full of pennies and an aged bottle of Old Spice after-shave.

VISUAL SENSORY INJECTION

Research scientist Eckhard Hess has observed involuntary changes in the eyes of people viewing sexual material. The size of their pupils altered significantly in response to seeing erotic pictures (*The Tell-Tale Eye*). Their eyes were not passive; they self-adjusted to the situation, trying to get the best view.

Other studies have found that showing a picture of a familiar face can cause a change in the electrical conductivity of the surface of the skin—*even though the face cannot be identified* ("Where Is the Self?" Bernard L. Strehler, *Synapse*, 1991). According to this research, we can experience *physical* reactions to what we see, heightened by emotional associations we may have formed, even when large chunks of information are missing.

Phenomena like this are formally studied in university laboratories by a newly evolved species called the white-coated, grant-eating wizard. The same phenomena are accessible to regular folks through experience.

Once, while we were waiting to speak before a large convention audience in Atlantic City, New Jersey, Shannon confessed to an intense dislike for an individual on the sponsoring organization's staff. That was uncharacteristic of her. What was the cause of her acrimonious reaction? Instead of providing a socially acceptable explanation for her behavior, she continued hurling a zoo-full of animal traits at her innocent target (negative traits, it should be pointed out, that she usually reserved for her coauthor).

She verbally proceeded to lacerate her unsuspecting victim, killing him softly through the slightest of smiles, all the while maintaining the innate self-control of a hard-headed southern belle trying to justify racial segregation to a group of black people. "Look at him," she whispered, while pointing surreptitiously. "Don't you just know he's vain as can be?" She continued her monologue without pausing for a reply. "He's probably dishonest. Lecherous, too. You think he's some kind of politician or something?"

After some gentle questioning, we learned this gentleman's only offense was his rather bushy eyebrows. They had provoked the entire episode. Why? Years ago, Shannon had an unpleasant experience with a fellow who also had bushy eyebrows. She had long since forgotten the experience, but the sensations were encoded into her memory and were still capable of being recalled by a benign pair of bushy eyebrows. Have you ever found yourself similarly reacting to someone you have only seen and never met?

Can what you see influence how you feel? Let's try an informal experiment. Find a picture of yourself as a child and look at it for a few minutes. What feelings are you aware of? Are they good feelings? Strong feelings?

People experience a range of feelings when they see pictures of themselves as children. If they were happy as children, they feel happy. If they were troubled, they feel troubled—all triggered by seeing the pictures.

Other things we see around us also invite emotional reactions.

- Explicit sexual material (movies, video tapes, magazines) remain consistently hot sales items because *seeing* them results in specific, measurable, *physical* changes. These changes are associated with heightened sexual readiness which, according to unverified reports, is not altogether unpleasant.

- Seeing a fresh puddle of vomit is enough to cause some people to throw up.

- Crosses, crucifixes and shiny St. Christopher medals dangle from car mirrors because they are associated with feelings of comfort, security and well-being.

- Seeing a freshly made chocolate eclair can make your mouth water.

- The sight of a green, putrid oyster can have the opposite effect.

- Brightly colored Christmas decorations can lift the spirits of the most cantankerous old misers.

- Research psychologist Manuel J. Smith, author of *Kicking the Fear Habit*, describes a common experience every parent has (with implications for Visual Sensory Injection). "Go to the municipal park in your area on Sunday," Smith writes. "Look for a two-year-old child crying, and what is mommy saying? 'Look at the white birds on the lake. Aren't they pretty? See them all swimming together? See the little baby ducks following their mommy?' Mom is getting her child to orient (switch attention) to the many things in his environment and she does it simply, successfully and with minimum effort."

- Newspaper columnist Dick Hitt reported a device that uses vision to directly influence physical relaxation. Called the Mind Mirror, Hitt said it worked by "displaying a full spectrum, real-time image of the electrical activity in both brain hemispheres." ("Brain Enhancer Leaves Curious With an Idea," *Dallas Times Herald*, June 11, 1989)

- John T. Malloy (*Dress For Success*) is the patron saint of the look-successful, be-successful crowd. His enormously popular book introduced readers to the strategic importance of proper business attire. Many salespeople attribute large production increases to the advice in Malloy's book. We agree. But Visual Sensory Injection tells us there may be more to the story. The clothes you wear not only help you position yourself for better access to the people you wish to influence, but they also dramatically influence *you*. Professional actors confess that it's much easier to simulate the personality of characters they portray once they're in costume. When salespeople wear costumes *they associate* with success, they tend to behave as if they were accomplished and successful. That may be why they prospect more boldly, behave more decisively, and produce more income.

The Yellow Dot Technique

The instructions for using Visual Sensory Injection are the same as Sensory Injection using smell which we have already described. First, select the feeling state you wish to later reproduce on cue. (For the Yellow Dot, we suggest relaxation.) Produce the feeling state and pair it with a visual cue. We use small yellow dots with adhesive backing. After sufficient practice, take your visual cue (yellow dot) to work with you. When you need to relax prior to prospecting, put your visual cue in your line of vision. The rest is automatic.

You can attach your visual cue to your telephone, briefcase, sales proposals, desk top, automobile dashboard, almost anywhere you can see it when you need to. We still use our yellow dots, and we surreptitiously attach them to microphones all over the world. If you happen to attend one of the conventions at which we're featured to speak, look closely. You may catch us fixing the yellow dot to our microphone. When we look out at the audience, we're actually looking out over our yellow dot which is poised in our field of vision, signaling us to relax.

Never use your visual cue when you don't need it. If you do, you risk developing a tolerance to it, thus reducing its effectiveness.

Visual Sensory Injection is effective, but its potency varies from person to person. Usually, when it fails, it's because of insufficient or inconsistent practice. Sometimes it's due to undiagnosed call reluctance impostors. But if you're sufficiently motivated, goal-focused, and follow the guidelines we have outlined, Visual Sensory Injection should help you learn to relax while prospecting.

TASTEFUL SENSORY INJECTION

Your sense of taste can also help you form a new, more positive orientation to prospecting. Why? You may "be what you eat," but you *feel* what you taste. Taste can influence mood.

Taste triggers various body-state changes, some of which are powerful enough to "interfere with your thinking brain." (Manuel J. Smith, *Kicking the Fear Habit*) Arthur Henley says, "Our taste buds affect not only the way we feel about certain foods, but also the way we feel—period!" (*Phobias: The Crippling Fears*)

Unconvinced? You don't see how taste could have a very *substantial* influence on how you feel? Maybe the following informal experiment will help.

The Feel of Taste?

Food has physical and chemical properties. It also has an emotional dimension.

- Are there certain tastes you associate with comfort? What are they?

- Are there tastes you associate with confidence and well-being? What are they?

- Do certain tastes bring to mind childhood memories? Which tastes?

- Do you consider certain tastes sensual? Which ones?

For the next few seconds, just think about eating a *bad* oyster and read the following text aloud, slowly:

The putrid, green-colored morsel slides from its half shell into my open mouth. To my surprise it feels warmer than room temperature, not cool like I expected. As I bite down, starting to chew, I realize it lacks consistency. It has turned into a foul, slimy liquid.

How about it? Do you feel any different? Are you ready for a big meal? Probably not. Taste, and the mental associations we bring to it, can contribute to what we feel and how much we feel it. We can't speak for you, but just having to write about eating a bad oyster was enough to make us queasy. If you need more evidence, find it somewhere else.

Food and Mood

The chemical composition of what you eat and drink can alter your mood. That has been well established by academics and nutritional practitioners alike. Massive inroads have been made in this area. The following six factoids are examples.

- Caffeine and Tryptophan "can directly affect brain function and consequently behavior..." (H. R. Lieberman, "The Behavioral Effects of Foods," lecture, Department of Brain and Cognitive Science, Massachusetts Institute of Technology, 1987)

- The artificial sweetener Aspartame can "cause mood changes in depressed individuals." ("The Sweet Taste of Distress," *Science News*, April 19, 1986)

- A 1990 study reported that food consumption and taste preferences of adult females change across the menstrual cycle—most likely due to endocrinological factors. (Bowen and Grunberg, "Variations in Food Preference and Consumption Across the Menstrual Cycle," *Physiology and Behavior*, February 1990)

- Researchers at the Massachusetts Institute of Technology discovered that some people have an unconscious *biochemical* need for a pick-up which can be readily supplied by eating something sweet, like a lollipop.

- Beer affects the mood of self-restrained and problem drinkers differently. Restrained beer drinkers become less aggressive and enjoy the taste of the beverage more than unrestrained drinkers. (Lillian S. Bensley, "The Heightened Role of External Responsiveness in the

Alcohol Consumption of Restrained Drinkers," *Cognitive Therapy & Research*, December 1989)

- Popular Waco, Texas, nutritional counselor Dr. Fran Connor sums it up: "Stressful career conditions, irregular and haphazard eating habits, staccato fad diets, and fast food living can contribute to the undoing of the most stable mind, and the malaise of the most healthy body." ("Nutrition and the Bottom Line," *Journal of Agent and Management Selection and Development*, Vol. 1, No. 3, 1981)

The slippery mental connections between what we *taste* and how we feel is another matter. Considerably less effort has gone into investigating that subject. Consequently, much less is known. But that seems to be changing.

What you eat doesn't just get gulped in, chewed up, and then routed down to your stomach where it's chemically dissolved into nutritional categories. There's more to it than that. We taste what we eat. After speeding along electro-chemical pathways to the brain, sensory signals from taste provoke memories and associations which have been formed by prior experience. They allow us to classify what we taste as comforting, obnoxious, stimulating or exciting. Taste stimulates neuro-chemical messages which have emotional connotations.

- The authors of a Canadian study confirmed that certain moods tend to be affiliated with different tastes. (Lyman and McCloskey, "Food Characteristics Thought Desirable During Various Imagined Emotions," *Journal of Psychology*, March 1989)

- Some chronically overweight people eat to fight off gloomy feelings. They compulsively eat to taste foods they associate with feeling loved, cared for, or comfortable. To them, hunger or nutrition is superfluous.

- One expert, discussing the difficulty of getting adults to change unhealthy eating habits which could be cancer-causing, said children's taste buds have to be trained early because "the foods we eat later in life invoke the sensations associated with the foods we learned to eat as kids." ("Diet and Cancer," *Innovations*, Public Broadcast Service, 1988)

Using taste to evoke positive feelings prior to prospecting is straightforward. The implications for our well-being run further and deeper.

Training Sequence

Applying Sensory Injection via your sense of taste is easy. The step-by-step instructions parallel those outlined earlier for using your sense of smell. First, select the feeling state you want to reproduce later on cue. Then produce that feeling state and pair it with your taste cue. After sufficient practice, take your taste buds prospecting. When you need to fortify yourself with your feeling state, put your taste cue in your mouth. The rest is automatic, compliments of your nervous system and the effort you invested in practice.

Like smell, taste can be paired to *any* feeling state you wish. Potential taste cues are abundant, limited only by your imagination and what you can safely put in your mouth.

Some tastes are particularly suited for wrenching your attention away from call reluctance cues. Bitter or sour flavors work like Thought Zapping rubber bands for the taste buds because you can't efficiently fear something and battle a disagreeable taste at the same time.

Other, less aggressive tastes, are better suited for engineering alternative feeling states such as relaxed composure or positive expectation.

To jar your attention loose from call reluctance cues, try:

- A cold, bitter pickle
- Biting a lemon
- Persimmon
- Bitter lime
- Durian

Noteworthy alternatives include:

- Chocolate
- Chewing gum
- Mints
- Cinnamon
- Nuts
- Dried fruits

One of the best mediums for delivering tasteful Sensory Injection is hard candies with highly flavored center sections. They're accessible, great as taste cues, highly portable, inexpensive, and quite effective.

Biting down on a taste cue with a soft center releases an explosion of flavor which can instantly summon an alternative feeling state.

Learning Fear Sideways

Some commercial sales training vendors pitch the viewpoint that consequential learning results from traumatic or intense life situations—so-called "significant emotional events."

This is *one* way things get learned, but it is certainly not the only way or even the most common way. In terms of call reluctance, as we have said repeatedly, initial prospecting fears can be acquired by just experiencing low level anxiety in a prospecting situation. The anxiety doesn't have to be "significant." *It doesn't even have to be related to prospecting!* It usually isn't.

This phenomenon was verified several years ago by University of Amsterdam researchers J.T. Barendregt and F.S. van Dam. They demonstrated that hypnotized volunteers could be made to fear benign common occurrences like tones sounding or lights being turned on. Once hypnotized, the investigators used posthypnotic suggestions to instruct their subjects—or victims, depending on your point of view—that lights and tones would *continue* to cause a fear reaction even after they had been awakened from their experimental trance-state. Interesting but not remarkable since the two scientists had not demonstrated anything that's not routine for any common stage hypnotist. But Barendregt and van

---

Durian: The "King of Fruit"?

What is Durian? Durian is a fruit about the size of a football, very thickly skinned with a mass of sharp spikes. To some, it is a gross, awful-tasting substance eaten with impunity by residents of Singapore. They enjoy eating it while watching television—like Texans enjoy beer and potato chips. Durian has been mercifully banned from airplanes and hotel rooms in the area because of the lingering stench it leaves behind.

Perhaps the only thing that native Singaporians, such as our friend Debbie Teo, probably enjoy more is feeding the stuff to unsuspecting authors, like us, while videotaping their heroic efforts to remain diplomatic and tactful.

We heartily recommend visiting Singapore. We do not recommend trying Durian.

Dam are scientists, not entertainers. They continued to present the trained light cue over and over, even after their research subjects had awakened. Right before the light cue was turned on, however, they also handed their subjects a common, innocuous star-shaped object. After presenting the star and the light *together* a few times, the star began to acquire a behavior-shaping ability on its own. No longer dependent on the light cue, the star made the research subjects as nervous as the light—*all by itself*. In fact, the indirect training was so effective that one individual had trouble holding the star in her hand—*even when she was offered relatively large amounts of money to do so.*

Most forms of call reluctance are learned in the same indirect but powerful way. When connections of this type are formed, then reinforced, words alone don't have the jurisdiction to sever them. You can't simply talk yourself out of it.

Capital procedures, like Thought Zapping and Sensory Injection, are needed to repel the habit. Then it can be replaced with new habits which are more likely to move you closer to your performance goals.

SONIC SENSORY INJECTION

Physically, sound is just a wave-like mechanical vibration of air, an energy flux over a given area. In terms of human experience, sound is much more. Its significance towers sublimely above its simple physical properties: pitch, level, tone and timbre. Today, scientific investigators seek to better understand how the physical properties of sound intermix with brain functions, like memory and learning, to influence feelings. Understanding sound only in terms of its physical properties is fruitless and foolish, like searching for knowledge without reference to truth.

Upon waking in the morning, the hearing ear is greeted by an uninterrupted ensemble of sounds. They can be witless and incoherent or stimulating and arresting. Sounds can alert us to attention or cause us to inwardly reflect. At days end, sounds can help quiet the musings of our mind and lull us off to sleep.

- A scream terrifies or startles.

- A siren alerts.

- Hearing someone yawn can move you to yawn, too.

- Hearing someone cry invokes sympathy or sadness.

- A bugle call stirs you to action.

- You tap your feet to certain rhythms—often without even realizing you're doing it.

- Fingernails screeched across a blackboard surface can cause your skin to crawl.

- Hearing someone uncontrollably laugh can be enough to set off a whole room of uncontrolled laughter.

- Hearing a certain melody can deluge your mind with visceral images of a past romantic adventure.

Sounds and emotions are intertwined, an arrangement that is not peculiar to any particular group of individuals such as *auditories*. (Auditories are individuals who are alleged to weigh the information they get from their sense of hearing more than the information they obtain from their other senses. It has "the sound." The concept should sell to gullible people with money to spend—it passes for fact on the pop-psych speaking circuit. But it finds no such support in credible scientific literature. The term "auditory" is used most often by a talkative group of sectarian, self-help evangelists called *neurolinguistic programmers*. Adequate scientific backing has failed to support many of their claims.)

Feel the Sound

Sound and emotion are traveling buddies, they hang out together. Where you find one, you are likely to find the other. Poignant sounds may actually serve as *memory markers*, helping us divide important stages of our lives so we can recall significant life events. Who can forget the sound of school bells?

The sound of a school bell ringing the end of class may still signal the student in us to change rooms—like the guests at the Mad Hatter's tea party. "Clean cups! Move down!" (*Alice In Wonderland*, Lewis Carroll) More than 71 recent academic studies confirm the connection between what we hear and how we feel. Practical applications range from marketing to mental health.

Years ago, Ivan Pavlov, the famous Russian physiologist, used a sound to bring modern learning theory to life. He discovered that a simple tone could become the psychological equivalent of a piece of meat. He taught his dogs to drool at the sound of a bell as if the bell was food. More recently, Frank Pacetta (*Don't Fire Them, Fire Them Up*) recommends a nautical cousin of that idea to sales managers—install a ship-captain's bell and give it a good, loud ring whenever someone lands an order. Drooling is, presumably, optional.

- Music therapy, a technique based on using music to help facilitate recovery from physical or emotional impairments, is gaining acceptance as an adjunct clinical treatment.

- Popular writers Robert Ornstein and David Sobel think music may help control some of the hormones that influence the immune system. ("Coming To Our Senses," *Advances*, Fall 1989)

- An Oklahoma educator says music can be used to establish mood, lessen anxiety, encourage calmness, ease loneliness, and soothe irritability. (Betty Harper, "Say It. Review It. Enhance It With a Song," *Elementary School Guidance and Counseling*, February 1985)

Sensory Tales

Two snapshots from our own experience illustrate the link between what we hear and what we feel.

Orchestrated Relaxation:

Recently, while waiting in a Brisbane, Australia, cocktail lounge for an important press interview, an unexpected change came over us. We always over-prepare for interviews and we try to stay reasonably alert. But on this occasion we both sank into our chairs tranquilized and inert. We didn't know why. We were neither drunk nor drugged. After some lifeless conversation on the matter we simultaneously figured out what had happened. It was the music. The selections piped through the hotel lounge sound system were the same pieces Mary Marsella, our massage therapist, plays while dispersing her acutely relaxing massages. It is our practice to get two massages per week when writing or supervising strenuous research projects. Apparently, that was sufficient for a powerful connection to be formed between the background music Ms. Marsella plays and the profound physical relaxation her massages produce.

Agitated Alert:

Coauthor George Dudley is not inclined to sit still for long, enjoyable meals. Regardless of the fare, he can be relied upon to quick-step through the occasion. There's a reason—in addition to his reputed lack of social sophistication. Finding out what it was

continues

Sensory Tales *continued*

required knowledge of Sensory Injection, sound cues, and the discovery of a U.S. government conspiracy to experimentally alter the eating behaviors of unsuspecting young men.

While still in his formative years, Dudley's body and soul were entrusted to surrogate father figures—drill instructors at the dreaded U.S. Marine Corps Recruit Depot at Parris Island, South Carolina. There, for 16 weeks, the future author was not permitted to casually walk to his meals—or anywhere else for that matter. He, along with his comrades, either *marched* or *ran*. Arriving at the dining hall, the young marines dined to the luxurious sounds of Sousa military marches, incessantly blaring out over the ceiling speakers. No time was allocated for visiting or savoring the taste of food. Everything moved double-time. Dudley's young nervous system became confused and he generalized quick-stepping through meals, all meals, everywhere. To this day, he quick-steps through his meals, out of step with everyone else.

- Music not only influences our temperament, but as consumers it also induces moods, influences memory, and manipulates purchasing decisions. "Human beings," one researcher concluded, "nonrandomly assign emotional meaning to music, and music used in marketing-related contexts is capable of evoking nonrandom affective (feeling) and behavioral responses in consumers." (Gordon C. Bruner, "Mood, Music and Marketing," *Journal of Marketing*, October 1990)

- Alpert and Alpert agree. They found that music influences product evaluations and may have a significant impact on purchasing intention. (Alpert and Alpert, "Music Influences on Mood and Purchase Intentions," *Psychology and Marketing*, Summer, 1990)

  (If you need an example, go to any major mall during the pre-Christmas shopping season. What do you hear? Christmas carols. They commemorate the advent of Christendom in every store—even those operated by heathens, heretics, and pagans! Carols cover anti-Christian sentiment like a sonic layer of makeup. They make everyone feel like a celebrant while justifying multiple purchases and inviting customers to "shop till you drop." They have a significant impact on purchasing intention.)

- Morning *drive-time* radio may be mangling your mood before you get to work. Israeli researchers Caspy, Peleg, Schlam and Goldberg report that *sedative* music is highly related to calmness, tenderness, and contentedness while *stimulative* music is more related to tension and anger. ("Sedative and Stimulative Music Effects," *Motivation and Emotion*, June 1988) Earlier, a pair of researchers found that *calm* and *exciting* music may be guilty of sex discrimination, reserving some of its influence for women. (Fisher and Greenberg, "Selective Effects Upon Women of Exciting and Calm Music," *Perceptual and Motor Skills*, June 1972)

Fear-Busters

Certain sounds can be transformed into sound cues by Sensory Injection training. They can then be used to mobilize feeling states capable of fighting call reluctance toxins, like germ killing antibodies.

Applying Auditory Sensory Injection is easy. Like the other forms of Sensory Injection, it requires only the cerebral effort needed to boil water. Just follow the training sequence we outlined for using fragrance cues, making only minor adjustments when needed. In general, the procedure consists of only five steps.

Select. First, select the feeling state you wish to reproduce later on. Do you want to be more upbeat, attitudinally tweaked to perform at your optimum? Or would you rather be more relaxed, composed, and self-controlled? The choice is yours, but only one cue can be trained at a time. (Theoretically, more than one cue can be trained simultaneously. But doing so demands a more complicated training paradigm.) If you only wish to use sound to startle yourself back to prospecting reality, you should understand what you are doing but no actual training or practice is required.

Designate. Next, select a sound cue. You can use sounds you produce yourself such as a handclap or whistle. Alternately, you can play prerecorded sounds such as church bells, musical selections, recordings of tropical rain forest sounds, auditorium applause, thunderstorms, waterfalls, ocean waves, Gregorian chants, etc.

Produce. Once you have chosen your sound cue, produce the feeling state by carefully following the instructions provided earlier in the section on smell.

Pair. Hitch your feeling state to your sound cue by listening to your sound cue immediately upon achieving the feeling state you wish to cue at a later time.

Practice. Practice the last step enough times for the sound to produce the feeling state *by itself*. That will probably require two or three repetitions per day, every day, for three to five days. It will take some of you more than five days, some of you less. Make certain the connection between your sound cue and feeling state is sturdy before trying to use it to counter call reluctance.

Use your sound cue to fortify your attitude whenever you need to, preferably right *before* anxiety-producing prospecting situations.

Break the Sound Barrier

Sound cues can ring, rumble, boom, bang, buzz, clink, clank, and crash. They startle, soothe, or mobilize. They may also be heard by others who are not privy to Sonic Sensory Injection. To them, such sounds will seem bizarre and they might exile you to the edge of social respectability. As a precaution, you should explain what you're doing to the people closest to you at home and work.

The sound you choose for your sound cue is a matter of taste, preference, and function. Hopefully, you will also consult with your imagination and your sense of humor because working with sound cues can be fun. Here are some ideas to get you started.

Whistle Loud. The maxim, "Whistle While You Work," contains some truth. Whistling can be a sound cue. It can be paired with an appropriate feeling state and then used later when needed. Vigorous whistling requires serious effort and attention. Just trying can jar your attention loose from the grips of call reluctance cues.

Sing Loud. You're in your car driving to meet a prospective buyer. You sense a twitch of call reluctance. What can you do? Raise your voice in song! Pretend you're Willie Nelson, Nelson Eddy, Janis Joplin, Julio Iglesias, Olivia Newton-John, Elton John, Mick Jagger, the Righteous Brothers, or if you have loftier ambitions, gospel singer Sandi Patti. Call-reluctant salespeople with 13 or more distinct personalities might consider emulating the choir at King's College, Cambridge. Hyper-Pros should find singing operatic arias consistent with their social pretensions. If you have Oppositional Call Reluctance, you've probably already started grumbling. But grumbling is the melody of malcontentedness you've *been* singing. Try Willie Nelson.

Shout Loudly. Variations on this theme have been around for a long time. Psychotherapist Arnold Lazarus suggested yelling "Stop It!" at the first sign of fear. (*Multimodal Behavior Therapy*) Through the years, countless other practitioners have made their mark by making small, cosmetic changes. But the rationale remains the same. Shouting "Stop it!" works just like a verbal Thought Zapping rubber band.

Hum. Humming is a softened variation of the first two suggestions. You can hum a melody, mantra, or nonsense syllable as you approach potential call reluctance cues.

Fantasy Audio. When you listen to fantasy audio, the music is heard only in your head. You just *imagine* listening to it. Coauthor George Dudley has suggested this technique to others and regularly uses it himself. He *imagines* listening to Bach's *Jesu, Joy of Man's Desiring* prior to a stressful experience. Several years ago he paired the music to relaxing. Since then he imagines hearing this melody whenever his blood pressure readings are taken. Contrary to his extremely demanding lifestyle, he has no record of high blood pressure.

Play an Audio Cassette. Link your favorite music to the feeling state you wish to optimize. Moody salespeople with Role Rejection Call Reluctance tend to like the theme from *Rocky*. But your choices are limitless. Coauthor George Dudley, who tirelessly experiments on himself with Auditory Sensory Injection, listens to Christmas music *every morning of the year*! He has learned to be extremely protective of the sounds he listens to in the morning. He wants them to be bright and renewing, not loudmouthed or profane. What he listens to first thing in the morning is more important to him than what he has for breakfast. Christmas music? Every morning?

Turn On Your Car Radio—Loud. About to leave on a prospecting sales call? Are your thoughts drifting toward call reluctance? If so, use your radio to get them back on track. Switch on your radio. Then turn the volume up *loud, but just for five seconds*. "But which program should I listen to?" Over-Preparers ask. It doesn't matter. Music, news, talk radio—at a window rumbling volume, they all liquefy into noise which insults your eardrums and shatters your concentration. Like smelling salts for fainting spells, a loud, offensive burst of sound can shock you back to prospecting reality.

Sound Advice

Sounds are commanding agents of change. They can startle, uplift, or call to action. Sound cues are distinctive. Linked by training to a goal-enhancing feeling they can deliver concentrated doses of sonic energy strong enough to sweep call reluctance cues from your prospecting pathway.

We hope you try Auditory Sensory Injection. It can help open new doors of prospecting comfort, permanently eliminating the need for call reluctance escape hatches. You've got ears. Use them.

TACTILE SENSORY INJECTION

Touch is the last of the five major senses you can use to give yourself Sensory Injection. Though described last, you will quickly discover it is far from being least important.

- Michelangelo's depiction of God reaching out to touch Adam with life transcended the ceiling of the Sistine Chapel to help shape the artistic and religious sensitivities of our culture.

- "Whenever I want to recall that moment, that high moment of military triumph, I have only to close my eyes and open a window and let the wind blow steady and a little cold across my cheeks and lips. I do it sometimes in moments of uncertainty. Then I become young again, and mighty." (*The Autobiography of Henry VIII*, Margaret George)

- "*Just kiss yourself!*" admonished one of the speakers participating in a National Association of Female Executives teleconference.

- Mothers communicate with their newborn infants primarily through the sense of touch.

- Some salespeople are taught that gently touching their customers can facilitate rapport and increase sales.

- Touch can melt away distracting forces and improve creativity. "Only the person who is relaxed can create," wrote the ancient philosopher, Cicero. His words are being heeded. Some progressive organizations are using the sense of touch to jump-start the creative process with a hands-on massage. ("Creativity Process Often Starts with a Good Massage," *Marketing News*, April 1991)

- Some businesses report that empathetic touch, again in the form of massage, improves worker efficiency. (*Wall Street Journal*, April 23, 1991)

- Does it matter which pajamas you wear to bed, or whether you wear any at all? According to an article in *Men's Health* ("Help for Insomniacs," February 1991), it does. Wearing sleepwear similar to what you wore as a child will transport you back to a time when your biggest worry was not call reluctance or the state of the economy, but whether *Bonanza* would be a rerun next weekend.

- Faith healers—charmers, cranks, charlatans, and true believers—all ritualistically underwrite their practice by skillful *laying on of hands*.

- Attila the Hun and his warriors, returning from battle, jumped and danced around, vigorously shaking their limbs to prevent fear from building up in their muscles.

Our skin doesn't just keep our insides in. It's not just our birthday suit, the outer hide we're born in and destined to wear for the rest of our life on earth. Skin is a properly credentialed sense organ. A living antenna of sorts, it continuously feeds streams of sensory data to our brain where it is processed into watchful intelligence about what's happening out in the world.

Touch and emotion operate closely together under a reciprocal agreement to share data. This arrangement is recognized intuitively even when it is unknown to our intellect. Certain things *touch* us emotionally. Certain people, such as clowns, mystics, and the mentally ill, are *touched*. Physical contact often has direct, intense emotional consequences.

- A threatening shove

- An angry poke

- A tap on the shoulder to get attention

- A pat on the back to signal praise

- A slow, relaxing stroke from a skilled massage therapist

- A sexually intimate caress

If someone touches you, you know it, fast. Depending on how and where you were touched, you respond.

Sensory data streaks to the brain for evaluation through dedicated groups of specialized cells called *neurochemical receptors*. They function like microscopic computer keyboards. When the right kind of signal hits the right kind of nerve cell the signal is relayed to the brain. Otherwise, it is largely ignored.

When you see light, it's because light rays push dedicated neural receptors on your retinas located on the back of your eyeballs. That's how your brain knows, for example, when the color red is being detected. The same light, however, leaves the nerve receptors on your skin and your taste buds completely unmoved unless you're a perpetual mouth-breather, wheezing through life open-mouthed like a human air filter gathering up light rays, sonic vibrations, pollen, mold spores, insects, diesel exhaust, and classified telecommunications. If you meet someone like that, delicately remind them to close their mouth. They'll feel better.

The same type of neurochemical receptors associated with the brain mechanisms that regulate emotions have been found at various *other* locations throughout the body. Neuroscientist Candace Pert reported that neuropeptides, biochemical substances associated with these neuro-chemical receptor sites, formed a communications link between the brain, emotions, and our immune system. Not coincidental to our purpose, these emotion-related chemical receptors tend to be concentrated at the body's sites for *touch*. "Emotions are not just in the brain, they're in the body," says Pert. Massage therapy guru Clyde Ford claims that when he touches the body, "doorways to the mind open and images and memories enter conscious awareness." (*Where Healing Waters Flow*) "Thus," he reasons, "the neuropeptide system can be affected through touch, and emotions can be stored and recalled through (touching) the body." (*Where Healing Waters Meet*) If true, the sense of touch can be used to manage behaviors like call reluctance.

Call Reluctance Applications

Like other forms of Sensory Injection, touch can be used to snatch attention from call reluctance fear cues. Alternatively, it can be used to trigger positive feeling states you associate with optimum performance.

No Pain, No Gain

Who wants pain? Perhaps you do if you want to overcome call reluctance but don't want to master any of the primary fear management techniques.

Ford Motor Company's motto says "Quality is Job One." Job one for your nervous system is "Detect and report pain." Nerve fibers detecting the presence of pain have absolute priority over everything else. Period.

Readers suffering from migraine, cluster, or vascular headaches—conditions far more disabling than call reluctance—already know that. Those conditions force attention onto themselves and away from everything else. They're painful, incapacitating, and have little redeeming value except perhaps one: They illustrate a little used call reluctance management technique. Self-generated physical discomfort can take your mind off your fears. No kidding. One pain can block another. Physical pain can block emotional pain. You can shake off your call reluctance fears by making your body protest. That's what Carla did.

Carla Yamamoto works for a moderately successful California medical supplies company where she is the sole woman sales representative. Before she began selling medical supplies, her company provided un-remarkably ordinary sales training. Preventive call reluctance training was not included. Her managers considered sales call reluctance "a negative concept," so it didn't exist. It was like a scandalous second cousin, never mentioned. Stout requirements for obtaining new accounts did exist, however, and each salesperson, including new ones, was assigned a quota.

A dedicated sales management staff was available to help. The company's "culture" was fashionably dedicated to excellence, customer service, and team building. "Every single salesperson," the corporate credo read, "is an important member of our corporate team." Of course, salespeople achieving their quotas were considered *more* important members of the corporate team, but that's another issue.

Carla didn't sleep much the night before her first day of prospecting. She was anxious. She got up earlier than normal and more anxious than usual, but she was ready. In the shower she recited product specifications. While getting dressed she rehearsed her prospecting presentation. Without realizing it she put on an uncomfortable old bra she thought she had thrown away.

Preoccupied with the day ahead, Carla didn't notice her bra was garroting her chest until she had almost reached her office. It was too late then to return home to change. There wasn't enough time. Going braless was not an alternative. She had to suffer her situation in silence. As the morning progressed, her discomfort increased. After making several prospecting contacts she realized her nervousness had disappeared. Where? When? How? She didn't know.

Her uncomfortable old bra had taken her attention completely off her emotional distress and forced it onto her physical discomfort. Pain blocking pain provided her the opportunity she needed to experience prospecting without emotional distress. In effect, she counter-conditioned herself. Call reluctance, ever the opportunist, was unable to exploit the situation and develop further.

Today, Carla is as industrious and exuberant as ever. She is still employed by the same company where she competes head-to-head every month with two other salespeople, both men, for "sales*man* of the month." She threw her old bra away.

Behavior modification pioneer Dr. Joseph Wolpe used one of Pavlov's principles, *external inhibition*, when he applied electric shock to a patient's skin to demolish phobic anxieties. Fortunately, less drastic measures may be as effective.

- Put a small pebble in your shoe

- Wear uncomfortable underwear (like Carla)

- Slightly over-tighten your belt

- Weigh down your wallet or purse

- Put sharp-edged keys in your pocket (*Be careful! One salesman almost stabbed himself in a most delicate place.*)

You don't have to inflict pain on yourself to overcome call reluctance. There are gentler, equally effective ways to use touch to apply Sensory Injection. A detailed training sequence is found in the earlier section on fragrance cues.

Call Reluctance SWAT Team

The following suggestions may stimulate you to think of creative ways to sidestep your fears. The first group is recommended for shifting your attention away from call reluctance fear cues. *They are not recommended as cues for triggering alternative feeling states.*

Whack! One way to end a frenzied call reluctance attack is with an attention-busting slap in the face. It's about as enjoyable as recalling your last tax audit, but it restores attention to more important matters like prospecting. Try it. Next time you find yourself drifting into a prospecting panic, give yourself a good, swift slap in the face. You can escalate your attack by doing it in front of a mirror. Notice the expression on your face.

Precaution: If you are a semi-sadistic sales manager, be prudent. Only use this method *occasionally* when it is *absolutely* called for and appropriate. You could be sued. If you're a call-reluctant salesperson with masochistic leanings, or British, be equally careful. Improper use could induce enjoyment, an uncourtly situation which might arouse you to sue yourself.

Rapid fire neck-slapping. Just before entering a situation in which there may be fear cues, rapidly slap yourself on the back of the neck a few times. Be careful! Use the soft, blunt underside of your fingers. Don't make a fist. No Karate chops. You're trying to jar yourself loose from fear, not punch yourself out or injure yourself for life.

Pinch yourself. This is a tried-and-true variation of the neck slap. Though less intense, it's probably just as effective, if not more civilized. Prospecting on the phone or in person? Notice your mind starting to dwell on your fears? Try *covertly* giving yourself a convincing pinch on your thigh, underside of your arm, or another sensitive body area. Try to inflict just enough pain to collar your attention but not enough to impose agony; and, by all means, don't blow your cover by yelping out loud. If your sensitivities won't allow you to pinch yourself, find a confederate who will. Pinchers are not an endangered species. Experts are plentiful. Try Mexico City or Rome.

Bite your tongue. If you have trouble locating a sensitive body part to pinch, or a pincher to pinch it, try pinching your tongue with your *teeth*.

Zap your wrist with a rubber band. If you're alert, you have probably wondered if the Thought Zapping rubber band, introduced in an earlier chapter, is actually a variation of Sensory Injection. It is. Sadly, however, since we released the first edition of *The Psychology of Call Reluctance*, the technique has been recklessly over-prescribed by lightweight experts looking for a new marketing gimmick. We've listened to numerous complaints from individuals and organizations who have been victimized by presentations featuring rubber bands "to zap your call reluctance away." Regrettably, *our* names were offered as the authoritative voice behind these ill-advised applications. With good intentions, but inadequate insight, gullible victims of these presentations were hustled into little more than mindless self-flagellation. Before you do the same, *reread the entire chapter on Thought Zapping.*

Precaution: If you've endured child abuse or any other incident where physical pain could have left emotional scars, use these procedures *only* with the knowledge and guidance of a properly trained mental health professional, i.e., a clinical psychologist or psychiatrist. This is imperative if you're currently undergoing treatment for psychological or emotional problems. Though not probable, inappropriate use *could* aggravate dormant psychological difficulties or impair current treatment efforts. If you have *any* doubt, ask your mental health advisor *first*.

A friendly touch. Ask a friend to sit beside you while you prospect or, if necessary, to actually accompany you on a few prospecting calls. He or she should be asked to gently touch your arm, hand, neck, or face for *five seconds* every time you begin to experience distress.

Touch Cues for Alternative Feeling States

The previous group contained suggestions for attentional distraction. Here are some potential touch cues you can use to engineer feeling states you can recall later when you need them.

Tactical touch. Why not use your index finger to touch your forearm or your hand, or touch your fingers together? Almost any part of your body can function as a touch cue. If you want your touch cue to trigger relaxation, review the instructions for "relaxing on cue" in the chapter on Threat Desensitization. Or you can use the instructions provided in the section on fragrance cues.

A friendly touch. Human touch can be an awesome touch cue. Ask your friend to touch you in some agreed upon manner each time you achieve the positive feeling state you wish to engineer. Once trained, ask your friend, now technically a touch cue, to accompany you while you prospect. He or she should cue-up your positive feeling state whenever you need it, by touch. If you don't have a friend, make one. Or borrow one. If absolutely necessary, rent one.

Rock and roll. Most people have a rocking chair somewhere in their past. Do you? Perhaps you remember snuggling up in a parent's lap while being rocked to sleep. Maybe you remember your grandmother, or perhaps an old aunt, sitting in a rocking chair knitting while watching television or engaging in soft conversation. Maybe your grandfather, while sitting in his favorite rocking chair, lured you into his lap so he could romance your imagination with far-flung tales about Uncle Remus, Bear Swamp, the Wizard of Oz, and the Mad Hatter. Or maybe you just remember yourself as a child rhythmically rocking away, entranced by your own deep imaginings. For most of us, rocking chairs are pretrained, natural touch cues. So why not put a rocking chair back into your life? Get one for your office and sit in it before you start prospecting. Better yet, if possible, sit in it while prospecting!

Toe wiggling. Surreptitiously wiggling your toes can be a good touch cue.

Chew on something. Chewing can be transformed into a touch cue. For Touch Sensory Injection, the taste is irrelevant. The *muscle action* of chewing is paired with a positive mood state. Try licorice, beef jerky, dried fruit, or bubble gum. One salesman used leather, but he had a particularly resistant case of call reluctance.

Pocket/Purse Diversion

Here's a technique that's fun and almost guaranteed to take your mind off call reluctance. But, like earning frequent flyer miles, "certain restrictions do apply." Here's how to play. Ask your spouse to *secretly* put something into your pocket or purse before you go to work. They must not tell you what it is and it cannot be something obvious or ill fit, like a battleship. (If you don't have a spouse, ask the individual that sociologists and city folks would refer to as your "special other." If you have neither a spouse nor a special other, pause here. Get one.)

Each time you experience prospecting distress, stop. Without looking, put your hand into your pocket or purse for *one minute*. No longer. During that minute, feel around and try to guess what the object is *using only your sense of touch*. When your minute is up, *return to prospecting immediately, whether you have guessed what the object is or not*. This method can't be easily used to cue-up alternate feeling states but it's fun and effective. It will take your mind off your prospecting woes. You may guess what the object is, but not before you lose your prospecting fear in the process. Here are some things that have been used to play pocket/purse diversion. Show them to your spouse or special other, or both if that should be your fate.

- Shape-changing objects, like Silly Putty

- Intimate objects (Special note to Minnesota home siding salesman John T.: No, John, we really don't consider one of your monogrammed handkerchiefs an intimate object. Think harder.)

- Hairy, fake insects

- Artificial worms

- Objects from your past (childhood or adolescence)

- Paper money (if you correctly guess the denomination by the end of the day, you keep it)

- Divorce papers

If you carry a purse, have your spouse secretly put an object into a *smaller* bag first, along with some decoys like a pen, some paper, and a few buttons. Then put the small bag into the purse. Otherwise, you may inadvertently feel the object at inappropriate times, like reaching in to get your car keys.

Does sales call reluctance sit lodged in your prospecting pathway like an undigested meal on a queasy stomach? If so, Sensory Injection using your sense of touch can help. It can help you bypass clogged-up prospecting attitudes when necessary—or clear them by force if required. Try using touch. It makes sense.

Final Word on Sensory Injection: Touch

Your senses can help expel your fears. They can fortify your prospecting heart. Use of the sense of touch as an effective behavioral management technique has been established. It gloats in scholarly respectability. But somewhat more importantly, this sense may have also played a critical, but heretofore unheralded, role in shaping western civilization as we know it.

A small, uncelebrated group of touch receptors vigilantly safeguards your social well-being. Right now. Dedicated and tireless, this concentrated bundle of no-name, neurochemical sentries has but one entry in its job description: faithfully distinguish solids from vapors, mass from gas, substance from smoke. If it sounds like some kind of consumer protection circuitry you should take to hear the next gee-whiz, cassette-selling sales training guru you sign up to hear, you're right. But not exactly right.

Nearly omnipotent management professors will have surmised by now that the neural outpost we honor is positioned strategically in your anus. Granted, this may seem like a relatively low-grade neural assignment—shades of neurochemical Siberia. But can you fathom the profound social improprieties that would occur if these valiant neurochemical civil servants were not at their post, doing their job, distinguishing mass from gas? It would mean the end of western civilization as we know it.

The sense of touch is a crucial behavioral management tool. It unselfishly helps you maintain your social standing, and it can help you overcome your call reluctance.

TARGET REVERSAL

PRIMARILY AFFECTS:	PRESCRIBED FOR:
Thoughts	✓ **Doomsayer**
	✓ **Over-Preparation**
Feelings	✓ **Hyper-Pro**
	Stage Fright
✓ **Actions**	Role Rejection
	Yielder
	Social Self-Consciousness
	Separationist
	Emotionally Unemancipated
	Referral Aversion
	✓ **Telephobia**
	Oppositional Reflex

According to the *1990 Statistical Abstract of the United States of America*, 13,747,000 people are in sales or sales related positions. That's a lot of salespeople, several times the entire population of New Zealand (excluding sheep and tourists). Most of these salespeople set goals. Those that don't undoubtedly have goals set for them in the form of quotas.

For most sales professionals goal-setting is helpful. Along with time management and stress management, goal-setting has become an inviolate part of modern sales training practice. Miniature fortunes have been made packaging goal-setting advice and aggressively selling the programs to salespeople. Most sales managers consider goal-setting an essential segment of the sales training process. Goal-setting is extremely popular, far outshining other programs such as preventive call reluctance training. Is there a sales pro anywhere who has not heard, "If you don't know where you're going, you won't know when you get there?"

That oft quoted, cerebral slug pertains best to families arguing over vacation plans, but that's not the point. Goal-setting is, and it's much too important to entrust to a clutter of cliches.

Goals, Aspirins and Allergies

Most salespeople benefit from setting goals, but not all. Some are *tainted* by the goal-setting process. For them, it is prospecting poison. High-level sales performance requires rigorous concentration. The key to concentration is attention management. Goal-setting helps us to zoom-in and focus attention upon what we are trying to accomplish. But goals are like aspirin tablets: Some salespeople don't tolerate them well. Instead of helping, they make matters worse. These salespeople are *goal-allergic*.

Goal-allergic salespeople are spooked by goals. They have trouble letting them function as behavior guiding beacons. Instead of using goals to navigate around distractions which could lure them off course, goal-allergic salespeople become transfixed by them. They're stunned by goals like deer dazed by approaching headlights. Goal-allergic salespeople are blinded by the beacons set to guide them.

Goal-allergic reactions fall into the category of psychological misdemeanors called performance anxieties. Lots of people have them. If you have ever experienced math anxiety you know the feeling. Knowledgeable, capable people suffering from math anxiety intellectually freeze up whenever the subject confronts them. They panic, their eyes roll wildly in their sockets while a white froth drips indecently from their mouths. They can't add, subtract, multiply or divide. They can't solve algebraic equations. They can't balance a checkbook. When they aim for the keys on their pocket calculator, they miss. Differential calculus is out of the question. Multivariate statistical analysis would cause certain coronary arrest. All mathematical reasoning scares them. They can only run.

Students with test anxiety know the feeling, too. They study and prepare only to hyperventilate when they're asked to complete a test. Their scores make them look like unmotivated underachievers. They're not. They're just afraid to take tests. What happens when test anxious students marry math anxious mates? The marriage must be immeasurably screwed-up, which brings up the next category.

Many adults—of both sexes—suffer from performance anxiety indelicately linked to sexual functioning. Narrowly focused on performing superlatively, these adults can barely perform at all. For them, goals have stopped being helpful. They've started to interfere.

Antidotes

One of the common and most effective behavioral treatments for adults suffering from sex-related performance anxiety is called non-demand pleasuring. Non-demand pleasuring involves changing perspective. Over-concern about endpoint *results* is *decreased* while focus on the *process* of pleasure-giving is *increased*. It works. Conceptually akin to Target Reversal, this principle also works in the sales office—and on the rifle range.

Home on the Range?

We tell audiences that we developed the concept of Target Reversal after listening to Black Sabbath albums—backwards. That's not true, of course. The seeds for Target Reversal were sown years ago in a real inferno.

Young military recruits in the U.S. receive intensive weapons training. Minimum competence must be demonstrated with firearms on the rifle range. Failures are recycled, which is a fate worse than death at the legendary U.S. Marine Corps Training Depot, Parris Island, South Carolina.

Marine recruit George Dudley was a few minutes away from failure. The year was 1961. A watchful and uncharacteristically perceptive drill instructor phoned down to the target pits. He ordered Dudley's target turned over. Backwards. At 1000 yards it's hard to see the target. Now he couldn't see the bull's-eye. There was little use in trying.

"It's no use worrying now. You're going to fail anyway, you little maggot," the DI growled from beneath his "campaign hat," the fabled logo of U.S. Marine Corps drill instructors. No father figure, his voice was raspy, low pitched and egotistically self-certain, like the demon-possessed girl in *The Exorcist*. "Forget it! Just guess where the center is," he said sarcastically. "See if you can hit it."

It was over. Dudley leaned into his rifle accepting the inevitable. At one thousand yards he started firing at the imaginary center of the target. Bull's-eye! Another bull's-eye! Another! The young Marine began scoring bull's-eyes, one after another. The first of his life. Miraculously, he passed the test, qualifying his first year as a Rifle Marksman. It was a start. Before his military obligation was over he would qualify for the highest designation attainable—Rifle Expert. It came from reversing a target and shooting at imaginary bull's-eyes.

Imaginary Bull's-Eyes Today

We have observed and studied the same phenomenon many times since. During workshops or convention presentations, we have asked call-reluctant salespeople (verified in advance by call reluctance testing) to come to the front. Once there we asked them to throw darts at a target board.

Like magicians inspecting tricked-up equipment, we deceptively stacked the deck by usually picking salespeople we knew had Stage Fright or Doomsayer Call Reluctance. These two types tended to produce the most dramatic effect. It made us look brilliant.

Most of the uptight dart throwers missed the bull's-eye—and the target board. Their darts went sailing into walls, but when we turned their targets over, exposing only a blank piece of target-sized paper, something wonderful happened. Call-reluctant salespeople, so uptight they couldn't hit the board, started throwing tight clusters near the center. Many hit bull's-eyes for the first time ever.

Target Reversal and Goal-Setting

If you're spooked by the goals you set, target reversal can help. It's quick, easy and effective. But it only works for some people. Will it work for you? Section one below will help you find out.

Section One

1. Get a dart board. Hang it at an appropriate height.

2. Cover the dart board with a clean, unused piece of target paper. The bull's-eye should be visible, facing outward. (Paper targets are available from most sporting goods stores.)

3. Stand back and throw three to six darts. Try your best to hit the bull's-eye.

4. Count the number of bull's-eyes you hit. If you did not hit any, see if your darts formed little groups or clusters.

5. Remove the paper target. Take a clean, unused target and cover the dart board as before, but this time turn the target side over so it faces the dart board. All you should see is a blank piece of paper.

6. Throw three to six more darts from the same distance. Since you can't see the bull's-eye, use your imagination. Just aim for where you think the bull's-eye is.

7. Compare your accuracy. If you get more darts near the center of the target or in a tighter group on the second try, then Target Reversal will probably work for you. If you did better the first time when you could plainly see the bull's-eye, then Target Reversal won't hurt you, but it probably won't help you either. Don't waste your time.

Using Target Reversal

Target Reversal can help you detraumatize your goals. Here's how.

1. Determine your performance goal. It should be observable and quantifiable like, "number of prospecting phone calls made every

fifteen minutes." Avoid using vague statements such as, "I would like to have a better attitude about prospecting." This statement is a declaration, not a performance goal.

2. Write down your goal on a moderate to large piece of paper.

3. Set a realistic time frame for reaching your goal. Target Reversal works best with short-term goals not longer than one month. Write your time frame below your objective: "I will try to perform at this level within 20 workdays."

4. Tape your goal statement on the wall where you can easily see it, but turn it over so it faces the wall. You will not be able to see what you wrote.

5. Forget about the bull's-eye. Aim for the *imaginary center*. Focus on things you can do to move you closer to your goal, not the goal itself. Like the drill instructor ordered, "Guess where the center is." Then start firing.

Let us know if you hit any prospecting BULL'S-EYES!

THE HOT WATER BOTTLE TECHNIQUE

PRIMARILY AFFECTS:	PRESCRIBED FOR:
Thoughts	✓ **Doomsayer**
	Over-Preparation
✓ **Feelings**	Hyper-Pro
	✓ **Stage Fright**
✓ **Actions**	Role Rejection
	Yielder
	Social Self-Consciousness
	Separationist
	Emotionally Unemancipated
	Referral Aversion
	✓ **Telephobia**
	✓ **Oppositional Reflex**

The body temperature of most humans is about 98.6 degrees Fahrenheit (37 degrees Centigrade). Love psychologist Leo Buscaglia is probably warmer, attorneys correspondingly colder. This figure refers only to body core temperature, however, which is the temperature in your body cavity (heart blood temperature to physicians and vampires). Stomach, rectal, and oral thermometer readings are measures of body core temperature.

How Cool Are You?

How cool are you? According to authors Willis and Grossman (*Medical Neurobiology*), there is no normal core temperature. Body core temperatures follow cycles fluctuating during the day and over time. Some people have higher body core temperatures than others. They're hot. Your body core temperature probably spans a normal range between 96.8 to 100.4 degrees Fahrenheit (36 to 38 degrees Centigrade).

Skin temperature is usually 6 to 8 degrees cooler than core temperature. Cutaneous cold and warm receptors relay information to your brain about temperature conditions on your skin. (Body core thermostats are controlled by thermodetectors. They dwell in a thermodetector ghetto located in your central nervous system. Look them up in the yellow pages under anterior hypothalamus. That's where they hang out.)

Call Reluctance and Skin Temperature

Prospecting for new business rarely involves actual physical danger. If you look both ways before crossing busy streets like your parents taught you, you will avoid most of the physical danger you might be exposed to. (Salespeople in Singapore will also avoid stiff jaywalking fines.) Yet call-reluctant salespeople tend to react to threatening prospecting situations as if they contained life-threatening physical danger. It goes downhill from there.

Like a werewolf when the moon is full, you're not yourself when a call reluctance episode transforms you. You become a different person. Your body abruptly changes, invoking up to 1400 physiological changes (Danskin and Crow, *Biofeedback*). Your heartbeat accelerates, pumping reserve blood supplies to your muscles and brain so you can think better while running faster. But supplying blood during call reluctance is like supplying oil during wartime: it has to come from somewhere.

During call reluctance episodes, blood is rerouted from your extremities to your vital organs. That's why your hands tend to turn clammy and cold when you're distressed. They have less blood to warm them. There's a second benefit built into the system. If you find yourself in a fist fight during a call reluctance episode, be of good cheer. You may take a pounding, but you'll bleed less.

Call-reluctant salespeople are subjected to many unwanted bouts of distress which are related to prospecting. Some scholars, most notably Thomas Ravenscroft, believe the elevated fears associated with sales call reluctance correspond to proportionately elevated levels of GBSH, a brain-based hormone secreted by the Anterior Corpus Locatum (ACL). The ACL is the brain structure thought by some to be responsible for regulating the "flight" or "fight" response.

After a few passive repetitions, prospecting distress can become paired with cold, clammy hands. Soon, clammy hands while prospecting (even though you may not be distressed) may be enough to trigger your call reluctance button. Your brain checks your fingertips and finds them cooler than they ought to be. Since you are prospecting, the inference is made that prospecting produces distress because your fingertips have cooled down.

Experiments conducted with sales managers attending management training workshops illustrate the point. Initial fingertip temperatures were obtained from all participants. Then the group was told that two of them would be selected at random to make cold calls. A second series of fingertip temperatures were taken, revealing an average drop of six to ten degrees for the group. Call reluctance is merciless. It even saps the blood from your fingers.

Neuroscientists Discover
New Pathways to Emotions

Mechanical explanations for call reluctance justify using non-word-based countermeasures. That's our approach, but how does it square with other speakers and writers, or psychological practitioners? Not very well.

These individuals still maintain that most problems, such as call reluctance, come from repressed desires, twisted beliefs, irrational ideas, or other faulty thought processes. Read a self-help book or turn on your radio or television and you can see for yourself. Their old, shopworn mentalistic ideas currently enjoy booming talk-show popularity. But we believe their days are numbered. Their concepts are inevitably fading into psychological antiquity, soon to be maintained, like old cars, by a few devoted collectors.

Why? We argued for our brain-based bias concept of call reluctance earlier. An article in *U.S. News & World Report* supports this viewpoint: "The brain appears to be *programmed* to size up the emotional importance of certain stimuli, such as a flash of light, much more quickly than scientists once thought. Researchers previously thought that information taken in by the senses travels to the thalamus (an early sensory processing station) then to the cortex, where it is consciously taken in and relayed to subcortical areas of the brain such as the amygdala. These interior regions then send messages back to the cortex, and also set in motion physiological responses. But neuroscientist Joseph LeDoux has found an additional and more direct pathway between the thalamus and amygdala, that bypasses the cortex completely. In primitive emotions like fear, nerve impulses transmitted along this route reach the amygdala two to three times faster, allowing for a quick and dirty judgment of whether the stimulus is something to be afraid of—probably even before it is consciously perceived. This assessment is then elaborated by thinking and memory." (M. Zang, "Brain Circuits," *U.S. News & World Report*, June 24, 1991)

Sounding the All Clear

Ever notice how a hot bath at the end of a long day seems to restore your mind as much as your body? Researchers have studied the matter. In one study, forty adults were submerged in whirlpool baths for ten minutes. Significant changes in pulse rate and finger temperatures were found. These changes produced "increased feelings of well-being and decreased... anxiety" (William N. Robiner, "Psychological and Physical Reactions to Whirlpool Baths," *Journal of Behavioral Medicine*, April 1990). Uptight? Soak down.

We have been observing a similar phenomenon in ourselves and others for some time. We don't have access to whirlpool baths every time we feel stressed out, but there is an insider's secret we use that helps us counter call reluctance cool-downs. It's quick and easy. It requires little conscious thought. It is also controversial.

Before making any major presentation before large audiences or television cameras, we make a quick detour to the rest rooms. Aside from the customary reasons for such visits, we douse our hands in warm water for several minutes. Then, beaming self-assured smiles, we are ready to return to our purpose. Some of you will also be amazed when you see what a pair of warmed-up hands can do. It's as if call-reluctant sensations are melted away before they can take hold. Author George D. Fuller wrote that "warmer sensations coincide with calmer feelings" (*Biofeedback Methods and Procedures In Clinical Practice*). We agree.

You can't always make a detour to the rest room, but you can prepare a hot water bottle before you start prospecting, especially by phone. Before starting, warm your hands and rewarm them as necessary. If a hot water bottle is not available, try using alternative warming sources such as a cup of warm coffee or chemical warming packets sold in sporting goods stores.

The call reluctance "Hot Water Bottle" technique is powerful and can be used to block many episodes of call reluctance before they get started. The real judge, however, is not us or other researchers, or even other salespeople. It's you. Give it a try. See what you think.

Is Religious Transformation an Authentic Behavioral Change Technique?

Our inventory of methods for managing call reluctance would be incomplete if we did not at least mention religious transformation. In one of our research projects we interviewed some highly productive salespeople who attributed their success to their religious faith (Dudley and Goodson, *Call Reluctance Research Report for the Million Dollar Round Table*, 1988). Other salespeople have made similar assertions since then. Some even claim their call reluctance was purged (along with various other unwanted behaviors) by a life-transforming religious experience.

For some, the turnabout assumed the form of a gentle illumination which followed a soul-searching, mystical experience. For others, it resulted from an amalgamated "peak experience." The majority, however, claim their "conversion experience" was harsh and abrupt, like a frame-bending pothole encountered at highway speed. Despite differences in the contour of their experiences, all the beneficiaries vocally insist their call reluctance was corrected by a *spiritual* event, not psychological self-management.

What should we make of this? Should religious experience be included in a catalog of behavior change techniques? They never are. Perhaps they should be.

Writing this book took five years of preparation and about two-and-one-half years of actual writing. During that time we reviewed scores of self-help books and audio cassettes. In total, we invested well over a thousand dollars listening to and reading about how to be positive, establish instant rapport, use subconscious processes, manipulate others, read "representational systems," use subliminal messages, walk on hot coals, visualize success, hypnotize ourselves and other people, set goals, manage time, overcome objections, mimic winners, win by intimidation, swim with sharks, be ethical, and many other nostrums promising to change our lives. There were occasional, condescending references to God, *but not one allocated a single sentence to direct religious transformation as an agency of behavioral change.* Not one. To the self-help crowd the issue is too hot to handle, so it's best to treat it like it doesn't exist at all. Most scientifically minded psychologists also stand clear of the issue, but they justify their

continues

Religious Transformation *continued*

positions by clinging to the scientific method which finds religion an especially difficult subject to explain.

It is extremely difficult to adequately and fairly study subjective religious experience with secular instruments and measures. When science approaches religion it is usually from a safe, abstracted distance after it has been reformatted into lightless historical questions or sketchy cultural patterns. When it comes to studying religion, scientists are (as theologian Hans Kung noted about Sigmund Freud) "strictly amateurs." (Hans Kung, *Freud and the Problem of God*)

Curiously, some of the same scientists who find it difficult to take the study of religion seriously, experience no such discomfort while handling nebulous scientific concepts such as population explosion, extraterrestrial intelligence, generation gap, or unconscious mind. These notions, and many other trendy conjectures sacred to the daily ritual of science, also require an audacious leap of faith. Some, such as the speculative assumptions about mental illness which are used to treat emotional distress, currently demand titanic leaps of faith—of an order of magnitude sufficient to make an African witch doctor cringe in sarcastic disbelief.

Religion, with its great institutions and practices, aroused many of the notions which paved the way for western civilization. It gave us our concept of the individual, government, laws, ethics, and even its two greatest modern rivals, science and technology. Preached in small country churches and chanted in great towering cathedrals, religion satisfies the spirit in a way no self-help book, including this one, ever can. Predating psychology, it articulates our ancient cravings to understand ourselves and our circumstances. Unlike psychology, which is supposed to narrow its vision and assume the bit, bridle and blinders of the scientific method, religion has a broader, more universal obligation.

Where scientific psychology rightfully helps call-reluctant salespeople manage their behavior, religion reaches deeper. It penetrates our soul and transforms our character.

EPILOGUE

The journey from the first few paragraphs in the preface to the last few instructions for Sensory Injection was a long one. For some sales professionals it was a treacherous one. They didn't make it, but *you* made it and that's what counts. Hopefully you learned something about call reluctance—and yourself—along the way.

Was it worthwhile? We don't know. The value of this book to your career depends on you. It is not like a general purpose self-help book. The ultimate test is not how you *feel* now, but what you *do* now.

So why are you still reading? Why aren't you prospecting?

APPENDIX

THE RESEARCH

Though far from perfect, the relationship between call reluctance and sales performance is more predictable than the daily fluctuations in the Dow Jones Average or weather forecasts three days in the future.

Call Reluctance Research

SHOULD YOU READ THIS CHAPTER?

Most readers skip over or run at full gallop from chapters on research. They think the words are too difficult, the concepts too dull, and the topics too irrelevant to apply to business in general or sales in particular. To them, reading about research would be tortuous, like studying medieval politics or 18th century English literature.

They may be right. Some readers don't need to know the research behind the principles and techniques in this book. They need to be prospecting. Others, however, should find the information fascinating, enlightening and perhaps even helpful. This group includes:

- Sales managers
- Sales assessment and selection departments
- Sales trainers
- Sales consultants
- Motivational speakers
- Mental health practitioners
- Marketing officers
- Sales support personnel
- Reputable academics
- Disreputable academics
- Students
- Literate politicians

Though not soap opera silly, the Research Appendix is not out of your intellectual reach. At times the research will tickle your cortex a little, but it's not difficult to understand unless you're a backward reader who begins reading books at the end and then browses forward. (If that describes you this chapter won't make much sense. So put the book down. Pick it up again and turn to the front. Start reading from the beginning. Then, when you get to this section it will make more sense. Trust us. It works like magic.)

If you decide to skip this chapter, you won't be alone. Most readers will probably scuttle it. Sadly, formal research has a bad reputation among practical thinking, quick acting business people. The reputation is fully earned and rightly deserved.

Like fine cuisine, most self-respecting research articles must project intellectual "presentation" values. Research is usually served to other researchers only after it has been properly warmed with linguistic vanity, scientific pretension and mysterious incomprehensibleness. That's how academics promote (prospect) for job security and gain visibility, while simultaneously trying to get money from somebody else (usually government agencies) to pay for their prospecting efforts. Results have to be sufficiently erudite to intimidate genuinely curious scholars and to discourage them from trying to duplicate results. That could be disastrous. At the same time, academic research articles must appear to warmly invite all scientists to try. With promotional skills like that, they should be in sales.

Research doesn't have to be word-proud or stuffy. It can be fun. When it's stripped of institutional pretense and scholastic affectation it's just a way to ask a question and then try to answer it as conclusively as you can by following certain rules of measurement. Anyone can do research. Anyone can learn the rules. You don't have to be smart. You have to be curious.

What kinds of questions can you ask? You can ask any question you want to. But certain questions are better than others because they're easier to break down into statements you can confirm or deny by taking measurements.

Here are some of the raw, red meat questions we asked about call reluctance. The answers we got from our research are scattered throughout this appendix.

- *Are sales managers less call reluctant than the salespeople they manage?*
- *Do men experience more call reluctance than women?*
- *Are certain companies or industries given to more call reluctance than others?*
- *Is call reluctance a problem in Asia, too, or is it confined to the U.S.?*
- *Does call reluctance stay the same, or does it change with age?*
- *Does the effort Hyper-Pros put into looking professional pay off?*
- *Does Oppositional Reflex Call Reluctance limit how much you can earn or is it just a personality style?*
- *Is Stage Fright Call Reluctance one thing or two?*
- *How much income will you lose if you're an unreformed Yielder trying to sell automobiles?*
- *How effective are inspirational speakers?*
- *Are call reluctance scores stable or do they change from week to week?*
- *Does all the extra time Over-Preparers put into learning technical information help them project a more competent image?*
- *Which group has the most call reluctance?*

Call reluctance research is not meaningless. To be sure, it often disappoints us. Most of our real-world investigations produce enough ambiguous, inconsistent, unintelligible or unexpected results to make us question continuing the project, but we do continue because call reluctance research has another side. It is a mine field of surprises. It is never dull.

Most of our research centers around the Call Reluctance Scale. The Call Reluctance Scale is a super high-tech assessment device which is based on more than 20 years of systematic research and development. It has been completed by tens of thousands of sales and non-sales people from scores of industries located on five continents. Yielding 21 separate call reluctance scales, it is the only formally developed assessment device built to quantify:

- Total prospecting energy lost due to call reluctance

- The Call Reluctance Impostors

- All twelve types of Call Reluctance

- All four Call Reluctance sub-types (which can add statistical "noise" to other sales assessment efforts, resulting in distorted information and misguided training and selection decisions)

Call Reluctance Scales are mailed, faxed, or sent by modem for computer scoring. They arrive 24 hours a day, every day, 365 days a year. They come from various countries and almost every imaginable industry—including at least one for a prison door salesman! The result of all this activity is the only computer archive of call reluctance information in the world. Information which sheds light, solves problems, and points to the future.

Our approach to this chapter will be non-technical but not superficial. Some precision will be sacrificed, but that's unavoidable. Precision is lost when research results are communicated with words. We'll just lose more. Brief technical additions, such as correlation coefficients and statistical significance tests, will be provided when they are appropriate and the information is available, but they will be enclosed in parentheses. (Statistical significance is just a numerical index that tells technical researchers whether the impressive result they're celebrating probably would have happened anyway. To scientists and personnel managers affecting to appear scientific, a result is important (significant) if it's expected to occur by chance alone five times or less per 100 occurrences. That rigor is required in science, but it's far too restrictive for business. A research result which might occur 10 or even 20 times by chance alone could still have extraordinary practical business significance. It could be worth hundreds of thousands of dollars per year in new income.)

NATURAL HISTORY OF CALL RELUCTANCE

We are militant people-watchers. We watch all kinds of people in all kinds of settings. Some have call reluctance, some don't. We watch them with our eyes and scrutinize them with expensive research instruments which extend our reach by amplifying our natural senses.

Our studies take us to uncharted regions of human enterprise where, hiding in the researcher's version of a duck hunter's blind, we use our eyes, ears, and specialized equipment to observe talented people caught in their own mental traps. But unlike the hunter we do not observe for sport or entertainment. We measure and graph, calculate and classify so we can help people avoid the lures and traps of career self-destruction.

Call Reluctance and Non-Sales Personnel

Two of our earlier studies suggest the fear of self-promotion is not just prejudiced against salespeople. It can impair professionals in many career settings.

To most outsiders, corporate data processing departments are not typically thought of as fun places to be. They have a reputation for being dispassionately procedural and predictably answering "no, it can't be done" to all questions originating from the sales and marketing departments. Poking around several years ago we discovered that the same natural laws which regulate self-promotion and career advancement in sales were also at work governing career advancement in corporate data processing departments. To our astonishment we found post-training supervisory ratings of *technical* competence were highly influenced by *non*-technical personality variables associated with self-promotion.

These results didn't fit the image, so we figured we made a mistake. Maybe we used the wrong experimental design, maybe we made a computational error. Maybe we better try again. So we tried again. On our second try we used another sample of non-sales types, corporate administrative management personnel. Another fun group.

The results were similar. Over a five year period, the number of promotions and the amount of salary increases in non-sales, administrative management personnel were directly correlated with one and only one personality factor—willingness to self-promote. Individuals moving up the corporate ladder the fastest and landing the biggest salary increases were not necessarily the best on-the-job technicians. They were most willing to self-promote. In sales terms they "prospected" for pay increases. In political terms they "ran" for promotions. Those not faring so well sat and waited to be recognized. They're still waiting.

What conclusions can be drawn from studies like this? Call reluctance is not restricted to sales and marketing. It can hit anyone in any department right in the wallet. Has it hit you?

TAKING A CENSUS

Which type of call reluctance is most common? That's a question drenched in difficulty because it depends on how you see things.

Observers who cannot or do not seek assistance from objective measurement devices tend to see the world only in terms they are familiar with. Their observations are interpreted to force-fit their limited experiences. For example, sales managers having difficulty themselves using the telephone to prospect

Weird Science

Anyone can do science, but not all science is good science. How can you spot the difference? Some unscrupulous marketeers use the word "science" as a positioner, for its credibility value. You may know some of these marketeers. They're not hard to find. They're the folks who announce scientific breakthroughs on a weekly basis, solve perplexing scientific problems with aplomb, and claim unique resources, skills and abilities not available to merely mortal scientists. You may have guessed it. They're the "great pretenders," unethical self-promoters pretending to be scientists. Pretenders leave tracks. You can spot them.

Self-referencing. Like cult leaders, pretenders continually make self-references. Legitimate scientists don't. They don't have to. They have something else to talk about—their data.

Weird bibliographies. Pretenders decorate their claims with obscure, pretentious research citations like the "distinguished College of Metaphysical Enquiry, at Uttergurgen." A few years ago we stumbled across two sales selection tests claiming to perform wonderful things. They were, they said, nearly 80-90% accurate (an outrageously high number which was bound to make them money and get our attention). Both contained research citations which we wrote down and attempted to locate and acquire. One consisted of obscure foreign entries which could not be located or did not exist. The other was based on initial research done with 30 fraternity brothers at a university in the early 1950's! Unquestionably related to sales success, right?

Cousins. Pretenders play verbal shell games. They illustrate when they should explain. Proof comes in the form of stories they tell about their mothers and fathers, sisters and brothers, aunts and uncles, cousins and obscure third-party acquaintances. Pretenders have as many stories about friends and relatives as preachers have "illustrations." There's nothing wrong with telling stories. There's nothing wrong with telling stories about your friends and relatives. You just don't need an advanced degree in science to do it.

Cosmeticians. Pretenders don't like to originate research or supervise long-term projects. That takes too much time and effort. They prefer to carefully excise the work of others and claim it for their own—but only after making tasteful cosmetic changes. Ask to see proof of authorship, and if you're a prospective buyer, proof of ownership.

Declaration of Independence. Science is collaborative. It takes time to become an expert, and assistance supplied by many people. Pretenders don't like to commit years to studying one thing, so they just declare themselves to be experts. In lieu of formal research projects they depend on popular magazine articles to keep them current. Ask them about their research.

continues

Weird Science *continued*

Absolutely Right. Pretenders are inclined to speak in absolute terms. They give definitive answers to questions, while reputable scholars offer only hypotheses and more questions. Science is a system of probabilities. There's always room for error. Absolute truth and absolute knowledge are properly deferred to matters of religious faith. Observe the verbal habits of your favorite "scientific" gurus. Are their words conditioned with a proper respect for being wrong?

No Regrets. Pretenders never make mistakes. Legitimate scientists do. Most research projects are mistakes, and many fail to find anything conclusive or of value. Pretenders always seem to get positive results.

Fringe Dwellers. Pretenders tend to stay clear of other scientists. Run-ins could be embarrassing. So they graze in greener pastures beside scientifically naive business people and gullible consumers. They make easier prey. Don't be counted among them. Get a work sample. Take it to the psychology department of your local university. Ask for their opinion.

In the past you could judge scientific claims by researching publications in refereed journals. Not any more. Like killer bees, fake research results have been discovered in respected, heretofore sacred, academic research journals.

What can you do? The best way to verify scientific claims is not with reams of paper, columns of data or requests for validity. As sales management professionals you have a better solution available. You can test out reasonable sales development programs by purchasing a few and trying them out in pilot studies *before* signing your name or committing your company to long term purchases. Legitimate operators will welcome opportunities to demonstrate the utility of their program in your company. Pretenders will squawk.

When a program works it earns more money for your company than it costs. You should continue using it, expanding its use throughout your organization. If it doesn't, trash it. Ignore scientific credibility, academic degrees, or pretenders groveling at your feet. Junk it. That's how we think business decisions should be made. Science can play a role, but pious appeals to scientific credibility alone should never be the deciding factor.

think Telephobia is the most common form of call reluctance. One Oppositional sales selection consultant *recommends* hiring Oppositional candidates for sales positions. His approach may suit his needs, but it runs contrary to the conclusions drawn from objective studies.

General opinion holds that Stage Fright is the most common social fear. It may be. Our data is mute on people in general. We have assessed enough salespeople, however, to know the generalization about Stage Fright is unsound when it is applied to salespeople. Senior sales and marketing executives know it too. Many say their marketing efforts are continuously thwarted by Social Self-Consciousness, not Stage Fright. Who is right? Which type is most common? The answer depends on which statistical lens is used to snap the picture.

When arithmetic averages are used to sketch a call reluctance profile for the typical sales professional you get an image like the one shown in Table 1.

Table 1   Call reluctance profile for 1,865 sales professionals.

Call Reluctance Type	Average Score
Total Call Reluctance	39
Doomsayers	17
Over-Preparation	39
Hyper-Pros	40
Stage Fright	42
Role Rejection	28
Yielders	32
Social Self-Consciousness	35
Separationist	47
Emotionally Unemancipated	46
Referral Aversion	27
Telephobia	37
Oppositional Reflex	8.9 *

* Due to a technical difference in scale construction the average for Oppositional Reflex is understated in this chart. It is actually much higher but expressed in different units of measurement, like comparing degrees and centigrade.

Though Hyper-Pros take first place honors in other tables, Separationists and Emotionally Unemancipated take first in this study. Stage Fright and Hyper-Pros follow close behind. Doomsayers are usually anchored safely somewhere at or near the bottom regardless of how you compute it, so we can safely conclude that they are comparatively rare in sales.

When this sample is further condensed by purging everyone except *severe* call reluctance "basket cases," as demonstrated in Table 2, Separationists still claim first place, but Hyper-Pros run a respectable second.

Profiles based on arithmetic averages can be perilously misleading. They may obscure more than they illuminate, and produce a false sense of statistical security. For example, a few salespeople with unusually high scores can ruin the party for everyone. They disproportionately influence averages, shifting them upwards. They single-handedly make all salespeople look more call reluctant than they really are. But more importantly, extremely wide variations in call reluctance exist across industries, individual companies within industries, and even across sales departments within the same company.

Table 2 Call reluctance types suffered by 242 sales professionals: ranked in descending order of frequency.

Call Reluctance Type	Marker Behavior
Separationists	Fears losing friends
Hyper-Pro	Fears being humiliated
Emotionally Unemancipated	Fears loss of family
Telephobia	Fears using the telephone
Stage Fright	Fears group presentations
Social Self-Consciousness	Fears being intimidated
Over-Preparation	Fears being under-prepared
Referral Aversion	Fears losing a closed sale
Yielder	Fears being pushy

Table 3 testifies to that point. It illustrates the incidence of call reluctance in two different sales offices from the same company, located in the same geographic area of the country. Although total call reluctance is approximately the same in both operations, the profile of types for the two organizations varies considerably, probably reflecting the influence of district sales management personnel. Production for both groups is roughly equivalent. Neither has posted increases for the last 34 months, but other branches in their company have. So have their competitors.

Table 3 Call reluctance types occurring most frequently in two branches of one company.

Call Reluctance Type	Locality A	Locality B
Total call reluctance	38%	35%
Doomsayer	18%	20%
Over-Preparation	23%	21%
Hyper-Pro	38%	30%
Stage Fright	29%	47%
Role Rejection	22%	18%
Yielder	41%	33%
Social Self-Consciousness	11%	35%
Separationist	43%	32%
Emotionally Unemancipated	39%	20%
Referral Aversion	25%	8%
Telephobia	44%	39%
Oppositional Reflex	11%	19%

Call Reluctance Scores fall along a 100%-point scale. The higher the score, the more call reluctance is indicated. The average total call reluctance score for productive salespeople in the same industry is about 34%.

The table shows both organizations have somewhat higher call reluctance averages than they should, but for different reasons. Branch A is stumbling because of unredeemed Telephobics who are afraid to prospect by telephone because they are afraid they might intrude (Yielders), especially on people they know (Separationists). Salespeople in Branch B are not comfortable prospecting to groups (Stage Fright) or using the phone as a prospecting tool (Telephobia), especially to contact up-market buyers (Social Self-Consciousness).

Most Popular Type

The mode is another statistical measure of central tendency. In reality it's just the most popular number among a group of other numbers, like "best dressed," "best personality" or "most likely to succeed." In the case of call reluctance, it is calculated by counting the highest type which occurs most frequently.

Table 4 Call reluctance types which occur most frequently.

Call Reluctance Type	Number Having as Highest Type	Percent
Doomsayers	13	1%
Over-Preparation	116	10%
Hyper-Pros	188	16%
Stage Fright	150	13%
Role Rejection	2	.02%
Yielders	19	2%
Social Self-Consciousness	68	6%
Separationist	130	11%
Unemancipated	165	14%
Referral Aversion	25	2%
Telephobia	112	10%
Oppositional Reflex	1*	.01%*

* Due to a technical difference in scaling, Oppositional Reflex is under-represented by this chart. It actually appears far more frequently, and poses a far greater problem than this chart indicates.

Table 4 provides another perspective, but it also contains biases which distort. The data was collected primarily from people who were already *in* sales. It does not adequately reflect the call reluctance characteristics of *prospective* salespeople. That requires another sample. Additionally, 32% of the participants in this study either had, or were disposed to get, more than one type of call reluctance. These data do not reflect the incidence of types in salespeople experiencing a double or triple blast of call reluctance.

Most Common Form of Call Reluctance

What is the most common type? As you might have guessed by now, we don't know. But experts, we are told, are supposed to know everything, so we cheated. We forced a conclusion by mixing some statistical know-how (scale impact differential weighting), with poetic license (intuitive extrapolations) and bound them with common sense. We arrived at an answer (Table 5). It helps us sound more intelligent when we're asked "What type is most common?" on the radio, and it seems to parallel real-life experience. That's always a nice touch.

Table 5   Call reluctance ranked by overall frequency of occurrence.

Call Reluctance Type	Rank	Marker Behavior
Yielders	1	Fears being pushy
Over-Preparation	2	Fears being underprepared
Emotionally Unemancipated	3	Fears loss of family approval
Separationists	4	Fears losing friends
Hyper-Pros	5	Fears being humiliated
Role Rejection	6	Ashamed to be in sales
Social Self-Consciousness	7	Fears being intimidated

Based on our calculations, Yielder, the fear of being seen by others as pushy or intrusive, is the most common type of call reluctance found in salespeople. Comparatively speaking, Doomsayers are relatively rare. Characterized by outward signs such as shyness and social awkwardness, Doomsayers are easily screened out by even the poorest sales selection interviews and tests. Ironically, Doomsayers have a disproportionate influence on many sales selection consultants, supplying most of what consultants know about sales call reluctance. Their screening procedures are grossly over-populated with behaviors found only in Doomsayers. Sadly for them and their clients, Doomsayers are actually quite rare.

Emotionally Unemancipated and Separationists appear to be frequent, but they're not. When their scores are adjusted for industries (like stockbrokers who are actually taught *not* to make sales calls on family members or friends), they drop nearly out of sight.

CROSS CULTURAL STUDIES

Serious work with call reluctance is not limited to the United States. Interest in call reluctance research is growing steadily in other countries as well. At present, some of the most influential and representative work is found in Australia, New Zealand and Canada. Singapore, Malaysia and the U.K. are showing signs of interest.

Trained call reluctance specialists in progressive firms in these countries are supervising innovative applications which will benefit sales organizations everywhere. In Auckland, HRD psychologist Peter Sullivan has pioneered new industry applications and supplied additional data we needed to explore the relationships between call reluctance types and well-respected, multipurpose psychological tests such as the California Psychological Inventory (CPI) and the 16PF. These findings have been considerably expanded with the help of American Ph.D. psychologist Dr. Carroll Thomas. Australian psychologist Dr. Norm Rees has been doing some pioneering work of his own, integrating call reluctance management technology into clinical practice. Although there are some important cultural and language differences, results to date have been enlightening and encouraging.

Our work with international sales populations has demonstrated that all salespeople are not alike when it comes to what makes them—and their careers—tick. The implications for optimizing sales training strategies are significant. What plays in Peoria may sputter in Singapore. A recent study is particularly illuminating.

What motivates salespeople around the world? What makes them hit the road, pick up the phone, and go for the close, day after day? We asked 2800 sales professionals in six countries to define what they want most from their career. Their responses indicate that no monolithic, global definition of "success" exists. What one salesperson, or one culture, sees as a career breakthrough—moving into management, for example—others may perceive as a step backward in terms of opportunity, prestige, and earning potential. If there is anything like a universal motivator, however, it's money. Overall, about 1 in 4 salespeople in our sample called "the opportunity to earn a lot of money" their single greatest motivation for being in sales. Unsurprisingly, Americans outdo all other countries in their craving for financial success: almost 38% called money their number-one motivation. British salespeople feel almost as strongly about financial reward (37%). Twenty percent of Canadians, and 27% of South African salespeople, feel the lure of big commissions most strongly. At the other end of the scale are the altruistic Australians. Only 15.6% of Aussie sales reps say they went into sales primarily to earn a lot of money. Kiwis were close behind at about 17%.

What accounts for these cultural differences? We don't know. But this study underscores our assertion that success and failure are *artistic* terms, not scientific formulae. Organizations worldwide that wish to helm effective, productive sales forces will abandon narrow definitions of success that fire up small portions of their salespeople but leave others in the cold.

An early study found that data processing sales representatives in a large international company operating in Australia are more likely to struggle with Hyper-Pro Call Reluctance than other types. In that respect, they resemble their U.S. counterparts, matching them score for score (and probably beard for beard). Before that, a study correlating Hyper-Pro scores with annual sales quotas found as Hyper-Pro goes up, sales production goes down. In Philadelphia or Perth, it's the same: It *costs* to be a Hyper-Pro. Another early study found the average sales quota attained for the three most call reluctant sales reps was 45%. Attained quota for the three reps with the lowest Hyper-Pro scores was 118%.

Australian capital (heavy) equipment salespeople tend to be similar to their counterparts in the U.S., with one notable exception: The Australians tend to be slightly more inclined toward Over-Preparation. In the insurance industry, Australian home office personnel still tend to mimic some of the same call reluctance behaviors which impede U.S. insurance companies. A visit to Macquarie Bank, Rankine & Hill, Edward Rushton or Nelson Joyce would help.

Consulting engineers have little use for sales related technologies such as call reluctance, right? Wrong. Rankine & Hill Pty. Limited is a prominent Sydney consulting engineering firm. Marketing coordinator Susi Barber explains, "There is a close liaison with clients by the engineering staff. At present, the principals of the firm conduct the major portion of the client development work by developing relationships with prospective clients, and expanding and developing personal networks. This programme will shortly be broadened to include all levels of the firm (including engineers)." Sounds like consulting engineers have to prospect for new business like everyone else. Senior executives at Rankine & Hill, such as Director Richard Mesley, are setting the pace for their competitors. He realizes that consulting engineering firms who wish to grow can no longer be satisfied with constructing the best buildings they can for clients; they must also construct a sales-oriented vision throughout their own organization. Sooner or later, other consulting engineering firms will learn that as well. Rankine & Hill won't have to. They anticipated, took preemptive action and got underway. They are fortifying the foundation for their own future.

Nelson Joyce is Managing Director (president) of Nelson Joyce & Co., Pty. Limited, a Sydney firm which markets industrial adhesives and plastic film products. Joyce provides a comfortable mix of practical and progressive business savvy, including call reluctance support for his sales team. "The awareness of call reluctance," he writes, "has enabled us to pick (spot) call reluctance behavior and provide suitable counseling to improve performance." A business veteran, Joyce is more authentically forward looking than many younger managers half his age.

John Burrows, Managing Partner for Arthur Andersen, Australia, sponsored the first application of call reluctance machinery in his industry. (Accountants and business consulting services organizations have steadily increased their interest in call reluctance in the last several years. Like banks, technically trained staff members must now help compete for new accounts.)

John Rae, Managing Director of Edward Rushton, an international valuing company, claims call reluctance management procedures are not just for traditional sales areas, but for "any part of the organisation which is in any way involved in selling products or services."

International Norms

Data samples organized according to national origin provide interesting macro views of how call reluctance operates in different countries and cultures. Many such samples already exist. Many more are being collected, almost daily. These emerging international call reluctance norms may help senior sales and marketing executives anticipate call reluctance problems within their own cultures, while suggesting how to deal with them as well.

- Overall, sales professionals in Singapore appear more inclined to Social Self-Consciousness (53%) and Stage Fright (54%). Emotionally Unemancipated (51%) was elevated and Telephobia (48%) was unexpectedly high. Total call reluctance (prospecting Brake score) was 41%. Referral Aversion (10%) was low.

- Aross the China Sea, in Hong Kong, salespeople project a similar call reluctance pattern. Emotionally Unemancipated (60%) is high, as is Social Self-Consciousness (50%) and Telephobia (50%). Interestingly, scores on Separationist Call Reluctance in both Hong Kong and Singapore were comparatively low, confirming once again that Separationist (friends) and Emotionally Unemancipated (family members) are separate dimensions. You can't forecast one from knowing the other.

- Overall, Australians tend to be slightly less call reluctant than their Kiwi neighbors located just across Tasman Sea in New Zealand.

- With the exception of French-speaking Quebec, Canadians are indistinguishable from their U.S. counterparts. (We have no data from Quebec Province. It remains a mystery.)

- We're just beginning to gather call reluctance data on salespeople in Spain and Italy. Still missing are data for ancient Etruscans.

- In recent years, with the assistance of some of the largest firms in the United Kingdom, we've begun to unlock the mysteries of British salespeople. While they tend to be somewhat less impaired by call reluctance than their counterparts in other countries, they do boast royal levels of Hyper-Pro Call Reluctance, as evidenced by their fondness for wearing braces (which, we found out, have nothing to do with orthodontia, but are in fact what we call "suspenders"). Despite the formidable language barrier, we continue to study this intriguing group.

INDUSTRY STUDIES

Global views tantalize call reluctance scholars, practitioners and a few curious bystanders. But they're not nearly as practical as call reluctance cross sections taken from various industries and sales cultures. Normative data exists for many of these, but space limitations do not permit listing them all. We'll sketch some of the most interesting ones and discuss a few in detail.

The data we will describe are real data taken from the real experiences of real companies. Most of these companies do not wish to be identified by name. They use persuasive arguments to assert their position. First, they believe mentioning their name in the context of call reluctance could impair their ability to recruit new sales talent. Secondly, they think the aggressive anti-call reluctance technology they're using gives them a hidden advantage over their competitors. Third, they said they will sue us if we do.

Stockbrokers

We have received invaluable assistance from some of the most forward thinking companies in this industry since the early 80's. Our studies could not have been done without their cooperation, and though they prefer to remain nameless, we know who they are and owe them a debt of gratitude.

In terms of type sensitivity, stockbrokers fear humiliation. They're inclined to be Hyper-Pros. As a group, they are vulnerable to a self-sabotaging fear that some current or prospective client might question their professional competence, or even their integrity. Brokers refuse to network through their friends (Separationists) or their family (Emotionally Unemancipated). A respectably sized sub-group hone their technical skills to a fine edge, while neglecting their prospecting skills altogether. They're Over-Preparers.

The average stockbroker in the U.S. acquires about 70 new accounts per year and earns gross commissions approaching $200,000 annually. The call reluctance profile illustrated in Table 6 is based on 395 new and experienced brokers.

Table 6   Call reluctance profile of 395 new and experienced stockbrokers.

Call Reluctance Type	Average Score
Total Call Reluctance	36
Doomsayers	11
Over-Preparation	45
Hyper-Pros	45
Stage Fright	34
Role Rejection	29
Yielders	32
Social Self-Consciousness	28
Separationist	51
Emotionally Unemancipated	55
Referral Aversion	32
Telephobia	37
Oppositional Reflex	6

Total call reluctance for the sample was about average for salespeople in general. Separationist and Emotionally Unemancipated scores were much higher than expected. Those elevations have been traced to commercial sales training programs for brokers. If you are a broker, watch who you let near your mind! Average Hyper-Pro and Over-Preparation scores were also high. This is undoubtedly due to the technical/financial features of the sales culture plus the over-emphasis brokers traditionally put on appearing professional. For stockbrokers, moderately high Hyper-Pro scores can be positively related to production, indicating that image projection, or Image-Oriented selling, can contribute to success in this field (Dudley, G.W., Goodson, S.L., *Selling Styles Profile Analysis*, Behavioral Sciences Research Press). Image-Oriented Sellers highlight what *they* can do for buyers, instead of what the product can do, how good the service will be, how warm the relationship will be, or what the buyer's needs may be.

Reducing the data down a step reveals some interesting differences between the new and established brokers. Table 7 illustrates the "catch 22" relationship between earnings and tenure. Those who stay longer make more money. But only money-making new brokers get to stay. New stockbrokers must function in a hostile, non-forgiving sales environment. Call reluctant salespeople don't survive. Everyone loses.

This table also confirms that Separationist and Emotionally Unemancipated scores are significantly lower for the neophytes than the veteran brokers. The new ones have not yet learned to feel uncomfortable networking through their relatives and friends. As an aside, higher Goal Level scores and lower Goal Diffusion scores suggest the new generation of brokers may be more ambitious. They may quickly outperform the old guard.

There are few Doomsayers among experienced stockbrokers, but those with the highest Doomsayer scores who managed to hold on, produced poorly. Brokers with the lowest Doomsayer scores, produced in the highest amounts and earned the most commission dollars. The highest producers also had the lowest Stage Fright scores. The lowest producers had the highest, indicating the importance of group presentations to commission dollars of stockbrokers.

Table 7 Call reluctance profile for experienced vs. inexperienced stockbrokers.

Call Reluctance Type	Experienced	Inexperienced
Brake	37	33
Doomsayers	11	10
Over-Preparers	42	50
Hyper-Pros	44	46
Stage Fright	33	35
Role Rejection	29	28
Yielders	31	34
Social Self-Consciousness	29	27
Separationist	57	40
Emotionally Unemancipated	59	46
Referral Aversion	38	21
Telephobia	39	33
Oppositional Reflex	5	6
Motivation	68	66
Goal Level	58	63
Goal Diffusion	58	51
Gross Commissions:	215,000	56,000

Brokers with the highest Yielder scores were the lowest producers. Those scoring between 0-22% averaged $35,000 of commissions per quarter, while scores from 23-38% averaged $20,000 of income. Brokers with Yielder scores of 39% or higher earned only $9,438.

This conclusion was confirmed by a second, separate study of brokers who marketed solely by telephone. High Yielder scores produced $10,000.00 of commissions. Brokers low on the Yielder scale averaged $15,000.00 more per person.

As expected, Social Self-Consciousness was very important. Brokers with the highest scores (averaging only 39.4%) were anchored in the lowest production group. Low scorers (24%) soared to the highest production category.

The call reluctance type most linked to the survival (retention) of new brokers (less than one year) was Role Rejection (t=2.0839, P<.0223, for the difference between terminated and retained new hires).

The relationship of Motivation Level scores to actual production dollars (Table 8) had the kind of stair-step linearity scientists dream of finding. This conclusion held when confirmed by a second group of brokers. The brokers with the highest motivation scores averaged $25,500 per person per quarter in commissions, while those with the lowest scores averaged only $14,000.

A third study looked at 250 telemarketing stockbrokers. Unlike the first group who needed to promote themselves visibly in the community, this group was phone-bound. Brake scores for this group, (total call reluctance) were significantly related (P<.05) to production.

Table 8 Average Motivation scores by production category.

Average Score	Production Category
64%	Lowest
68%	Middle
73%	Highest

Their Telephobia scores were not as neatly textbook linear, as we would have preferred, but they added worthwhile confirmation. Brokers with the highest levels of Telephobia Call Reluctance earned the lowest incomes ($17,000 per quarter). Those with average levels of Telephobia produced average amounts of business, earning about $19,000 per quarter in commissions. The group with the lowest Telephobia scores earned the highest incomes, averaging $22,000 per quarter in commissions each.

The difference in commissions between the highest and lowest producers in this particular sample averaged only $5,000 per person. But that's certainly not unimportant. Put a pencil to it. If this company employed only 10 brokers with elevated Telephobia scores, it would cost each of them $20,000 per year in lost commissions. It could cost the company many times that amount in lost profits, depending on the percent paid out in commissions. Even slight Telephobic scratches can open major prospecting wounds, causing massive financial hemorrhaging.

Another independent study focused on stockbrokers who succeed early in their careers. We took production figures for 346 stockbrokers and analyzed them in terms of their call reluctance scores. The correlation between total call reluctance (Brake score) and production was upside down and highly significant (r=-.22, P<.01.) As call reluctance increased, production for these new brokers dramatically decreased. As in the other studies, Yielders produced harmony, not profits.

Banks and Savings & Loans

In the recent remembered past, trust officers and other bank officials psychologically distanced themselves from the sales function. They were above it. "Selling" was a near-obscenity. They could not easily pronounce it.

Insulated by tradition, many U.S. banks were studies in obstinacy, arrogance and neglectful mismanagement. In some organizations the human resources department was even elevated above sales. They were actually permitted to shape sales policy, often even circumventing the sales management professionals who were accountable for sales results!

Sound incredible? It's not. This industry is an example of what happens when competent employees contribute, but don't manage visibility. A "recognition vacuum" develops which is quenched by less deserving people. Some are call reluctant. For example, when Hyper-Pros, who look the part of leadership, migrate to the top of these institutions they immediately begin to insulate themselves. They add unnecessary layers of staff and build intra-company empires. Over-Preparers reaching the same heights bog their organizations down in the muck of petty, incessant meetings. In some financial centers, the absence of deserving, ethical, self-promoting employees competing for top positions clears the way for unethical self-promoters. They just walk in and take over. Banks must re-shape their organizations and overhaul their attitudes toward sales if they wish to meaningfully compete with traditional sales-driven financial organizations. Sporadic, research-based snapshots we've taken of this industry over the years suggest it won't be easy.

As a group, old-style trust officers are Hyper-Pros and Over-Preparers spiced up with toxic levels of Role Rejection Call Reluctance. That's a heavy load, but it shouldn't be surprising. Most of them came from technical backgrounds. They neither expected nor desired to become involved with the sales process. They certainly didn't expect to be part of it.

When they started their careers, financial institutions like banks and savings & loans didn't have or need sales professionals. Many still insist they don't. Why should they? They have "relationship managers." No joke, folks.

But the banking industry seems to be undergoing a metamorphosis. Once safely consigned to "relationship" selling and other teflon-surfaced prospect-hugging sales philosophies, banking now represents one of the most aggressive industry-wide migrations toward a no-excuse prospecting culture. Competitive industries should take notice.

While managing an important division for Australia's prestigous Macquarie Bank, Executive Director Andrew Ipkendanz underscored the new emphasis in banking. "Everyone at Macquarie Bank is in sales.... from the managing director to the tellers," he said. It made a difference, and he has the numbers to prove it. Working with New Zealand psychologist Megan Brice, his team recorded a 500% increase in sales.

That's not an isolated case. Other organizations which were ready to swap the comfort of rapport-building for the revenues which come from closed sales posted similar results. A banking study we completed in 1992 confirmed that a sales organization's attitude toward new business acquisition makes a difference which can be counted.

We measured the presence, type and degree of sales call reluctance in all 125 employees of an investment banking organization. We found that commissions earned were negatively related to Over-preparer and Yielder scores. Earnings were positively related to motivation scores as measured by the Call Reluctance Scale.

Table 9   Call reluctance profile for financial center sales personnel (banks, savings & loans).

Type of Call Reluctance	Average Score
Brake	40
Doomsayers	19
Over-Preparation	41
Hyper-Pros	39
Stage Fright	55
Role Rejection	31
Yielders	35
Social Self-Consciousness	38
Separationist	39
Emotionally Unemancipated	50
Referral Aversion	20
Telephobia	41
Oppositional Reflex	8

A statistical composite was built from unequal parts of the most important ingredients. It was found to significantly distinguish the highest from the lowest producers in terms of attitude toward prospecting ($p < .01$).

Salespeople with the best attitudes toward prospecting earned an average of $80,000 per year, per person. Those with the worst attitudes toward prospecting earned only $49,000 each during the same time period.

Bankers used to lament, "If I had wanted to go into sales I would have." Some still do. But now we know how much it's likely to cost.

Macquarie Bank and other forward-thinking banking institutions are industry leaders. They're not waiting for conditions to improve, or for luck. They don't have to. By actively seeking new business, they're creating opportunity and harvesting it. That's what financial planners should have done.

Financial Planners

A few years ago, financial planners were the hottest new addition to the financial services industry seen in decades. Their advent was touted with corporate sponsored advertising. Cryptic, ceremonial letters were affixed to business cards of normal people we had known for years. Any consumer could see, this wasn't business as usual. It was serious drama, like science fiction movies from the 1950's. A small town's entire population would disappear, or better still, all the kids, especially those in puberty, would go missing. When they showed up again, they talked differently and had weird looks in their eyes. They probably formed their own professional association, too.

We think that's what happened to large numbers of young stockbrokers, bankers and insurance agents a few years ago. One day, probably during a total eclipse, they de-materialized. Disappeared. When they recomposed and, like the sunshine, came back again, they were not the same. They had a strange look in their eyes, and talked funny. "I'm not a salesman," one protested, robotically. "I'm a 'Financial Planner'."

They were better trained and more credentialed than common salespeople. Some charged a fee to hear their sales presentation. That made them more objective. No longer salespeople, some stopped prospecting for new business. "We don't have to prospect," the editor of one of their publications told our publicist, "We're professionals. We're Financial Planners."

Things changed. Three years later we were the featured speakers at a convention for financial planners. By then their numbers had decreased dramatically. When we told the audience what the editor had said three years before, they hooted, hissed and howled. They were frustrated. They needed new business desperately but had forgotten how to prospect comfortably to get it. What a difference a few years can make.

In our judgment that editor was catastrophically wrong. Authors like us have to prospect for readers, or the books we write don't sell. Scientists have to prospect for research grants or their efforts go unfunded. Ivory towered academics have to prospect to deliver their fair share of visibility to the department. (Of course, they don't call it "prospecting." The maxim for survival in academia is "publish or perish.") The military has to prospect for funds to purchase new weapons. City governments, actors, university undergraduates looking for a date, gurus and cult leaders, politicians and Christ himself while he was on this earth all had to prospect. So do Financial Planners.

To be more precise, so *did* financial planners. Members of that persuasion are difficult to locate these days. Like dinosaurs, they used to walk the earth in great numbers. But it seems like all but the heartiest have died out, qualifying them for a place, if not in history, at least on the endangered species list. Researchers should have been more alert. We should have identified them with ear tags or implanted transmitters under their skin so their migratory habits could be tracked. But that might not have helped. What if they just de-materialized again? Vanished? Whichever, all we have are a few blurry snapshots taken of salespeople reputed to be financial planners during their stay in these parts.

From these statistical snapshots we know the financial planner designation tended to attract hard core Over-Preparers. But that conclusion is tentative. It was difficult for us then and it is still difficult for us now to determine what a "financial planner" was. From our admittedly confused perspective, it appears they were actually an amalgam of Over-Preparer escapees from other financially oriented sales disciplines. The designation "financial planner" was awarded to individuals who successfully completed one or another specialized course of study. Most we talked with confessed to prospecting, selling, and closing like other salespeople, but it was confided in hushed, secretive tones, like Southern Baptists making plans to go out drinking and dancing. A vocal, non-representative minority insisted financial planners were prototype professionals. They did not sell, did not prospect, and did not collect commissions. That was certainly providential, since they definitely did have call reluctance.

Insurance

The insurance industry is a large, moving target. Static generalizations useful one day may be obsolete the next due to the fallouts, shakeouts, scandals and other traumas which have plagued this industry. But some generalizations are possible, some are warranted, and one is inescapable: *call reluctance remains a big problem in the insurance industry.*

Large scale, within-industry samples like the one illustrated in Table 10, tend to smooth out blemishes like call reluctance. Hovering statistically above, the insurance industry does not appear to be any more contaminated by sales call reluctance than other industries. It looks emotionally hygienic. Don't be deceived.

Table 10 Call reluctance profile for 575 insurance agents.

Call Reluctance Type	Average Score
Brake	37
Doomsayers	20
Over-Preparation	40
Hyper-Pros	44
Stage Fright	41
Role Rejection	28
Yielders	29
Social Self-Consciousness	33
Separationist	48
Emotionally Unemancipated	50
Referral Aversion	21
Telephobia	38
Oppositional Reflex	9

For a start, the table does not show that call reluctance data from the insurance industry tends to be bimodal, meaning the data coagulates like two blobs of grease into two clusters, or groupings, not one. Tossing the data into a single statistical composite yields a middle of the road compromise, not really applicable to either.

One group is under the influence of quick fix shortsightedness which is reflected in their sales management philosophy and practices. The second group consists of authentically sophisticated, well-run insurance and financial services organizations. Both struggle with call reluctance, but in different ways with radically different effectiveness.

A Tale of Two Companies

Honored as the lone commercial enterprise on Capitol Hill, the Acacia Financial Group does not have the size or influence of bigger financial services insurance companies. Most insurance executives visiting the U.S. from other countries probably never heard of it. Yet the Acacia Financial Group, piloted with insight and sensitivity by company president Tuck Nason, boasts a long history, full range of financial products and a restless dissatisfaction with the status quo.

Nason, a successful ex-branch manager himself, helps other seasoned sales management pros, such as regional vice-president Jim Andrepont and consultant-psychologists Ed Timmons and Bruce Merrick, sustain Acacia's militant prospecting heartbeat. Acacia has provided call reluctance support company-wide, for all of their agents, longer and more consistently than any other company—of any type. They pioneered their call reluctance philosophy back in 1976 under management visionaries Rusty McGlasson and Duane Adams. If you call Acacia and ask them their retention figures, they will probably tell you.

Another insurance conglomerate, which need not be named, advertises regularly on television. It has a much bigger image, supported by massive advertising budgets. It also has, we suspect, a much worse agent retention history. But unlike the Acacia Financial Group, you'd never know it. Then how do we know? One of their most successful managers told us.

The manager was a pathological Hyper-Pro. To him, image was everything. A stuffed olive of a man, he used to proudly announce his company's astronomically high retention rate for new agents. The figure implied his agents were happier than other agents, so they stayed longer—much longer. He used the felicitous situation to help him recruit new agents, who stayed longer, too. Neat.

Competitors flying nearer the earth were justifiably dismayed. How did they do it? Envious dignitaries visiting the states from foreign insurance companies were visibly impressed. Regular streams of such pilgrims visited the home office, where retention figures were brought out and displayed like the Shroud of Turin. We were even impressed—then confused. How did they do so well? All the behavioral evidence indicated that they were no better at managing the sales function than other insurance companies, and in some cases, like the silly grid-based attitude scale they touted for agent selection, they were not even in the same league as their competitors. We decided to check.

At least once a year, this company co-sponsored an image orgy for its Hyper-Pro sales managers. An advertisement was placed in the newspaper which

Call Reluctance? No Problem.

Our data suggest that the insurance industry provides asylum for more low motivation impostors than other industries. Some of them have survived long enough to migrate into sales management, and in some companies to senior sales management.

Faithful to the spirit of Low Motivation Impostors, these executives don't seem to care if call reluctance exists in their sales force or not. Other things are more important, such as tee-up times, executive perks and biweekly upheavals (called "organizational restructuring.") They provide no substantial programs for detecting, assessing, or correcting call reluctance. They are not interested in the subject either. But then, they don't seem interested in learning much of anything. They think their agents are clones of themselves (they often are). All they really need is to be "pumped up, paid on time and entertained." The incidence of call reluctance in these companies is many times higher than comparable companies within the same industry.

included prominent color portraits of the management staff surrounded by little black and white pictures of all their agents. The agency we monitored was reputed to be one of their biggest and perennially most successful, though we discovered later that most all of their agencies said that. Nevertheless, we saw our chance and took it.

The verification we sought would be simple. Yet it would demand a patient vigil. You see, each year we compared the pictures with the previous year's to see who was new and who was missing. After two years we had a troubling suspicion; after three, a scientific hypothesis; after four, the inconsistency between the retention figures they published and the faces in the pictures was unavoidable. Our work was done. The actual retention percentage for the branch was in the low 20's, not the high 80's or low 90's.

If you're a foreign observer visiting U.S. insurance companies, don't be too impressed too quickly. Verify. Read between the lines. Be especially wary of unrealistically high claims. Well run companies on genuine, prudent growth tracks, like The Acacia Financial Group, have effective agent recruiting, selection and training practices. They don't have to give their statistics a steroid shot.

Call Reluctance: Premium With No Benefits

Some insurance companies fit the preceding description, but not all. The insurance industry also houses companies which have developed some of the finest sales organizations anywhere. Their salespeople rank among the highest level sales professionals anywhere. They are nourished by some of the most sophisticated sales training programs of any industry.

Some of our earliest work on call reluctance was done for an insurance company, the old Southwestern Life Insurance Company in Dallas, Texas. The beneficiary of not one, or two, but decades of high quality people in senior management positions, this company was rightly distinguished for its leadership in agent recruiting, selection training, and development technologies. Highly experimental programs, like our call reluctance research, were not only tolerated, but patronized and encouraged.

The first two individuals ever subjected to our efforts were failing agents for the old Southwestern Life Insurance Company. Both had approximately three months of tenure, and neither had a production heart beat in that they had produced essentially nothing during their first three months. In the early 1970's, we referred to these challenges as "autopsy cases."

After receiving call reluctance training, agent "A" steadily increased from zero to $2,000 of production (per month) in only four months. Agent "B" went from near zero to $3,000 per month during the same time period.

Both individuals regained prospecting consciousness. Both resurrected their sales careers. Since then, one has matured into a highly successful young sales manager. We don't know what happened to the other. We learned a lot about call reluctance from these two early cases. We learned more about how much a company can care about its salespeople.

In 1988 we were honored with access to members of the insurance industry's Million Dollar Round Table (MDRT) organization. MDRT is an international body with members from 48 nations. They represent an elite group, the top-most insurance producers in the world. Membership confers a special status. Desire for membership helps focus the ambitions of all new agents.

The MDRT Call Reluctance Research Project was planned as a supplement to our platform presentation at their 1988 annual convention in Atlanta, Georgia. We were initially skeptical about becoming involved in another research project of this magnitude because we were not certain the topic was appropriate to sales professionals earning up to a quarter million dollars per year. Besides that, we had already studied many VHPs (Very High Producers) in other industries.

Soon after the project began, our skepticism ended. We had anticipated indifference. Instead, we got stacks of unsolicited letters and hours of un-scheduled spontaneous interviews, both in person and on the phone. The result was an unexpectedly rich flow of practical information about the influence of call reluctance on sales success in the insurance industry. The results were published the following year.

By unselfishly participating in this study, members of MDRT helped detail the contrasts between salespeople who say they want to reach the top of their profession, and those who actually produce at that level.

Each MDRT participant completed the Call Reluctance Scale. Scores were returned to Dallas for computer processing. Scores were compiled and examined in terms of age, MDRT commissions category, and tenure in insurance sales. Scores from a contrast group were used for comparison. The contrast group was a second, independent sample of insurance salespeople matched by age and tenure in insurance sales to approximate the MDRT sample. They represented several different agencies, companies, training philosophies, and sales selection programs. None produced enough new business to warrant MDRT membership.

Score profiles for Top of the Table, the best of the best, are especially illuminating and bring differences into sharp relief when juxtapositioned next to members in the contrast group.

- Top of the Table members averaged 39% on Over-Preparation Call Reluctance. Their counter-parts in the contrast group averaged 47%. The highest insurance producers prepare, but don't over-prepare.

- Hyper-Pro scores for Top of the Table members averaged 46.88%. The contrast group averaged 53.67%. High producers project a professional image.

- Stage Fright scores for Top of the Table members averaged 41.61%, while marginal producers in the contrast group averaged 53.67%. High producers are less likely to fear group presentations, therefore, more likely to make use of group, "seminar selling" strategies.

- Top producers have more authentic pride in their profession. We cannot infer from the data that they have it because they produce more, or they produce more because they have it, but one thing is clear: They have it. They averaged 29.5% on Role Rejection, while members of the contrast group were busy pretending to be positive (46.67%).

- Like most people, top MDRT producers don't want to be intrusive. But they don't let the fear of being considered intrusive block their prospecting path. Their average Yielder score was 23.67%. Also-rans in the contrast group weighed in at a hefty 38.14%.

- Very high producers ask for referrals. Top MDRT producers averaged 18.72% Referral Aversion Call Reluctance. The contrast group shot up to 38.89%.

- Average Motivation Level scores (the higher the better) for the MDRT categories approximated a stair-step linear pattern (Table 11).

Table 11 Average Motivation scores and MDRT production category.

MDRT Production Category	Average Motivation Score
Non-MDRT Contrast Group	42.16%
Entry Level MDRT	64.44%
Middle Group MDRT	67.02%
Top of the Table MDRT	73.72%

- Goal Level scores were also linearly related to production (Table 12).

Table 12 Average Goal Level scores and MDRT production category.

MDRT Production Category	Average Goal Level Score
Non-MDRT Contrast Group	38.53%
Entry Level MDRT	45.53%
Middle Group MDRT	57.20%
Top of the Table MDRT	64.11%

Perhaps the most telling measure of all was Oppositional Reflex Call Reluctance. MDRT members welcomed the opportunity to learn more about themselves. They wanted to see what they could improve. Members of the contrast group were contentious, argumentative and highly opinionated. We had never met a larger or more vocal group of experts on sales assessment. "Is it valid?" they asked. "How long will it take?" "Why do you want me to take it?" "What are you going to do with the results?" "Aren't tests like that illegal?" "I have to get permission from our home office." "I don't believe in tests."

Entry level MDRT members scored only 5.7% on Oppositionality. The industry average is about 8%. The middle MDRT group scored roughly in the middle, at 4.4%. Super producers in the Top of the Table group scored 1.8%. That's not a typo. They scored only 1.8%.

The contrast group scored five times higher. They averaged 10% (actually higher, we were rounding generously that day), but they had a lot of interesting questions and wild excuses for why they were not MDRT members and how the questionnaire didn't really pinpoint them. Too bad. The only thing standing between many of them and Top of the Table productivity was Oppositional Reflex Call Reluctance.

Insurance sales managers can learn from these data. So can trainers, consultants and new agents. But the people who can learn the most are veteran agents who are still not earning what they are worth.

For some, MDRT producers may be an idealized standard, not applicable to the experiences of most insurance salespeople. Perhaps. Let's review some more data.

We looked at the first year commissions earned by a group of 37 new agents and found essentially, the same patterns. Motivation, Stage Fright (P<.05) and Role Rejection (P<.01) were all linked to income level. New agents with this company with high total call reluctance averaged $10,562 in commissions their first year. Their less reluctant peers earned $14,337. Yielders produced $11,395, while non-Yielders got $15,347. Those with the highest Motivation Level scores earned $14,543. Their less urgent counterparts settled for $7,945.

In a third study, early production was examined for 387 new insurance agents. Agents scoring high in total call reluctance averaged only $185.00 per person, per month of tenure. Those less hesitant to prospect enjoyed $756 per person, per month of tenure. Call Reluctance can keep you poor.

What happens when an insurance company applies call reluctance technology? One company decided to find out. They overhauled their sales selection process, retrofitting it with the Call Reluctance Scale. Their new agent selection model was based on a three-pronged model we developed for assessing sales selection procedures in the late 1970's. (Dudley, G.W., & Goodson, S.L., & Haynes, J.R.,"Testing the Test," *Journal of Agent and Management Selection and Development*, Vol. 1, No. 1, 1981)

Our method does not endorse or condemn the use of any particular assessment procedure. Instead, it offers sales managers a conceptual discipline they can use to hold the methods they use for selection accountable for results. (We find that managers not using such a model tend to over-rely on test scores, subverting their management prerogative to the output of a test. Managers are ultimately accountable for the accuracy of selection decisions. Sales selection tests are not.) Therefore, we teach managers not to over value buzz words like ego or dominance. Instead, ask the tests producing these scores to help answer one or more of three questions: ***How Much? How Soon? What Cost?***

1) How much *money* is this individual likely to make for me?
2) How *soon* is this individual likely to produce at that level?
3) What is it going to *cost* me to get that production within that time frame, in terms of additional management *time*, *effort*, and *money*?

If your sales assessment techniques are not helping you to substantially reduce uncertainty about one or more of the three preceding questions, fire them. Get new ones. That's what one insurance company did. The new guard was tested for fitness before the old ones were replaced. After all, making a change is not necessarily making an improvement. The old procedures were retained, but set aside, while the new ones were proving their mettle. The results were impressive. The preceding year, 60 new agents had terminated before completing 12 months in sales.

As you can see in Table 13, the difference between the old way and the new way was stunning. I wish we could take credit for the dramatic improvement in retention, claiming it was all due to our Call Reluctance Scale, but we can't. The scale made a respectable contribution, but the real improvement probably came from exposing the sales managers to our conceptual model. Once that model was understood, the managers had an "a-ha!" experience of the first order. They were more careful about how they used selection procedures, using the Call Reluctance Scale, for example, to help prune obviously call-reluctant candidates—who would have been hired under the old method.

While the MDRT study was probably the high point of our work with the insurance industry, the study we did with 50 zero producers was probably the low. This sample consisted entirely of new agents who, after three months on the job, had yet to sell their first policy. Members of this distinguished fraternity had been acquired by the managers of a company with high visibility, but no authenticated means of assessing call reluctance. (The selection procedure the company used claimed to be valid for predicting the fear of rejection, but it was apparently suffering from an injury, perhaps a cerebral hemorrhage.)

Table 13 The effects of call reluctance screening on agent attrition.

Month	Call Reluctance Screening	
	Before	After
January	7	2
February	15	2
March	21	2
April	26	2
May	26	2
June	30	2
July	35	3
August	38	3
September	42	3
October	47	5
November	51	5
December	60	5

The sample consisted of both men and women. Average age was 32 years, average years of formal education was seventeen, one year beyond the basic four-year university degree. Before becoming agents, they had earned an average salary of almost $30,000.00, a feat not to be duplicated as agents since they had produced absolutely nothing during their first three months of tenure. The senior vice-president of sales and marketing gave his seal of approval to our study. Eighteen months before, he had listened to his director of agent selection give a melodramatic presentation on behalf of the "fear of rejection" test they were presently using. A quiet, nervous man, he looked, to us, like he was about to explode.

Using a battery of formal, reputable psychological tests, we found that intelligence was higher than average. Ego-strength measures indicated no problems with self-esteem. They liked themselves. They were more dominant than average, and more sociable and outgoing. They had higher than average doses of impulse restraint (self-discipline), no abnormal levels of stress or nervous tension were present, and optimism was higher than average. So were scores on "locus of control" or attributional style. Sociability was high as well. On paper, this particular group looked great. So why were they failing?

- The average total call reluctance score (Brake) for this group was bimodal: 36 for one group and 44 for the other. If you squeezed the two averages down into one, like two oranges into one glass of orange juice, the taste would be bitter: somewhere around 40-41. That's high.

- Stage Fright wandered upwards to near 50%.

- At 54%, Yielders tipped the scales.

- The *average* Hyper-Pro score for the group was a mirror shattering 50%! You aren't likely to get an average Hyper-Pro score that far out in the stratosphere by accident alone. There had to be help. Something had to *systematically* tilt the hiring decisions in the direction of call-reluctant Hyper-Pros, who also happened to have Stage Fright and be Yielders. (Definitely not MDRT material.)

Perhaps it was something in the local water supply. No, that's not probable because the sample was sea-to-shining-sea national. Could it be the hand of God? Not likely. Even Old Testament accounts say God only got mad enough to drown everyone, he never lost his sense of propriety and attacked insurance companies. Besides that, if providence was involved, we would know about it. This company's quasi-distinguished chairman of the board delights in giving stem-winding, red, white and blue patriotic speeches, wherein he implies having regular policy meetings with God.

As it turned out, the bandit was made of paper. It was the new selection test the company had been using. Unwisely talked into de-emphasizing the Career Profile, the standard test the insurance industry recommends for assessing prospective agents, the company had been duped by a glitzy series of presentations featuring copious claims of validity and pages of testimonial endorsements. The recognition-starved director of agent selection had not been overlooked either. He had been generously wined and dined, his ego inflated along with his head size, until he became "all hat, no cattle." The sales strategy worked. The test didn't.

We pieced things together by correlating selection test scores, hiring recommendations, and call reluctance measures. The equation which emerged affirmed what we suspected. The test, constructed using non-sales samples, was easily faked and weighted in the wrong direction. High call reluctance type scores, especially Hyper-Pro, were positively related to hiring recommendations. The more Hyper-Pro Call Reluctance you had, the more likely you were to succeed as an insurance agent, this test said.

It's an understandable error. Hyper-Pros are pretty, remember? They look professional, successful. That's the image of success the selection test looked for, and that's what they found—an image, hollow on the inside, unable to prospect.

Sales Management Performance and Call Reluctance

Sales managers and trainers in the insurance industry tend to have higher call reluctance scores than the agents they manage. One study, for example, found that 26 regional sales vice-presidents averaged 14% more call reluctance than the agents in their company. Another study showed how call-reluctant sales managers can damage retention.

Call Reluctance Scale scores were obtained from 36 insurance sales managers. The sample consisted of new and experienced sales managers working with companies who distributed several financial services products. We studied how many new agents they recruited and how well they were able to retain the new agents they acquired. Hyper-Pro and Oppositional Reflex measures were *positively* related to the number of new agents recruited, but *negatively* related to new agent retention (P<.05).

We do not have an adequate explanation for this data. Perhaps projecting an image of professional strength helped them attract new talent, but was insufficient to help them keep the agents they recruited. We are not sure.

Role Rejection In the Insurance Industry

Perhaps no form of call reluctance is more troublesome to the insurance industry than Role Rejection. Over-sensitive about their public image, many companies have unwisely tried to dispose of the problem, like the banking industry, by calling the sales function by another name.

It won't work. Despite what these companies call their salespeople ("financial planners," "account executives," "client representatives"), Role Rejection Call Reluctance tenaciously retains its grip, short circuiting the sales function. Role Rejecting agents, calling themselves by another name to make themselves more emotionally acceptable (to themselves), produce significantly less than agents calling themselves agents. This phenomenon is illustrated by two agents we met at different times during different studies of insurance salespeople. Both gave us business cards. One producer proudly presented his ornate card which read "Senior Financial Services & Estate Planning Advisor." His name was followed by an ostentatious trail of cryptic letters, designating degrees and affiliations we did not recognize or understand. The other agent's card simply read "Insurance Agent." The first agent was participating in a study of marginal to barely adequate producers. The second was a veteran member of the Million Dollar Round Table.

Role Rejection seems to thrive in insurance companies where agents are called alternative names (financial planners, etc.), but training remains focused on sales. The resulting mixed message echoes across company affiliations, products sold, and markets worked.

Role Rejection in the insurance industry is characterized by uncertainty, shame, and guilt associated with being in sales. It often originates in the callous and insensitive stereotypes the general public, and often the companies themselves, mindlessly pin on insurance salespeople. Too often, when it first surfaces in the form of honest doubt or emotional confusion, misguided sales managers force it emotionally underground with heavy-handed, self-righteous indignation and rapid-fire platitudes. "Don't you believe in our business?" they ask. "Haven't you caught the vision?" Buried under a dung heap of clichés, it ferments, worsening, until it bursts.

Automobile Sales

Automobile retailers in the U.S. tend to lag far behind other industries in sales selection and training. Many owners and sales managers still don't recognize call reluctance as a problem, or comprehend its importance to them.

Backward, sometimes intellectually offensive showroom sales tactics, ("Excuse me. I have to check with my sales manager to see if he'll agree to a sensational price this low.") are given more time, money and attention.

Automobile agencies in other countries appear to have a more mature concept of sales as a profession and auto sales as a legitimate career. In general, they seem more open to ideas and technologies which can help boost sales and profits.

U.S. dealerships seem to be moving in the right direction, but it is still too early and the movement is still too slow to be certain. Movement is necessary, however. Times are tough for the auto industry. Radical changes are necessary. Salespeople are needed who do not depend on advertising-based floor traffic for the major portion of units sold. As in other direct sales industries, auto dealerships need unimpaired prospectors who will get onto the telephone, up from their seats, and out into the community to make sales happen. They can no longer sit and wait. The industry can no longer bear it. As the following table shows, it costs too much.

The profile illustrated in Table 14 was acquired by the automobile industry's Automotive Satellite Television Network (ASTN), sponsor of the project. It consisted of 75 auto salespeople who were geographically scattered throughout the U.S. and represented a wide range of automobile marques. Call reluctance was assessed in relation to *cumulative commissions* earned during the most recent quarter.

The average age of participants was 34 years old. Average sales experience was 72 months, with 24 of that in automobile sales. During their tenure in auto sales, they had worked only for one agency. Educationally, the average auto sales professional in this sample had attended college for two years, but had not completed a degree.

Table 14 Call reluctance and commissions: highlights for 75 U.S. automobile salespeople.

Call Reluctance Type	Commissions Earned	
	High CR	Low CR
Brake	4,360	8,438
Doomsayers	6,840	7,854
Stage Fright	6,904	8,245
Yielders	5,780	9,016
Separationists	6,525	8,189
Referral Aversion	6,649	9,269
Telephobia	6,500	9,000
Oppositional Reflex	5,912	7,978

The Impostor profile for this sample was similar to other industries. Highly motivated auto salespeople averaged $8,738.00 per person commissions during the most recent quarter. Their less motivated, more laid back colleagues earned $7,400.00.

Beyond the Statistics

We didn't know. A friend we have known for years sells cars, Cadillac cars, actually. We had just picked up two new, fully equipped Cadillac Fleetwoods. Hyper-Pro black, with darkly tinted privacy windows, the sinister looking machines are company perks we get for being warm and witty—fun people to know. (Actually the cars are near bribes, inducements to keep successful authors happy, writing and loyal.) We would have ordered the wheeled machines from our friend, but we didn't know he sold cars, Cadillacs at that! He never mentioned it.

Is it important for automobile salespeople to identify with their sales career, to want to succeed as automobile sales professionals? Yes. Goal Level scores formed the same stair-step pattern we have observed before in other industries. The salespeople with the highest Goal Level scores produced the most quarterly commissions ($9,414.00.) The least goal-directed producers earned less ($5,648.00 per quarter), and average, middle-of-the-roaders, occupied the middle ground. They averaged $8,289.00 in quarterly commissions.

Not to be ignored, Goal-Diffusion Impostors had something to say about selling cars, too. Motivated, but goal-scattered, they earned $1,373.00 per person *less* than sales pros who set priorities and steered the course. That's sobering. Goal-Diffusion Impostors trying to sell cars can expect to cough up $5,492.00 per person, per year to support their habit. That's expensive.

Cosmetics/In-home Party Sales

Some companies have successfully built international reputations on the basis of sales originating from small, in-home parties. Antecedents of modern seminar prospecting, these smaller, less formal in-house gatherings pre-date seminar selling by decades. They are currently used to market an entire spectrum of products ranging from artwork to pots and pans, esoteric vitamins to sexy lingerie, makeup to makeovers.

Like others, we thought Stage Fright would be the most troublesome call reluctance type for salespeople in this setting. It can be. But recent studies show it's not the demon it used to be. More virulent specters have surfaced.

We assessed 108 salespeople engaged in party sales. Our national (U.S.) sample consisted of men and women from more than one company selling a variety of different products. To succeed, they had to prospect for hosts to sponsor in-house parties and assure adequate attendance. Then, they had to change hats and present their products, give persuasive demonstrations, and take orders. It's not for the faint-hearted. (Coauthor Shannon Goodson claims most successful producers in this ultra-demanding sales field are women, a fact which seems to have been "irresponsibly edited out" of the section comparing call reluctance score

Which Sales Pros Are Most Honest?

How do salespeople stack up against preachers and politicians when it comes to stretching the truth? We devised an objective way to find out.

The Call Reluctance Scale, a computer-based assessment tool used to measure call reluctance, also features the unusual, covert ability to detect exaggeration behavior. We recently administered the test to 2,760 salespeople in Australia, New Zealand, South Africa, Canada and the United States to determine whether exaggeration is commonly used as a sales tactic and, if so, how much.

We don't know if exaggeration is actually taught as a legitimate sales practice in these countries, but we learned that it is widely practiced nonetheless. The average salesperson in our sample exaggerated more than 40% of the time. But some countries seem to breed more characteristically forthright salespeople than others. Those in New Zealand proved most honest, exaggerating an average of 34% of the time. Their counterparts in Australia did so 43% of the time. South Africans wandered from the straight and narrow 39% of the time, while Canadian sales pros exaggerated 48% of the time. The grand prize, not unexpectedly, goes to the Americans, who spun tales a whopping 55% of the time!

Are all salespeople who exaggerate unethical? Not necessarily. But we were so fascinated with these results that we are now developing a new instrument, the Potentia Response to Opportunity Scale™. It is specifically designed to produce an ethical profile of sales and non-sales professionals.

differences between men and women. So far, no one has accepted responsibility for this scandalous act.)

Total call reluctance in this industry is unusually high. The average total score is 45%, ranking it at or near the top when cross industry comparisons are made. This condition can be easily explained. Unlike most sales settings, such as insurance, commercial real estate, or capital equipment, the majority of salespeople in party sales are women. Most of them have no sales experience. They are trying it for the first time.

Industries that hire inexperienced salespeople must endure call reluctance levels which are higher than average. Almost everyone who wants a chance gets a chance to try in-house party selling. Lowering the fence means more varmints jump over. Many more. Large numbers of call reluctant salespeople are found in these organizations, many times more than most traditional sales organizations tolerate, though our data indicate that some companies, making a big fuss over how hyper-selective they are, actually produce call reluctance profiles which are even worse.

Social Self-Consciousness (65%) ruins the party for party salespeople. It is joined by Telephobia (49%) and Yielders (43%). Together, this triad spells disaster. It makes them easily intimidated by prospects with money to spend and hesitant to use the phone to prospect because they might offend someone. An average Goal Level score of only 47% makes quick work of many party sales careers. It suggests that these individuals have not yet made up their minds to succeed. Many never will.

Real Estate

Call reluctance has a telling influence on the real estate industry, but the impact shifts somewhat according to the type of real estate sold. People selling commercial real estate tend to be Over-Preparers. Residential real-estate salespeople are inclined to be Yielders. One study we conducted on 80 residential real estate salespeople produced a total call reluctance score of 51%. Telephobia was 43%. These scores are dangerously high, but probably more representative of the sloppy recruiting, selection and sales training practices characterizing the operation, than the industry as a whole. The industry is better observed from a more representative sample.

Table 15 shows call reluctance profiles for two groups of residential real estate salespeople. The first group is a normative sample. It can be used to make inferences about the real estate industry in general. The second, smaller sample consists only of high producers. Both are U.S. samples. Sadly, exact sample sizes for these two groups must be listed missing in action, because it wasn't recorded and the raw data can't be located. We believe there were 200-300 in the first sample, and about 100 in the second.

Table 15 Call reluctance profiles for two groups of residential real estate salespeople.

Call Reluctance Type	Average Producers	High Producers
Total Call Reluctance	42	32
Doomsayers	25	12
Over-Preparation	38	35
Hyper-Pros	37	46
Stage Fright	51	47
Role Rejection	29	25
Yielders	36	24
Social Self-Consciousness	39	26
Separationist	47	35
Emotionally Unemancipated	44	35
Referral Aversion	27	16
Telephobia	49	18
Oppositional Reflex	10	6

High producers were distinguishable from average producers on every measure but one, Hyper-Pro. On that score, they were higher. We don't know why. Several scores, such as Referral Aversion and Telephobia, were dramatically lower for high producers. Fortunately, that is as it should be.

Telemarketers

A recent sample of 123 telemarketers yielded a significant (P<.0472), relationship between the absence of call reluctance (total) and cumulative production. For telemarketers, as call reluctance increases, cumulatiave production decreases. But the thing which surprises us most about telemarketing organizations is the number of Yielders trying to sell exclusively by phone. Hesitant to be intrusive, many say they cope better prospecting by phone than they could prospecting face-to-face. Do they? We don't know. No study has ever been made comparing telephone and face-to-face prospecting effectiveness for a group of Yielders.

Telecommunications

We assembled data from 436 salespeople in the telecommunications industry. The salespeople were all active, full-time salespeople employed by major telecommunications companies. The sample consisted of men and women. U.S. telecommunications companies tended to dominate the sample, but non-U.S. companies were included as well.

Average total call reluctance was 41%. That is not particularly high given the variability of call reluctance within the companies making up the telecommunications industry sample, but two other head-scratching results produced a mild stutter. They will probably have the same effect on sales managers in the telecommunications industry when they read it. A significant number of their salespeople are probably Impostors.

Goal Level scores averaged only 45%. Scores that low are usually only discovered in clumps of salespeople who are angry or resentful towards their employers. It can indicate apathetic disinterest in the sales force. Companies undergoing turbulent organizational changes are prime candidates. The sales force thinks it can no longer trust company leadership, so it decides to wait it out, sitting on the sideline until things blow over. Production does not increase, and may decrease, a lot. To superficial observers, it looks like call reluctance.

Oppositional Reflex Call Reluctance averaged 12%. That is high for an industry average. It is about 50% higher than salespeople in other industries, and six times higher than high producers.

Some telecommunications giants, such as MCI in the United States and Telecom in Australia, are beginning to take a serious look at the impact of call reluctance on sales. Initial efforts with these companies, as well as other telecommunications companies, are showing positive signs of improvement.

Fundraisers

Fundraisers prospect for charitable donations. In the U.S., churches, fraternal groups, charitable associations, private universities, and other organizations depend on volunteers to solicit funds. Fundraisers tend to have considerably more total call reluctance (41%) than most professional salespeople, although as you have seen, some individual sales organizations easily exceed that number. Fundraisers struggle with Role Rejection more than other call reluctance types, a situation which should yield to preventative call reluctance training.

Hotel Services

Hotel services salespeople look remarkably like their counterparts in other industries. One small sample came from a high visibility, international hotel chain. Like the telecommunications industry, high Oppositional Reflex measures (12%) floated to the surface. But a larger sample (Table 16), gathered since then, paints a milder, more representative picture of salespeople in hotel services sales.

Table 16 Call reluctance profile for 62 hotel services salespeople.

Call Reluctance Type	Average Score
Total Call Reluctance	38%
Doomsayers	15%
Over-Preparation	40%
Hyper-Pros	37%
Stage Fright	45%
Role Rejection	27%
Yielders	38%
Social Self-Consciousness	30%
Separationist	53%
Emotionally Unemancipated	51%
Referral Aversion	24%
Telephobia	21%
Oppositional Reflex	10%

Chemical Sales

Salespeople selling industrial chemicals are a combustionable lot. Samples drawn, with care, from that industry suggest that it could easily qualify as a call reluctance toxic waste dump. Many salespeople in that industry struggle with multiple strains of call reluctance, not just one. According to the data, they probably caught it from their sales managers. To cope, they invite a manufacturer's rep to coffee. Manufacturer's reps can usually be found at their desks, especially when they should be out prospecting for new accounts. Weighted down by Over-Preparation (50%) and Hyper-Pro Call Reluctance (50%), they can't move.

Franchise Sales

American FastSigns, a leading international franchiser, helps assure success for their small business owners with serious call reluctance assessment and training. According to Director of Training, Leslie Gorman, at American FastSign's international headquarters, "It's not enough for franchisees to have good products. They have to make sure other people know they have good products. Small business owners have to manage visibility right at the start." Unlike most franchisers, American FastSigns helps their franchisees acquire sound business practices, and healthy prospecting hearts.

Advertising

Samples taken from two advertising organizations (Table 17), show important differences, but they also contain some striking similarities. Group A consisted of 50 salespeople, Group B of 120. Together, they provide an initial glimpse of call reluctance at work in the advertising industry. We're not sure we want a closer look.

Table 17 Call reluctance profile for two advertising organizations.

Call Reluctance Type	Group A	Group B
Total Call Reluctance	44%	38%
Doomsayers	30%	13%
Over-Preparation	43%	42%
Hyper-Pros	43%	47%
Stage Fright	50%	40%
Role Rejection	27%	27%
Yielders	41%	30%
Social Self-Consciousness	24%	29%
Separationist	14%	63%
Emotionally Unemancipated	45%	53%
Referral Aversion	36%	34%
Telephobia	25%	31%
Oppositional Reflex	21%	19%

As you can see, both organizations are inflated with enough Over-Preparing Hyper-Pros to begin a law practice. But, that's nit-picking. Astronomically high Oppositional Reflex scores hint that these are not really companies at all. They're bombed out craters. Prospecting for new accounts can't be optimal; there's no time. The salespeople are too busy arguing with prospects, customers, management and each other. Like Over-Preparers perpetually away from their desks "in a meeting," these organizations appear *out* for the *duration*. They're at war. They need help. But, according to our data, they probably won't get it from our next group, Psychologists.

Psychologists

Psychologists are a remarkable and picturesque lot. We know. They told us so. Psychology is the only profession we have uncovered to date whose members boast competence and charge admission for their expertise in mathematics, sex, electronics, politics, economics, religion, business, families, philosophy, physiology, biochemistry, physics, race relations, and rock and roll. It staggers the imagination.

They are able, and willing, to comment on just about any topic. Psychologists tend to be a little shy, however, when it comes to being tested themselves. We discovered that several years ago, while we were trying to gather call reluctance norms for psychologists. Truly one of life's great mysteries. Our data had to be obtained the hard way, piece-by-piece.

Table 18 Call reluctance profile for 318 psychologists.

Call Reluctance Type	Average Score
Total Call Reluctance	41%
Doomsayers	28%
Over-Preparation	49%
Hyper-Pros	55%
Stage Fright	23%
Role Rejection	52%
Yielders	31%
Social Self-Consciousness	18%
Separationist	30%
Emotionally Unemancipated	51%
Referral Aversion	10%
Telephobia	24%
Oppositional Reflex	33%

These call reluctance scores (illustrated in Table 18) are, shall we say, intense. While total call reluctance is no higher than any other topped-out sales group, some of the individual types are hefty. Over-Preparation (49%), Hyper-Pro (55%) and Role Rejection (52%) are high enough to consider cork linings for the walls. Stratospheric Oppositional Reflex scores, fifteen times higher than high producers, indicate a lethal dose of need to be right, conflicted self-promotion.

Most psychologists never earn what they're worth, and these figures help explain why. High Over-Preparation and Oppositionality indications suggest the situation may be futile. They won't easily admit to the problem, nor will they ask for help. They can't. They are more likely to spin their wheels, attacking the data.

You may have noticed that a disproportionate number of psychologists wear beards and moustaches. In case you haven't noticed, so do many other academics. It's the Einstein-Freud prototypic scientist look. Everyone with more than one university degree gets to wear one. But if you want hyper-science, look no further than our next group: motivational/inspirational speakers.

Motivational/Inspirational Speakers

Over the years we have had the opportunity to measure and observe many of the famous, and not so famous individuals in the business of trying to help other people aspire to higher levels of achievement. We have measured many of them. An equal number, however, refused. Another group won't return our phone calls.

They tend to be loners, working alone in consultancy/speaking practices. Most have some experience in sales or sales management, where they were good producers, but not very high producers. The majority are self-educated, a few university educated. Though frequently identifying themselves with science, most are mavericks, operating well outside any formal scientific alliances or constraints. We think it is safe to speculate that most could not comprehend a

---

Motivational Speaker Causes Brain Death

We watched a television program featuring one such individual who billed himself, as they all do, as a consultant, motivator and sales trainer. He was speaking to a group of salespeople. We do not recall the industry. "He is," the baritone announcer intoned, "one of America's most sought-after business consultants. He has been called one of America's five best speakers and his clients currently include IBM, Prudential-Bache, Digital Equipment, Citibank and Merrill Lynch." These appeals to authority got our attention. We were impressed.

The first few minutes consisted of four platitudes and two jokes. We didn't get the jokes. But he caught our attention anyway. "Scientists," he said "have proven that thousands of your brain cells are killed by looking at television for a half hour." That was interesting.

Sadly, this gentleman must have been watching television before his presentation, because the irony of what he was saying completely passed him by: He was scheduled to be on for an hour. According to him, by the time he was finished his audience would be brain dead, murdered as it were, by his hour long presentation. We switched him off, doing our small part for humanity while preserving our valued cerebral functions.

What do real scientists think? We played the recorded segment to C. A. Dudley, author of legitimate, eye-glazing studies like "Solitary Hypothalamic Neurons Inherently Express Vasopressin and Tyrosine Hydroxylase" (*Peptides*, 1989). She laughed.

---

legitimate scientific journal nor would most care to. The freewheeling result can be flamboyant, and not infrequently funny and bizarre.

It took years to chase down call reluctance data for this group. But that's understandable, because they do not come from any particular group, such as consumer electronics salespeople, so they had to be stalked, one-by-one like slippery game.

Role models for success, they look, act and speak about what to do and how to be. A diagnosis of call reluctance would be as welcome, and possibly as damaging, to their career as a case of syphilis. Why risk it? Most didn't. We're still trying to gather more data.

Table 19 Call reluctance profile for 54 motivation/inspirational speakers.

Call Reluctance Type	Average Score
Total Call-Reluctance	32%
Doomsayers	12%
Over-Preparation	23%
Hyper-Pros	57%
Stage Fright	18%
Role Rejection	36%
Yielders	8%
Social Self-Consciousness	20%
Separationist	30%
Emotionally Unemancipated	31%
Referral Aversion	10%
Telephobia	24%
Oppositional Reflex	45%

It is apparent, as the profile in Table 19 illustrates, why motivational speakers are loners. Extremely high Hyper-Pro scores and Oppositional Reflex scores do not make them very suitable team players. Their needs to be center stage and get their way would be like working with a preening adolescent who throws temper tantrums if he doesn't get his way. It is not altogether clear if this is a problem. No production data exist for this group.

Summary

We hope this brief tour of the call reluctance outback provided some overview of how call reluctance affects different companies and different industries. Many, many more samples have been taken representing companies, industries, and other weird groupings of people. We regret that space and time limitations prevented us from including more of them. If we missed one you are in, or interested in, we apologize. If you contact us through the publisher we will try to see you get the information you need.

Table 20 Call reluctance summary by industry.

Industry or Group	Most Threatening Call Reluctance Type
Stock Brokers (U.S.)	Hyper-Pro
Banks (International, Mixed)	Over-Preparation
Savings & Loans	Over-Preparation
Telemarketers	Yielder
Advertising Sales	Hyper-Pro
Automobile Sales	Yielder
Cosmetics	Social Self-Consciousness
Consultants/Speakers	Hyper-Pro
	Oppositional Reflex
Psychologists	Hyper-Pro
	Oppositional Reflex
Personnel	Oppositional Reflex
Financial Planners	Over-Preparation
	Role Rejection
Hotel Services	Over-Preparation
General Sales Management	Hyper-Pro
Real Estate, Residential	Yielder
Real Estate, Commercial	Over-Preparation
Insurance Agents	Role Rejection
Office Equipment	Social Self-Consciousness
Computer Hardware	Over-Preparation

ENVIRONMENTAL FACTORS

Call Reluctant Sales Managers

High call reluctance levels in sales managers can influence bottom-line considerations such as the tenure of their sales reps. A study of call reluctance attitudes in sales managers found that, as a group, sales managers tend to be Over-Preparers. Many, especially those in technical sales areas, unintentionally contaminate some of their most promising new salespeople with small but deadly doses of unnecessary meetings, petty reports and an assortment of daily forms to complete. But when sales managers are tainted with a mixture of Oppositional Reflex and Hyper-Pro Call Reluctance, retention takes a dive. Average tenure of sales reps increased in organizations where Hyper-Pro and Oppositionality in the sales managers decreased. Managers averaging high amounts of these two call reluctance types tended to keep their new sales reps less than six months. Managers averaging low amounts tended to keep their new recruits an average of almost twelve months. Call reluctance attitudes in sales managers and training consultants can have an effect on more than just prospecting. They can also influence retention. This is a potentially volatile discovery since training consultants, as a group, have more Hyper-Pro and Oppositional Reflex Call Reluctance than most other groups we have observed.

Sales Training Programs

We have also found some highly respected sales training programs that transmit subtle call reluctance messages. More importantly, we are shocked to learn that sales training departments, which would not knowingly poison their salespeople with spoiled food, are failing to check the content of their sales training programs for call reluctance contamination. Well-intended programs often contain subtle call reluctance messages embedded within the content. In more than a few cases, we have found call reluctance detonators emphasized in certain sales training materials. Once exposed, salespeople who were not call reluctant, soon learned how to be.

Sales Management Style

Companies utilizing highly inspirational, feeling-based sales training approaches are spawning grounds for call reluctance. Those stressing technical sales fundamentals within a formal training program seem to produce less call reluctance than is typical for their respective industries.

Table 21 Call reluctance profile by age group.

Call Reluctance Type	Age 20-29	Age 30-39	Age 40+
Total Call Reluctance	33	33	31
Doomsayers	13	11	10
Over-Preparation	36	39	39
Hyper-Pros	43	44	44
Stage Fright	37	30	30
Role Rejection	23	25	25
Yielders	28	29	29
Social Self-Consciousness	24	29	26
Separationist	45	32	26
Emotionally Unemancipated	47	36	36
Referral Aversion	22	18	13
Telephobia	27	36	32
Oppositional Reflex	8	9	4

DEMOGRAPHICS

Age

Some forms of call reluctance appear to be influenced somewhat by age, but as Table 21 shows, the contribution varies by type.

The total sample consists of 169 salespeople grouped by age. There were 48 salespeople in age group one, 63 in the second group, and 58 in the third. Age group sample sizes approximate the distribution of age in the general population of full-time, active, professional salespeople.

Some types of call reluctance show changes across the age group samples, while others appear immune to age differences. For example, Social Self-Consciousness decreases a little, reflecting an increase in sales *self* confidence. Yielder scores, on the other hand, show little change from group to group. Most changes can probably be explained by exposure factors such as corporate sales training environments, sales training content, sales role models, and general life changes. Decreases in Separationist Call Reluctance can probably be understood in terms of better integration of life and career interests. The steady decline in Oppositional Reflex and Doomsayer tendencies may have physiological explanations.

Sexual Habits of Call Reluctant Sales Professionals

Red heads are temperamental. Bald heads are sexy. Latins make the best lovers. What about call reluctant salespeople? What's the inside gossip about them?

Gentlemen prefer blondes. So do BMW-driving, carefully mustachioed, Hyper-Pro men (named Brian or Kevin).

Hyper-Pro women prefer their men taller than Brian or Kevin (regardless of hair color).

Strong-willed women are initially attracted to Yielder men, only to be repulsed by them shortly thereafter.

Oppositionals of both sexes don't court the opposite sex. They romance disappointment, flirt with disaster. New lovers are romantically hoisted to unrealistic highs, then reduced to worm-level lows, all within a few weeks. Then, with the predictability of the seasons, then the cycle repeats all over again.

There. Now that we have your attention, we can safely move on to the real, more interesting, topic of this section: *call reluctance*. Does one sex have more of it than the other? If so, how much, which forms, and why?

Gender

Table 22 lists the average scores for each call reluctance type for a group of 1137 men and 556 women. (Statistically-minded spirits will find these averages followed by their "t" values and the probability computed for "t" based on a two-tailed hypothetical distribution.) The samples were randomly drawn from diverse industries, countries and sales settings. No attempt was made to further break down the samples into sub-groups (experienced women vs. experienced men), because we were only interested in studying sex-reflected differences, not national, industry, age, or other influences. The sample sizes are unequal because there are more men in sales than women.

In summary, the samples used for this study represent various nations, ages, levels of experience, education, races, religions, political viewpoints, shoe sizes and sales settings. But the most compelling justification for using these data is that the test scores were already in the computer and didn't have to be punched in again. That's real science.

Table 22   Call reluctance profile for 1137 men and 556 women.

Call Reluctance Type	Males	Females	"t"	P
Total Call Reluctance	36.45	39.17	5.20	.0000
Doomsayers	16.18	19.16	2.75	.0060
Over-Preparation	39.58	40.91	1.71	.0883
Hyper-Pros	42.00	37.98	4.17	.0000
Stage Fright	41.02	45.06	3.43	.0006
Role Rejection	28.09	28.42	.63	.5257
Yielders	31.04	34.90	4.79	.0000
Social Self-Consciousness	33.93	36.36	1.87	.0619
Separationist	45.35	48.91	2.46	.0141
Emotionally Unemancipated	46.07	45.65	.27	.7873
Referral Aversion	25.05	30.74	4.59	.0000
Telephobia	36.24	37.21	.67	.5028
Oppositional Reflex	8.56	8.88	.51	.6092
Impostors				
Motivation	65.70	66.63	1.07	.2837
Goal Level	49.88	45.94	3.14	.0017
Goal Diffusion	59.87	64.21	3.31	.0009

What conclusions can be drawn from these scores? It depends on your point of view. Our own perspective on the differences between male and female salespeople has evolved steadily since we first began to gather data on the subject.

Initially we found little difference in Call Reluctance Scale scores between men and women, a phenomenon we attributed to male-biased selection protocols which favored females who most resembled (or successfully emulated) their male counterparts. Later, as the number and influence of saleswomen increased, we found they experienced generally higher levels of call reluctance. Searching for an explanation that was both credible and fair—at the insistence of co-author Shannon Goodson—we credited professional "growing pains," a temporary affliction as women sought appropriate role models and crafted their own identity in sales. And now? We're prepared to offer a less sweeping assessment and look at saleswomen the same way they see themselves: as multilayered, multidimensional beings, not easily compartmentalized into sales and non-sales identities. Women carry more societal baggage into the workplace than men. They don't leave their upbringing, their cultural values, or the expectations of society at the door when they go to work in the morning. Their call reluctance scores reflect that. Total call reluctance is higher for these women than for their male counterparts. Many may still rely on outdated "myths of success," encouraged by consultants and gurus who continue to assure women that hard work alone will blast them through the fabled glass ceiling. A 1993 university study, reported in *New Woman* magazine, found that women with MBAs are taking less time to climb the corporate ladder to upper management than male colleagues. The researchers' rationalization: "The women must have been more competent and/or hardworking (than the men)." Yielder scores are higher among women. They hesitate to appear pushy or intrusive. Interestingly, a *Fortune* survey of CEOs found that only 8% of top executives believe that women lack the aggressiveness and determination to succeed. Our own work with dynamic, successful women around the world has convinced us they don't. But traditional gender roles cast these behaviors as "unladylike." Many otherwise modern, forward-thinking businesswomen still subconsciously buy into that premise. Erecting not just a glass ceiling but an emotional wall, they deny themselves access to the very attributes which could propel them to the top. Women's goals tend to be less clearly defined, and more conflicted, than men's. In the 1990's, the spectre of "superwoman" still lingers over many women juggling careers with homes and families. Due to custom, circumstance, or financial necessity, they don't have the luxury of devoting themselves to their career at the expense of traditional domestic duties. Recent studies show that married women continue to carry greater responsibility for housework and child care than their husbands (even when both work full-time.) The social, genetic, physical, and cultural factors at work are simply too complex and uncharted at this point to definitively explain the disparities between men and women in this study. We're not sure we want to produce a definitive explanation. We do not aspire to become sociologists. We're merely interested in the relationship between sales call reluctance and financial success.

To explore gender differences further, we recently gathered data on another group of women: executives. Table 22a lists scores for 225 male executives and 97 female executives representing a diverse sampling of industries and countries. As we expected, overall call reluctance for both men and women at this level is lower than for non-executives of *either* gender. In fact, the executive group experienced lower levels of *all* forms of call reluctance and impostors—except one. Not unexpectedly, executives, both male and female, tend to have higher levels of Hyper-Pro.

Attention to image apparently is less of a hindrance (and may even be somewhat beneficial) to getting promoted into executive positions. That may explain the prevalence of "pretty" if not productive men and women in top management positions.

Table 22a   Call reluctance profile for 225 male and 97 female executives.

Call Reluctance Type	Males	Females	"t"
Total Call Reluctance	31.15	33.53	1.88
Doomsayers	13.60	15.46	.79
Over-Preparation	37.98	44.34	3.12
Hyper-Pros	45.77	43.49	.94
Stage Fright	25.58	28.04	1.15
Role Rejection	25.47	27.67	1.69
Yielders	26.30	28.13	.96
Social Self-Consciousness	27.66	24.04	1.28
Separationist	39.81	44.18	1.28
Emotionally Unemancipated	40.42	42.33	.52
Referral Aversion	18.48	22.29	1.41
Telephobia	30.39	30.82	.13
Oppositional Reflex	5.10	4.88	.20
Impostors			
Motivation	71.64	72.49	.42
Goal Level	59.56	58.87	.25
Goal Diffusion	57.34	63.14	1.72

RESEARCH ODDS AND ENDS

If you think uncorrected call reluctance could be having a negative impact on your behavior, you're probably right. How do we know? That's what the data we harvested from some of our studies whispers in our ears. As you will see, the studies themselves are studies of research tenacity. They range from pristine to outlandish. They probably should have been neatly stitched into earlier sections. In order to include them at all, we had to send them to the back of the bus.

Sales performance is the result of many positive influences. Call reluctance is a spoiler. Though far from perfect, the relationship between call reluctance and performance is more predictable than daily fluctuations in the stock market or weather forecasts three days into the future. For example:

The average number of new life insurance cases (orders) submitted by a group of insurance agents with the highest total call reluctance scores was seven per month. Another group with the lowest call reluctance scores averaged in excess of ten new cases per month.

The average annual production quota rank for new telemarketers with high call reluctance scores was 38th. The rank for telemarketers with low call reluctance scores was 28th, more than ten points better.

Certain types of call reluctance have their greatest impact on early performance. Second month (cumulative) earnings of one sample of new sales reps trying to sell to up-market clients illustrates the point. Those with low Social Self-Consciousness averaged over $3,000 while those with high Social Self-Consciousness averaged only $600 for the same time period.

Call Reluctance and Early Performance

Call reluctance has a dramatic and predictable impact on early performance, and early performance is probably the best single indicator of later performance. We know it is not uncommon for some commercial testing organizations to recklessly claim predictive accuracy at five years. Ridiculous. We have never seen anything which even approaches high predictive accuracy at five years, or four, or three, or even two for that matter. Not psychological tests, not mystical intuitions, not astrological signs, not handwriting analysis. Nothing. Hopefully, we never will. Why? Because any test boasting high three year predictive accuracy raises a very touchy question: If a test's scores, obtained prior to hiring, are so deterministically linked to later outcomes, what are the sales managers, sales training department, and marketing support functions being paid for in the meantime? The implication is nothing. They have no influence. It's all in the scores.

We have far more modest intentions. We try to measure and forecast the influence of call reluctance on *early performance*. Why? Studies we repeated several times in different companies, clearly showed that early sales performance is the best single predictor of later sales performance. When tenure effects are held constant, ninth month production rank is almost perfectly correlated with end of 12th month production rank. The correlation across these studies is about r=.97 P<.007. Furthermore, sixth month production rank is almost as highly correlated to the 12th. More importantly, however, third month production rank is almost as accurate as the sixth. Very little forecasting accuracy is lost.

The correlation is high, not perfect. Miraculous transformations in a salesperson's production can occur, but they are exceptions, not the norm. You wouldn't want to bet on them. Neither would we. That's why we unapologetically calibrate our call reluctance forecasting efforts to early production. That's hard enough, and we know that if we get that part right, the sales management staff can step in and do its part to guide the successful new producer on to greater success.

Using this logic, we have found that the Call Reluctance Scale can be used to help predict performance as early as the end of the first month of selling. This was shown by first assessing prospective sales reps, and then putting the information aside, unused. Later, we went back and gathered additional information on those who were hired to see what, if anything, predicted their production at the end of the first month. Again, those with high Social Self-Consciousness averaged only $260 by the end of their first month, but those with low Social Self-Consciousness averaged more than $2,500 during the same time period. Similar relationships have been observed between other types of call reluctance and early performance. We have even found strong, unexpected relationships between sales performance and Separationist and Unemancipated Call Reluctance in sales environments where family and personal friends are not even considered part of the market. This gives added support to our belief that the broader dimension, the fear of self-promotion, is what we are actually measuring. That's why it has been so successful in sales and non-sales applications.

Ignorance is Bliss

Most sales executives still don't know what call reluctance really is, where it comes from, how to measure it, or what to do about it. We discovered this using a "pre" and "post" call reluctance instruction questionnaire.

Several groups of active sales managers were asked to estimate how effective their companies were at detecting call reluctance and managing it once it had been found. The companies represented various industries. Before instruction, the managers tended to rate their current call reluctance practices effective or highly effective. After exposure to call reluctance instruction, company effectiveness ratings plummeted.

Call Reluctance From Your Ears?

The term "fear of rejection" has many origins, all of them remote and barely touchable. Repressed ego, low self-esteem, external locus of control, lack of self-confidence, and other equally literary, and untouchable explanations have been claimed to be the cause. Call reluctance pales by comparison. It's either passed along by contact or, according to some of our most recent studies, your genes.

While most mental health professionals accept mentalistic explanations for emotional distress, a few seek *physical* ties that bind. We stand with the minority. A recent author, writing from the majority view point, said social fears come from poor social skills. Studies by eminent personality theorists, such as R. B. Cattell, showed that certain personality dimensions, such as protension and low dominance, were traceable to hereditary influences. These dimensions are first cousins, several factor orders removed, to our Yielders, Hyper-Pros, and Oppositionals.

In 1986 we began asking sales pros some questions included on an unnamed research appendix. They agreed to answer them, but the questions struck them as rather strange. For the next four years, we tagged these questions onto so many call reluctance projects that today, we can't be certain how many completed the research supplement. Hundreds, probably well over a thousand, were included.

"Are you clumsy or klutzy, always bumping into things?" we would ask. "Were you prone to motion sickness or dizziness when you were a kid?" "Do people think you're spaced out or scatter brained?" "Do you find yourself checking and re-checking things, for example, to make sure the doors are locked at night?" The questions were adapted from Levinson's 1986 book on clinical phobia (Harold N. Levinson, *Phobia Free*).

Levinson is a medical doctor and psychiatrist who believes many phobias may actually be outward signs of physical illness, primarily of the inner ear. The questions in our research supplement were all symptoms associated with inner ear problems. Numerous salespeople, checking multiple symptoms, were not aware they had an inner ear disturbance. We suggested they see a qualified medical professional. Many, but not all, did. Of those who did, many had allergies, ear infections, or structural problems affecting their inner ears. We took all the completed research supplements and correlated them with Call Reluctance Scale scores. The results were surprising. Table 23 lists the number of call reluctance types associated with each inner ear symptom cluster. The table includes only the numbers of call reluctance types meeting or exceeding the conventional scientific burden of proof (P<.05 or better).

Table 23 Number of call reluctance types associated with symptoms of inner ear disturbances.

Symptom Cluster	Number of Types
Balance and Coordination	2
Vision and Hearing	3
Sense of Direction	0
Sense of Time	5
Motion Sensitivity	3
Memory and Recall	5
Distractibility	6
Hyperactivity	1
Obsessions and Compulsions	5
Academic Problems	3
Related Mental Symptoms	4

Several call reluctance types had one or more links to the inner ear symptoms, but one kept popping up: Doomsayer. Interestingly, Doomsayer Call Reluctance is the most phobic-like of all the call reluctance types.

Anecdotal evidence provided additional support. For four years, during workshops, seminars, lectures, and formal presentations, we routinely asked how many people had higher than average Doomsayer scores. Though the absolute number was always low compared to other types, we were able to pursue the matter by asking a second question. How many high scoring Doomsayers suffer from inner ear infections, allergic reactions, and other maladies thought to influence inner ear functioning? Most of the Doomsayers admitted to chronic bouts with the symptoms. Only random numbers of the other call reluctance types did.

Today, we feel confident that at least one type of call reluctance, Doomsayer, is due to an underlying physical problem. Discovering that the offending mechanism is probably an inner ear disturbance, guides us to recommend that Doomsayers, in sales careers, make a visit to their family physician. The cure they seek is not likely to be found in pep talks or psychological mumbo-jumbo. It may be a simple over the counter antihistamine.

We have always believed that some of the other call reluctance types *also* have physical causes. We just don't know what they are yet. But, we're optimists. We know they will eventually be found.

Rated Effectiveness of Self-Help Media and Programs

We have been superficially exposed to many different sales training programs. Although it has little influence on our sub-speciality, we have listened to many speeches, observed workshops, read books, listened to audio cassettes, and watched television programs, all professing to make the listener "a winner." We were curious. Were they effective? To find out, we asked.

First, the academics. One study used university students (*not* salespeople) to evaluate a 15 minute segment of a national pharmaceutical sales training program. (Some academics need to take a trip to town because they seem to be having difficulty distinguishing between acne-fighting students and product presenting salespeople.)

Lectures, supplemented by color slides, failed to produce content recognition scores better than the scores obtained by lecture alone. Videotaped presentations "designed to carry the main points of the message in a dynamic way" enhanced retention, even after one week. Video presentations, featuring action, elevate long-term retention of training program content (R. E. Gehring & M. P. Toglia, "Relative Retention of Verbal and Audiovisual Information in a National Training Programme," *Applied Cognitive Psychology*, July-September, 1988).

We thought for a while. Then, we made an awesome intellectual breakthrough. Why not by-pass university sophomores, and just ask people who actually buy and use sales training materials? We did. We learned.

Our sample consisted of 196 U.S. sales managers, trainers, and professional sales training consultants. None had noticeable acne. Some non-U.S managers were included, but not enough to justify generalization to non-U.S. markets.

Within the last twelve months an average of:

- 8.56 sales training workshops/seminars had been attended
- 7.45 self-help/sales training books were purchased
- 7.23 self-help/sales training audio cassettes were purchased
- 6.94 self-help/sales training videos were watched
- $579.67 was spent by the average manager on workshops
- $329.20 was spent on video presentations
- $87.85 was spent on audio cassettes
- $26.55 was allocated to buying books

Twelve times more dollars were invested in videos than books. Do the managers think their payoff was twelve times more production?

Ranked order of helpfulness/effectiveness:

- Workshops/seminars   1
- Books   2
- Audio cassettes   3
- Videotapes   4

The subject rated most effective:

- Practical sales techniques (how to sell procedures, not conceptual principles about selling)

The subjects rated least effective were:

- Time management
- Goal-setting

Industries making greatest use of commercial self-help, sales training books, cassettes, videos, and workshops:

- Air freight
- Security systems

Industries making least use:

- Banking
- Airlines

If you're a consultant searching for a new product area, you can put this intelligence to immediate use. *Avoid* time management and goal-setting. Like stress management and walking across hot coals, their time has come and gone. Consider instead, step-by-step, procedural, how-to sell information. By all means, keep it practical. Avoid being conceptual. Don't use this book as a role model, and don't be disappointed if banks and airlines won't buy it.

Stage Fright and Perceived Subject Mastery

Salespeople measuring high on Stage Fright Call Reluctance rate their own fear of speaking before groups high. In several small group studies, sales managers, trainers, and salespeople were asked to independently estimate how much fear they experienced when speaking before groups of people. Those subjectively rating their fear the lowest, averaged the lowest objective Stage Fright Call Reluctance scores (average=15.86%). Participants reporting the highest distress levels, averaged Stage Fright Call Reluctance scores more than two times higher.

Stage Fright makes capable people look stupid. In one study, we assigned practice teaching assignments to 63 sales training professionals. The assignments were equal in length and approximately equal in content complexity. The sample consisted of sales managers, trainers, professional sales training consultants, and psychologists.

Participants anonymously rated each instructor on subject mastery. Each individual's ratings were correlated with objective Stage Fright Call Reluctance scores from the Call Reluctance Scale. Instructors with the *highest* average Stage Fright Call Reluctance scores were given the lowest competency ratings by their peers. Those with the *lowest* objective Stage Fright scores were rated the most competent.

What does this mean to you? A lot. It means that in group presentation situations, *people tend to misinterpret fear as ignorance or incompetence*. When you show signs of discomfort when speaking before groups, people think you don't really know what you're talking about. We have confirmed the results of this study several times.

Over-Preparation Scores and Peer Ratings of Subject Mastery

In a similar study, we wanted to see if all the extra time Over-Preparers devote to getting ready, paid off. To find out, we used a similar group of sales training professionals. Subjective peer ratings of subject mastery were compared to objective Over-Preparation Call Reluctance measures. As Over-Preparation scores went up, ratings of technical competency went down. Are you an Over-Preparer? Lighten up. Adequate preparation is necessary. Too much is counterproductive.

Hyper-Pro Scores and Presentation Skills Ratings

Hyper-Pros are people who stand in front of mirrors—a lot. Carefully projecting a professional image, checking, then projecting some more, they invest enormous amounts of energy into image-management behavior. Combing their hair, straightening their clothes, practicing their voice tone modulations (for effect, not content like Over-Preparers), they live and work to have others respect and approve their appearance. Does it make a difference?

To find out, we used another group of sales training professionals. The group consisted of men and women and each was assigned an instructional segment to teach. The segments were matched for length, and approximately matched for content level. Subjective peer ratings of presentation skills were obtained for each presenter, and compared to objective Hyper-Pro Call Reluctance measures we had acquired previously. The results were stoically received, the Hyper-Pros hiding behind a facade of aloof dignity, like they do when you pick a piece of lint from their clothes and show it to them.

The sales training professionals with the lowest Hyper-Pro scores on the Call Reluctance Scale received average presentation skill ratings of 46.67% (out of a possible 100%). Those with moderate scores gathered peer ratings of 46%. Those with the highest Hyper-Pro scores, had the most to say about "proper" instructional design, what salespeople need to know, and how to teach them. They were given peer ratings of 46.36%.

Fail to see any difference? That's because there isn't any. Hyper-Pros can plant themselves in front of mirrors all day long if they want to. They can fine tune their voice and their words, their clothes and their image, but it won't make much difference. Like everyone else, to be rated an effective presenter, they have to present effectively. Just looking the part isn't enough.

Financing Levels and Call Reluctance

Salespeople with high Hyper-Pro *and* Oppositionality measures look and act forcefully successful. Repeated studies with new insurance agents show that Oppositional Hyper-Pros achieve *above* average starting salaries and/or financing levels. It's probably due to their skillful use of image manipulation and subtle intimidation. Whatever it is, it works. Diplomatically speaking, it's the most impressive sale they make. Actual production rarely justifies above average starting salaries. On the other hand, companies committing the error tend to have the most successful *looking* agents.

Oppositional Reflex and the Need to Critique

Salespeople with Oppositional Reflex Call Reluctance are an opinionated lot. They have more to say than other salespeople, and an urgent need to say it. Anecdotal reports from sales managers confirm that Oppositionals are in fact more prone to verbal outburst over relatively inconsequential things, than other salespeople. That is interesting but not persuasive or scientifically useful, so we resolved to study the matter further. Actually, circumstances defined the project for us.

Glancing through piles of Call Reluctance Scales, we found several instances where hostile remarks about the test had been scribbled on the answer sheet. Since the questionnaire format was entirely multiple choice, and no commentary had been requested, we attributed the phenomenon to the humidity index. That was met by skeptical resistance and some name-calling, so we decided to pursue the matter in two ways. First, we took all the answer sheets and counted how many words of commentary we found on each. Most had none. The number of words of commentary was compared with all call reluctance scale scores. Nothing surfaced from the study except for: Oppositional Reflex. Salespeople with Oppositional Reflex Call Reluctance averaged 24 words of unsolicited commentary, and furthermore, as objective Oppositional Reflex scores increased, so did words of commentary.

To take things a step further, we added a second part to our study. Independent judges subjectively evaluated answer sheets containing unsolicited commentary for degree of *critical* content. Comparing these ratings with objective Oppositional Reflex scores, we found that salespeople writing the most critical comments had the highest Oppositional Reflex scores. Oppositionals are easy to spot. They have a lot to say, and most of it critical.

Physical Responses to Call Reluctance

We have literally wired sales managers, trainers and professional consultants up to multi-channel physiographs and other sinister looking pieces of laboratory equipment. Most recently, we have been gathering data to help us determine if there is a relationship between electrical conductivity on the surface of the skin and total call reluctance. Decades ago, scientists learned that electrical conductivity on the skin surface is a good, some say the best, indicator of emotional excitability or "idling speed." So far, our research shows some encouraging trends, but lacks the definition we would like to see.

Call reluctance should leave physical tracks in the snow if it is a physical event, as we claim it is. To illustrate the point, sales professionals were given temperature sensitive biocards, specially calibrated to detect small drops in finger temperature, a sure sign of distress. To help personalize the application and produce supporting data for one of our call reluctance countermeasures, some groups of participants were asked to record their finger temperature readings. The readings were taken right after they received their biocard on a form which was specifically designed for this study.

After initial (baseline) readings had been recorded, each participant was asked for his or her business card. All the cards were dropped into a small container. Next, they were told the purpose of dropping their business cards into the container. Two participants were going to be picked at random to demonstrate their cold calling technique to the group.

Two cards were about to be randomly drawn. A cold, dead silence overpowered the previously animated room. Right before the cards were drawn, everyone was asked to re-check their biocard readings. The new readings were recorded along side their baseline readings. Then, each participant was asked aloud if there was a difference between the first and second readings, and if so, how much.

The situation was designed to induce call reluctance feelings. It did. It also made believers of doubters. The average finger temperature change was six degrees. The diving finger temperatures accompanied a drop in the blood supply to the extremities. Blood was being diverted away from fingers and toes to body core areas, where emergency preparations were underway for a potentially dangerous threat. Of course, the only "threat" was making a cold call, but when it comes to call reluctance, that's all it takes.

Self-Referencing

Do natural self-promoters like to verbally decorate themselves? You bet they do. In one study, we examined the self-referencing statements appearing in the written text of sales training gurus destined to appear on any list of natural self promoters. No effort was made to determine if they were ethical or unethical. That was not the purpose.

In one case, every seven and one-half lines of text bulged with five self-referencing statements. He "wrote the book," he said. He's also a "renowned speaker, trainer, author." And don't forget two other staples: "Most sought after speaker," and "Fortune 500 clients." (Did you ever write down all the consultants, authors, and "most sought after speakers" who claim to do business with Fortune 500 companies? We did. In an informal study, we listed them by promotional claim. Interesting. The phrase should probably be revised to read "Fortune Hundred Thousand.")

Natural self-promoters do not hesitate to let people know who they are, and what they do well (or at least what they *say* they do well). They generously spice their rhetoric with flamboyant self-referencing statements.

Rated Competency of an Inspirational Speaker

Motivational speakers claim to have the keys to your success, they know people in high places, and they are scheduled to give a presentation in your town. You need to hear them—or, do you?

As sub-specialists, firmly entrenched in our own narrow area, we have little interaction with motivational speakers, but salespeople do, and since we study salespeople, we wanted to learn more about their attitudes toward some of the things they are exposed to.

We acquired a video-taped presentation of one "internationally renowned" motivational speaker. (They all say that.) He was billed as one of the "world's most sought after speakers," and "internationally recognized as an authority" (on at least a half-dozen different topics). He is single-handedly responsible for motivating salespeople to *record* levels of production. Besides, a friend of a friend of ours who is in sales, says he's great.

A small but diverse sample of 59 sales pros were asked to view the tape. The sample was national, and represented a cross section of companies and industries. The tape was about one half hour long, but participants did not have to watch the whole thing if they did not wish to. They could signal by raising their hand when they wished to stop, at which time they could get up and leave the room for the duration of the tape.

Viewers were asked to subjectively rate the presentation on four important criteria. Total time watched was recorded for individuals who did not wish to view the whole tape. None had seen the tape before, although most were familiar with the speaker and some had heard him before.

Relevancy. The speaker received an average relevancy rating of 7.07 (out of a possible 10). Relevancy means how applicable or important the subject is to success in sales. A score of zero would mean the subject was worthless. Ten would mean the subject was crucial. This speaker's subject was considered very important.

Integrity. Integrity was a judgment of the speaker's character. Was he trustworthy? Believable? Honest? Did he seem to apply what he said to himself? On this measure, there was some doubt. The speaker received an average rating of only 5.64.

Originality. Originality measured the uniqueness of the content. Had the participants heard this or a similar presentation from others? Did the speaker actually create the content, or was he just repeating ideas originated by others? The average rating from our sample was 5.08. They had heard it all before.

Effectiveness. Effectiveness assessed the utility of the content. Could it really make a difference in sales production? Could the participants put what they learned to use? Probably not. An average rating of 4.93 signaled considerable doubt.

Subjective ratings are impressions, not facts. But it *is* a fact that these are the impressions our sample had of the motivational video presentation they watched—or could have watched. Actually, most were quickly bored, and left within the first ten minutes.

If you plan large meetings or conventions, take note: Modern sales professionals are not stupid, gullible or passive. According to our data, they no longer consider old style motivational pep talks very worthwhile. Yet there are exceptions. Some salespeople still prefer motivational presentations, abundantly spiced with jokes and anecdotes. Who are they? Low Motivation Impostors. They prefer entertainment over education and training. To them, good, old fashioned, motivation presentations are great.

Three Kinds of Stage Fright?

Mention stage fright and everybody presumes they know what you mean. We thought we knew what we meant, and found out we didn't. Very recent studies show that stage fright, like call reluctance itself, actually consists of at least three sub-groups. Each is distinguishable by what is feared, how it is feared, and the countermeasures which should be used to correct it.

Studies like these surface when call reluctance countermeasures don't work according to plan—which is not altogether uncommon. Then, it's back to the drawing boards to finish what we should have done better the first time. Fine tuning our understanding of Stage Fright Call Reluctance was not an easy undertaking. It required a special questionnaire. The form we devised only had three questions, but the questions were very carefully formulated. To paraphrase, the first asked participants to rate how much fear they typically experience when speaking before groups. Ratings went from zero (none) to 100% (bone shaking incapacity). Comparisons with objective Stage Fright scores produced the expected high correlations. The second question asked participants to rate how much fear they might experience, if they gave a presentation to people who could see them, but not hear them. The third question asked them to rate how much fear they would anticipate having, if they gave a presentation to people who could hear them but not see them.

If Stage Fright Call Reluctance is, indeed, only one-sided, (unidimensional= null hypothesis), then individual ratings across the three questions should have been about the same. As expected, based on intuitions, hunches and prayers (we were paying for the project ourselves), they were not. The first, small sample of

26 sales professionals produced widely varied ratings. The ratings were statistically compared to objective call reluctance measures. Some participants feared giving presentations where they could be seen, more than giving presentations where they could be heard. Others the reverse. They feared giving presentations where they could be heard more than presentations where they could be seen. We had found enough support for our hypothesis to continue. Comparatively large numbers of individuals have completed the research form since then, convincing us that Stage Fright does indeed consist of three sub-factors. Like all forms of call reluctance, the countermeasures most appropriate depend on the particular version you are trying to correct.

According to our data, type "X" Stage Fright is characterized by general over-excitation. The primary marker behavior is worrying. Salespeople with "X" type Stage Fright tend to worry more about everything. It should be no surprise then, that they worry more about speaking before groups than salespeople without Stage Fright. Type "X" Stage Fright statistically tends to bond to Doomsayers more than other call reluctance types.

Type "Y" Stage Fright Call Reluctance is characterized by intense concerns about saying something which would sound stupid, unprepared, superficial or foolish. Their primary marker behavior is rigid content delivery. They cope by preparing ponderous notes, which they laboriously adhere to when speaking before groups. Salespeople with "Y" type Stage Fright tend to be statistically related to Over-Preparers.

The last sub-type of Stage Fright, type "Z," centers on the body. It is identifiable by intense physical "packaging," which covers for a fear of physical exposure. They don't care what they say or how they sound so much, but they are mortified that you might be able to see through their clothes somehow, and see them for who they really are. They suffer from a poor body image. The primary marker behavior is over-investment of energy in checking appearance related matters. Nothing awkward allowed. Fly zipped? Slip showing? Panty lines? Watch the posture. Don't trip. Be graceful not klutzy, and don't forget: absolutely no nose-picking. Salespeople with type "Z" Stage Fright tend to be linked by correlation to Hyper-Pro Call Reluctance.

Hyper-Pro Call Reluctance is Not One Thing

Some of our most recent studies discovered that Hyper-Pro Call Reluctance, like Stage Fright, is not a one-sided affair. It consists of two fear-sensitive alloys, mixed in an emotional blender to formulate one case of Hyper-Pro Call Reluctance. Unlike Stage Fright, however, the new insights do not complicate things. They actually make Hyper-Pro Call Reluctance conceptually easier to understand, less likely to be confused with other call reluctance types, and more likely to be successfully managed. Countermeasures for Hyper-Pro Call Reluctance still apply. No major alterations are needed.

Hyper-Pro Call Reluctance is a short-hand term for "Distended Professionalism." It occurs when salespeople invest too much effort into projecting a high toned, professional image. Things, like prospecting, which are necessary to become successful in sales, are crowded out and de-emphasized.

Hyper-Pros spotlight either their voice and/or their body when they project their "look." We have christened Hyper-Pros who primarily use their voice, "Voice-Proud" (or "Word Proud"). Hyper-Pros trying to project the image of success primarily through physical appearance are called "Body-Proud." Some Hyper-Pros over-cook both. They constitute a third, "Mixed" group.

All Hyper-Pros can be considered vain to some degree, but the placement and degree of their vanities differ. Voice-Proud Hyper-Pros focus on the sound of their own voice. They like to hear themselves talk. In contrast, salespeople who are not Voice-Proud Hyper-Pros don't care how they sound.

Highly defined Voice-Proud Hyper-Pros enjoy using high-minded, multi-syllable words, some of which they may not fully understand themselves. It's the sound that counts. It makes them sound intelligent. But word size alone is not enough, and can occasionally be misleading. Sound duration is also needed. Sound duration is how much sonic space they take up with their words. Some people speak with great economy. Others scrawl the words they speak pretentiously, dragging out last syllables like gaudy, ornate flourishes appended to the end of handwritten script. General Douglas MacArthur wrote and spoke with melodramatic affectation. Nowhere is this more evident than in the strident love letters he composed to his wife. A motivational speaker we heard sounded like a Pentecostal revivalist. He stretched his last syllables until they filled the void between his words—almost as if he was afraid of silence.

Body-Proud Hyper-Pros are like adolescent boys dressing for the prom. They spend too much time in front of mirrors, inspecting their own image. They comb, trim, preen, and adjust. To Body-Proud Hyper-Pros, costume is more important than content. Ask General Custer. According to the documentary, "The Civil War," U.S. Army General George Armstrong Custer immediately bought himself a flashy new uniform. Then, he put it on and had his photograph taken. He had just graduated from the U.S. Military Academy at West Point—at the bottom of his class. Custer went on to more noteworthy achievements, the most notable perhaps, losing the Battle of Little Big Horn, where he also lost his life.

Body-Proud Hyper-Pros use status symbols as pointers. By conspicuously flashing them, they direct attention to the image they're trying to project, like traffic cops in Hamilton, Bermuda direct traffic. Flashy cars, designer clothes, gold neck chains, expensive watches (or look-alike watches that look expensive), even participation in club house sports, can all be used to push the "look."

Highly defined Mixed Hyper-Pros are Voice-Proud and Body-Proud. In salespeople, that formula produces self-absorption to the point of disabling vanity, and that spells blocked talent and lost opportunities.

CURRENT AND FUTURE PROJECTS

Analogical Fear Replacement

Several new research projects are in progress or in the planning stages. Call reluctance countermeasures can't rest on past accomplishments. We never promised them job security. While they are being subjected to continuous testing and refinement, we are simultaneously on the lookout for their replacements.

Some forms of call reluctance are tricky to work with. That's understandable, because call reluctance is fear-based, and therapists everywhere know how difficult fears can be to work with. Admittedly, we're looking for shortcuts. We are presently experimenting with an alternative approach for dealing with heavily defended fear systems. We have tentatively called the technique Analogical Fear Replacement.

This experimental procedure was initially provoked by our failures. Certain highly resistant cases of call reluctance get hyper-defensive and return our best efforts like buckshot ricocheting off bulletproof glass. Unable to pass through the front door, we've gone around to the side looking for unlocked windows and doors. We may have found one. Analogical Fear Replacement works by totally withdrawing from the primary call reluctance area. Instead, efforts are concentrated on a similar, but unassociated fear which has no apparent connection to call reluctance. It has a precedent, some motivated people have used it intuitively.

George Dudley has a fear of heights. It used to be incapacitating, but his fear was de-fanged years ago when he was a young Marine at Parris Island Marine Corps Depot. While a recruit, he was required to successfully complete a "confidence course." The run included climbing and maneuvering—at telephone pole heights. He had to gut up, but he faced off against the fear, pushed himself through, and did it well. Today, he still has a fear of heights, but fear no longer has him. That's not the end of the story. By successfully assaulting his fear of heights, he learned how to overcome other hesitations—such as speaking to large groups of people, which would have been far more difficult to deal with, if it had been approached head-on.

During the early 1980's, film actress Kim Basinger was home-bound with agoraphobia. Her escape was complete, but it didn't come from hypnosis, talking therapy, or positive thinking. Her breakout came from posing nude for *Playboy* magazine. It was difficult, but when her clothes came off, so did her agoraphobia.

Similarly, a highly motivated young business woman was frozen in place by Stage Fright Call Reluctance. She could not speak in front of groups and believed herself incapable of creative work. She wanted to be able to create and speak comfortably to groups, but could do neither. So Basinger-like, she determined to go to a nude beach and disrobe. It took several false starts, but one day she stepped out of her clothes *and* her fears in one defiant gesture.

Psychological learning theory might explain these changes in terms of Thorndike's spread of effect, the tendency of learning to generalize to adjacent areas. Others might understand the approach as a variation of Threat Desensitization, but it's not. Threat Desensitization is bottom up, vertical. It works by first removing small fears, and progressing up to large ones. As each step is successfully completed, the effect generalizes upwards, deflating the big fears proportionately.

Analogical Fear Replacement doesn't work that way. It appears to work by radiating learning sideways. Well-defended types, such as Oppositional Reflex Call Reluctance, might be approached obliquely, by working on some other fear, like heights. We don't know why it should work. We just know it has. Perhaps it involves the underlying structure of fear. We're not sure, but we sure are trying to find out.

New Applications for Call Reluctance

- A clinical psychologist who treats social fears is already using the Call Reluctance Scale to forecast and diagnose dating anxiety. He claims the problem is very similar to call reluctance and quite widespread. People from all walks of life, including at least one government official, have been successfully treated. We have been exploring the application and expect to add a section on inhibited flirting and dating behaviors. Flirting is just one of the many derivative forms of self-promotion which we are including in our forthcoming book on the non-sales applications of our work.

- It is estimated that more than half the people who purchased our first call reluctance book, and made it enormously successful, were not in sales. They were students and small business owners, accountants, military personnel, psychiatrists, and career counselors—people in all kinds of settings. Unmet needs and generous word-of-mouth endorsements sent them to our book on call reluctance, written essentially for salespeople. Most found what they were looking for, but many commented that the fit was a bit awkward. So we're crafting them their own book, diagnostic test, and collateral materials.

- Sales call reluctance could have societal implications beyond the narrow confines of measured sales results. In 1994 we completed a study of 124 management-level professionals for Dallas-based outplacement specialist John McDorman. Each had been "downsized," "right-sized," or "re-engineered" out of his or her position. The group consisted of middle to high level management, but included no salespeople. According to leading international personnel/ recruitment specialists, encountering high numbers of qualified clients who fail to quickly find new employment because they will not merchandise themselves consistently is a chronic source of frustration. Is it, they ask (and so did we), due to the same reasons talented salespeople fail—because they don't prospect consistently? To find out, we administered the Call Reluctance Scale. Scores were correlated with the number of employment interviews scheduled during the subsequent two weeks. Seven statistically significant scores were identified. Call reluctance is not, it seems, limited to sales professionals.

- Are "client-centered" sales practices more effective than product-advocating approaches? Not according to the evidence. In 1995 we compared actual sales results of salespeople in the direct marketing industry who endorsed "consultative" selling with results of those who did not. The difference was staggering. The consultative group produced an average of $35,210. The non-consultative group averaged $46,076, an extremely significant difference ($p < .00007$). These results are consistent with objective data reported in other studies such as "The Effects of Empathy on Salesperson Effectiveness" (*Psychology & Marketing*, July/August 1992). Consultative selling may make the sales process more acceptable to *call reluctant* (Yielder, Hyper-Pro and Role Rejecting) sales organizations. But it does not make them more productive.

- We will be exploring the incidence of attention deficit disorders in salespeople. Data from procedural tasks indicate that some salespeople have trouble managing their attention. Consequently, they under-perform in academic situations, such as product training and other learning areas. It is not uncommon in such cases for poor performance to be impulsively attributed to intellectual inability, not disability.

- In 1994 we examined the statistical relationship between Call Reluctance Scale scores and the most highly regarded clinical instruments in use today by professional psychologists and psychiatrists. These included the Sixteen Personality Factors Questionnaire, the Millon Clinical Multiaxial Inventory, and the Minnesota Multiphasic Personality Inventory. Many important, statistically significant correlations were found between Call Reluctance Scale scores and the other "benchmark" instruments.

- An electronic research archive is now available for individuals who need quick access to the latest research-based information about sales call reluctance. Call Reluctance Research On-Line is the world's only repository for independent scholarly research on sales call reluctance. However, it is not suitable for everyone. Research summaries are presented in a technical format required by scholars and journalists.

Call Reluctance Neural Networks

We are currently absorbed in switching call reluctance diagnostic procedures from traditional (multi-linear, differentially weighted) statistical procedures, to state-of-the-art *neural networks*. What is a neural network? A neural network is a new way to approach complex problems. It is based on innovative new computer programs (algorithms) which allow computers to simulate, though not duplicate, many of the problem-solving abilities of the human brain.

Your brain is composed of billions of specialized cells called neurons. Each neuron works like a primitive biological computer. Neurons cannot keep a secret. They broadcast everything they are told, no matter how intimate, to every other neuron they are in contact with. The result is a lot of gossipy nerve chatter, and a very intelligent problem-solving system—you. By using the same architecture as your brain, but on a somewhat more modest scale, neural networks make computers behave like brains. They can be taught to recognize faint patterns, spot vague trends, and find meaning in data that traditional correlational techniques might sail past in ignorant bliss.

Call reluctance neural networks notice patterns, spot trends, and find hidden relationships in data just like you do—by going to school and learning about the past. Once the network learns enough to understand "facts" about call reluctance, it can make judgments and generalize, diagnose, and predict future performance. Some organizations have already installed experimental networks. They are being used to predict the price of petrochemicals (94% accuracy), corporate bond ratings (100% accuracy), horse races (17 winners per 22 races), jury panel selection, solar flares, breast cancer, liver transplants and the chemical composition of beer. Call reluctance in sales and sales management personnel is being added to the list.

Summary and Conclusions

We hope the research base you just sampled gives you an overview of our call reluctance projects. More importantly, we hope you can appreciate that call reluctance is not just a flashy idea. It is real. It can be measured and quantified. It has a history and it has physical, emotional, and financial costs.

As you are reading, Call Reluctance is still about its business. It is swindling corporate organizations and robbing individual sales professionals. Left unattended, it is parasitically gorging itself with their energy, spirit, and money. But knowledge gained from egg-headed research programs, such as those we sketched above, can help stop call reluctance. Its spawning grounds can be cleared and decontaminated. But if and when that happens depends on you and your organization.

Are you ready to earn what you're worth?

QUANTITY
BOOK DISCOUNTS

Quantity discount prices are available to companies, educational, civic and religious organizations wishing to place large volume orders. For more information, please contact:

Corporate Sales Division
Behavioral Sciences Research Press
12803 Demetra Drive
Dallas, TX 75234

Toll Free: 1-800-323-4659
FAX: (972) 243-6349
www.bsrpinc.com
e-mail: webmaster@bsrpinc.com

FEAR FREE PROSPECTING & SELF-PROMOTION
W O R K S H O P

Fear-Free Prospecting & Self-Promotion Workshops™
are available throughout the United States, and a growing number of foreign countries.

No Platitudes. No Tricks. No Gimmicks.

It's the only workshop of its kind. Anywhere. Based on over twenty years of documented research and development, it packs the firepower you need to help you prospect with pride and persistency. The Fear-Free Prospecting & Self-Promotion Workshop is the *only* call reluctance workshop endorsed by authors, George W. Dudley & Shannon L. Goodson.

To us, call reluctance training is never a footnote, or a last minute add-on. It's our entire mission. We do more call reluctance training—and do it better—than anyone else in the world.

Call Reluctance Specialists

You don't get paid increased commissions for what you learn, only for what you do. That's why our objective is to help you to increase the *number of contacts you initiate with prospective buyers*.

We'll equip you with serious, high octane countermeasures you can use immediately. Step-by-step, authorized call reluctance training *specialists* will walk you through the new generation of exciting call reluctance countermeasures.

Is the Fear-Free Prospecting & Self-Promotion Workshop for you? Frankly, we don't know. But, if you've read all the books, been to all the workshops, listened to all the cassettes and you're still not earning what you're worth, maybe we can help. Call, fax, or write for more information about **Fear-Free Prospecting & Self-Promotion Workshops** in your area.

FEAR-FREE PROSPECTING &
SELF-PROMOTION WORKSHOP™
12803 Demetra Drive
Dallas, Texas 75234
(972) 243-8543
FAX (972) 243-6349
www.bsrpinc.com
e-mail: webmaster@bsrpinc.com

ABOUT THE AUTHORS

George W. Dudley and **Shannon L. Goodson** are recognized as the world's leading authorities on sales call reluctance and the fear of self-promotion. For almost twenty-five years they have studied the reasons why so many talented, hard-working people fail to earn what they are worth. With backgrounds in science, research to them is not a hobby. It's a lifestyle.

Dudley holds a Master's degree in experimental psychology from North Texas State University. He began his career in the Field Testing and Evaluation unit of the U.S. Marine Corps. He later directed Field Testing and Research for a Fortune 500 company. He is listed in *Who's Who in America* and *Who's Who in Science and Engineering*.

Goodson holds a Master's degree in organizational psychology from Lamar University. An experienced psychotherapist, author, researcher, and counselor, she is also a noted expert on women in the business world. Her research has been presented to professional associations all over the globe. She is listed in *Who's Who of American Women*.

BIBLIOGRAPHY

The American Journal of Clinical Hypnosis. St. Paul, MN: The North Central Publishing Company, 1981, Vol. 23, No.4.

Diagnostic and Statistical Manual of Mental Disorders. The American Psychiatric Association, 1980.

Proceedings of the 1988 Annual Meeting: Million Dollar Round Table. Des Plaines: Million Dollar Round Table, 1988.

Ackerman, Diane, *A Natural History of the Senses*. New York: Random House, 1990.

Adler, Mortimer J., *How to Think About God*. New York: Macmillan Publishing, 1980.

Ailes, R. & Kraushar, J., *You Are The Message*. New York, NY: Doubleday, 1988.

Alberti, R. E. & Emmons, M. L., *Your Perfect Right: A Guide to Assertive Behavior (2nd ed.)*. San Luis Obispo, CA: Impact Press, 1974.

Alper, Joseph, Our Dual Memory. *Science*, July/August 1986.

Alpert, Judy I. & Alpert, Mark I., Music Influences on Mood and Purchase Intentions. *Psychology and Marketing*, Summer 1990, Vol. 7, No. 2.

Bandler, R. & Grinder, J., *Frogs into Princes*. Moab, Utah: Real People Press, 1979.

Bass, C.D., *Banishing Fear From Your Life*. Garden City, NY: Doubleday & Co., 1986.

Beck, A. T., Emery, G. & Greenberg, R. L., *Anxiety Disorders and Phobias*. Basic Books, 1985.

Bensley, Lillian S., The Heightened Role of External Responsiveness in the Alcohol Consumption of Restrained Drinkers. *Cognitive Therapy & Research*, December 1989, Vol. 13, No. 6.

Benthall, J. & Polhemus, T., *The Body As A Medium of Expression*. New York: E. P. Dutton & Co., 1975.

Bischof, Ledford J., *Interpreting Personality Theories*. New York: Harper & Row, 1964.

Bloomfield, H. H. & Felder, L., *The Achilles Syndrome*. New York: Random House, 1985.

Bloomfield, H. H., Cain, M. P., Jaffe, D. T., & Kory, R. B., *TM Discovering Inner Energy and Overcoming Stress*. New York, NY: Dell Publishing Company, 1975.

Bok, Sissela, *Lying: Moral Choice in Public and Private Life*. New York: Pantheon Books, 1978.

Bolles, E. B., *Remembering & Forgetting*. New York: Walker and Company, 1988.

Bowen, Deborah, J. & Grunberg, Neil M., Variations in Food Preference and Consumption Across the Menstrual Cycle. *Physiology and Behavior*, February 1990, Vol. 47, No. 2.

Bower, S. A. & Bower, G. H., *Asserting Your Self*. Menlo Park, CA: Addison-Wesley Publishing Company, 1976.

Brenman, M. & Gill, M. M., *Hypnotherapy*. New York, NY: International Universities Press, 1947.

Brito, T., Call Reluctance. *Pacific Way—Air New Zealand*, April 1989.

Brucker, P., The Negative Side of Positive Thinking. *Viewpoint*, Summer 1987.

Bruner, F. I. & Gordon, C., Music, Mood, and Marketing. *Journal of Marketing*, October 1990, Vol. 54, No. 4.

Bry, A., *A Primer of Behavioral Psychology*. New York, NY: The New American Library, 1975.

Bry, A., *How to Get Angry Without Feeling Guilty*. New York: New American Library, 1976.

Burns, D. D., *Feeling Good*. New York, NY: New American Library, 1980.

Butler, P., *Self-Assertion for Women*. San Francisco, CA: Harper & Row, 1981.

Buzzotta, V. R., Lefton, R. E., & Sherberg, M., *Effective Selling Through Psychology*. Cambridge, MA: Ballinger Publishing Company, 1982.

Canavan-Gumpert, D., Garner, K., & Gumpert, P., *The Success-Fearing Personality*. Lexington: Lexington Books, 1978.

Caspy, T., Peleg, E., Schlam, D., & Goldberg, J., Sedative and Stimulative Music Effects. *Motivation and Emotion*, June 1988, Vol. 12, No. 2.

Cattell, Raymond B., *Human Motivation and the Dynamic Calculus*. New York: Praeger, 1985.

Cattell, Raymond B., *The Scientific Analysis of Personality*. Chicago: Aldine Publishing Company, 1965.

Cattell, R. B., Eber, H. W., & Tatsuoka, M. M., *Handbook for the Sixteen Personality Factor Questionnaire (16PF)*. Champaigne, IL: Insititute for Personality and Ability Testing, 1970.

Cattell, Raymond B., *Abilites: Their Structure, Growth, and Action*. Boston: Houghton Mifflin Company, 1971.

Cattell, Raymond B. (editor), *Handbook of Multivariate Experimental Psychology*. Chicago: Rand McNally & Company, 1966.

Centers, Richard, *Sexual Attraction and Love*. Springfield: Charles C. Thomas, 1975.

Charlesworth, E. A. & Nathan, R. G., *Stress Management*. New York: Atheneum, 1984.

Cialdini, Robert B., *Influence*. New York: William Morrow and Company, 1984.

Combs, S., A Local Sales Doctor Treats the Timid Prospector. *Orlando Business Journal*, February 1989.

Comer, M. J., Price, D. H., & Ardis, P. M., *Bad Lies in Business*. London: McGraw-Hill, 1988.

Connor, Dr. Fran, Nutrition and the Bottom Line. *Journal of Agent and Management Selection and Development*, 1981, Vol. 1, No. 3.

Connor, Dr. Fran, Nutrition and the Bottom Line: Part Two. *The Journal of Agent and Management Selection and Development*, 1983, Vol. 1, No. 4.

Corsini, Raymond (editor), *Current Psychotherapies*. Itasca, IL: F. E. Peacock Publishers, 1974.

Cox, Richard H. (editor), *Religious Systems and Psychotherapy*. Springfield: Charles C. Thomas, 1973.

Cumming, M., Phoney Illness Has Salespeople Scared. *Sunday*, October 18, 1987.

Daldrup, Dr. Roger J. & Gust, Dodie, *Freedom From Anger: The Daldrup Method*. Aptos, CA.: Living Business Press, 1988.

Danskin, David G. & Crow, Mark A., *Biofeedback*. Mayfield Publishing Company, 1981.

Darrow, T., Call Reluctance: A Career Stopper. *Kiwanis Magazine*, February 1989.

Darrow, T., Conquering Call Reluctance. *Delta Sky Magazine*, May 1988.

Darrow, T., Learning to Toot Your Own Horn. *National Business Employment Weekly*, November 4, 1990.

Darrow, Terri L., Bragging Rights. *Entrepreneurial Woman*, July/August 1991.

Didato, S. V., *Psychotechniques*. New York: Playboy Paperbacks, 1980.

Dudley, C. A., University of Texas Health Science Center, Dallas, Texas, Private Communication.

Dudley, G. W. & Goodson, S. L., *The Psychology of Call Reluctance: How to Overcome the Fear of Self-Promotion*. Dallas: Behavioral Science Research Press, 1986.

Dudley, G. W. & Goodson, S. L., The Fear Factor: Notes on the New Psychology of Call Reluctance. *Managers Magazine*, July 1987.

Dudley, G. W., Agent and Management Selection in the Life Insurance Industry: Separating the Myths from the Realities. Presentation, Annual Southwest Management Conference, Austin, TX, 1985.

Dudley, G. W. & Goodson, S. L., Call Reluctance: The Missing Term in the Performance Equation? MDRT Research Project, Behavioral Science Research Press, 1988.

Dudley, G. W. & Goodson, S. L., Call Reluctance: The Missing Term in the Performance Equation? *GAMC News*, January/February 1989.

Dudley, G. W., Call-Reluctance Clinic: A Method of Early Prediction. *The Journal of Agent and Management Selection and Development*, 1981, Vol. 1, No. 3.

Dudley, G. W. & Goodson, S. L., Don't Be Afraid! Overcome Your Fear of Prospecting. *Life Association News*, January 1989.

Dudley, G. W. & Goodson, S. L., Facing Your Prospecting Fears. *Personal Selling Power*, March 1985.

Dudley, G. W. & Goodson, S. L., High and Low Producers: What's the Difference? *Real Estate Selling Strategies*, March 1989.

Dudley, G. W., Identification is the First Step. *The Journal of Agent and Management Selection and Development*, 1981, Vol. 1, No. 1.

Dudley, G. W., Protensive Call Reluctance. *The Journal of Agent and Management Selection and Development*, 1983, Vol. 1, No. 4.

Dudley, G. W., Reluctance Inhibits Agents' Sales Success. *National Underwriter*, October 13, 1987.

Dudley, G. W., Sales Performance: The Missing Link, October 1986.

Dudley, G. W., Secrets of Self-Promotion. *In Business*, August 1987.

Dudley, G. W. & Goodson, S. L., The Fear of Prospecting. *Training Magazine*, 1984.

Dudley, G. W., The Typical Agent Selection Test. *The Journal of Agent and Management Selection and Development*, 1983, Vol. 1, No. 4.

Dudley, G. W., The Varieties of Call-Reluctance. *The Journal of Agent and Management Selection and Development*, 1981, Vol. 1, No. 2.

Dudley, G. W., *Personality Patterns in Call-Reluctant Direct Sales People*, Unpublished Manuscript, 1978.

Dudley, G. W. & Goodson, S. L., *Predicting Success and Failure in Life Insurance Sales with the Sixteen Personality Factors Questionnaire*, Unpublished Manuscript, 1978.

Dudley, G. W., *Predicting Success and Failure in Life Insurance Sales: Comparison of Three Psychological Methods*, Unpublished Manuscript, 1974.

Dudley, G. W., *Predicting Success and Failure with the Motivation Analysis Test*, Unpublished Manuscript, 1974.

Dudley, G. W., *The Motivation Analysis Test: Case Study*, Unpublished Manuscript.

Dunn, Albert H. & Johnson, Eugene M., *Managing Your Sales Team*. Englewood Cliffs, NJ: Prentice-Hall, 1980.

Ekman, Paul, *Telling Lies*. New York: Berkley Books, 1986.

Ellis, A., *Reason and Emotion in Psychotherapy*. New York: Lyle Stuart, 1967.

Ellis, A. & Grieger, R., *Handbook of Rational Emotive Therapy*. New York: Springer Publishing Company, 1977.

Emery, G., *Own Your Own Life*. New York: New American Library, 1982.

Erickson, M. H., Rossi, E. L., & Rossi, S. I., *Hypnotic Realities*. New York, NY: Irvington Publishers, 1976.

Erickson, M. H. & Rossi, E. L., *Hypnotherapy*. New York, NY: Irvington Publishers, 1979.

Feder, B. & Ronall, R. (editors), *Beyond the Hot Seat*. New York: Brunner/Mazel, 1980.

Fisher, Seymour & Greenberg, Roger P., Selective Effects on Women of Exciting and Calm Music. *Perceptual and Motor Skills*, June 1972, Vol. 34, No. 3.

Frank, I., Overcoming the Fear. *Dallas Times Herald*, June 15, 1986.

Freeman, Walter, J., The Psychology of Perception. *Scientific American*, February 1991.

Frichtl, P., Fear of Phoning. *Industrial Distribution*, January 1986.

Fuller, G. D., *Biofeedback*. San Francisco, CA: Biofeedback Press, 1984.

Fuller, George D., *Biofeedback Methods and Procedures in Clinical Practice*. San Francisco: Biofeedback Press, 1984.

Gardner, Martin, *Science: Good, Bad, and Bogus*. New York: Avon, 1981.

Goffman, E., *The Presentation of Self in Everyday Life*. New York: The Overlook Press, 1973.

Goodman, Charles S., *Management of the Personal Selling Function*. New York: Holt, Rinehart and Winston, 1971.

Goodman, D. S. & Maultsby, M. C., *Emotional Well-Being Through Rational Behavior Training*. Springfield, IL: Charles C. Thomas, 1978.

Goodson, S. L., A Situational Approach to Achievement Behavior as a Function of Fulfilling Other's Expectations. Paper presented Annual Convention: Southeastern Psychological Association, Atlanta, GA, 1978.

Goodson, S. L. & Journal Research Staff, The Male and Female Agent: Are They Really the Same? *The Journal of Agent and Management Selection and Development*, 1981, Vol. 1, No. 1.

Goodson, S. L., Personality Differences Between Male and Female Career Agents: Implications for Sales Trainers. Paper presented Annual Convention: Southeastern Psychological Association, New Orleans, LA, 1980.

Goodson, S. L., Predicting Success and Failure in Life Insurance Sales Management. Paper presented Annual Convention: Southeastern Psychological Association, Washington, D.C., 1981.

Goodson, S. L., *Tenure and Production Characteristics of Women Career Agents*. Unpublished Manuscript, 1980.

Goodson, Shannon L. & Wagley, Ronald F., Intelligent Use of Intelligence Scores. *The Journal of Agent and Management Selection and Development*, 1981, Vol. 1, No. 2.

Grimes, B. & Grimes, L., Is Call Reluctance Limiting Your Success? *Real Estate Today*, July 1989.

Guion, Robert M., *Personnel Testing*. New York: McGraw-Hill, 1965.

Guthrie, R. D., *Body Hot Spots*. New York: Van Nostrand Reinhold Company, 1976.

Hampden-Turner, C., *Maps of the Mind*. New York: Macmillan Publishing Company, 1981.

Handly, R. & Neff, P., *Beyond Fear*. New York: Fawcett Crest, 1987.

Handly, R. & Neff, P., *Anxiety & Panic Attacks*. New York: Fawcett Crest, 1985.

Harper, Betty Q., Say It. Review It. Enhance It With a Song. *Elementary School Guidance and Counseling*, February 1985, Vol. 19, No. 3.

Hauck, P., *Overcoming Worry and Fear*. Philadelphia: The Westminster Press, 1977.

Haynes, Jack & Journal Research Staff, The Key to Successful Testing. *The Journal of Agent and Management Selection and Development*, 1981, Vol. 1, No. 1.

Henley, Arthur, *Phobias: The Crippling Fears*. New York: Avon, 1988.

Hitt, Dick, Brain Enhancer Leaves Curious With an Idea. *Dallas Times Herald*, Sunday, June 11, 1989.

Hollans, L., Is Selling Just a Numbers Game? *Birmingham Business Journal*, August 4, 1986.

Hollans, L., Why Sales People Fail: They Fear the Phone. *Birmingham Business Journal*, September 3, 1986.

Hoover, K., Death of a Salesman: 'I was going to call but...'. *Atlanta Business Chronicle*, November 30, 1987.

Hunt, D., *No More Fears*. New York, NY: Warner Books, 1988.

Jeffers, S., *Feel The Fear and Do It Anyway*. New York: Fawcett Columbine, 1987.

Johnstone, G., Any Problems Just Give This Pair a Call. *The Sun*, Brisbane, Australia, July 26, 1989.

Journal Research Staff, Why Can't Tests Predict? *The Journal of Agent and Management Selection and Development*, 1981, Vol. 1, No. 1.

Karrass, Chester, *Give & Take*. New York: Thomas Y. Crowell, 1974.

Karrass, Chester, *The Negotiating Game*. New York: Thomas Y. Crowell, 1970.

Kennedy, Marilyn Moats, *Office Politics*. New York: Warner Books, 1980.

Kipnis, David, *Character Structure and Impulsiveness*. New York: Academic Press, 1971.

Knuckey, D., Fear of Taking Risks Short-Circuits Success. *The Australian*, October 20, 1990.

Kohn, P., Call Reluctance: The Sales Pitch Killer. *Australian Jewish News*, August 10, 1989.

Konner, M., *The Tangled Wing*. New York: Holt, Rinehart and Winston, 1982.

Kranzler, G., *You Can Change How You Feel*. Eugene, OR: RETC Press, 1974.

Krasner, L. & Ullmann, L. P. (edited and introduced by), *Research in Behavior Modification*. New York: Holt, Rinehart and Winston, 1965.

Kung, Hans, *Freud and the Problem of God*. New Haven: Yale University Press, 1979.

Laker, B., Why Some Won't Make That Sales Call. *Dallas Times Herald*, June 15, 1987.

Lange, A. J. & Jakubowski, P., *Responsible Assertive Behavior*. Champaign, IL: Research Press, 1976.

Lant, Jeffrey, *How to Make a Whole Lot More Than $1,000,000*. Cambridge: JLA Publications, 1990.

Lant, Jeffrey, *Cash Copy*. Cambridge: JLA Publications, 1989.

Lasden, M., Mind Probing: Science or Science Fiction? *Computer Decisions*, April 1984.

Lasden, M., The Trouble With Testing. *Training Magazine*, May 1985.

Lazarus, A. & Fay, A., *I Can If I Want To*. New York: William Morrow and Company, 1975.

Lazarus, A. A., *Multimodal Behavior Therapy*. New York: Springer Publishing Company, 1976.

Lazarus, Arnold A., *Behavior Therapy & Beyond*. New York: McGraw-Hill Book Company, 1971.

Leib, J., Many Sales Pros Afflicted with Call Reluctance. *The Denver Post*, June 25, 1989.

Leman, Dr. Kevin & Carlson, Randy, *Unlocking the Secrets of Your Childhood Memories*. Nashville: Thomas Nelson Publishers, 1989.

Lester, David, *A Physiological Basis for Personality Traits*. Springfield: Charles C. Thomas, 1974.

Ley, D. & Forbes, *The Best Seller*. Newport Beach: Sales Success Press, 1984.

Lipsett, L., Rodgers, F. P. & Kentner, H. M., *Personnel Selection and Recruitment*. Boston: Allyn and Bacon, 1964.

Little, J., Our Workers Too Shy to Get Ahead. *Sunday Mail*, Australia, July 23, 1989.

Loo, G., Help for the Unsung Office Worker. *Singapore Today, The New Paper*, September 6, 1989.

Lykken, D.T., *A Tremor in the Blood*. New York: McGraw-Hill Book Company, 1981.

Lyman, Bernard & McCloskey, James, Food Characteristics Thought Desirable During Various Imagined Emotions. *Journal of Psychology*, March, 1989, Vol. 123, No. 2.

MacKenzie, I., New Program Helps Agents Conquer Fear. *National Underwriter*, February 20, 1982.

Mann, S., *A New Approach to Self-Motivation*. Englewood Cliffs, NJ: Prentice-Hall, 1987.

Masson, Jeffrey Moussaieff, *Against Therapy*. Atheneum, New York: Macmillan Publishing, 1988.

McMullin, R. & Casey, B., *Talk Sense to Yourself*. Lakewood, CO: Counseling Research Institute, 1975.

Miller, Robert B., *Strategic Selling*. New York: William Morrow and Company, 1985.

Molloy, John T., *Molloy's Live For Success*. Toronto: Bantam Books, 1981.

Monagan, C.A., *The Neurotic's Handbook*. New York: Atheneum, 1982.

Moore, J., Reducing Reluctance. *Dallas*, Feburary 23-March 1, 1987.

Morgan, G., Banks, A. & Zilko, J., *Going Up: How to Get, Keep and Advance Your Career*. Sydney Collins Publishers, 1988.

Mullin, R. E., *Handbook of Cognitive Therapy Techniques*. New York: W. W. Norton & Company, 1986.

Nichols, M. P., *No Place to Hide*. New York: Simon & Schuster, 1991.

Nirenberg, Dr. Jesse S., *How to Sell Your Ideas*. New York: McGraw-Hill, 1984.

Nolan, S., Treatment for a Career Disease. *Australian Woman*, May 20, 1987.

Ornstein, Robert & Sobel, David, Coming to Our Senses. *Advances*, Fall 1989, Vol 6, No. 3.

Padovani, M. H., *Healing Wounded Emotions*. Mystic, CT: Twenty-Third Publications, 1987.

Patterson, C. H., *Theories of Counseling and Psychotherapy*. New York: Harper & Row, 1966.

Perls, F., Hefferline, R., & Goodman, P., *Gestalt Therapy*. New York: Dell Publishing, 1951.

Phelps, S. & Austin, N. *The Assertive Woman*. San Luis Obispo, CA: Impact, 1976.

Pillar, D., How to Hang Up on Fear. *Fort Worth Star Telegram*, February 16, 1988.

Polster, Erving & Polster, Miriam, *Gestalt Therapy Integrated*. New York: Brunner/Mazel, 1973.

Powell, B., *Overcoming Shyness*. New York: McGraw-Hill Book Company, 1979.

Rabkin, R., *Strategic Psychotherapy*. New York, NY: New American Library, 1977.

Rathus, S. A. & Nevid, J. S., *Behavior Therapy*. New York, NY: Doubleday & Company, 1977.

Reed, M., Is Selling Yourself a Nightmare? *Panorama ANSETT Inflight Magazine*, June 1987.

Reilly, R. R. Ed.D. & Johnson, J. A., An Effective Approach in Dealing with Call Reluctance. *National Underwriter*, 1983.

Rethlingshafer, Dorothy, *Motivation as Related to Personality*. New York: McGraw-Hill, 1963.

Richardson, D., Identifying Sales-Call Reluctance. *Maintenance Sales News*, September 1990.

Ricketts, C., Is Call Reluctance Holding You Back? *Dallas Business Journal*, February 26, 1990.

Ries, Al & Trout, Jack, *Positioning: The Battle for Your Mind*. New York: Warner Books, 1986.

Ritchie, Berry & Goldsmith, Walter, *The New Elite*. London: Penguin Books, 1988.

Roane, S., *How To Work A Room*. New York, NY: Warner Books, 1988.

Robeson, J., Mathews, H. L., & Stevens, C. G., *Selling*. Homewood, IL: Richard D. Irwin, 1978.

Robiner, William N., Psychological and Physical Reactions to Whirlpool Baths. *Journal of Behavioral Medicine*, April 1990, Vol. 13.

Roessler, Robert & Greenfield, Norman S. (editors), *Physiological Correlates of Psychological Disorder*. Madison: The University of Wisconsin Press, 1962.

Salupo, Victor, *The B.S. Syndrome*. Cleveland: The Bull Buster Press, 1985.

Sampson, A., Call Reluctance - The Salesperson's Social Disease. *Rydge's Sales and Marketing*, May 1986.

Sanford, A.J., *Cognition & Cognitive Psychology*. New York: Basic Books, 1985.

Satir, V., *Peoplemaking*. Palo Alto, CA: Science and Behavior Books, 1972.

Schur, Edwin, *The Awareness Trap*. New York: McGraw-Hill Book Company, 1976.

Shapiro, D., Barber, T. X., DiCara, L. V., Kamiya, J., Miller, N. E., & Stoyva, J. (editors), *Biofeedback and Self-Control*. Chicago: Aldine Publishing Company, 1972.

Simon, S. B., Howe, L. W., & Kirschenbaum, H., *Values Clarification*. New York: Hart Publishing, 1978.

Smith, D., Prescription for Call Reluctance. *The Orlando Sentinel*, October 13, 1987.

Smith, J. D. & Desimone, D., *Sex and the Brain*. New York, NY: Warner Books, 1983.

Smith, Manuel, Jr., *Kicking the Fear Habit*. New York: The Dial Press, 1977.

Staff, Best (and worst) of Health 1991- Help for Insomniacs. *Men's Health*, February 1991, Vol. 6, No. 1.

Stone, Judith, Scents and Sensibility. *Discover*, 1989, Vol. 10, No. 12.

Strehler, Bernard Q., Where Is the Self? *Synapse*, 1991.

Stroebel, C. F., *QR The Quieting Reflex*. New York: Berkley Books, 1983.

Stuart, Richard B., *Trick or Treatment*. Champaign, IL: Research Press, 1970.

Szymanski, D., Overcoming Fear of the Phone. *The Tampa Tribune*, November 5, 1989.

Teiberman, H. R., The Behavioral Effects of Foods. *Department of Brain & Cognitive Science*, Massachusettes Institute of Technology, 1987.

Thurman, C., *The Lies We Believe*. Nashville, TN: Thomas Nelson Publishers, 1989.

Trevarthen, C. (editor), *Brain Circuits and Functions of the Mind*. New York: Cambridge University Press, 1990.

Ullmann, Leonard P. & Krasner, Leonard, *Case Studies in Behavior Modification*. New York: Holt, Rinehart, and Winston, 1965.

Verner, Gayle, A Way to a Sound Mind and Body? *USA Weekend*, July 1-3, 1988.

Walker, C. E., *Learn to Relax*. Englewood Cliffs, NJ: Prentice-Hall, 1975.

Watkins, D., Overcoming Fear in Sales and Marketing. *Australian Institute of Management Magazine*, 1990.

Weekes, C., *Simple, Effective Treatment of Agoraphobia*. Sydney: Angus & Robertson, 1983.

Weeks, C., *Peace From Nervous Suffering*. New York: Bantam Books, 1972.

Weinberger, N. M., McGaugh, J. L. & Lynch, G. (edited by), *Memory Systems of the Brain*. New York: The Guilford Press, 1985.

Whitney, R. A., Hubin, T. & Murphy, J. D., *The New Psychology of Persuasion and Motivation in Selling*. Englewood Cliffs: Prentice-Hall, 1965.

Willis & Grosman, *Medical Neurobiology*. St. Louis: C.V. Mosby Company, 1981.

Wolman, Benjamin B. (editor), *Handbook of General Psychology*. Englewood Cliffs, NJ: Prentice-Hall, 1973.

Wolpe, Joseph, *The Practice of Behavior Therapy*. New York: Pergamon Press, 1974.

Yates, A., *Behavior Therapy*. New York: John Wiley & Sons, 1970.

Zane, M. D. & Milt, H., *Your Phobia*. Washington, D.C.: Warner Books, 1984.

Zilbergeld, B. & Lazarus, A. A., *Mind Power*. New York: Ballantine Books, 1987.

Zimbardo, P. G. & Radl, S. L., *The Shyness Workbook*. New York, NY: A & W Publishers, 1979.

Zimbardo, P. G., *Shyness*. Menlo Park, CA: Addison-Wesley Publishing Company, 1978.

Index

". . .internationally acclaimed."

–REAL ESTATE SELLING STRATEGIES

"Help for unsung office workers."

–SINGAPORE TODAY

"How about a book which presents an up-to-date review of the current research in a psychological topic of interest to all sales trainers which not only covers the topic in detail but also presents concrete remedies to employ in the field — and what if this book were written in plain English? Too good to be true? Well, Dudley and Goodson have done an outstanding job distilling some high level research studies into a breezy, humorous and helpful primer."

–TRAINING TRACKS

"Explicit step-by-step instructions."

–TEXAS BANKING

"...focuses on solutions."

–REGISTERED REPRESENTATIVE

"Describes the call reluctance profiles which predominate in various industries."

**–SUCCESSFUL SALESMANSHIP
(SOUTH AFRICA)**

"Ways to overcome the problem..."

–SUCCESS!

"Startling...(information) you simply can't afford to miss."

**–ARIZONA ASSOCIATION
OF LIFE UNDERWRITERS**

"The bedrock of what separates success from failure."

–THE DOMINION (NEW ZEALAND)

"Clear-cut guide to earning what you're worth."

–KXAS-TV, DALLAS

"Salesperson's Bible."

–KGTO–AM, TULSA, OK

"With (this book) in hand, you'll have a fighting chance to solve one of the most unnerving problems any salesperson ever has."

–FINANCIAL SERVICES TIMES

"Quickly becoming the salesperson's Bible."

–THE JOURNAL RECORD

"Gives people the tools to understand…and the techniques to do something about (call reluctance)."

–THE AUSTRALIAN

"Not only pinpoints call reluctance…but provides ways to correct it."

–MAINTENANCE NEWS

"Vitally important to business people."

–DAILY TELEGRAPH (AUSTRALIA)

"Help is at hand!"

–SUCCESSFUL SELLING (AUSTRALIA)

"A must…(Dudley and Goodson) are pioneers in call reluctance research."

–KIWANIS MAGAZINE

"YOU NEED THIS BOOK…START MAKING MONEY NOW!"

**–JEFFREY LANT, Ph.D., AUTHOR OF
THE UNABASHED SELF- PROMOTER**

"…The only work that has any real value in helping sales folks get their rubber in solid contact with the road."

**–EDWIN O. TIMMONS,
NOTED CONSULTING PSYCHOLOGIST**

"Vast findings…a must for every contact-dependent professional …absolutely invaluable for salespeople…managers, sales training professionals, telemarketers, personnel directors, management consultants, mental health and marriage and family professionals as well as fund-raisers and public speakers."

–AGENCY SALES

"New product line not selling? New sales training system producing the same old results? Maybe it's not your products or your training, or market conditions or economics. Maybe it's call reluctance."

–SALES AND MARKETING EXECUTIVE REPORTS

"Businesses can expect to increase their revenue up to 500%."

–THE NATIONAL BUSINESS REVIEW (NEW ZEALAND)

"Accomplishes a goal too many self-help books miss."

–DALLAS/FT. WORTH BUSINESS JOURNAL

"This book will fascinate general readers and professionals alike."

–SMALL PRESS

"Although written for sales professionals, the book has attracted almost as many non-sales readers with similar fears that hold them back from promoting themselves at work."

–ORLANDO SENTINEL

"Whole new insights into what makes salespeople and non-salespeople tick."

–"BUSINESS WORLD," TV–NEW ZEALAND

"Call reluctance affects thousands of sales professionals, preventing them from making new contacts—the bread and butter of direct sales."

–DENVER POST

"Uncover your hidden prospecting fears and learn how to overcome them."

–REAL ESTATE TODAY

"Psychologically sophisticated tips on how to overcome call reluctance."

–ATLANTA BUSINESS CHRONICLE

"…will find a respected home in our library and be of great assistance to our sales personnel."

–PIERIE STEYN, DEPUTY CHAIRMAN AND CEO, SANLAM (LIFE INSURANCE), SOUTH AFRICA

"Not just positive thinking."

–FORT WORTH STAR-TELEGRAM